Corsica

THE ROUGH GUIDE

Rough Guide credits

Text editor:	Jonathan Buckley
Series editor:	Mark Ellingham
Editorial:	Martin Dunford, John Fisher, Greg Ward, Jules Brown, Graham Parker, Samantha Cook, Jo Mead
Production:	Susanne Hillen, Andy Hilliard, Gail Jammy, Vivien Antwi, Alan Spicer, Melissa Flack
Finance:	Celia Crowley, Simon Carloss
Publicity:	Richard Trillo

Theo would like to thank: Janine Serafini, Jean Pandolphi, Jean Raffali, Sophie Hastings, Len Taylor, Felicity Taylor, Marie-Claire Roccaserra, Sam Taylor, Ghjuvan'Francescu Luciani (wherever he is), Caroline Kelly, everyone who has worked on the book and all my supportive friends.

Thanks from the editor to Michael Müller Verlag, Micromap Ltd, Gail Jammy, Margaret Doyle and especially Miranda Davies.

The publishers and authors have done their best to ensure the accuracy and currency of all the information in *The Rough Guide to Corsica*; however, they can accept no responsibility for any loss, injury or inconvenience sustained by any traveller as a result of information or advice contained in the guide.

This first edition published 1994 by Rough Guides Ltd, 1 Mercer Street, London WC2H 9QJ.
Distributed by The Penguin Group:

Penguin Books Ltd, 27 Wrights Lane, London W8 5TZ
Penguin Books USA Inc., 375 Hudson Street, New York 10014, USA
Penguin Books Australia Ltd, 487 Maroondah Highway, PO Box 257, Ringwood, Victoria 3134, Australia
Penguin Books Canada Ltd, 10 Alcorn Avenue, Toronto, Ontario, Canada M4V 1E4
Penguin Books (NZ) Ltd, 182–190 Wairau Road, Auckland 10, New Zealand

Rough Guides were formerly published as Real Guides in the United States and Canada.

Typeset in Linotron Univers and Century Old Style to an original design by Andrew Oliver.
Printed in the UK by Cox & Wyman, Reading, Berks.

Illustrations in Part One and Part Four by Edward Briant
Basics and Contexts illustrations by Henry Iles.
Front cover photo: Place Gaffori, Corte. Back cover photo: Bonifacio.

240pp.
Includes index.

A catalogue record for this book is available from the British Library

ISBN 1-85828-089-3

Corsica

THE ROUGH GUIDE

Written and researched by
Theo Taylor

THE ROUGH GUIDES

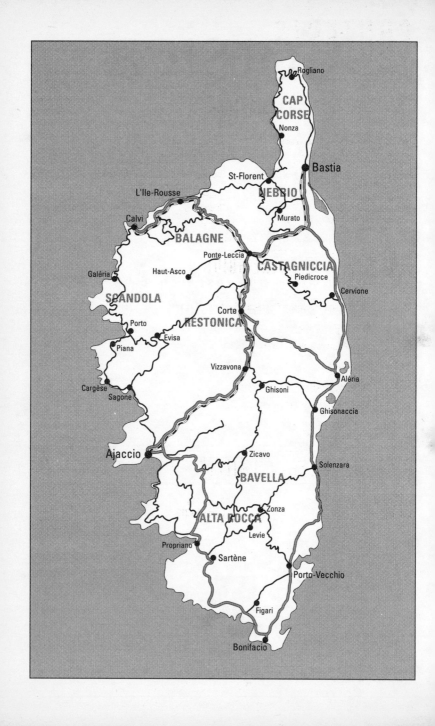

CONTENTS

INTRODUCTION

A round one and a half million people visit Corsica each year, drawn by a climate that's mild even in winter and by some of the most astonishingly diverse landscapes in all of Europe. Nowhere in the Mediterranean has beaches finer than Corsica's perfect half-moon bays of white sand and transparent water, or seascapes more inspiring than the mighty granite cliffs of Corsica's west coast. Inland, crystalline rivers cascade from the island's central peaks, rushing through dense forests of colossal pines that have been untouched for centuries. In the north of the island, exquisite Romanesque churches overlook olive groves and ranks of vines, while to the south prehistoric statues lurk on moon-stark plains or in green valleys cloaked in aromatic maquis shrubs.

Even though the annual influx of tourists now exceeds the island's population sixfold, tourism hasn't spoilt the place. There are a few resorts, but over-development is rare and high-rise blocks non-existent, thanks largely to local resistance – sometimes violent – to the approaches of foreign speculators. Although they are obliged to import practically every consumer durable from the French mainland, many Corsicans regard themselves as a people apart, and a history of repeated invasion has only strengthened their **self-identity**. Through the Saracen raids of the Middle Ages and the periods of Spanish, Italian and French rule, the Corsicans have tenaciously held onto their heritage, and continue to preserve their **ancient culture** in the face of the modern world. Unearthly choral chants sung in the native language can still be heard in some remote regions, and a belief in the supernatural remains a potent force. A continuing preoccupation with death is attested by the mausoleums that you'll see on hillsides all over the island, while the fierce sense of family pride preserves more than a vestige of the feeling which fired the notorious vendettas of the past. The code of honour that protected the island's bandits right into the present century persists in a culture that tends to regard collaboration with the police as something shameful, and in which virtually every male carries a knife. Yet the Corsicans' reputation for hostility to foreigners is largely undeserved. They might not be immediately approachable, but a deep hospitality is easily discovered if you make the effort – especially if you admire their island.

Where to go

Two hundred years of French rule have had limited tangible effect on Corsica, an island where Baroque churches, Genoese fortresses, fervent Catholic rituals and an indigenous language saturated with Tuscan influences show a more profound affinity with neighbouring Italy. During the long era of Italian supremacy the northeast and southwest of Corsica formed two provinces known as *Diqua dei monti* – this side of the mountains – and *Dila dei monti*, the uncontrollable side beyond. Today the French *départements* of *Haute-Corse* and *Corse du Sud* roughly coincide with these territories, and remain quite distinct in feel.

Capital of the north, **Bastia** was the principal Genoese stronghold and its fifteenth-century old town has survived almost intact. Of the island's two large towns, this is the more purely Corsican, and commerce rather than tourism is its main concern, which makes it an attractive alternative to some of the southern towns. Also relatively undisturbed, the northern **Cap Corse** harbours inviting sandy coves and coastal hamlets such as Erbalunga and Centuri Port – friendly fishing villages which provide hotel accommodation for the few tourists who make it up here. Within a short distance of Bastia, the fertile region of the **Nebbio** contains a plethora of churches built by Pisan stoneworkers, the prime example being the cathedral of Santa Maria Assunta at the appealingly chic little port of **Saint-Florent**.

To the west of here, **L'Île-Rousse** and **Calvi**, the latter graced with an impressive citadel and fabulous sandy beach, are major targets for holidaymakers – and their hilly hinterland, the **Haute-Balagne**, offers plenty of hilltop villages to explore, as well as access to the northern reaches of the vast **Parc Naturel Régional**, an astounding area of forested valleys, gorges and peaks. The spectacular **Scandola** nature reserve, a part of the northwest coast that lies within the boundaries of the park, can be visited by boat from the tiny resort of **Porto**, from where walkers can also strike into the magnificently wild **Gorges de la Spelunca** and **Fôret d'Aitone** – where you might spot the island's delicacy, wild boar, if you keep your eyes peeled.

Sandy beaches and rocky coves punctuate the **west coast** all the way down to **Ajaccio**, Napoléon's birthplace and Bastia's traditional rival. Its pavement cafés and palm-lined boulevards are thronged with tourists in summer, most of whom take the opportunity to sample the watersport facilities of the expansive and beautiful **Golfe d'Ajaccio**. Slightly fewer make it to nearby **Filitosa**, greatest of the many prehistoric sites scattered across this, the most heavily visited half of the island. Brash **Propriano**, the spot that has perhaps suffered most from the tourist boom, lies close to Filitosa and to stern **Sartène**, seat of the wild feudal lords who once ruled this region, and still the quintessential Corsican town.

More megalithic sites are to be found south of Sartène on the way to **Bonifacio**, a comb of ancient buildings perched atop furrowed white cliffs at the southern tip of the island. Equally popular **Porto-Vecchio** provides a springboard for excursions to the amazing beaches of the south, or alternatively to the oak forest of **Ospedale**, or even to the astounding **Col de Bavella**, where flattened pines spring from the bald granite needles. The **eastern plain** has less to boast of, but the Roman site at **Aléria** is worth a visit for its excellent museum, while to the north of Aléria lies the **Castagniccia**, a swathe of chestnut trees and alluring villages.

Corte, standing at the heart of Corsica, is the best base for exploring the stupendous mountains and gorges of the interior, with the remote valleys of the **Niolo** and **Asco** a stone's throw away. Dominating these valleys, **Monte Cinto** marks the northern edge of the island's spine of high peaks; the experienced hiker could attempt the **GR20**, an epic trail that traverses this magnificent ridge, past Monte d'Oro and Monte Renoso, as far as Monte Incudine in the south.

When to go

Whatever kind of holiday you intend to take, the **best times of year** to visit Corsica are the **late spring** and **late summer or early autumn**, when you're guaranteed sunshine without the stifling heats of July and August. The wild flowers carpeting the island in April and May make these delightful months to come, and the autumn is just as good for scenic colour – the Castagniccia in particular is a riot of russet tones at this time of year. Beachgoers will be ensured a tan as late as October, and even if you plan a visit in the depths of winter you're unlikely to encounter much rain, though snow on the high mountains can restrict driving through the passes in January, February and March, when visibility is often obscured by mists.

Crowds are only likely to be a problem in the major resorts such as Porto-Vecchio and L'Île Rousse, especially in August, when the whole of Italy and France take their annual holiday. In the remoter areas you should book ahead if you want to be certain of staying in the place you're heading to, for the simple reason that there is rarely more than a single hotel in any village. For most of the island, however, you can rely on finding a place to stay at any time.

CLIMATE CHART – AJACCIO											
	Jan	Feb	Mar	April	May	June	July	Aug	Sept	Oct	Nov	Dec
Average Daily Max Temperature °C	13	14	16	18	21	25	27	28	26	22	17	14
Average Monthly Rainfall mm	76	65	53	48	50	21	10	16	50	88	97	98

GETTING THERE FROM BRITAIN AND IRELAND

Flying is obviously the easiest way to reach Corsica, and you'll find a range of inexpensive deals on offer from London and Manchester. Fares inevitably vary according to the season – Easter and June to September are the peak times. The main destinations are Ajaccio, Bastia and Calvi, with some flights going to the smaller airport of Figari in the south of the island.

Travelling by rail or car and ferry will work out much more expensive than flying, and is only worth considering if you want to tour mainland France on your way to Corsica.

BY PLANE

Air France and *British Airways* are the only airlines operating **scheduled flights** to Corsica from Britain, and all involve changing at either Paris or Nice. *Air France* do a daily flight from London Heathrow to Paris Charles de Gaulle, connecting with an *Air Inter* flight from Orly Airport to Ajaccio, Bastia or Calvi. *British Airways* run a daily flight from London Heathrow to Nice, connecting with a *Compagnie Corse Mediterranée* flight to Calvi. *Air France* and *British Airways* also fly from Manchester to Paris daily.

The cheapest *Air France* or *British Airways* ticket is an **Apex** return fare, costing around £260 in low season, rising to around £415 during July and August. From Manchester the prices are slighly higher. Apex tickets must be reserved two weeks in advance and your stay must include one Saturday night. Your return date must be fixed when purchasing and there are no refunds.

AIRLINES IN THE UK

Air France, 177 Piccadilly, London W1V OLX (☎081/742 6600).

British Airways, 156 Regent St, London W1R 5TA (☎081/897 4000).

FLIGHT AGENTS

Campus Travel, 52 Grosvenor Gardens, London SW1 (☎071/589 5599); with branches in Birmingham, Bristol, Cambridge, Edinburgh, Oxford. Also branches at *YHA* shops and university campuses.

Thomas Cook, 45 Berkeley St, London W1 X 5FP (☎071/499 4000); with branches all over the UK.

Council Travel, 28a Poland St, London W1V 3DB (☎071/267 3337).

CTS Travel, 44 Goodge St, London W1 (☎071/637 5601).

Nouvelles Frontières, 11 Blenheim St, London W1Y 5LE (☎071/629 7772).

STA Travel, 86 Old Brompton Rd, London SW7 3LH; 117 Euston Rd, London NW1 2SX (☎071/937 9921); with branches in Manchester, Leeds, Bristol, Cambridge and Oxford.

CHARTER COMPANIES IN THE UK

Air 2000, 2nd floor, Astley House, 33 Notting Hill Gate, London W11 3JQ (☎071/229 7711).

Euro Express, 30 Baker Street, London W1 (☎071 935 0504).

Falcon, 33 Notting Hill Gate, London W11 3JQ (☎071/757 5500).

Direct charter flights work out far cheaper, though it's advisable to book well in advance for July and August; at other times of the year it may be worth waiting until the last moment as the later you leave it the cheaper the price. *Air 2000* fly from London Gatwick to both Calvi and Figari airports every Sunday from May to October. *Euro Express* operate three flights a week from Gatwick to Ajaccio, one a week to Bastia, and three weekly to Calvi and Figari from Gatwick and Manchester. There's also one flight a week from **Edinburgh** to Calvi. *Falcon* run regular summer flights to Corsica, flying from Gatwick to Ajaccio, Calvi and Figari airports. Current costs are around £170 in high season, falling by £20 in low season.

Even cheaper flights are sometimes available through a specialist **agent** – bargains start at around £100 return to Calvi. There are dozens of sources. Look in the classified sections in the Sunday newspapers – the *Sunday Times* especially – and if you live in London, *Time Out* magazine and the *Evening Standard*. Or contact one of the big youth/student travel specialists like *STA Travel* or *Campus Travel*, good for cheap deals if you're under 26 or a student. Consider also a **package deal** which takes care of flights and accommodation for an all-in price (see p.6); package operators can also be a source of cheap one-off flights.

OVERLAND

There are numerous routes from England to the continent, and several ferries from the French mainland over to the Corsican ports (for details, see box opposite). If you don't want the hassle of driving between the north and southern French ports, you might consider using British Rail's motorrail service, whereby you can put your car on the train at London's Victoria Station and travel with it as far as Nice, but the cost is considerably higher – currently working out at around £700 one way, for vehicle plus passengers. After numerous delays, the **channel tunnel** is scheduled to open from the autumn of 1994. Coaches, cars and motorbikes will be loaded onto a freight train known as *le Shuttle*, which will take 35 minutes to get between the loading terminals at Folkestone and Calais. The service is planned to run every fifteen minutes at peak periods, hourly at quieter times such as late night. Fares are charged per vehicle – from £220 to £310 return for vehicle plus passengers.

BY RAIL

Travelling by train to Corsica won't save you money; an ordinary return fare to the ferry ports of **Nice**, **Marseille** or **Toulon** currently costs around £150 from London, including the channel ferry crossing. If you're **under 26**, you can get a slightly discounted Explorer ticket from *Eurotrain* (address below), or a *BIJ* ticket from student and youth agents and some high street travel agents – these tickets are valid for up to two months and give as many stopovers as you like. You can also arrange connecting fares at a discount from outside London, or qualify for reduced-price tickets if you join the train at the channel ports.

All in all, if you are planning to travel around Europe, it might be an idea to invest in an **InterRail** pass. If you're **under 26**, this costs £249 for one month's unlimited rail travel throughout Europe, plus discounts on cross-channel services and some ferry routes; the 15-day version costs £179. The pass for over-26s costs £269 for a month and £209 for 15 days. **InterRail** passes are available from British Rail stations and youth/student travel agents; to qualify, you need to have been resident in Europe for at least six months.

Whichever method you choose, it's well worth reserving a seat (£3.50) or a couchette bed (around £10) for your trip – something you should do well in advance in season.

> ### RAIL AGENCIES
>
> **British Rail European Travel Centre**, Victoria Station, London SW1 (☎071/834 2345).
>
> **Thomas Cook**, 45 Berkeley St, London SW1 (☎071/499 4000) and many regional offices.
>
> **Eurotrain**, 52 Grosvenor Gardens, London SW1 (☎071/730 3402); and regional *Campus Travel* offices.

BY BUS

In the unlikely event that you'd want to take a coach to Corsica, there is a direct service to Nice operated by **Eurolines** (164 Buckingham Palace Rd, London SW1; ☎071/730 0202), leaving once a week from London Victoria Coach Station throughout the year and three times a week from June to September. Fares are £90 return with small reductions for under 26s and students.

FERRIES FROM UK TO FRANCE

Of the numerous cross-channel ferries, hovercrafts and high-speed catamarans, the most useful for **drivers** are those to France, Belgium or the Netherlands from Dover, Folkestone, Ramsgate, Newhaven, Portsmouth, Southampton, Plymouth, Felixstowe, Harwich and Hull. The fare structures are bewilderingly complex, with countless variations according to date of crossing, time of crossing and size of vehicle, but the box below gives a rundown of the essential information on services and their costs – a return ticket is generally priced as two singles.

FERRIES FROM FRANCE TO CORSICA

Ferries to Corsica from Marseille, Nice and Toulon (see next page) are run by *SNCM Corsica Marittima*. Crossings take between seven and twelve hours, costing around 250F per passenger, plus 550F per car. (There are also ferries from the Italian ports of Genoa, La Spezia and Livorno – useful if you're doing a tour of Europe, but otherwise unlikely to be convenient. These services are detailed on p.6.) You can contact the companies directly to reserve a space in peak season (essential with a car), or you can reserve places with *SNCM* at the *Air France* office in London (see p.3).

FERRY CROSSINGS FROM BRITAIN

Route	Company	Frequency	Length of Crossing	Single Fare Car	Single Fare Passenger
Dover–Calais	Stena Sealink	6–22 daily	1hr 30min	£70–155	£24
Dover–Calais	Hoverspeed	7–20 daily	35–45min	£82–180	£26
Dover–Calais	P&O	15–25 daily	1hr 15min	£70–155	£24
Dover–Ostend	P&O	2 daily	5hr 45min	£70–145	£24
Hull–Zeebrugge	North Sea Ferries	1 daily	14hr 30min	£151–159	£47–55
Hull–Rotterdam	North Sea Ferries	1 daily	14hr	£151–179	£45–55
Felixstowe–Zeebrugge	P&O	2 daily	5hr 45min	£70–145	£24
Folkestone–Boulogne	Hoverspeed	6 daily	1hr	£60–144	£21
Newhaven–Dieppe	Stena Sealink	2–4 daily	4hr	£68–160	£28
Plymouth–Roscoff	Brittany Ferries	1–2 daily	6hr	£73–170	£22–37
Poole–Cherbourg	Brittany Ferries	1–3 daily	4hr 30min	£65–168	£22–38
Portsmouth–Caen	Brittany Ferries	2–3 daily	6hr	£69–165	£20–38
Portsmouth–Cherbourg	P&O	1–4 daily	4hr 45min	£63–150	£20–35
Portsmouth–Le Havre	P&O	2–3 daily	5hr 45min	£69–137	£20–35
Portsmouth–St Malo	Brittany Ferries	1–7 weekly	9hr	£73–172	£23–40
Ramsgate–Dunkerque	Sally Line	5 daily	2hr 30min	£59–120	£15
Southampton–Cherbourg	Stena Sealink	1–2 daily	6–8hr	£84–146	£18–35

CROSS-CHANNEL FERRY COMPANIES

Brittany Ferries, Wharf Rd, Portsmouth PO2 8RU (☎0705/827 701).

Hoverspeed, Maybrook House, Queens Gardens, Dover CT17 9UQ (☎0304/240202).

North Sea Ferries, King George Dock, Hedon Rd, Hull HU9 5OA (☎0482/795141).

P&O European Ferries, Channel House, Channel View Rd, Dover CT17 9TJ (☎0304/203388);

London office, telephone enquiries only (☎081/575 8555).

Sally Line, Argyle Centre, York St, Ramsgate, Kent CT11 9DS (☎0843/595522); 81 Piccadilly, London W1V 9HF (☎071/858 1127).

Stena Sealink, Charter House, Park St, Ashford, Kent TN24 8EX (☎0233/647047).

FERRY CROSSINGS FROM FRANCE TO CORSICA

Route	Frequency	Length of Crossing	Period of Operation
Marseille–Ajaccio	4–7 weekly	12hr overnight, 9hr daytime	year round
Marseille–Bastia	3–4 weekly	12hr overnight, 7hr daytime	year round
Marseille—Porto-Vecchio	1–3 weekly	12hr overnight	July to September
Marseille—Propriano	1 weekly	12hr overnight	April to September
Marseille–L'Île-Rousse	2 weekly	8hr daytime	April to September
Nice–Ajaccio	1–6 weekly	12hr overnight	year round
Nice–Bastia	3–6 weekly	12hr overnight	year round
Nice–Calvi	1–3 weekly	5hr daytime	April to September
Nice—L'Île Rousse	1–3 weekly	5hr daytime	April to September
Toulon–Ajaccio	1–4 weekly	10hr overnight	April to September
Toulon–Bastia	1–3 weekly	12hr overnight	April to September
Toulon–Propriano	1 weekly	12hr overnight	June to September

SNCM ADDRESSES

Marseille: 61 boulevard des Dames, Marseille 13002 (☎91 56 30 10).

Nice: Gare Maritime, quai du Commerce, Nice 06000 (☎93 13 66 66).

Toulon: 21 & 49 avenue de L'Infanterie de Marine, Toulon 83000 (☎94 16 66 66).

PACKAGES

Most travel agents will be able to provide details of packages to Corsica, which vary from the standard travel-plus-hotel deals to more specialist trips such as walking tours. Alongside the large tour operators there exists a handful of small independent travel companies who offer pricier but more rewarding packages. Packages mostly fall into one of the following categories:

Fly-drive If you want to rent a car in Corsica, it's well worth checking with tour operators before you leave as most deals work out much cheaper than renting on the spot.

Hotel packages These deals can be excellent value, usually featuring a good three-star hotel. All-in prices for a week's bed and breakfast in Calvi, for example, start at around £300 per person per week, rising by about £50 in high season.

Self-catering Some companies offer villa or farmhouse accommodation in combination with charter flights or fly-drives, but it's generally possible to book just the house. Accommodation prices start at £300 per week – the shortest bookable period – for an average four-bedroomed house. Rental prices usually include insurance, water and electricity. Also available are holidays in self-catering town apartments, which tend to be slightly less expensive than the rural options.

Specialist holidays Some operators offer walking tours in Corsica, none of which come cheap; flights, accommodation, food, local transport and the services of a guide can cost up to £800 per person per week. Holidays based around watersports activities are also offered by many companies; for these reckon on paying around £700 weekly per person.

GETTING THERE FROM IRELAND

No airline offers direct flights from Ireland to Corsica. The cheapest way is to get to either London or Paris and connect to a flight to Corsica from there. There are numerous daily flights **from Dublin** to both London and Paris operated by *Ryanair*, *Aer Lingus*, and *British Midland* – the cheapest fares, which cost from around IR£160 for a return to Luton or Stansted, though the cost of the bus and underground journeys across London may make the total cost greater than *Aer Lingus* or *British Midland* fares to Heathrow. Flights to Paris will set you back around IR£200. **From Belfast** there are *British Airways* and *British Midland* flights to Heathrow, but the cheapest service is the *Britannia Airways* run to Luton, at around £70 return. *British Airways* fly daily to Paris for £120 return and *British Midland* also do a daily flight for around

PACKAGE TOUR COMPANIES IN BRITAIN

Air France Holidays, 69 Boston Manor Rd, Brentford, Middlesex (☎081/568 6981). Flight and accommodation, fly-drive and air-and-rail packages from London, Birmingham, Aberdeen, Manchester, Bristol, Edinburgh and Southampton. Flight plus a week in a hotel in Ajaccio, Calvi or Porto-Vecchio.

Allegro Holidays, Vanguard House, 277 London Rd, Burgess Hill RH15 9VQ (☎0444 235 678). Fly-drive deals and self-catering apartments, cottages and hotels.

Bladon Lines, 56/58 Putney High St, London SW15 1SF (☎081/785 3131). Accommodation in beach hotels and catered villas. Tennis, sailing and water-skiing included in the price. Special deals off-season.

Corsican Affair, George House, 5–7 Humbolt Rd, London W6 8QH (☎071/385 8438). Fly-drive, hotel packages and self-catering.

Cresta Holidays, 32 Victoria Street, Altrincham WA14 1ET (☎061/926 9999). Basic hotel-and-flight deals.

Euro Express, 1 Charlwood Ct, County Oak Way, Crawley, West Sussex (☎0293/511 125). Good deals for flights, hotel and villa accommodation.

Falcon Holidays, 33 Notting Hill Gate, London W11 3JQ (☎071 221 6298). Good range of low-cost packages.

France Voyages, 145 Oxford St, London W1R 1TB (☎071/494 3155). Expensive package deals including flight and hotels, villas and self-catering apartments. Also walking tour packages.

French Affair, 5–7 Humbolt Rd, London SW6 1TN (☎071/385 8438). High-priced packages specializing in farmhouses and villas in rural areas inland.

French Expressions, 2–4 Belsize Crescent, London NW3 (☎071/794 1480). Upmarket holidays in the poshest resorts on Corsica. Also special walking tours.

French Life Holidays, 26 Church Rd, Horsforth, Leeds LS18 5LG (☎0532/390 077). Package deals including flights and hotel accommodation.

Simply Corsica, 3 Chiswick Terrace, Acton Lane, London W4 5LY (☎081/747 3580). Self-catering and hotel accommodation; good value for money.

Sovereign Corsica, Astral Towers, Betts Way, Crawley RH10 2GX (☎0293/ 599 950). Upmarket specialists offering flights plus accommodation ranging from self-catering apartments to posh villas. Helpful and knowledgeable service.

Vacances en Campagne, Bignor, nr Pulborough, West Sussex RH20 1QD (☎07987/411). Self-catering accommodation all over Corsica, from apartments and cottages to large mansions. High standards and good value for money.

VFB Holidays, Normandy House, High St, Cheltenham GL5 3HW (☎0242/580187). Fly-drive family holidays with hotels and self-catering apartments. Sports facilities included in the price.

Voyages Ilena, 7 Old Garden House, The Lanterns, Bridge Lane, London SW11 3AD (☎071/ 924 4440). Classy hotels and self-catering accommodation all over Corsica; flight and fly-drives too.

Mark Warner, 20 Kensington Church St, London W8 4EP (☎071/938 1851). Upmarket beach-club style hotels and apartments with sailing and windsurfing thrown in.

AIRLINES AND AGENCIES IN IRELAND

Aer Lingus, 42 Grafton St, Dublin 2 (☎01/370 011); 46 Castle St, Belfast (☎0232/245 151).

British Airways, 9 Fountain Centre, College St, Belfast (☎0232/240 522).

British Midland, 54 Grafton St, Dublin 2 (☎01/ 798 733); Suite 2, Fountain Centre, College St, Belfast (☎0232/225 151).

Britannia Airways, no reservations office in Ireland – bookings from Luton Airport, Luton, Beds (☎0582/424 155).

Budget Travel, 134 Lower Baggot St, Dublin 2 (01/613 122).

Ryan Air, College Park House, 20 Nassau Street, Dublin 2 (☎01-797 444 or ☎01-770 444).

USIT, 19–21 Aston Quay, O'Connell Bridge, Dublin 2 (☎01-679 8833); Fountain Centre, College St, Belfast (☎0232/324 073).

the same price. From Dublin you can slightly undercut the plane fare by getting a *Eurotrain* ticket, but from Belfast you'll save nothing by taking the train and the ferry. For the best student/youth deals from either city, go to *USIT* (see box above).

GETTING THERE FROM NORTH AMERICA

From North America, Corsica is one of your more obscure European destinations. Discount travel agents – normally the mainstay of budget travellers – concentrate on high-volume routes and are unlikely to be able to ticket you beyond Paris, or perhaps Nice. By all means give it a shot, but you'll probably end up paying a published fare to Corsica.

DIRECT FLIGHTS

Air France is the only airline that flies all the way to Corsica (using its domestic subsidiary, *Air Inter*, for the final leg). However, most other transatlantic carriers have flights to Paris and can ticket you from Paris to Ajaccio or Bastia on *Air Inter* or *Air Afrique* – the total fare might not be any more than what *Air France* charges, especially in winter (or even in summer, if you can find a good promotional fare to Paris). Check the box opposite for airlines and their North American "gateway" cities.

The cheapest scheduled tickets are **Apex** tickets. These carry certain restrictions: you have to book – and pay – at least 21 days before departure and spend at least seven days abroad (maximum stay three months), and you're liable to get penalized if you change your schedule. There are also winter **Super Apex** tickets, sometimes known as "Eurosavers" – slightly cheaper than an ordinary Apex, but limiting your stay to between 7 and 21 days. Some airlines also issue **Special Apex** tickets to those under 24, often extending the maximum stay to a year.

Fares are also heavily dependent on **season**, and are highest from around early June to the end of August, when everyone wants to travel; they drop during the "shoulder" seasons (Sept–Oct & April–May); and you'll get the best deals during the low season, November through March (excluding Christmas). Figure on the following approximate Apex **fares** to Ajaccio, based on midweek travel (flying on weekends ordinarily adds about $50 to the round-trip fare): New York, $820 in winter, $1000 in summer; Washington, $900/$1080; Miami, $920/$1120; Chicago, $900/$1120; Houston, $970/$1170; LA or San Francisco, $1070/$1220; Montréal or Toronto, CDN$960/$1180.

STOPOVER ROUTES

If you don't mind spending a few days in Paris or London first, or if you were planning to visit other parts of France anyway, you might consider nabbing a cheap transatlantic flight through a discount travel agent and sorting out your onward travel when you get there.

Discount outlets, advertised in Sunday newspaper travel sections such as the *New York Times*, can usually do better than any Apex fare to Paris or London. They come in several forms. **Consolidators** buy up large blocks of tickets that airlines don't think they'll be able to sell at their published fares, and sell them at a discount. Besides being cheap, consolidators normally don't impose advance-purchase requirements (although in busy times you'll want to book ahead just to be sure of getting a ticket), but they do often charge very stiff fees for date changes. Also, these companies' margins are pretty tiny, so they make their money by dealing in volume – don't expect them to entertain lots of questions. **Discount agents** also wheel and deal in blocks of tickets offloaded by the airlines, but they typically offer a range of other travel-related services such as travel insurance, rail passes, youth and student ID cards, car rentals, tours and the like. These agencies tend to be most worthwhile to students and under-26s, who can often benefit

AIRLINES IN NORTH AMERICA

Only gateway cities are listed for each airline; other routings are always possible using connecting flights.

Air Canada (☎800/776-3000). Montréal, Toronto and Vancouver to Paris and Nice.

Air France (☎800/237-2747). New York, Washington, Miami, Montréal, Toronto, Chicago, Houston, San Francisco and Los Angeles to Paris or Nice; connections to Ajaccio on *Air Inter.*

American Airlines (☎800/433-7300). New York, Miami, Dallas-Fort Worth, Chicago and Los Angeles to Paris.

British Airways (☎800/247-9297; in Canada ☎800/668-1080). Many North American cities to Paris and Nice (via London).

Canadian Airlines (☎800/665-1177). Montréal, Toronto and Vancouver to Paris.

Continental Airlines (☎800/231-0856). Newark, Houston and Denver to Paris.

Delta Airlines (☎800/241-4141). Atlanta, Cincinnati and New York to Paris.

Northwest Airlines (☎800/225-2525). Los Angeles, Minneapolis and Detroit to Paris.

PIA Pakistan International Airways (☎800/221-2552). New York to Paris.

TWA (☎800/892-4141). New York, Boston, St. Louis and Washington to Paris.

United Airlines (☎800/538-2929). Chicago and Washington to Paris.

from special fares and deals. Some agencies specialize in **charter flights**, which may be even cheaper than anything available on a scheduled flight, but again there's a trade-off: departure dates are fixed, withdrawal penalties are high (check the refund policy), and the plane is likely to be packed.

If you're looking to regroup somewhere in Europe before continuing on to Corsica, **London** is a good place to aim for: there are plenty of flights from there, and of course language is no problem. For advice on getting from London to Corsica, see pp.3–6. The other obvious stopover is **Paris**, where you can avail yourself of *Air Inter*'s standard Paris–Ajaccio fare of about $135 one way.

PACKAGE TOURS

Corsica is way off the beaten path for most North American **tour** companies. Your choices basically come down to a couple of outfits that can arrange short-term rentals of villas ($500 and up for a week for two people) and a couple of adventure-travel companies that do hiking trips in

TOUR OPERATORS IN NORTH AMERICA

Adventure Center, 1311 63rd St., Suite 200, Emeryville, CA 94608 (☎800/227-8747). Corsican village treks.

Himalayan Travel, 112 Prospect St., Stamford, CT 06901 (☎800/225-2380). Trekking in the Corsican interior.

Interhome, 124 Little Falls Rd., Fairfield, NJ 07004 (☎201/882-6864). Short-term villa and chateau rentals.

Vacance En Campagne, PO Box 299, Elkton, VA 22827 (☎800/327-6097). Short-term rentals of chateaux and country houses.

Corsica (about $900 for a week's trek). If you're set on going with a package tour, you might want to consider contacting a tour operator in Britain, where Corsica is a much more popular destination (see box on p.7). Alternatively, you could deal directly with *Ollandini Voyages*, Corsica's biggest tour operator – they're at 3 Pl. de Gaulle, BP 304, 20176 Ajaccio, France (☎01133/95 21 72 21).

GETTING THERE FROM AUSTRALASIA

There are no direct flights from Australia or New Zealand to Corsica – the best you can do is fly direct to Britain, France or Italy and change planes there. If you qualify for student/youth discounts, it's best to book through an agent like *STA* (see box below).

Return fares **to London** start at around A$1600 with *Aeroflot* (via Moscow) from Sydney, leaving twice weekly. Slightly more expensive are seats from Sydney and Auckland on *Garuda* (via Indonesia and Bangkok), *Japanese Airlines* (overnighting in Tokyo), or direct on *British Airways*, all costing from $A1800/NZ$2600.

Air France fly from Sydney and Auckland to **Paris** (CDG) via Jakarta and Singapore at least once a week from around A$2000/NZ$2200, and includes a return "side trip" within France which can be used to reach Nice or Marseille. Marseille and Paris can also be reached on *Aeroflot*'s bi-weekly service from Sydney via Moscow for A$1600.

Qantas fly three times a week from Auckland via Sydney **to Rome**; the fare, from around A$2000/NZ$2200, allows two return "side trips" that can get you to Nice, Marseille or Genoa. Rome can also be reached on *Aeroflot*'s bi-weekly service from Sydney via Moscow for A$1600.

Finally, a *Qantas* **global explorer** allows six stopovers in Europe from A$2200/ NZ$2400.

AIRLINES IN AUSTRALIA AND NEW ZEALAND

Aeroflot, 88 George St, Sydney (☎02/233 7911). No NZ office.

Air France, 12 Castlereagh St, Sydney (☎02/233 3277); 57 Fort St, Auckland (☎09/303 3522).

British Airways, 64 Castlereagh St, Sydney (☎02/258 3300); Dilworth Building, cnr Queen and Customs streets, Auckland (☎09/367 7500).

Garuda, 175 Clarence St, Sydney (☎02/334 9900); 120 Albert St, Auckland (☎09/366 1855).

Qantas, International Sq, Jamison St, Sydney (☎02/957 0111/236 3636); Qantas House, 154 Queen St, Auckland (☎09/303 2506).

AUSTRALIAN DISCOUNT AGENTS

Anywhere Travel, 345 Anzac Parade, Kingsford, Sydney (☎02/663 0411).

Brisbane Discount Travel, 360 Queen St, Brisbane (☎07/229 9211).

Discount Travel Specialists, Shop 53, Forrest Chase, Perth (☎09/221 1400).

Flight Centres, Circular Quay, Sydney (☎02/241 2422); Bourke St, Melbourne (☎03/650 2899); plus other branches nationwide except the Northern Territory.

STA Travel, 732 Harris St, Sydney (☎02/212 1255); 256 Flinders St, Melbourne (☎03/347 4711); other offices in Townsville and state capitals.

Topdeck Travel, 45 Grenfell St, Adelaide (☎08/ 410 1110).

Tymtro Travel, Suite G12, Wallaceway Shopping Centre, Chatswood, Sydney (☎02/411 1222).

Passport Travel, 320b Glenferrie Rd, Malvern, Melbourne (☎03/824 7183).

NEW ZEALAND DISCOUNT AGENTS

Budget Travel, PO Box 505, Auckland (☎09/309 4313).

Flight Centres, National Bank Towers, 205–225 Queen St, Auckland (☎09/309 6171); Shop 1M, National Mutual Arcade, 152 Hereford St, Christchurch (☎09/379 7145); 50–52 Willis St, Wellington (☎04/472 8101); other branches countrywide.

STA Travel, Traveller's Centre, 10 High St, Auckland (☎09/309 9995); 233 Cuba St, Wellington (☎04/385 0561); 223 High St, Christchurch (☎03/379 9098); other offices in Dunedin, Palmerston North and Hamilton.

RED TAPE AND VISAS

Citizens of EU countries, Japan, New Zealand, Canada and the United States do not need any sort of visa to enter France for a stay of up to ninety days. The British Visitor's Passport, obtainable over the counter at post offices, is also valid for France.

Nationals of all other countries must obtain a visa before arrival in Corsica – the addresses of the major French embassies and consulates are given below. Three types of visa are currently issued: a transit visa, which is valid for only three days; a short stay (*court séjour*) visa, valid for ninety days after date of issue; and the *visa de circulation*, which allows for multiple stays of ninety days over three years (maximum of 180 days in any one year).

For stays longer than ninety days you are officially supposed to apply for a *Carte de Séjour*, for which you'll have to show proof of income at least equal to the minimum wage. However, EU passports are rarely stamped, so there is no evidence of how long you've been in the country, and if your passport is stamped you can legitimately cross the French border, to Belgium or Germany for example, and re-enter for another ninety days.

FRENCH EMBASSIES AND CONSULATES

AUSTRALIA 303 Angas, Adelaide (☎08/231 8633); 492 St Kilda Rd, Melbourne; (☎03/820 0921); 10 Eagle, Brisbane (☎07/229 8201).

BRITAIN 6a Cromwell Place, London SW7 (☎071/823 9555); 7–11 Randolph Crescent, Edinburgh (☎031/225 7954); 523–35 Cunard Building, Pier Head, Liverpool (☎051/236 8655).

CANADA 42 Promenade Sussex, Ottawa ON K1M 2C9 (☎613/512 1715). There are consulates in Edmonton, Quebec, Toronto and Vancouver.

IRELAND 36 Ailesbury Rd, Dublin 4 (☎01/694 777).

NETHERLANDS Vyzelgr. 2, Amsterdam (☎20/624 8346).

NEW ZEALAND Corner Princes St and Eden Crescent, Auckland (☎09/302 7629).

USA 4101 Reservoir Rd NW, Washington DC 20007 (☎202/944 6000); 934 Fifth Avenue, New York NY 10021 (☎212/606 3688); 540 Bush St, San Francisco, CA 94108 (☎415/397 4330). Consulates in Boston, Chicago, Detroit, Houston, Los Angeles, Miami and New Orleans.

HEALTH AND INSURANCE

No visitor to France requires vaccinations of any kind, and general health care in Corsica is of the highest standard. There are hospitals in all the main towns, and smaller places like Porto-Vecchio have clinics serving the surrounding area. EU nationals can take advantage of the French health services under the same terms as the residents of the island, as long as you're in possession of a form E111, which can be picked up at most major post offices. However, because the French health system provides subsidized

rather than free treatment, travel insurance – covering health plus loss or theft of baggage – remains essential.

HEALTH PROBLEMS

Under the French social security system, every hospital visit, doctor's consultation and prescribed medicine is charged – though in an emergency you won't be presented with the bill up front. Although all employed French people are entitled to a refund of 75–80 percent of their medical expenses, this can still leave a hefty shortfall, especially after a stay in hospital (accident victims have to pay even for the ambulance or helicopter that takes them there).

To find a **doctor**, stop at any *pharmacie* and ask for an address – we've given *pharmacie* addresses throughout the guide. Consultation fees should be from 80–90F, and after the visit you'll be given a *Feuille de Soins* (Statement of Treatment) for later documentation of insurance claims. **Prescriptions** should be taken to a *pharmacie* which is also equipped, and obliged, to give first aid, for a fee. The medicines you buy will have little stickers (*vignettes*) attached to them, which you must remove and stick to your *Feuille de Soins* together with the prescription itself. In serious **emergencies** you will always be admitted to the local hospital (*centre hospitalier*), whether under your own power or by ambulance.

INSURANCE

Before you purchase any insurance, check what you have already – **North Americans** may find themselves covered for medical or other losses while abroad as part of a family or student policy. Many bank and charge accounts include some travel cover, and some credit cards offer insurance benefits if you use them to pay for your holiday tickets. Canadians especially are usually covered by their provincial health plans, and holders of *ISIC* cards are entitled (outside the USA) to be reimbursed for $3000-worth of accident coverage and 60 days of in-patient benefits up to $100 a day for the period the card is valid.

If you do want a specific travel insurance policy, there are numerous kinds to choose from: short-term combination policies covering everything from baggage loss to broken legs are the best bet and cost around $50–70 for 15 days. One thing to bear in mind is that none of the currently available policies covers theft; they only cover loss while in the custody of an identifiable person – and even then you must make a report to the police and get their written statement. Two companies you might try are *Travel Guard*, 110 Centrepoint Drive, Steven Point, WI 54480 (☎715/345-0505 or 800/826-1300), and *Access America International*, 600 Third Ave, New York, NY 10163 (☎212/949-5960 or 800/284-8300).

If transiting via Britain, North Americans might consider buying a policy from a British travel agent. British policies tend to be cheaper than American ones, and routinely cover thefts – which are often excluded from the more health-based American policies.

In **Britain**, as well as those policies offered by travel agents, consider using a specialist, low-priced firm like *Endsleigh* (Cranfield House, 97–107 Southampton Row, London WC1; ☎071/436 4451), who offer two weeks' basic cover in Europe for around £20.

With all policies, for **medical treatment and drugs**, keep all the bills and claim the money back later. If you **have anything stolen** (including money), register the loss immediately with the local police – without their report you won't be able to claim.

MONEY, BANKS AND COSTS

French currency is the **franc** (abbreviated as F or sometimes FF), divided into 100 **centimes**. Francs come in notes of 500, 100, 50 and 20F, and there are coins of 20F, 10F, 5F, 2F, 1F, 20 centimes and 10 centimes. The exchange rate is prone to fluctuations, with the franc veering between 7F and 9F to £1, and between 3.50F and 5F to $1.

Normal **banking hours** are 9.30am–noon and 2–4pm, closed on Sunday and either Monday or, less usually, Saturday. **Rates of exchange** and **commissions** vary from place to place – the **post office** is the best place to change money, as they charge a minimal commission of around 5F, a huge saving on the 50F charged by banks for changing travellers' cheques. However, many village post offices no longer offer an exchange service, due to the incidence of robberies, and many **banks** also refuse to do currency exchange – so your best advice is to take advantage of the post offices in the major towns, and make sure you have a good supply of francs when you arrive.

Many of the major French banks, including *Crédit Agricole*, *Crédit Lyonnais*, *Societé Générale* and *Banque Populaire Provencale et Corse* have branches in Corsica, with the largest concentration in Ajaccio and Bastia. There is no *American Express* office.

Travellers' cheques, one of the safest ways of carrying your money, are available from almost any of the principal banks, whether you have an account there or not, usually for a service charge of one percent on the amount purchased, though some go as high as five percent. (Your own bank may offer cheques free of charge provided you meet certain conditions.) *Visa* and *American Express*, equally accepted, are the most widely recognized brands. It's best to buy travellers' cheques in your home currency, as it's common practice for Corsican exchanges to charge more for cashing cheques in francs.

Alternatively, Europeans can use **Eurocheques**, now offered by most British banks for a flat fee. These cheques can be written for the precise amount you wish to withdraw, and are liable to just one percent commission on each cheque, though Corsican banks do occasionally try to charge the rate for standard exchange. You can also use *Eurocheques* in many restaurants and shops, and you can withdraw cash from certain cash-dispensers using your *Eurocheque* card.

The major **credit cards and charge cards** are usually accepted in tourist-concentrated areas, but it's best to have cash for the remoter hotels and restaurants. *Visa* is the most widely recognized; *American Express* and *Access* rank considerably lower – only the *Crédit Agricole* bank provides facilities for *Access*, and many restaurants and hotels won't accept it because of the huge commissions they have to pay.

COSTS

Accommodation will probably constitute your main expense during your stay in Corsica, and even then it won't come to much. The majority of hotels charge 200–300F for a double room, and 200–250F for a single. Luxury places and cheap *pensions* are rarer, and where this type of accommodation exists it is listed in the guide. Staying in campsites can be a money-saver as long as you stick to the basic sites found in rural areas, which charge between 50 and 100F per day, and avoid the flashy complexes which are found along the coast, which can cost almost as much as a hotel.

As for **food**, in any town you'll find restaurants with three- or four-course meals for between 75F and 100F. Picnic fare, obviously, is less costly, especially if you buy from small local shops or supermarkets rather than markets or specialist food shops aimed at tourists. More sophisticated meals using takeaway salads and ready-to-heat dishes, bought in *rotisseries* or *charcuteries*, can be put together without stretching the wallet too far. If you're on a budget, you need to beware of the expense of beer and coffee in bars, cafés and clubs – though cigarettes are far cheaper here than on the mainland.

Public transport costs around 100F for 100km, whether you're travelling by buses or by the *micheline* train (Bastia–Ajaccio is currently around 100F). Petrol prices are amongst the highest in Europe, at just over 5F per litre for leaded and just under 5F for unleaded (approx. 25F per imperial gallon, 20F per US gallon). Car rental will set you back anything upwards of 2000F per week, depending on the season and company. Bicycles cost about 150F per day.

Museums and monuments won't prove too much of a drain on your resources, for the simple reason that there are relatively few on the island. Most charge around 15F and give discounts for holders of *ISIC* cards or to under-26s on presentation of a passport.

Thus a **minimum daily requirement** would be around 150F per person, if camping and doing your own catering; to do things comfortably you'd need about 300F per person, if travelling in a couple and staying in budget hotels; and in order to have no worries at all, count on spending around 600F per day.

INFORMATION AND MAPS

The foreign branches of the **French Government Tourist Office** give away maps and glossy brochures, including lists of Corsican hotels, campsites, sports facilities and public transport services. In Corsica every major town has a tourist office (*Office du Tourisme*), addresses of which are detailed throughout this guide. Usually only open in summer (May–Sept),

these offices give out specific local information, including free town plans, lists of leisure activities, bike hire, and countless other things. Many tourist offices also publish hotel and restaurant listings, as well as driving and walking itineraries for their areas. In mountain areas they share premises with the local hiking and climbing organizers, who can give detailed advice about the best routes to take. Map information about forest trails can be found on boards outside *maisons forestières* (forest huts) – the only one open to the public is in the Forêt d'Aitone.

In addition to the various free leaflets – and the maps in this guide – the one extra map you'll definitely want is a detailed **road map**. The *Michelin* yellow map series 1:200,000 (no.90) is the best map of the whole island for drivers. If you're planning to **walk or cycle**, check the three series of *IGN* maps: 1:100,000 (green), 1:50,000 (also green), and 1:25,000 (blue). The *IGN* 1:100,000 maps, the smallest-scale contoured maps available, are essential for cyclists, who tend to cycle off 1:25,000 maps in a couple of hours.

MAP AND GUIDE OUTLETS

London

National Map Centre, 22–24 Caxton St, SW1 (☎071/222 4945).

Stanfords, 12–14 Long Acre, WC2 (☎071/836 1321).

The Travellers Bookshop, 25 Cecil Court, WC2 (☎071/836 9132).

Edinburgh

Thomas Nelson and Sons Ltd, 51 York Place, EH1 3JD (☎031/557 3011).

Glasgow

John Smith and Sons, 57–61 St Vincent St (☎041/221 7472).

Chicago

Rand McNally, 444 N Michigan Ave, IL 60611 (☎312/321-1751).

New York

British Travel Bookshop, 551 5th Ave, NY 10176 (☎1-800/448-3039 or ☎212/490-6688).

The Complete Traveler Bookstore, 199 Madison Ave, NY 10016 (☎212/685-9007).

Rand McNally, 150 East 52nd St, NY 10022 (☎212/758-7488).

Traveler's Bookstore, 22 West 52nd St, NY 10019 (☎212/664-0995).

San Francisco

The Complete Traveler Bookstore, 3207 Filmore St, CA 92123 (☎415/923-1511).

Rand McNally, 595 Market St, CA 94105 (☎415/777-3131).

Seattle

Elliot Bay Book Company, 101 South Main St, WA 98104 (☎206/624-6600).

Toronto

Open Air Books and Maps, 25 Toronto St, M5R 2C1 (☎416/363-0719).

Vancouver

World Wide Books and Maps, 1247 Granville St.

Washington DC

Rand McNally, 1201 Connecticut Ave NW, 20036 (☎202/223-6751).

Note that *Rand McNally* now have 24 stores across the US; phone ☎1-800/333-0136 (ext 2111) for the address of your nearest store, or for **direct mail** maps.

Adelaide

The Map Shop, 16a Peel St, SA 5000 (☎08/231 2033).

Brisbane

Hema, 239 George St, QLD 4000 (☎07/221 4330).

Melbourne

Bowyangs, 372 Little Bourke St, VIC 3000 (☎03/670 4383).

Sydney

Travel Bookshop, 20 Bridge St, NSW 2000 (☎02/241 3554).

Perth

Perth Map Centre, 891 Hay St, WA 6000 (☎09/322 5733).

ACCOMMODATION

At most times of the year accommodation is plentiful in the major towns and around the Corsican coast, with the exception of the eastern plain, where rooms are scarce. However, from June to August it's a good idea to book your room in advance wherever you're heading, and booking is always advised in the more remote parts of the island. August is the most problematic month, as the French and Italians take their holidays en masse at this time. The

"Language" section at the back of this book should help you make your reservation, as few hoteliers or campsite managers speak any English. We've detailed a range of accommodation wherever such a range exists, but you'll find there are very few luxury places and only a couple of hostels in the whole of Corsica (at Propriano and Calvi).

HOTELS

All French hotels are graded on a scale that rises to three stars, and the price of the room corresponds roughly to the number of stars, though unfortunately this system isn't very reliable in Corsica, as some hotels give themselves the stars regardless of whether they've been visited by inspectors.

At the **one-star** level you can expect to pay 200–250F for a double, without a private bathroom, around 30–50F more for a private shower. **Two-star** places charge around 250–350F for a double including a private bathroom, and **three-star** hotels usually cost 300–450F for a double room with bathroom and in many cases a television with satellite channels – though there are a few plush villa-hotels where the bill can rise to 600F or even higher.

Breakfast can add 30–50F per person to a bill, although there is no obligation to take it and you will nearly always do better at a café. The cost of eating **dinner** in a hotel's restaurant can be a more important factor to bear in mind when picking a place to stay. Some places insist that you take at least one full meal with them (*demipension*), especially in the mountains, where food is usually of a high quality.

Single rooms are only marginally cheaper than doubles, so sharing always keeps down the cost. Some hotels will provide extra beds for three or more, charging around 25 percent per bed. Note that many hotels are **open only in summer**, usually from May to September – we've indicated in the guide those establishments that close for the winter. The ones that do stay open in winter often offer discounts to off-season visitors.

FERME-AUBERGES

Bed and breakfast accommodation doesn't yet exist in Corsica, as the notion of a having a fee-paying guest in one's home runs counter to

Corsican traditions of hospitality. The nearest equivalent is full-board farmhouse accommodation in one of the island's **Ferme-Auberges**, where the main attractions are rural calm and the chance to sample authentic Corsican cooking. These aren't a cheap option, however, averaging out at 300F per person per day. We've included some of these in the guide, but for a full list you should contact the *Maison de l'Agriculture*, 19 av Noel-Franchini, 2000 Ajaccio (☎95 29 42 31).

RENTED HOUSES

If you're planning to stay a week or more in any one place it might be worth considering **renting a house**. The easiest and most reliable way of finding a property is to use the official French government service *Gîtes de France* (☎071 493 3480). Membership, obtained through the tourist office and costing £3, gets you a handbook listing a wide variety of houses all over France, including Corsica, each entry having a photograph and description of the house. A computerized booking service enables you instantly to reserve a place for any number of full weeks, for a cost that ranges from around £150 to £600 a week.

Another way of finding a place is to try one of the package holiday firms listed on p.7, though these tend to be at the upper end of the market, or to look for properties advertised in the Sunday newspapers. Finally, you can wait until you arrive in Corsica and ask any local tourist office for a list of accommodation to rent in the region – these will work out less expensive, but there's obviously the risk that nothing suitable will be on offer.

GITES D'ETAPES AND REFUGES

If you're planning a hiking trip you may want to make use of the network of **gîtes d'étapes** and **refuges** designed exclusively for ramblers and situated at crucial stages along the main hiking trails of the GR20, the *Tra Mare e Monti* and *Da Mare a Mare*. The terms *gîte d'étape* and *refuge* are sometimes used interchangeably, as each offers pretty basic accommodation, but the principal difference between them is that some *gîtes d'étapes* provide meals for around 150F, and charge around 30–40F for a night's accommodation if there's a warden in charge, which isn't always the case. At all *gîtes d'étapes* and *refuges* you'll need a sleeping bag, and while some *gîtes d'étapes* provide fairly comfortable dormitories of bunk beds as well as primitive kitchen and bathroom facilities, many *refuges* – especially high in the mountains – are little more than shelters, barely converted from shepherds' crofts or ancient stone dwellings. You can usually camp in the vicinity of these refuges, if they turn out to be full up or closed – if you want to be certain of a roof over your head, check with the local tourist office before setting out.

All *refuges* and *gîtes d'étapes* are marked on the large-scale *IGN* maps and listed in the *Walks in Corsica* book (see p.217).

(see p.217)

CAMPING

Practically every locality has at least one **campsite** to cater for the thousands of French and Italians who spend their holiday under canvas. The cheapest – at around 50–60F per person per night – are usually found in deep countryside,

and are very basic. On the coast especially there are superior categories of campsite, where you'll pay prices similar to those of a one-star hotel for facilities such as bars, restaurants and swimming pools. People spend their whole holiday in these places – if you plan to do the same, and particularly if you have a caravan or a big tent, it's wise to book ahead. A booklet listing all campsites in Corsica is available from the French Tourist Board (see p.14).

Lastly, a **word of caution**: never camp rough (*camping sauvage*) on anyone's land without first asking their permission. Besides the fact that it's illegal, you're liable to get a bullet flying your way. Camping on beaches is illegal as well, though a lot of people do it. Wherever you camp, be careful with **fires**, as the maquis – which creeps down to the coast in many areas – burns quickly.

GETTING AROUND

If you want to see a lot of Corsica in a fairly short time, the only way to do it is to drive, and car rental firms are found in all the main towns. This can work out expensive, but even if your budget will only stretch to a few days, it's worth renting a vehicle of some kind. Bus services are adequate for linking the main towns but dwindle in the countryside. Approximate journey times and frequencies are given in "Travel Details" at the end of each chapter, but bear in mind that timetables are often unreliable. As for the train, it's worth taking in order to admire the small part of the scenery it crosses, but not if you're in a hurry. Walking is one of the best ways of exploring the island, which has an extensive network of footpaths and forest trails.

DRIVING

Driving in Corsica can cause a few headaches. Once you're off the relatively smooth main roads, the twisting mountain or coastal routes offer plenty of hazards for the unwary. Corsicans delight in seeing tourists nearly pushed off the narrow tracks, but aren't so pleased when you hinder their progress by driving too slowly. Camper vans are particular targets for abuse and heavy honking. Considering the restricted breadth of most roads, it's best to ignore the jeering and take the corniche and mountain routes at a steady pace. Another reason to drive slowly are the great potholes which pit many of the roads. Roaming pigs and goats present a further problem.

Rules of the road are fairly straightforward. You drive on the right and give way to anybody coming out of a side-turning on the right, unless you see a roadsign showing a red square on a white background – this means that you have priority. At traffic roundabouts the cars on the roundabout have priority. *CEDEZ LE PASSAGE* means "Give Way", a *STOP* sign means come to a complete halt.

The **minimum age** to drive a car in Corsica is eighteen, and during the first year after passing your test you must not exceed 90kph. If your car is right-hand drive, you must have your headlight dip adjusted to the right before you go. Painting your headlights yellow is a courtesy rather than a requirement these days.

Speed limits are 110kph (68mph) on two-lane highways, 90kph (56mph) on other roads in non-urban areas, and 60kph (37mph) in towns. **Fines** for driving regulations are exacted on the spot, and only cash is accepted – 1300F is the minimum for speeding. There are no toll roads in Corsica.

As regards **documentation,** if you're bringing your own car, or intend to rent one, you'll need a valid driving licence. British, EC and US licences are all vaild, but the new pink EU licences are especially helpful if you come across a police officer unwilling to peruse a document in English. You must carry your car registration document and insurance papers in your vehicle. Although the international Green Card is no longer compulsory, it does provide fully comprehensive cover, so it's a good idea to get hold of one from your insurer.

To **rent** a car you'll usually need to have held a licence for over a year, although Corsican firms aren't as fussy as their British counterparts. Renting a car in Corsica will generally cost in the region of £300 per week, unless you're booking for a period of a month or more, whereas a pre-booked vehicle should cost no more than £250. In addition to the main rental firms, whose phone numbers are given in the box below (*Holiday Autos*'s price should be unbeatable), you might consider a **fly-drive** deal from a tour operator or an airline (see p.3 & p.7). Should you want to take a chance with a local Corsican company, you'll find them at the airports, the main towns and the resorts – we've detailed the most useful ones in the guide.

If you **break down**, your only option is to hail a passing car and get them to take you to the nearest garage, so check that the cost of repairs is covered by your rental agreement, or – if you're in your own vehicle – consider taking out extra insurance cover to meet this eventuality. If you have an accident or break-in you should make a report to the local police (and keep a copy) in order to make an insurance claim; in the event of an accident you are also obliged to complete a *constat à l'aimable* (jointly agreed statement), which your car insurers should give you. As for **fuel**, note that in remote country areas – such as Cap Corse and the interior – fuel stations are especially scarce, so remember to fill up in the towns. Unleaded fuel (*sans plomb*) is available everywhere.

BICYCLES AND MOPEDS

Cycling is a popular sport in Corsica, and you'll see many teams of cyclists streaming along the mountain roads. Corsicans are used to parties of cyclists clogging the roads, and will go out of their way to make room for you, while hotels are quite obliging about looking after your bike, even to the point of allowing it into your room. However, as a way of getting around the island it's only to be considered if you're in good shape.

If you want to **bring your bike** from home, flying is by far the easiest way – most airlines will charge just £10 for transporting the machine, provided you pack it in the prescribed way. Car ferries carry bicycles for free, but the French railway *SNCF* charges a flat fee of 150F for transporting your bike, which cannot be taken on the train you're travelling on; usually there's a three- or four-day time lag between your arrival at a given place and your bike's arrival. If you are taking your own bike from the UK, it's a good idea to join the *Cyclists' Touring Club*, which will suggest routes and supply advice to members; they also run a particularly good insurance scheme. The cost of membership is £24 a year, £12 for students, the unemployed and under-12s, and their address is Cotterell House, 68 Meadrow, Godalming, Surrey GU7 3HS (☎0483/417217).

CAR RENTAL FIRMS

Britain		North America	
Budget	☎0800/181 181	Avis	☎800/722 1333
Hertz	☎ 081/679 1799	Dollar	☎800/421 6868
Avis	☎081/848 8733	Europe by Car	☎800/223 1516
Europcar	☎071/834 8484	Hertz	☎800/654 3131
Holiday Autos	☎071/491 1111	Holiday Autos	☎800/422 7737
		National Car Rental	☎800/CAR RENT

DRIVING VOCABULARY

to park the car	*garer la voiture*	puncture	*la crevaison*
car park	*un parking*	to inflate	*gonfler*
no parking	*defense de stationner*	battery	*batterie*
fuel station	*station de service*	plugs	*bougies*
fuel	*essence/super*	to break down	*tomber en panne*
fill it up	*faire le plein*	petrol can	*bidon*
oil	*huile*	insurance	*assurance*
air line	*ligne a air*	traffic lights	*feux*
tyre	*le pneu*	red light	*feu rouge*
wheel	*la roue*	green light	*feu vert*

CYCLING VOCABULARY

to adjust	*ajuster*	handlebars	*le guidon*
axle	*l'axe*	inner tube	*la chambre à l'air*
ball-bearing	*le roulement a billes*	loose	*dévissé*
battery	*la pile*	to lower	*baisser*
bent	*tordu*	mudguard	*le garde-boue*
bicycle	*le vélo*	pannier	*le pannier*
bottom bracket	*le logement du pédalier*	pedal	*le pédale*
		pump	*la pompe*
brake cable	*le cable*	rack	*la porte-bagages*
brakes	*les freins*	to raise	*relever*
broken	*cassé*	to repair	*réparer*
bulb	*l'ampoule*	saddle	*la selle*
chain	*la chaîne*	spanner	*la clef*
frame	*le cadre*	to straighten	*rédresser*
gears	*les vitesses*	stuck	*coincé*
grease	*la graisse*	tight	*serré*

In view of the toughness of the terrain (and the relative scarcity of shops supplying spares for touring bikes), you might prefer to **rent a bike** for a short trip from one of the main towns and tourist resorts, where you'll find plenty of outlets – we've listed many of them in the guide. One day's rental of a mountain bike *(Vélo Tous Terrains* or *VTT)* should cost around 150F, with a 500F deposit.

Mopeds are ideal for checking out secluded beaches and villages, and are generally available from places that rent out bicycles. The minimum age for riders is 14, and you can expect to pay 150F a day. Crash helmets, included in the price, are highly advisable although only compulsory for machines over 125cc.

BUSES AND TRAINS

Buses are Corsica's main public transport service, covering many areas which the train doesn't reach. The main routes are Bastia–Ajaccio (direct), Bastia–Porto-Vecchio (stopping at Ghisonaccia), Bastia–Calvi (stopping at L'Île Rousse), Ajaccio–Bonifacio (stopping at Propriano and Sartène), Calvi–Porto (direct) and Porto–Ajaccio (stopping at Cargèse). In rural areas the timetable is constructed to suit working and school hours, which means there's often just one bus a day in any direction, departing at a dauntingly early hour.

Corsica's diminutive **train**, *la micheline* or *Trinighellu* (little train), crosses the mountains from Ajaccio to Bastia via Corte, with a subsidiary line running from Ponte Leccia, north of Corte, to Calvi. The train follows a rattling precarious route across the island and is far slower than the bus (the 100km from Ajaccio to Bastia takes four hours, as opposed to three by bus) – due largely to delays caused by cows and goats roaming onto the lines, and by the driver having a chat with the "officials" posted at each station. **Tickets** cost about the same as the buses, ie 100F per 100km.

If you can provide proof that you're a student you get a discount on all tickets, and often if you're travelling to or from the university town of Corte you don't even need a card.

WALKING

One of the best ways to explore the mountains and forests of Corsica's amazing interior is by **walking**, and a huge variety of walks are practicable here, from a gentle stroll alongside a bubbling torrent to a strenuous climb up one of the mighty peaks. Many walks are best attempted from early spring through to late summer, principally to profit from the long daylight hours and avoid the mists and snow which descend over the hills in winter.

Whatever length of walk you're planning on tackling, take a sturdy pair of walking **boots**, as even on the shortest walks you may well be crossing streams and clambering over boulders. On the more ambitious long-distance hikes – the **GR20**, the **Tra Mare e Monti** and the **Da Mare a Mare** (detailed on p.87 and p.164) – you'll need to be equipped for a full day's exertion, and

an ice axe wouldn't go amiss for the highest granite needles, which reach up to 2000m. Accommodation for hikers is provided by **gîtes d'étapes** and **refuges** (see pp.16–17), and a cooking stove and a small tent would come in handy if these are full, which is a strong possibility in July and August.

New trails are being created all the time, with 600km of paths already clearly waymarked with orange paint or wooden arrows showing the distance to the nearest village or refuge. All these footpaths are described in the *Walks in Corsica* guide (see p.217), and tourist offices can provide information on their local paths – some of them organize climbing and walking expeditions with professional guides.

In Ajaccio the office of the **Parc Naturel Régional**, rue Général-Fiorella 20184 Ajaccio (☎95 21 56 54), gives excellent advice on all aspects of rambling in Corsica. Another useful Ajaccio address is the *Muntagne Corse in Liberta*, Immeuble le Rond Point, 2 av de la Grande Armée (☎95 20 53 14), which organizes hiking expeditions lasting from a couple of days to a week, at different levels of expertise.

EATING AND DRINKING

Corsican cuisine is not delicate, but its hearty rich stews and seafood dishes can provide some exceptional meals. Wherever you go you'll be offered a range of *charcuterie* (cured ham and smoked sausages), and as you'd expect on a Mediterranean island, you'll find plenty of oysters, mussels, lobster

and prawns on the menu. Freshwater fish and game also feature prominently, with such specialities as blackbird paté and roast kid appearing on special occasions. Snack food is primarily French, with Italian influence almost as evident (ie pizzas), and there's a wide choice of restaurants to cater for the tourist population. Menus are always in French, occasionally with translations, and you'll find some classic French dishes featured alongside the regional food.

BREAKFAST AND SNACKS

A croissant, *pain au chocolat* (a chocolate-filled croissant) or a sandwich with hot chocolate or coffee is the standard **breakfast**, which is best taken in a bar or café – you'll pay through the nose in any hotel.

At **lunchtime** you may find cafés offering a *plat du jour* (chef's daily special) at between 40F and 50F for a limited or no-choice menu. The *croque-monsieur* or *croque-madame* (variations on the toasted cheese sandwich) is on sale in cafés and street stands, along with *frites, crêpes, galettes* (wholewheat savoury pancakes), *gauffres* (waffles), *glaces* (ice creams), slices of pizza and all kinds of fresh sandwiches. Cafés in the mountains will make you up a *casse-croûte*, a large sandwich often filled with a generous slice of *lonzu* (cured ham) or local *saucisson*.

For **picnics**, local shops and occasional supermarkets can provide you with almost anything you need from fruit to paté, and a visit to a *rotisserie* or *charcuterie* is always rewarding. Cooked meat, ready-made dishes, cheese, quiches and assorted salads can all be bought by weight from the latter, or you can ask for a *tranche* (a slice), *une barquette* (a carton), or *une part* (a portion).

Salons de thé, though few and far between, serve brunches, salads and the like as well as cakes and ice cream and a wide selection of teas. They tend to be a good deal pricier than cafés as you pay for the swish decor. *Patisseries* do wonderful cakes and local sweet delicacies such as chestnut cake and *fiadone* (see box p.26), as well as some savoury snacks like pizza and *tartelettes* (mini-quiches) and *canistrelli* (shortbread-style biscuits).

FULL-SCALE MEALS

You'll find a sprinkling of excellent restaurants scattered about the island, with the best generally found in the villages. Fine fish restaurants predominate on the coast, as you'd expect, and inland you can get excellent trout at cosy *auberges*, where local game will also be on offer (for more on Corsican dishes, see below and p.26). Otherwise, there's an abundance of pizzerias and crêperies for those on a budget, and many of these places also often offer a wider choice of dishes than their name would suggest – regional cuisine, salads and pasta might all feature on the menu.

For country restaurants it's a good idea to reserve a table, although for most places in towns and resorts you won't need to bother. In many places it may be impossible to find anything after 10pm, although in the larger tourist resorts there's always something open in summer. Don't forget that hotel restaurants are usually open to non-residents, and are often good value.

Prices are posted outside the restaurant, and usually the least expensive option is the *menu fixe*, where the number of courses has already been determined and the choice is limited. These

revolve around standard dishes such as steak and chips (*steack frites*), chicken and chips (*poulet frites*), or fried fish of some kind (*friture du golfe* is common) and cost an average 80–100F. The *plat du jour*, often a regional dish, might well be featured on the *menu fixe*, but for unlimited access to the chef's specialities you'll have to go *à la carte*, when you can expect to pay upwards of 80F for the main course. In Corsica, as in the rest of France, any salad (sometimes vegetables too) comes separate from the main dish, and you will be offered coffee, which is also charged extra, to finish off the meal.

Service compris or *s.c.* means the **service charge** is included. *Service non compris, s.n.c.* means that it isn't and you need to calculate an additional fifteen percent. **Wine** (*vin*) or a **drink** (*boisson*) is unlikely to be included, although occasionally it is thrown in with cheaper menus. When ordering wine, ask for *un quart* (0.25 litre), *un demi-litre* (0.5 litre), *une carafe* (a litre) or *un pichet* (a jug). You'll normally be given the house wine unless you specify otherwise; if you're worried about the cost just ask for *vin ordinaire*.

Vegetarians will have problems in Corsican restaurants, as many dishes are meat-based. A good idea is to have a variety of starters which include salads and *crudités*, or resort to the pizza and pasta places. Remember the phrase *je suis végétarien(ne), il y a quelques plats sans viande?* (I'm a vegetarian; are there any non-meat dishes?).

CORSICAN SPECIALITIES

It's the maquis herbs and plants – thyme, marjoram, basil, fennel and rosemary – which give Corsican cooking a unique flavour that's enhanced by olive oil and spices, especially in the south of the island, where flavours are less subtle than in the north.

You'll find the best **charcuterie** in the north, where pork is smoked and cured in the cold cellars of the village houses – it's particularly tasty in the **Castagniccia**, where wild pigs feed on the **chestnuts** which were once the staple diet of the region's inhabitants. Here you can also taste chestnut fritters (*fritelli a gaju frescu*) and chestnut cake (*pulenta*) sprinkled with sugar or *eau de vie*. **Brocciu**, a soft *fromage frais* made with ewe's milk, is found everywhere on the island, forming the basis for many dishes, including omelettes stuffed with *brocciu* and mint, and

FOODS AND DISHES

Basic terms

Pain	Bread	*Poivre*	Pepper	*Verre*	Glass		
Beurre	Butter	*Sel*	Salt	*Fourchette*	Fork		
Oeufs	Eggs	*Sucre*	Sugar	*Couteau*	Knife		
Lait	Milk	*Vinaigre*	Vinegar	*Cuillère*	Spoon		
Huile	Oil	*Bouteille*	Bottle	*Table*	Table		

Snacks

Un sandwich/
une baguette ... **A sandwich**
  jambon   with ham
  fromage   with cheese
  saucisson   with sausage
  à l'ail   with garlic
  au poivre   with pepper
  pâté (de   with pâté (country-style)
   campagne)
  croque-monsieur   Grilled cheese and ham
     sandwich
  croque-madame   Grilled cheese and bacon,
     sausage, chicken or an egg

Oeufs   **Eggs**
  au plat   Fried eggs
  à la coque   Boiled eggs
  durs   Hard-boiled eggs
  brouillés   Scrambled eggs

Omelette ...   **Omelette** ...
  nature   plain
  aux fines herbes   with herbs
  au fromage   with cheese

Salade de ...   **Salad of** ...
  tomates   tomatoes
  betteraves   beets
  concombres   cucumber
  carottes rapées   grated carrots

Crêpe   **Pancake**
  au sucre   with sugar
  au citron   with lemon
  au miel   with honey
  à la confiture   with jam
  aux oeufs   with eggs
  à la crème de marrons   with chestnut purée

Other fillings/salads
Anchois   Anchovy
Andouillette   Tripe sausage
Boudin   Black pudding
Coeurs de palmiers   Hearts of palm
Epis de maïs   Corn on the cob
Fonds d'artichauts   Artichoke hearts
Hareng   Herring
Langue   Tongue
Poulet   Chicken
Thon   Tuna fish

And some terms
Chauffé   Heated
Cuit   Cooked
Cru   Raw
Emballé   Wrapped
A emporter   Takeaway
Fumé   Smoked
Salé   Salted/spicy
Sucré   Sweet

Soups (*soupes*) and starters (*hors d'oeuvres*)

Bisque   Shellfish soup
Bouillabaisse   Marseillais fish soup
Bouillon   Broth or stock
Bourride   Thick fish soup
Consommé   Clear soup
Pistou   Parmesan, basil and garlic
     paste added to soup
Potage   Thick vegetable soup
Rouille   Red pepper, garlic and
     saffron mayonnaise served
     with fish soup

Velouté   Thick soup, usually fish or
     poultry

Starters
Assiette   Plate of cold meats
 anglaise
Crudités   Raw vegetables with
     dressings
Hors d'oeuvres   Combination of the above
 variés   plus smoked or marinated
     fish

Fish (poisson), seafood (fruits de mer) and shellfish (crustaces or coquillages)...

Anchois	Anchovies	Daurade	Sea bream
Anguilles	Eels	Eperlan	Smelt or
Barbue	Brill		whitebait
Bigourneau	Periwinkle	Escargots	Snails
Brème	Bream	Flétan	Halibut
Cabillaud	Cod	Friture	Assorted fried fish
Calmar	Squid	Gambas	King prawns
Carrelet	Plaice	Hareng	Herring
Claire	Type of oyster	Homard	Lobster
Colin	Hake	Huîtres	Oysters
Congre	Conger eel	Langouste	Spiny lobster
Coques	Cockles	Langoustines	Saltwater crayfish
Coquilles St-	Scallops		(scampi)
Jacques		Limande	Lemon sole
Crabe	Crab	Lotte	Burbot
Crevettes grises	Shrimp	Lotte de mer	Monkfish
Crevettes roses	Prawns	Loup de mer	Sea bass

Louvine,	Similar to sea
loubine	bass
Maquereau	Mackerel
Merlan	Whiting
Moules	Mussels (with
(marinière)	shallots in white
	wine sauce)
Oursin	Sea urchin
Palourdes	Clams
Praires	Small clams
Raie	Skate
Rouget	Red mullet
Saumon	Salmon
Sole	Sole
Thon	Tuna
Truite	Trout
Turbot	Turbot

...and fish terms

Aïoli	Garlic mayonnaise served with salt cod and other fish	Fumé	Smoked
		Fumet	Fish stock
Béarnaise	Sauce of egg yolks, white wine, shallots and vinegar	Gigot de Mer	Large fish baked whole
		Grillé	Grilled
Beignets	Fritters	Hollandaise	Butter and vinegar sauce
Darne	Fillet or steak	A la meunière	In a butter, lemon and
La douzaine	A dozen		parsley sauce
Frit	Fried	Mousse/mousseline	Mousse
Friture	Deep fried small fish	Quenelles	Light dumplings

Meat (viande) and poultry (volaille)

Agneau (de pré-salé)	Lamb (grazed on salt marshes)	Langue	Tongue
		Lapin, lapereau	Rabbit, young rabbit
Andouille, andouillette	Tripe sausage	Lard, lardons	Bacon, diced bacon
		Lièvre	Hare
Boeuf	Beef	Merguez	Spicy, red sausage
Bifteck	Steak	Mouton	Mutton
Boudin blanc	Sausage of white meats	Museau de veau	Calf's muzzle
Boudin noir	Black pudding	Oie	Goose
Caille	Quail	Os	Bone
Canard	Duck	Porc	Pork
Caneton	Duckling	Poulet	Chicken
Contrefilet	Sirloin roast	Poussin	Baby chicken
Coquelet	Cockerel	Ris	Sweetbreads
Dinde, dindon	Turkey	Rognons	Kidneys
Entrecôte	Ribsteak	Rognons blancs	Testicles
Faux filet	Sirloin steak	Sanglier	Wild boar
Foie	Liver	Steack	Steak
Foie gras	Fattened (duck/ goose) liver	Tête de veau	Calf's head (in jelly)
Gigot (d'agneau)	Leg (of lamb)	Tournedos	Thick slices of fillet
Grillade	Grilled meat	Tripes	Tripe
Hâchis	Chopped meat or mince hamburger	Veau	Veal
		Venaison	Venison

Meat and poultry terms – dishes . . .

Boeuf bourguignon	Beef stew with burgundy, onions and mushrooms	*Coq au vin*	Chicken cooked until it falls off the bone with wine, onions, and mushrooms
Canard à l'orange	Roast duck with an orange-and-wine sauce	*Steak au poivre (vert/ rouge)*	Steak in a black (green/red) peppercorn sauce
Cassoulet	A casserole of beans and meat	*Steak tartare*	Raw chopped beef, topped with a raw egg yolk

. . . and terms

Blanquette, daube, estouffade, hochepôt, navarin and ragoût	All are types of stew	*Museau*	Muzzle
		Rôti	Roast
		Sauté	Lightly cooked in butter
Aile	Wing		
Carré	Best end of neck, chop or cutlet	**For steaks:**	
		Bleu	Almost raw
Civit	Game stew	*Saignant*	Rare
Confit	Meat preserve	*A point*	Medium
Côte	Chop, cutlet or rib	*Bien cuit*	Well done
Cou	Neck	*Très bien cuit*	Very well cooked
Cuisse	Thigh or leg	*Brochette*	Kebab
Epaule	Shoulder		
Médaillon	Round piece	**Garnishes and sauces:**	
Pavé	Thick slice		
En croûte	In pastry	*Beurre blanc*	Sauce of white wine and shallots, with butter
Farci	Stuffed		
Au feu de bois	Cooked over wood fire	*Chasseur*	White wine, mushrooms and shallots
Au four	Baked		
Garni	With vegetables	*Diable*	Strong mustard seasoning
Gésier	Gizzard	*Forestière*	With bacon and mushroom
Grillé	Grilled	*Fricassée*	Rich, creamy sauce
Magret de canard	Duck breast	*Mornay*	Cheese sauce
Marmite	Casserole	*Pays d'Auge*	Cream and cider
Mijoté	Stewed	*Piquante*	Gherkins or capers, vinegar and shallots
		Provençale	Tomatoes, garlic, olive oil and herbs

Fruit *(fruit)* and nuts *(noix)*

Abricot	Apricot	*Framboises*	Raspberries	*Pistache*	Pistachio
Amandes	Almonds	*Fruit de la passion*	Passion fruit	*Poire*	Pear
Ananas	Pineapple			*Pomme*	Apple
Banane	Banana	*Groseilles*	Redcurrants and gooseberries	*Prune*	Plum
Brugnon, nectarine	Nectarine			*Pruneau*	Prune
		Mangue	Mango	*Raisins*	Grapes
Cacahouète	Peanut	*Marrons*	Chestnuts		
Cassis	Blackcurrants	*Melon*	Melon	**Terms**:	
Cérises	Cherries	*Myrtilles*	Bilberries	*Beignets*	Fritter
Citron	Lemon	*Noisette*	Hazelnut	*Compôte de . . .*	Stewed . . .
Citron vert	Lime	*Noix*	Nuts	*Coulis*	Sauce
Figues	Figs	*Orange*	Orange	*Flambé*	Set aflame in alcohol
Fraises (de bois)	Strawberries (wild)	*Pamplemousse*	Grapefruit		
		Pêche (blanche)	(White) peach	*Frappé*	Iced

Vegetables *(légumes)*, herbs *(herbes)* and spices *(épices)*, etc

Ail	Garlic	*Endive*	Chicory	*Piment*	Pimento
Algue	Seaweed	*Epinards*	Spinach	*Pois chiche*	Chick peas
Anis	Aniseed	*Estragon*	Tarragon	*Pois mange-*	Snow peas
Artichaut	Artichoke	*Fenouil*	Fennel	*tout*	
Asperges	Asparagus	*Flageolet*	White beans	*Pignons*	Pine nuts
Avocat	Avocado	*Gingembre*	Ginger	*Poireau*	Leek
Basilic	Basil	*Haricots*	Beans	*Poivron*	Sweet pepper
Betterave	Beetroot	*Verts*	String (French)	*(vert, rouge)*	(green, red)
Carotte	Carrot	*Rouges*	Kidney	*Pommes (de*	Potatoes
Céleri	Celery	*Beurres*	Butter	*terre)*	
Champignons,	Mushrooms of	*Laurier*	Bay leaf	*Primeurs*	Spring
cèpes,	various kinds	*Lentilles*	Lentils		vegetables
chanterelles		*Maïs*	Corn	*Radis*	Radishes
Chou (rouge)	(Red) cabbage	*Menthe*	Mint	*Riz*	Rice
Choufleur	Cauliflower	*Moutarde*	Mustard	*Safran*	Saffron
Ciboulettes	Chives	*Oignon*	Onion	*Salade verte*	Green salad
Concombre	Cucumber	*Pâte*	Pasta or pastry	*Sarrasin*	Buckwheat
Cornichon	Gherkin	*Persil*	Parsley	*Tomate*	Tomato
Echalotes	Shallots	*Petits pois*	Peas	*Truffes*	Truffles

Dishes and terms

Beignet	Fritter	*Parmentier*	With potatoes
Farci	Stuffed	*Sauté*	Lightly fried in butter
Gratiné	Browned with cheese or butter	*A la vapeur*	Steamed
Jardinière	With mixed diced vegetables	*Je suis végétarien(ne).*	I'm a vegetarian. Are
A la parisienne	Sautéed in butter (potatoes); with	*Il y a quelques plats*	there any non-meat
	white wine sauce, and shallots	*sans viande?*	dishes?

Desserts *(desserts* or *entremets)* and pastries *(pâtisserie)*

Bombe	A moulded ice cream dessert	*Parfait*	Frozen mousse, some-
Brioche	Sweet, high yeast breakfast roll		times ice cream
Charlotte	Custard and fruit in lining of	*Petit Suisse*	A smooth mixture of
	almond fingers		cream and curds
Crème Chantilly	Vanilla-flavoured and sweet-	*Petits fours*	Bite-sized cakes/pastries
	ened whipped cream	*Poires Belle Hélène*	Pears and ice cream in
Crème fraîche	Sour cream		chocolate sauce
Crème pâtissière	Thick eggy pastry-filling	*Yaourt, yogourt*	Yoghurt
Crêpes suzettes	Thin pancakes with orange		
	juice and liqueur	**Terms:**	
Fromage blanc	Cream cheese	*Barquette*	Small boat-shaped flan
Glace	Ice cream	*Bavarois*	Refers to the mould, could
Ile flottante/	Soft meringues floating on		be a mousse or custard
oeufs à la neige	custard	*Coupe*	A serving of ice cream
Macarons	Macaroons	*Crêpes*	Pancakes
Madeleine	Small sponge cake	*Galettes*	Buckwheat pancakes
Marrons Mont	Chestnut purée and cream on a	*Gênoise*	Rich sponge cake
Blanc	rum-soaked sponge cake	*Sablé*	Shortbread biscuit
Mousse au	Chocolate mousse	*Savarin*	A filled, ring-shaped cake
chocolat		*Tarte*	Tart
Palmiers	Caramelized puff pastries	*Tartelette*	Small tart

And one final note: always call the waiter or waitress *Monsieur* or *Madame* (*Mademoiselle* if a young woman), never *garçon*, no matter what you've been taught in school.

CORSICAN DISHES

Starters

Cannelloni al brocciu	Pasta stuffed with *brocciu* and mint with tomato sauce	Suppa di Pesce/ Soupe de Poisson	Fish soup served with toast and garlic
Omelette al brocciu	Omelette filled with *brocciu*	Suppa Corsa/ Soupe Corse	Vegetable soup with beans

Charcuterie

Coppa	Smoked pork shoulder	Lonzu	Smoked pork fillet
Figatellu	Pork liver sausage	Prisuttu	Cured ham

Main courses

Aziminu	Rich, heavily spiced garlicky fish stew	Stifatu	A roll of stuffed meats – goat, lamb and sometimes
Bianchetti	Little fish fried in batter		blackbird –served with
Cabrettu a l'istrettu	Strongly spiced kid stew		grated cheese
Formaghju di porcu	Pork brawn seasoned with onion, garlic, pepper and maquis herbs	Tianu di Cingale / Sangliers en daube	Wild boar stew with potatoes
		Tianu d'agnellu	Lamb stew
Fritelle di gaju frescu	Fritters made with chestnut flour and *brocciu*	Tianu di fave	Pork and bean stew
		Tianu di pisi	Onions, carrots, peas and tomato stew
Lasagne di cignale	Wild boar lasagne		
Pivarunata	Peppery beef and potato stew with pimentos	Tripette	Tripe in tomato sauce

Cheese and puddings

Brocciu	Soft white cheese made with curds	Canistrelli	Soft shortbread-type biscuits made with white wine and honey
Fromage Corse	Uniquely flavoured indigenous hard cheese	Fiadone	Tart filled with *brocciu*
		Fritelli/beignets	Small doughnuts, sometimes made with chestnut flour

cannelloni al brocciu. *Suppa Corsa* is another delicious meatless choice; the precise recipe varies from region to region, but it's always packed with beans and garlic. *Fromage Corse* is also very good – a unique hard **cheese** made in the sheep-rearing Niolo and Asco regions, where *cabrettu a l'istrettu* (kid stew) is also a speciality.

Game – mainly stews of hare and wild boar but also roast woodcock, partridge and wood pigeon – features throughout the island's mountain and forested regions. Here blackbirds (*merles*) are made into a fragrant pâté, and **eel and trout** are fished from the unpolluted rivers. Red mullet (*rouget*), sea bream (*loup de mer*) and a great variety of **shellfish** is offered along the coast – the best crayfish (*langouste*) comes from around the Golfe de Saint-Florent, whereas oysters (*huîtres*) are a speciality of the eastern plain.

Many of the dishes listed above are only found in authentic Corsican places, but you'll always find one or two specialities on the menu of a standard restaurant. The French translation is given where the name will usually appear in French on the menu.

DRINKING

Cafés and bars line the streets and squares of Corsica's towns and tourist resorts, and these are where you'll likely do most of your drinking, whether as a prelude to food (*apéritif*) or as a sequel (*digestif*). Bars tend to be dark, functional places, whereas cafés are more open, often featuring a terrace where you can sit and watch life pass by. Every bar or café displays a price list with progressively increasing prices for drinks at the bar, at the table or on the terrace.

Wine (*vin*) is the regular drink, with *rosé* the type produced in greatest volume in Corsica. *Vin de Table* is generally drinkable and always inexpensive; restaurant mark-ups for quality wines, on the other hand, can be very high for a country where wine is so plentiful. In bars, you normally buy by the glass, and just ask for *un rouge*, *un blanc* or *un rosé*; *un pichet* gets you a quarter-litre jug.

Of the local products, you should be sure to try the **Santa Barba** or **Fiumicicoli** wines of the Sartène area, which come in both red and rosé, and the **Patrimonio**, a robust white wine from Cap Corse. The favoured aperitifs are the sweet muscat produced on Cap Corse, and the drink known as **Cap Corse**, a fortified wine flavoured with herbs.

Belgian and German brands account for most of the **beer** you'll find. Draught beer (*bière à la pression*) is the cheapest alcoholic drink after wine – ask for a *demi* (defined as 25cl). Bottled beer is exceptionally cheap in supermarkets.

Strong alcohol is drunk right through the day, the most popular drink being strong aniseed-based *pastis*, especially the local brand, **Casanis**. Brandies and *eaux de vie* are always available – the latter comes in a variety of flavours, such as *prune* (grape) and *cerise* (cherry), and is usually distilled locally in the villages. In many small restaurants and bars you'll be offered these free. You may also be offered **Cedratine** and **Myrthe**, which are locally made sickly sweet liqueurs.

On the **soft drink** front, you can buy cartons of unsweetened fruit juice in supermarkets, although in cafés the bottled nectars such as *jus d'abricot* (apricot) and *jus de poire* (pear) still hold sway. Some cafés serve tiny glasses of fresh orange and lemon juice (*orange/citron pressé*); otherwise it's the standard fizzy cans. Bottles of **mineral water** (*eau minérale*) and spring water (*eau de source*) – either sparkling (*pétillante*) or flat (*eau plate*) – abound. *Perrier* is popular but the island's own *Orezza* spring water is excellent. Note that tap water (*l'eau du robinet*) is particularly good quality in Corsica, coming from the fresh mountain streams.

Coffee is invariably *espresso* and very strong. *Un café* or *un express* is black, *un crème* is white, *un café au lait* (served at breakfast) is *espresso* in a large cup or bowl filled up with hot milk. Ordinary tea (*thé*) is Liptons' tea-bag tea, nine times out of ten; to have milk with it, ask for *un peu de lait frais*. Herb teas (*infusions*) are served in every café and can be a refreshing alternative. The more common ones are *vervaine* (verbena), *tilleul* (lime blossom) and *tisane* (camomile). ***Chocolat Chaud*** – hot chocolate – unlike tea, can be had in any café.

POST, PHONES AND MEDIA

Post offices – *postes* or PTTs – are generally open Monday to Friday 9am–noon and 2–5pm, plus 9am–noon on Saturday. However, don't depend on these hours: in the major towns you might find the main office open through the day, whilst opening and closing times vary enormously in the villages.

MAIL SERVICES

You can have letters sent to you by ***Poste Restante*** at any main post office on the island. The addresses of the principal offices are: Cours Napoléon, Ajaccio 20000, and Avenue Maréchal-Sebastiani, Bastia 20200. To collect mail you'll need a passport, and should expect to pay a charge of a few francs. If you're expecting mail, it's worth asking the clerk to check under all your names, as filing systems tend to be erratic. **Sending letters**, the quickest international service is by *aérogramme*, sold at all post offices. You can get ordinary **stamps** (*timbres*) at any *tabac* (tobacconist). If you're sending **parcels** abroad, try to check prices in the various leaflets available: small *postes* may need reminding of the huge reductions for printed papers and books, for example.

TELEPHONES

You can make domestic and international phone calls from any box (*cabine*), many of which only take **phone cards** (*télécartes*), obtainable for 20F and 50F from post offices and some *tabacs*. Coin-only boxes are still common in bars, cafés and villages, and take 1F, 5F and 10F pieces. For **calls within France**, whatever the distance, you should dial all eight digits of the number; for **international calls**, dial 19, wait for a tone, and then dial the country code (see box below), then the subscriber number minus its initial 0.

An alternative to dialling internationally from a *cabine* is to use the booths at main post offices, where you pay after making the call. If you do this, make sure you count your units, which are clearly displayed – mistakes are made in calculating the bill. To make a reverse-charge call to a number abroad, phone the international operator.

OPERATOR NUMBERS AND PHONE CODES

To call Corsica from abroad dial ☎01033 plus the number.

To call abroad from Corsica, the country codes are as follows:

Britain ☎44
Ireland ☎353
USA and Canada ☎1
Australia ☎61
New Zealand ☎64

To speak to the **operator** dial ☎10; the **international operator** is ☎19 33 11.

NEWSPAPERS AND MAGAZINES

The Corsican newspapers with the widest circulations are the two **local dailies**: the *Corse-Matin*, printed by *Nice-Matin*, and *Le Corse-Provencal*, which is more of a tabloid. These usually feature reports of gruesome shootings or holdups, which tend to be given greater prominence than news of the wider world, and are useful for listings. Of the **national dailies** *Le Monde* (Tues–Sun) is the most intellectual and respected, with no concessions to entertainment (such as pictures), but written in an orthodox French that is probably the easiest to understand. *Libération* (Tues–Sun), is moderately left wing and colloquial, with good selective coverage; *L'Humanité* is the Communist Party newspaper, with a constantly diminishing readership. All the other nationals are firmly on the right. British newspapers and the *International Herald Tribune* are intermittently available in the larger resorts and in Ajaccio and Bastia.

Weeklies, on the *Newsweek/Time* model, include the wide-ranging, left-leaning *Le Nouvel-Observateur* and its rightist counterweight, *L'Express*. The best and funniest investigative journalism is in *Le Canard Enchaîné*, but it's almost incomprehensible to non-natives. Corsican nationalists are represented by the weekly political magazine *Aritti*, with articles in French and Corsican, and there's also a general-interest Corsican monthly called *Kyrn*, which has some articles in Corsican.

TV AND RADIO

You get both **French and Italian television** in Corsica. French is slightly better quality, featuring a range of programmes from trashy quiz shows to intellectual discussions about wine. The third channel – **FR3** – features Corsican regional programmes, with a local news bulletin every lunchtime and evening and a sporadic schedule of documentaries. Italian television is less widely available; the RAI channels are the best, featuring documentaries and good news coverage. Many hotels also have **satellite** channels, which include at least one English-speaking station.

There are a few local **radio** stations in Corsica, many of them broadcasting within a tiny area. The best of these is Bastia's RCFM (*Radio Corse Frequenza Mora*; 103FM), broadcasting in French and Corsican and playing a good variety of music, including the traditional folk music and modern Corsican bands.

BUSINESS HOURS AND PUBLIC HOLIDAYS

Basic hours of business are 8am–noon and 2–6pm; almost everything in Corsica – shops, museums, tourist offices, most banks – closes for a couple of hours at midday. In remote parts of the island lunch breaks tend to be lengthier and opening times less reliable. Food shops all over the island often don't open until midway through the afternoon, closing around 7.30 or 8pm, just before the evening meal.

The standard **closing days** are Sunday and Monday, and in small places you'll find everything except the odd *boulangerie* (bakery) shut on both days. **Museums** are not very generous with their hours, tending to open around 10am, close at noon until 2pm or 3pm, and then run through until 5pm or 6pm – opening hours from mid-May to mid-September are generally slightly longer than during the rest of the year. Museum closing days are usually Monday or Tuesday, sometimes both. Most churches are open all day; if you come across one that's locked, you can ask for the key at the local *mairie* (town hall).

FESTIVALS AND EVENTS

Aside from the nationally celebrated religious festivals, such as the Assumption of the Virgin, local saints' days are celebrated in Corsican towns throughout the year, and often include fireworks and processions. Many events are music-

---

PUBLIC HOLIDAYS

There are twelve national holidays (*jours fériés*), when most shops and businesses, though not museums and restaurants, are closed.

January 1
Easter Sunday
Easter Monday
Ascension Day (forty days after Easter)
Pentecost (seventh Sunday after Easter, plus the Monday)
May 1 May Day/Labour Day
May 8 Victory in Europe Day
July 14 Bastille Day
August 15 Assumption of the Virgin Mary
November 1 All Saint's Day
November 11 Armistice Day
December 25

---

and arts-based affairs, with outdoor concerts and film festivals boosting the local tourist industry. There are also a few local country fairs where you can hear traditional Corsican singing and purchase regional specialities.

Of the innumerable Catholic feast days the most fervent are the **Easter** celebrations, almost invariably featuring a parade across town bearing a statue of the Virgin or of Christ, followed by

---

CALENDAR OF EVENTS

March 18 **Ajaccio** *Notre-Dame-de-la-Miséricorde* (see p.110).

Good Friday **Erbalunga** *La Cerca* (see p.52); **Sartène** *U Catenacciu* (see p.150); **Calvi** *La Granitola* (see p.77).

April **Bastia** English film festival (see p.46).

May 3 **Bastia** *Le Christ Noir* (see p.44).

June (third week) **Calvi** Jazz festival (see p.72).

June 2 **Bastia**, **Ajaccio** and **Calvi** *Saint-Erasme* Fishermen's festival celebrated with a mass and firework displays in the harbour.

July **Corte** *Ghjurnate di u Populu Corsu* Folk music festival.

August **Ajaccio** *Fêtes Napoléoniennes* Son et lumière in the Jardin du Casone.

August **Calvi** *Citadella in Festa* (see p.78).

August **Bonifacio** *Rencontres Mediterranéennes* (see p.153).

August 15 **Bastia and Ajaccio** *L'Assomption*.

September 8 **Lavasina** *Notre-Dame-de-Lavasina* (see p.51).

September 8–10 **Casamaccioli** *Santa di u Niolu* (see p.186).

September **Calvi** *Rencontres Polyphoniques* (see p.78).

October **Bastia** Mediterranean film festival (see p.46).

Mass and a street party with fireworks and music. Many of these rituals also include a procession called a *granitola*, an ancient rite whereby a line of penitents forms a spiral as it moves through the town. The most intense of all Corsican religious ceremonies is the **Catenacciu** in Sartène, an Easter procession led by a penitent who drags a cross through the streets in imitation of Christs' walk to Golgotha.

Of the island's plethora of folk festivals, one that is definitely worth attending is the September **Santa di u Niolu** in Casamaccioli, a riotous event involving much drinking, singing and gambling. Corte's *Ghjurnate di u Populu Corsu* summer festival brings together nationalist separatists from all over Europe for a week of concerts and political speeches. Mediterranean folk music festivals take place at various locations throughout the summer, and there's a two-week jazz festival at Calvi every June.

The box on the previous page gives a rundown on the main annual events, with cross-references to the places in the guide where you'll find more details.

TROUBLE AND POLICE

Despite Corsica's reputation for violence and extremist politics, you are unlikely to encounter any trouble during your stay on the island, provided you keep within the law and avoid confrontations with the locals. Petty crime is minimal, although it makes sense to keep a close eye on your valuables in the crowded tourist resorts. If you should get robbed, hand over the money promptly and start dialling the cancellation numbers for your travellers' cheques and credit cards. Vehicles are rarely stolen, but tape players and luggage left in cars are more vulnerable to thieves. Try not to leave any valuables in sight, and make sure you have insurance.

There are two main types of French police (popularly known as *les flics*): the **Police Nationale** and the **Gendarmerie Nationale**. For all practical purposes, they are indistinguishable; if you need to report a theft, or other incident, you can go to either. A noticeable presence in

---

EMERGENCY NUMBERS

Ambulance ☎18
Police ☎17
Fire service ☎18

CONSULATES IN MARSEILLE

Canada ☎91 37 19 37
Britain ☎91 53 43 32
Ireland ☎91 54 92 29
Netherlands ☎25 66 64
USA ☎91 54 92 00

Corsica are the **CRS** (*Compagnies Républicaines de Sécurité*), a mobile force of heavies, with whom you should have no contact unless you inadvertently get caught up in a riot.

The police have the right to demand identification from any citizen, so if you want to avoid all possible hassle, make sure you're able to produce your passport or something equally incontrovertible. For driving violations such as speeding, the police also have the right to impose on-the-spot fines. Should you be arrested on any charge, you have the right to contact your nearest consulate, which is likely to be in Marseille (see box above). People caught smuggling or possessing **drugs**, even a few grammes of marijuana, are liable to find themselves in jail and the consulate will not be sympathetic.

SEXUAL AND RACIAL HARASSMENT

Women are less likely to experience **sexual harassment** in Corsica than in mainland France or Italy. Men do tend to stare, but they rarely approach or pass audible comment. An inbuilt "respect" for the opposite sex means that men will never take advantage of a situation – if a woman is in any trouble she can rely on a Corsican (male or female) to help out. It's not unusual to be offered a drink in a bar, and accepting doesn't leave you open to any harassment – rather it's a case of people not liking to see you paying as a guest in their country. Walking around at night is usually safe, especially in mountain villages and major towns. You're more likely to encounter trouble from foreigners in tourist resorts.

You may, as a woman, be warned about "les Arabes", a standard instance of French **racism**. If you are Middle Eastern or black your chances of avoiding unpleasantness are unfortunately slim. Empty hotels claiming to be full, police demanding your papers and sometimes abusive treatment from ordinary people are all commonplace.

DISABLED TRAVELLERS

France has no exceptional record for providing facilities for disabled travellers, and Corsica lags far behind other regions in this respect. Accessible hotels do exist in the major resorts, and ramps or other forms of access are gradually being added to museums, but the situation is far from satisfactory. The organizations listed below can provide various forms of useful information.

TRAVEL WITH A DISABILITY: USEFUL ADDRESSES

APF (Association des Paralysés de France), 17–21 bd Auguste Blanqui, 75013 Paris (☎45 80 82 40). A national organization with regional offices all over France which can provide lists of accessible accommodation.

CNFLRH (Comité National Francaise de Liaison pour la Réadaption des Handicapés), 30–32 quai de la Loire, 75019 Paris (☎45 48 90 13). Information service for disabled travellers, with details of accessible accommodation, holiday centres etc. Also distributes various useful guides, including one to Corsica.

Holiday Care Service, 2 Old Bank Chambers, Station Rd, Horley, Surrey RH6 9HW (☎0293/ 774535). Information on all aspects of travel.

Kéroul, 4545 av Pierre de Coubertin, CP 1000, succ.M. Montréal, PQ H1V 3R2, Canada (☎514/ 2523104). Specializes in travel for mobility-impaired people.

Mobility International, 228 Borough High St, London SE1 (☎071/ 403 5688); PO Box 10767, Eugene, OR 97440 (☎503/343 1284). Information, access guides, tours and exchange programme.

RADAR (The Royal Association for Disability and Rehabilitation), 25 Mortimer St, London W1N 8AB (☎071/637 5400). Information on all aspects of travel.

Travel Information Center, Moss Rehabilitation Hospital, 1200 W Tabor Rd, Philadelphia PA 19141 (☎215/329 5715 x2233). Access information.

TRIPSCOPE, 63 Esmond Rd, London W4 1JE (☎081/994 9294). Phone-in travel information and advice service.

DIRECTORY

BEACHES are public property within 5m of the high tide mark; it's illegal to camp on them, however. Some beaches are protected areas, where you are prohibited from climbing on the dunes; and beware of the goats – an aggressive hazard in many spots.

CHILDREN are adored in Corsica and welcome in bars and restaurants. Hotels charge a small supplement for an extra bed or cot. Bus and train travel is free for the under 4s, half-fare for 4–12s.

CIGARETTES are the only consumer items cheaper than in mainland France, selling at 6F per packet.

CONTRACEPTIVES Pharmacists keep condoms (*preservatifs*) hidden under the counter, though there's an increasing number of dispensing machines in public places. You need a prescription for the Pill (*la Pillule*).

DIVING Clubs all over Corsica supply equipment and instruction for around 500F per day. At least bring a snorkel, as the sea is the clearest in the Med and packed with colourful fish.

ELECTRICITY is 220v, using plugs with two round pins.

LAUNDRY Self-service laundries in Corsica are extremely rare. *Pressing* services in Bastia and Ajaccio will do laundry for a high price and hotels will do it for around 50F per load. You could discreetly do your own in your hotel room, though technically it's forbidden to wash clothes in hotels.

LEFT LUGGAGE *Consignes* are found in the ports and train stations and charge around 15F per item per day.

PHOTOGRAPHIC FILM is expensive in Corsica, so bring as much as you'll need.

RIDING Former mule tracks converted into riding trails provide plenty of possibilities for riders. Long-distance rides, with accommodation provided along the way, are organized by the *Association Regionale pour le Tourisme Equèstre*, 20230 San Nicolao (☎95 38 56 70).

SKIING Although skiing is possible in the mountains, don't be fooled by tourist office advertising – snow is minimal and the prepared slopes are less than impressive. For information on cross-country skiing (*ski à fond*), contact *Montagne Corse in Liberta*, Parc Bilello, Immeuble Girolata, avenue Napoleon III 20000, Ajaccio (☎95 23 17 42).

TIME French summertime begins on March 28 and finishes on September 26, and therefore is an hour ahead of Britain for most of the year, except in October when times are the same. It's six hours ahead of Eastern Standard Time, nine hours ahead of Pacific Standard Time.

TOILETS Toilets, usually found at the back of bars, can be primitive hole-in-the-floor affairs, tending to lack paper. Outside public toilets are non-existent.

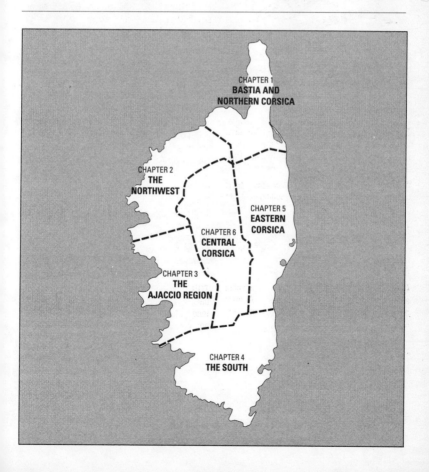

CHAPTER 1
BASTIA AND NORTHERN CORSICA

CHAPTER 2
THE NORTHWEST

CHAPTER 5
EASTERN CORSICA

CHAPTER 6
CENTRAL CORSICA

CHAPTER 3
THE AJACCIO REGION

CHAPTER 4
THE SOUTH

CHAPTER ONE

BASTIA AND NORTHERN CORSICA

Bastia, nowadays capital of the *département* of Haute-Corse, was the capital of the entire island under Genoa's colonial administration, and it was the Genoese who laid the foundations of northern Corsica's prosperity by encouraging the planting of vines, olives, chestnut trees and other more experimental crops – there's a village called Sparagaghjiu (Asparagus) in the hills above Saint-Florent. The long-term result of this development was that the peasant farmers of the north tended to be not just better off than their southern counterparts, but politically more ambitious too. Thus when Pascal Paoli recruited his rebel armies it was on this region's downtrodden rich that he concentrated his efforts, rather than on the downtrodden poor of the south, and even today there's a palpable difference in the political climate of the island's two halves, with northerners tending to see themselves as more radical, energetic and enterprising.

A thriving freight and passenger port, **Bastia** is the point of arrival for many visitors, and it can be a rather depressing experience at first, with industrial sprawl on the way into town from the airport, high-rise blocks on the hillsides above town, and no decent beaches. Yet, while Bastia lacks the appeal of sleek Ajaccio, this is the town to visit if you want to get to grips with modern Corsica, for a quarter of the island's population lives and works here and in the immediate surroundings. Moreover, despite suffering considerable damage in World War II, the city has retained its Italian character, especially around the **Vieux Port**, a horseshoe of vertiginous buildings dominated by the towers of the church of Saint-Jean-Baptiste and bulk of the Genoese citadel.

The nearest beaches are to the south along the unremarkable stretch of coast known as **La Marana**, which adjoins the **Étang de Biguglia**, a haven for migrating birds, and the beautiful Pisan church of **La Canonica**. To the north of Bastia, a single road follows the shore of the long rocky peninsula of **Cap Corse**, giving access to some exceptional coves and some diminutive ports, of which **Erbalunga** and **Centuri-Port** are the pick. At the base of the cape's finger, on the western side, lies **Saint-Florent**, a smart sailing centre and fishing village with most of the north's accommodation outside the capital. The hinterland of Saint-Florent, the **Nebbio**, is famed for the wines produced near **Patrimonio**, for dramatically sited upland villages such as **Oletta** and **Santo-Pietro-di-Tenda**, and for the finest Romanesque churches on the island – Santa Maria Assunta, on the outskirts of Saint-Florent, and the chapel of San Michele near Murato. West of Saint-Florent lies the uninhabited **Désert des Agriates**, a vast semi-barren expanse covered in massive clumps of rock, stands of cactus and the ruins of ancient stone dwellings. The coast here is generally wild and inaccessible, though the beaches of **Saleccia** and **Loto** are amongst the finest in Corsica.

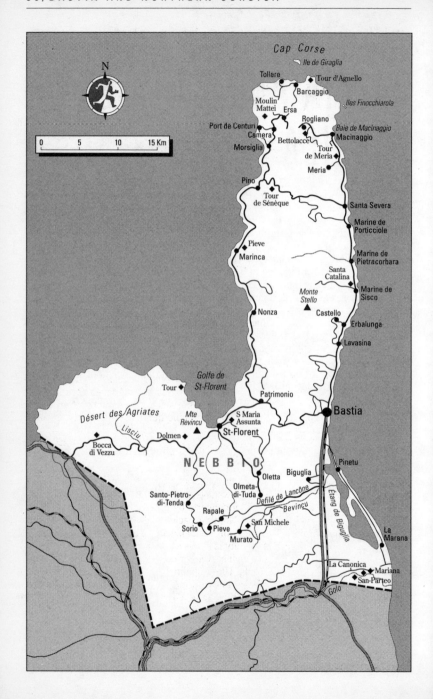

Public transport in the region is generally better than elsewhere on the island, but that isn't saying much. Corsica's train, the *micheline*, threads south from Bastia a little way, passing the Étang de Biguglia, but doesn't serve anywhere else covered in this chapter. Buses aren't common, but you can get one up into Cap Corse at certain times of the week, and daily into Saint-Florent. For the Nebbio villages you'll certainly need your own vehicle, and the same goes for the Désert des Agriates.

ACCOMMODATION PRICES

Throughout this guide, hotel accommodation is graded on a scale from ① to ⑥. These numbers show the cost per night of the **least expensive double room in high season**, and correspond to the following prices:

① under F200	③ F300–400	⑤ F500–600
② F200–300	④ F400–500	⑥ over 600F

Bastia

Paradoxically, the dominant tone of Corsica's most successful commercial town, **BASTIA**, is one of charismatic dereliction, as the city's industrial zone is spread onto the lowlands to the south, leaving the centre of town with plenty of aged charm. This charm might not be too apparent from the vast **place Saint-Nicolas** and the two boulevards parallel to it, which, though flanked by faded Art Deco shop fronts, are choked with expensive cars and busy shoppers. But to the south of here lies the old quarter known as the **Terra Vecchia**, a tightly packed network of haphazard streets, flamboyant Baroque churches and lofty tenements, their crumbling golden-grey walls set against a backdrop of fire-darkened hills. **Terra Nova**, the historic district on the opposite side of the old port from Terra Vecchia, is a tidier zone that's now Bastia's yuppie quarter, housing the island's top-flight architects, doctors and lawyers.

Young upper-crust Bastiais always used to be sent to Italian universities for their education, a traffic that has had a marked effect on the city's tradition of professional success and on its cultural life – it's here that you'll find Corsica's only purpose-built theatre. Modelled on Milan's La Scala, it was regularly visited by the great Italian opera stars, and nowadays, even though some of the gloss has gone, the place fills up for occasional concerts by touring companies from Italy, or for one of Bastia's film festivals. Nothing packs in the crowds quite like the recurrent nationalist rallies, however, for Bastia is something of a centre for dissidence. Discontent with the way the city is run is a constant feature of life here, as highlighted in 1989 when Bastia's civil servants rioted over the mysterious disappearance of local government funds. Highly politicized and busily self-sufficient, Bastia may make few concessions to tourism, but its grittiness makes it a more genuine introduction to Corsica than its long-time rival on the west coast.

A brief history of Bastia

In the twelfth century, when Corsica was under Pisan control, wine was exported to the Italian mainland from **Porto Cardo**, forerunner of Bastia's **Vieux Port**. Moorish raids made the area too vulnerable to inhabit, however, and it wasn't until the Genoese ascendancy that the port began to thrive. At first the Genoese governed from the former Roman base at Biguglia, to the south, but in 1372, when the fort was burned down by Corsican rebels, the Genoese governor abandoned the malarial site in favour of Porto Cardo, a spot close to Genoa and within easy trading distance of the fertile regions of the eastern plain, Balagne and Cap Corse. Before the end of the decade the governor, Leonello Lomellino, had built the *bastiglia* (dungeon) which gave the town its name; ramparts were constructed high on the escarpment above the port, and Genoese families, attracted by offers of free building land, began to settle within the fortifications in an area which became **Terra Nova**.

The sixteenth century saw the rise of a new class of merchants and artisans, who settled around the harbour on the site of Porto Cardo, the area now known as **Terra Vecchia**. The boom lasted until 1730, when Bastia was raided by an army of four thousand peasants, following similar attacks on Aléria and the Balagne settlements. Provoked to desperation by the corrupt despotism of the Genoese republic, the *paesani* went on the rampage for three days, annihilating most of the population of Terra Vecchia, who lacked the protection of the upper-class inhabitants of Terra Nova. Peace was finally restored by the intervention of the bishop of Aléria, but the remaining Genoese merchants promptly left for the safer ports of Bonifacio and Calvi, and Bastia went into decline.

During the **War of Independence** Bastia became a battleground. Pascal Paoli coveted the town for its strong position facing Italy, but it took two attempts and the efforts of the British fleet to take the town – the second assault was led by Nelson and Hood, who, though outnumbered by two to one, overcame the defenders in a long and difficult siege. In 1794, in the wake of this vistory, Bastia became home for English viceroy Sir Gilbert Elliot, who lived here for the two years of the Anglo-Corsican alliance. Bastia's hour of glory was short-lived, however, as the French finally gained full control of Corsica in 1796, and the island was divided into two *départements*.

Despite the fact that in 1811 Napoleon appointed Ajaccio capital of the island, initiating a rivalry between the two towns which exists to this day, Bastia soon established a stronger trading position with mainland France. The **Nouveau Port**, created in 1862 to cope with the increasing traffic with France and Italy, became the mainstay of the local economy, exporting chiefly agricultural products from Cap Corse, Balagne and the eastern plain. During World War II Bastia's economic prominence made it an obvious target, and it was the only town on Corsica to be severely bombed. A German division based here caused much of the destruction, but it was the Americans who caused the most damage, launching an attack as the people came out to celebrate their liberation. Many buildings were destroyed, including much of the old governor's palace, and the consequences of the bombing can still be seen in Terra Vecchia. Today Bastia's population has grown to 50,000, with the long-standing industries of freight handling and small-scale manufacture providing most of the employment, augmented by the burgeoning bureaucracies of local government.

Arrival, information and accommodation

Bastia's Poretta **airport** is 16km south of town off the Route Nationale; buses into the centre coincide with flights, dropping passengers at the **train station** for a fare of about 35F. **Ferries** arrive at the **Nouveau Port**, just a five-minute walk to

Regular car and passenger services operate all year round between Bastia and the French ports of Nice and Marseille, with a less frequent service to Toulon. Also served are the Italian ports of Genoa, La Spezia and Livorno, plus Piombino, Portoferraio and Porto Santo Stefano during July and August. In summer be sure to reserve a place, especially if travelling by car; vehicle supplements on all services are around 250F.

SNCM, Nouveau Port (☎95 54 66 88). To Nice (July & Aug 3 daily, May, June & Sept 3 weekly, rest of year 1 weekly); Marseille (July & Aug 1 daily, Sept 5 weekly, June 3 weekly, May 2 weekly, rest of year 1 weekly); Toulon (July & Aug 5 weekly, April–June & Sept–Oct 1 weekly). 350F per passenger; 9–12hr crossing.

Corsica Marittima, 15 bd de Gaulle (☎95 32 69 04). To Livorno (April–Sept 3 weekly; 3hr 30min; passengers 180F).

Corsica Ferries, Nouveau Port (☎95 54 66 99). To Genoa, La Spezia and Livorno (6 weekly all year; 3–5hr; passengers 180F); Piombino, Portoferraio and Porto Santo Stefano (June–Sept 1 daily; 3–5hr; passengers 200F).

Navarma, 4 rue Commandant-Luce-de-Casabianca (☎95 31 46 29). To Genoa (June–Sept 1 daily); La Spezia (April 4 weekly, May–Sept 5 weekly); Livorno (April 4 weekly, May–Sept 1 daily); Piombino (July 1 weekly, Aug to 1st Sat in Sept 1 daily); Porto Santo Stefano (mid-June to 1st Sat in Sept 1 daily). All services 180F passenger fare.

the centre of town. **Buses** from Ajaccio stop in boulevard Paoli, Bastia's main thoroughfare, whereas those coming from Porto Vecchio and Calvi stop in avénue du Maréchal Sebastiani, a wide street which leads from the station down to place Saint-Nicolas, the main square. There are two large **car parks**, one underground beneath place Saint-Nicolas, and one in the citadel, on the right as you enter the main town.

The **tourist office** is at the north end of place Saint-Nicolas (Mon–Sat 9am–noon & 2–6pm; ☎95 31 00 89). Although the staff won't fall over themselves to help you, they can provide a useful **bus timetable** for the Cap Corse services, which leave from the opposite side of the road. You can also get a map of the town and a list of **hotels** and **apartments** in the region.

You are usually guaranteed to find **somewhere to stay** in Bastia, but the choice of hotels is not great. Apart from the upmarket Posta-Vecchia, the classier places line the road to Cap Corse north of the port; the more basic ones are found in the centre of town, and there are a few even cheaper small *pensions* around the Nouveau Port.

Hotels

Du Cap, 11 rue du Commandant-Luce-de-Casabianca (☎95 31 18 46). The cheapest accommodation in Bastia, 3min from the port, near the church of Notre Dame. ①.

Le Central, 3 rue Miot (☎95 31 71 26). Rather austere but clean and comfortable and very central, off rue César Campinchi. ②.

Cyrnéa, Pietranera, 2km north of Bastia on the Cap Corse road (☎95 31 41 71). Clean and tranquil, with air conditioning in every room and sea views. It's on the right at the entrance to the hamlet. ④.

De l'Europe, 3 rue Campinchi (☎95 31 00 58). Small but adequate; has its own restaurant. ②.

Forum, 20 bd Paoli (☎95 31 02 53). Attractively chic, with spacious rooms and bar. ④.

Laetitia, 2 bd Paoli (☎95 31 06 94). Shabby but welcoming. Popular with students. ②.

Léandri, 47 bd Graziani (☎95 31 40 30). Near the post office. A friendly family-run place, on the first floor of a modern block. ①.

Napoléon, 43 bd Paoli (☎95 31 60 30). Small rooms but views all over town. ③.

De la Paix, 1 bd Général Giraud (☎95 31 06 71). Elegantly decorated. Worth the climb up the hill and the extra cost. ③.

Pietracap, route de San Martino, Pietranera (☎95 31 64 63). Luxury hotel with swimming pool. Closed winter. ⑤.

Posta-Vecchia, quai des Martyrs de la Libération (☎95 32 32 38). Large chic hotel with wonderful views across the sea. Open all year round. ③.

Riviera, 1 rue du Nouveau Port (☎95 31 07 16). Well-established comfortable hotel, handy for the port. ③.

Sud Hôtel, av de la Libération, Lupino (☎95 30 20 61). Charming place with own car park and friendly owners. About 1km south of town. ④.

Univers, 3 av du Maréchal Sebastiani (☎95 31 03 38). Opposite the post office. Noisy but convenient. ②.

Des Voyageurs, 9 av du Maréchal Sebastiani (☎95 31 08 97). In the touristy part of town – but useful for the buses going to Porto Vecchio. ②.

Campsites

Esperenza, route de Pineto (☎95 36 15 09). About 11km south of Bastia, beyond San Damiano (see below) and with fewer facilities. Hourly buses in summer from the Gare Routière.

Les Orangers, Miomo, 4km north along the route to Cap Corse (☎95 33 24 09). Shady and attractive site near the sea; the half-hourly bus to Erbalunga will drop you here.

San Damiano, Pineto, 10km south of Bastia (☎95 33 68 02). Huge and spacious with excellent facilities; take the road to the left across the bridge at Furiani roundabout. Buses as for the *Esperenza*.

Sables Rouges, on the beach (☎95 31 71 26). The closest campsite, situated 1km south of town at L'Arinella beach, but rather dirty and crowded.

The Town

Bastia isn't a large town and all its sights can easily be seen in a day without the use of a car. The spacious **place Saint-Nicolas** is the focus of town life: open to the sea and lined with shady trees and cafés, it's the most pleasant spot for soaking up the atmosphere. Running parallel to it on the landward side are **boulevard Paoli** and **rue César Campinchi**, the two main shopping streets, but all Bastia's historic sights lie within **Terra Vecchia**, the old quarter immediately south of the place Saint-Nicolas, and **Terra Nova**, the area surrounding the **Citadelle**. There's not much of interest in the **Nouveau Port** area, north of the *place*, other than restaurants and bars.

Terra Vecchia

From place Saint-Nicolas the main route into Terra Vecchia is **rue Napoléon**, a narrow street with some ancient offbeat shops and a pair of sumptuously decorated chapels on its east side. The first of these, the **Oratoire de Saint-Roch**, is a Genoese Baroque extravagance, built in 1604 and reflecting the wealth of the rising bourgeoisie. The walls are particularly remarkable, covered with finely carved wooden panelling. The chapel also possesses a magnificent **organ** decorated with gilt and wooden sculpture; hardly altered since it was built in 1750, it's played on religious festivals and in special concerts.

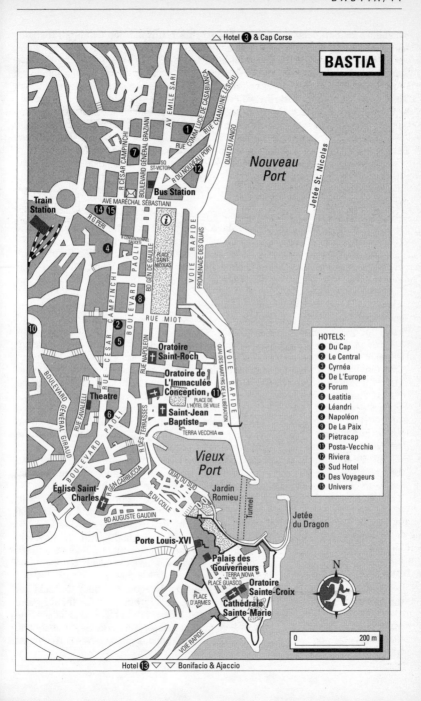

Hotel ③ & Cap Corse

BASTIA

Nouveau Port

Jetée St. Nicolas

Train Station

Bus Station

PLACE SAINT-NICOLAS

RUE MIOT

Oratoire Saint-Roch

Oratoire de L'Immaculée Conception

Saint-Jean Baptiste

PLACE DE L'HÔTEL DE VILLE

TERRA VECCHIA

Vieux Port

Theatre

Église Saint-Charles

Jardin Romieu

Tunnel

Jetée du Dragon

Porte Louis-XVI

Palais des Gouverneurs

TERRA NOVA

PLACE GUASCO

Oratoire Sainte-Croix

PLACE D'ARMES

Cathédrale Sainte-Marie

N

HOTELS:
❶ Du Cap
❷ Le Central
❸ Cyrnéa
❹ De L'Europe
❺ Forum
❻ Leatitia
❼ Léandri
❽ Napoléon
❾ De La Paix
❿ Pietracap
⓫ Posta-Vecchia
⓬ Riviera
⓭ Sud Hotel
⓮ Des Voyageurs
⓯ Univers

0   200 m

Hotel ⓭ ▽ ▽ Bonifacio & Ajaccio

A little further along stands the **Oratoire de L'Immaculée Conception**, built in 1611 as the showplace of the Genoese in Corsica, who used it for state occasions such as the inauguration of the governor. In later years, the English viceroy, Sir Gilbert Eliot, held parliamentary sessions here during the brief Anglo-Corsican alliance. Overlooking a pebble mosaic of a sun, the austere facade belies the flamboyant **interior**, where crimson velvet draperies, a gilt and marble ceiling, frescoes and crystal chandeliers create the ambience of an opera house. The unusually narrow nave terminates at an elaborate polychromatic marble altar, over which hangs an unimpressive copy of Murillo's *Immaculate Conception*. On the left stands a **statue of the Virgin** which on December 8 is paraded through the streets to the church of Saint-Jean-Baptiste. The sacristy houses a tiny **museum** (daily 9am–6pm) of minor religious works, of which the wooden statue of Saint Erasmus, patron saint of fishers, dating from 1788, is most arresting.

If you cut back through the narrow steps beside the Oratoire de Saint-Roch, a two-minute walk will bring you to **place de L'Hôtel de Ville**, commonly known as place du Marché because of the half-hearted **market** that takes place here each morning. Shouldering the south end of the square is the **Église Saint-Jean-Baptiste**, an immense ochre edifice that dominates the Vieux Port. Its twin campaniles are Bastia's distinguishing feature, but the interior is less than impressive – built in 1636, the church was restored in the eighteenth century in a hideous Rococo overkill of multicoloured marble. Decorating the walls are a few unremarkable Italian paintings from Napoléon's uncle, Cardinal Fesch, an avid collector of Renaissance art (see p.113).

Around the church extends the oldest part of Bastia, an oppressively secretive zone of dark alleys, vaulted passageways and seven-storey houses locked in isolation from the rest of town. By turning right outside the church and following rue St-Jean you'll come to **rue General-Carbuccia**, the heart of Terra Vecchia. Pascal Paoli once lived here, at no. 7, and Balzac stayed briefly at no. 23 when his ship got stuck in Corsica on the way to Sardinia. Set in a small square at the end of the road is the **Église Saint-Charles**, an august Jesuit chapel whose wide steps provide an evening meeting place for the locals; opposite stands the **Maison de Caraffa**, an elegant house with a strikingly graceful balcony.

The **Vieux Port** is the most appealing part of town: soaring houses seem to bend inwards towards the water, peeling plaster and boat hulls glint in the sun, while the south side remains in the shadow of the great rock that supports the citadel. Site of the original Porto Cardo, the Vieux Port later bustled with Genoese traders, but since the building of the ferry terminal and commercial docks it has become a backwater, deserted by day, when the clinking of a few fishing boats echoes around the harbour. It's livelier at night, with the glow and noise from the harbourside bars and restaurants, which continue round the north end of the port along the wide **quai des Martyrs**, where live bands clank out pop classics for the tourists in summer.

The best view of Bastia is from the **jetée du Dragon**, the quay that juts out under the citadel. To reach the citadel you can walk through the **Jardin Romieu**, the eighteenth-century terraced garden that ascends the cliff on this side of the harbour. Despite the elegantly sweeping stone steps, the gardens are dusty and unremarkable and are a notorious hang-out for dubious characters – certainly not the spot for a picnic.

Terra Nova

The military and administrative core of old Bastia, **Terra Nova** (or the *citadelle*) has a distinct air of affluence, its lofty apartments now colonized by Bastia's yuppies. The area is focused on **place du Donjon**, which gets its name from the squat round tower that formed the nucleus of Bastia's fortifications and was used by the Genoese to incarcerate Corsican patriots – Sampiero Corso was held in the dungeon for four years in the early sixteenth century. Next to the tower a strategically placed terrace **bar** commands a magnificent view that extends to Elba on a clear day.

Facing the bar is the impressive fourteenth-century **Palais des Gouverneurs**. With its great round tower, arcaded inner courtyard and battered orange paintwork, this building has a distinctly Moorish feel. During the Genoese heyday the governor and the local bishop lived here with an entourage of seventy horsemen, entertaining foreign dignitaries and hosting massive parties. When the French transferred the capital to Ajaccio it became a prison, then was destroyed during Nelson's attack of 1794. The subsequent rebuilding was not the last, as parts of it were blown up by the Americans in 1943, and today the restorers are trying to regain something of the building's former grandeur.

Part of the palace is given over to the **Musée d'Éthnographie** (Mon–Sat 9am–noon & 2–6pm; 25F), which presents the history of Corsica from prehistoric times to the present day. Its dusty vaulted chambers contain a motley collection of exhibits from rare rock specimens to Pascal Paoli memorabilia, an array that at first sight seems rather tired yet harbours some fascinating historical titbits.

In the first room there's one of the few Roman artefacts on show in Corsica, a diminutive **sarcophagus** decorated with hunting scenes – it was discovered in Bastelicaccia, near Ajaccio, where it was being used as a horses' drinking trough. In amongst the geological specimens are some rare minerals, including the unique greenish ring-patterned diorite found in Sainte-Lucie-de-Tallano, and an example of the orangey-brown sulphurous arsenic which the Germans used to make gas bombs in World War I. Busts of famous Corsicans are exhibited next door, along with the original 1755 **Flag of Independence**, an emblem of obscure origins. When the pope gave sovereignty of Corsica to Aragon in 1296, the new rulers adopted four Moors' heads with white head-bands as their coat of arms, possibly to mark a victory over the Saracens. The image was still used on maps of the island in the seventeenth century, and was then adopted by Theodor von Neuhof, who had the image of a single moor's head minted on coins during his short reign. Later on Pascal Paoli got hold of the emblem and declared it the official symbol of independent Corsica. Nowadays it's the unofficial national flag and is plastered all over the place – on car stickers, posters, pennants and football banners.

Another room houses an exhibition on daily life in different regions of Corsica, giving some idea of the harsh realities of existence on the land. Chestnut flour mills, farm instruments, olive presses and life-size mannequins of shepherds from the remote Niolo region provide the bulk of the display – explicating practices that are still continued in some regions of Corsica.

On the terrace of the museum stands the conning tower of the submarine **Casabianca**, which played a major part in the liberation of Corsica in World War II by ferrying weapons and ammunitions from Algeria. The sub was named after twelve-year-old Giocante de Casabianca, who died at Aboukir in 1798 when he refused to leave his father's ship after it had been attacked by Nelson's fleet – giving Felicia Hemans her inspiration for the poem beginning: "The boy stood on the burning deck".

Back in place du Donjon, if you cross the square and follow rue Notre Dame you come out at the **Eglise Sainte-Marie**. Built in 1458 and overhauled in the seventeenth century, it was the cathedral of Bastia until 1801, when the bishopric was transferred to Ajaccio. The over-restored facade is an ugly shade of peach, and there's nothing of interest inside except a small silver statue of the Virgin, which is carried through Terra Nova and Terra Vecchia on August 15, the Festival of the Assumption. Virtually next door, in rue de l'Evêché, stands the **Oratoire Sainte-Croix**, a sixteenth-century church decorated in Louis XV style, all rich blue paint and gilt scrollwork. It houses another holy item, the **Christ des Miracles**, a blackened oak crucifix which in 1428 was discovered floating in the sea surrounded by a luminous haze. A festival celebrating the miracle takes place in Bastia on May 3.

Beyond the church, the narrow streets open out to the tiny **place Guasco**, a delightful square at the heart of the citadel that typifies the exclusivity of Terra Nova. A few benches offer the chance of a rest before descending into the fray.

The beaches

Crowded with schoolchildren in the summer, the pebbly **town beach** in Bastia is only worth visiting if you're desperate for a swim. To reach it go left at the flower shop on the main road south out of town, just beyond the citadel. A better alternative is the long beach of **L'Arinella** at Montesoro, a further 1km along the same road, the beginning of a sandy shore that extends along the whole east coast. A **bus** to L'Arinella leaves from outside *Café Riche* on boulevard Paoli every twenty minutes; just get off at the last stop and cross the railway line to the sea. There are a couple of sailing and windsurfing clubs here, and a bar.

Leaving Bastia in the other direction, you will find sandy beaches about a kilometre along the road to **Cap Corse**, but these are rather polluted and the sea tends to be choppy.

Eating, drinking and nightlife

Lively place Saint-Nicolas, packed with cafés, is the place to be during the day. For a more sedate atmosphere boulevard Paoli and rue Campinchi are lined with chichi *salons du thé* offering elaborate creamy confections, local chestnut cake and doughnuts. Late-night clubbers can revive themselves with an early coffee and a *pain au chocolat* at one of the three cafés in the place de L'Hôtel de Ville which open at 4.30am for the market-traders. You'll find most cafés serve *croque monsieurs* at exorbitant prices, but for a better-value **snack** try the offbeat retro **kiosks** on place Saint-Nicolas, which sell hot dogs, crêpes and tasty *casse-croûtes* for a few francs. Numerous **pizza vans** are scattered about town until about 9pm (there's usually one outside the train station), evidence of a strong Italian influence that's also apparent in the predominance of pizzerias and pasta places in the Nouveau Port area. The town also boasts some excellent yet inexpensive **restaurants** serving Corsican specialities such as wild boar and *charcuterie*, and fish is inevitably prominent as well: the posh places on the quai des Martyrs do the best *aziminu*, a Corsican version of *bouillabaisse*. Most of the good restaurants are to be found around the Vieux Port and on the quai des Martyrs, with a sprinkling in the citadel.

Drinking is serious business in Bastia. The **Casanis** *pastis* factory is on the outskirts of town in Lupino, and this is indisputably the town's drink – order a "Casa" and you'll fit in well. There are many bars and cafés all over town, varying from the stark and brightly lit bars of Terra Vecchia that are the haunt of old men, to the elegant, dimly lit cafés on place Saint-Nicolas, where you can sip hot chocolate on low leather seats. The best place to buy wine is *Grand Vin Corse* at 24 rue Campinchi; the obliging proprietor will fill up plastic bottles of muscat from the barrels for you, at five francs per litre.

Bastia doesn't offer much in the way of **nightlife**. There are a couple of cinemas, a good theatre and a good central club. The best source of information about all events is the daily local paper *Corse Matin*, produced in Nice.

Restaurants

L'Ambada, Vieux Port. On the lively side of the port, opposite the citadel. Cheap set menus, salads and pasta.

U Cantarettu, Vieux Port. Corsican lasagne and sublime pizzas. A nightly concert of popular Corsican ballads courtesy of the owner; he doesn't do requests.

Casa Corsa, 1 quai des Martyrs. The freshest fish, and regional specialities such as *fiadone*, a kind of eggy cake.

Le Caveau du Marin, 4 quai des Martyrs. Welcoming little place decked out like a fishing hut, sharks' teeth and all. Seafood pasta a speciality.

Chez Gino, 11 av Emile-Sari. Five minutes north of place Saint-Nicolas in the Nouveau Port. Authentic Italian pizzas, well worth the queueing. Also sells delicious ice creams.

Chez Jack, 19 rue César Campinchi. Tiny but comfortable family bistro with inexpensive French cuisine and sardonic service.

Du Cous-Cous, 6 rue César Campinchi. Delicious cous-cous, popular with the locals; they do take-aways if you have a pot handy.

Le Depôt, 22 rue César Campinchi. Rich, delicious pizzas with *creme fraiche* and Roquefort toppings, baked in a wood oven. Trendy modern decor, loud music.

Le Dernier Métro, 3 rue des Zéphirs. Elegant restaurant with a good reputation for classic French cuisine. Expensive.

Fresch Pâtes, 18 av Emile-Sari. Recommended for inexpensive homemade pasta.

Le Paradou, place Galetta. Inexpensive pasta, pizzas and steaks, just behind the Vieux Port. Popular with young Bastiais.

A Scaletta, Vieux Port. Entrance on the steps leading from the port to Église Saint-Jean-Baptiste. Fresh fish, served on a precarious balcony overlooking the boats. Generous Corsican speciality menu at F65. Eau-de-vie on the house if you're lucky.

La Suerta, Villa Agostini, Suerta, 3km along the road to Saint-Florent. Traditional peasant food, hearty stews and pasta, an excellent *cannelloni al brocciu* in a homely environment.

U Tianu, 4 rue Monsigneur Rigo. Sparse, trendy nationalist hang-out in a small insalubrious street off quai des Martyrs. Excellent *charcuterie* and a different menu everyday, featuring local dishes such as blackbird paté and hare and olive stew. Not to be missed.

Bars and cafés

Bar Corsica, 2 rue Spinola. Tucked away behind the Vieux Port, this is the place to hear traditional Corsican singing.

L'Escale, 12 rue Luce-de-Casabianca. Spacious bar opposite the Nouveau Port. The only pool tables in town.

Le Goeland, Vieux Port. Another favourite bar with elderly locals.

L'Impériale, 6 bd Général de Gaulle. Busy café at the centre of place Saint-Nicolas. The only place which sells cigarettes late at night, so people are always coming and going.

Café Napoléon, 16 bd Général de Gaulle. Recently refurbished, elegant café, famous for its surly waiter, a character straight out of *Asterix*.

Les Palmiers, 8 bd Général de Gaulle. Popular café with young Bastiais. Good draught beer.

Bar Pascal, Vieux Port. Hang-out for hardened *pastis* drinkers.

Le Pigalle, Vieux Port. Serves the cheapest beer *à la pression* in Bastia.

Café Riche, 29 bd Paoli. Large and busy café that's a centre for gambling, next door to the first betting shop in Corsica.

Le Richelieu, 1 bd Général de Gaulle. Stark and unpretentious bar with a pinball machine and a huge picture of Bastia's football team. Open very late.

Nightlife

What there is of Bastia's **nightlife** centres around the bars, cafés and restaurants of the Vieux Port and place Saint-Nicolas. A couple of discos and cinemas add some variety to an evening, but you'll have to search hard for a crowded venue, as Bastiais seem to go for a quiet night in front of the television as their preferred entertainment.

If there is a concert in Bastia it will almost certainly be held in the **theatre** in place Favalelli (box office Mon–Sat 9am–noon; tickets 100–150F), west of rue Campinchi. Concerts of traditional Corsican singing and nationalist rallies are also regular events at the theatre and the Chambre de Commerce off place de l' Hôtel de Ville.

Of Bastia's two **cinemas**, the triple-screen *Regent* at 13 rue César Campinchi shows new films, always dubbed, whereas the *Studio*, in nearby rue Miséricorde, is a small outfit showing mostly subtitled art films. The ten-day *Festival du Film et des Cultures Méditerranéennes* takes place in November at the cinemas and the theatre, showcasing films, backed up by exhibitions, from all parts of the Mediterranean region. There's also a British film festival in the first two weeks in March, featuring fairly recent releases with French subtitles.

Nightclubs are few and far between. In the centre of town, the long-established *St Nicolas*, underneath the *place* at 14 bd Général de Gaulle, is the best place – the music is more varied than the usual endless Europop. Out of town, *L'Apocalypse* at La Marana is the disco to be seen at, but attracts a mainly teenage crowd. You'll need a car for this place, which is 10km along the La Marana stretch south of Bastia. Entry is free and drinks extortionate at both, which keep going till dawn (closed Mon & Tues).

Summer firework displays are a regular occurrence, with the most spectacular show happening in place Saint-Nicolas on **Bastille Day** (July 14), when street parties are held all over town. For the **Festival of the Assumption** (August 15), heralded by a solemn procession, the Vieux Port later becomes overrun by revellers. Other annual events include the **Fête du Christ Noir** on May 3 (see p.44), a **regatta** in June and the **Foire de Bastia** in July, which has stalls – mainly promoting local businesses – and live music in the evenings.

Listings

Airlines At the airport: *Air France* (☎95 32 10 29 or 95 54 54 95); *Air Inter* (☎95 54 54 95). **Airport enquiries** ☎95 54 54 54.

Banks and exchange Most of the main banks are on place Saint-Nicolas, at the bottom of bd Paoli and on rue César Campinchi. You can also change money at the *Change* at 15 av du Maréchal Sebastiani, which is only open July & Aug, till 7pm (closed Sun).

Bike rental *Locacycles*, 8 bd Graziani.

Bookshops The largest bookshop and stationers is *Temps de Vivre* on bd Paoli. You can pick up the *Herald Tribune* here and sometimes some other foreign newspapers. *Librairie Jean Patrice Marzocchi* in rue Saliceti, off the *place*, is a good bookshop selling many books about Corsica and also maps and books with walking routes.

Bus information For local routes call ☎95 31 06 65. For long-distance buses to Ajaccio call *Ollandini*, 9 av du Maréchal Sebastiani (☎95 32 22 05) or *Rapides Bleus* at no. 1 (☎95 31 03 79).

Car rental *Avis/Ollandini*, 9 av du Maréchal Sebastiani (☎95 32 57 30); *Europcar*, 1 rue du Nouveau Port (☎95 31 59 26).

Hospital *Centre Hopitalier de Falconaja*, rue Imperiale, Lupino (☎95 55 11 11).

Laundry *Pressing* at 4 rue César Campinchi does laundry and dry cleaning; the only self-service laundry is in Lupino, way out in the industrial zone.

Left luggage At the Nouveau Port (daily 7am–noon & 2–8pm; 15F per item).

Pharmacies Plenty on bd Paoli. In an emergency phone ☎95 31 99 17.

Post office The central post office is on av du Maréchal Sebastiani.

Taxis There is a taxi rank at the south end of place Saint-Nicolas (☎95 34 07 00).

Telephones There are phone booths outside the post office and in place Saint-Nicolas.

Watersports *Club Nautique Bastiais* is in the Vieux Port next to the jetée du Dragon (☎95 31 42 54); *Base Nautique de L'Arinella* is on L'Arinella beach (☎95 33 36 48).

South of Bastia

It's easy to be put off by the industrial sprawl south of Bastia, but amidst the built-up areas there are some hidden sights ideal for a half-day excursion. At the Furiani junction, about 3km along the N193, you can turn off the main road to follow the stretch of coast known as **La Marana**, where holiday villages and villas back a sandy beach lined with pine woods. Between this strand and the N193 lies the **Étang de Biguglia**, a wildlife-rich lagoon named after the ancient capital of Corsica, now an unremarkable village on the slopes above the main road. The lagoon stretches as far as the Roman site of **Mariana**, about 20km from Bastia, where you can see the remains of a twelfth-century basilica and the superb Pisan church of La Canonica.

There is no public transport direct to Mariana. **Buses**, which leave from opposite the Bastia tourist office at hourly intervals in summer, take you along La Marana as far as Pineto. From here it's a good three-kilometre walk to the Roman site.

La Marana and the Étang de Biguglia

Traditionally the summer haunt of prosperous Bastia families, the sixteen-kilometre littoral known as **LA MARANA** (pronounced "maran") is the beginning of the sandy stretch that continues uninterrupted all the way down to Porto Vecchio in the south. Largely the preserve of joggers and windsurfers, the beach offers shady pine woods, restaurants and bars, and even though the sea is quite polluted due to the proximity to Italy and the boat traffic, it's an agreeable excursion from Bastia when the heat gets too much.

All this part of the coast is divided into holiday residences or sections of beach attached to bars, the latter freely open to the public. Try **A Pagoda**, about 5km along the road – popular with the young crowd, it has a disco and a large open-air bar. Another good spot is **Pineto**, the furthest beach along the road and therefore the least crowded in the summer, where the bus terminates.

Fed by the rivers Bevinco and Golo, the Étang de Biguglia is the largest lagoon in Corsica and one of its best **birdlife** sites, thanks largely to the reed beds bordering the water. Of the birds that nest in the reeds various species of warblers are most common – in summer you'll find reed warblers at the southern end of the lagoon, as well as moustached warblers and cetti warblers, with their distinctive loud repetitive cry. In winter Biguglia is a stop-off point for migrating grey herons, kingfishers, great crested grebes, little grebes, water rails and various species of duck, such as the spectacular red-crested pochard, immediately identifiable by its red bill, red feet and a bright red head.

Mariana

The Roman town of **MARIANA**, just south of Étang de Biguglia, can be approached by taking the turning for the airport, 16km along the N193, or the more scenic coastal route through La Marana.

Founded in 93 BC as a military colony, Mariana had become a Christian centre by the fourth century, when its basilica was built. The settlement was damaged severely by the Vandals and Ostrogoths in the fifth and sixth centuries, and by the time of the Genoese occupation Mariana had become so waterlogged and malarial that it had to be abandoned. The **houses**, **baths** and **basilica** are now too ruined to be of great interest, but the square **baptistery** has a remarkable mosaic floor decorated with dancing dolphins and fish looped around a bearded Neptune – Christianized pagan images representing the Four Rivers of Paradise.

Adjacent to Mariana stands the church of Santa Maria Assunta, commonly known as **La Canonica**. Built in 1119 close to the old capital of Biguglia, it is the finest of around three hundred churches built by the Pisans in their effort to evangelize the island. Modelled on a Roman basilica, the perfectly proportioned edifice is decorated outside with Corinthian capitals plundered from the main Mariana site and with plates of Cap Corse marble, their delicate pink and yellow ochre hues fusing to stunning effect. The interior has been recently restored in a very plain style, and is used for concerts and for Mass on religious festivals.

About three hundred metres to the south of La Canonica stands **San Parteo**, built in the eleventh and twelfth centuries over the site of a pagan burial ground. A smaller edifice than La Canonica, the church also displays some elegant arcading and fine sculpture – on the south side, the door lintel is supported by two writhing beasts reaching to a central tree, a motif of oriental origins.

Cap Corse

Until Napoléon III had a coach road built around **Cap Corse** in the nineteenth century, the promontory was effectively cut off from the rest of the island, relying on Italian maritime traffic for its income – hence its distinctive Tuscan dialect. Ruled by feudal lords who retained substantial independence from the island's governors, it maintained a peaceful existence that greatly influenced the character of the **Cap Corsins**. For all the changes brought by the modern world, Cap Corse still feels like a separate country.

Forty kilometres long and only fifteen across, the cape is divided by a spine of mountains called the Serra, which peaks at **Monte Stello**, 1037m above sea level. The coast on the **east side** of this divide is characterized by tiny ports or *marines*, tucked into gently sloping river-mouths, alongside coves which become sandier as you go farther north. The villages of the **western coast** are sited on rugged cliffs, high above the rough sea and tiny rocky inlets that can be glimpsed from the corniche road. The wildness of Cap Corse remains virtually untainted by tourism: wild flowers grow in profusion on the mountainsides in spring, goats graze freely, the fishing villages are quiet and traditional, and many of the inland slopes are occupied by vineyards, producing the fragrant **wine** that's one of the cape's major exports. It's only in the last twenty years or so that hotels have appeared, with the highest concentration at **Macinaggio** and **Centuri-Port**, on either side of the northern tip. Unfortunately, though, much of the once verdant countryside is blackened by fire.

Many people tackle the hundred-kilometre corniche in a one-day tour from Bastia. A less arduous alternative is to cut across the peninsula at Santa Severa, thereby getting a taste of the interior and a look at the spectacular **Tour de Sénèque**, where popular legend says that the Roman poet-philosopher Seneca spent his exiled years. Best of all, of course, would be to spend a few days here. If you're driving, bear in mind that fuel stations are few and far between, so fill up in Bastia. For those without transport a **circular tour bus** operates daily from Bastia all year round. There's also a regular bus to **Erbalunga**, a placid fishing village 10km north of Bastia, where the buildings, ending in one of the ruined look-out towers for which the cape is famous, rise directly from the sea.

Even more conspicuous than these towers are the **convents**, **churches** and in particular **Romanesque chapels** that are scattered over the cape – it was on Cap Corse that some of the first Christian centres in Corsica were created, and this was the only region of the island where the Franciscan movement had any real influence. Elaborate marble **mausoleums** are also a common feature, often occupying lonely places on the inland hill-slopes and standing out strikingly white in a sea of green maquis.

A brief history of Cap Corse

Inhabited by various ancient civilizations – the Phoenicians, Greeks and Romans were all here – Cap Corse became significant in the tenth century, when the da Massa lords came over from Pisa and established fiefdoms across the region. By the following century Genoese settlers were being drawn to the cape's vineyards, and after Genoa's trouncing of Pisa at the battle of Meloria in 1284, the feudal lords of Cap Corse became important – if intermittent – allies of the island's new rulers. Two local families shared most of the cape from this time – the da Mare clan held the north whilst the da Gentile ruled the south, a situation that lasted into the late eighteenth century, when the French gained control of the island.

Although subject to the Genoese, the lords of Cap Corse were allowed a certain autonomy: largely ignored by the rest of the island, and well positioned for trading with the French and Tuscan ports, they were able to control their profits to a greater extent than their compatriots in the south. By the seventeenth century Cap Corse was economically more successful than any other region in Corsica, but piracy was a huge problem for the cape's tiny ports, which is why the coast is dotted with some thirty fortified towers, built as refuges for the local populations in times of trouble. An agricultural boom at the beginning of the nineteenth century spawned an outbreak of fancy palazzi and villas, which are still to be seen in villages over the cape, but a slump in the economy early this century

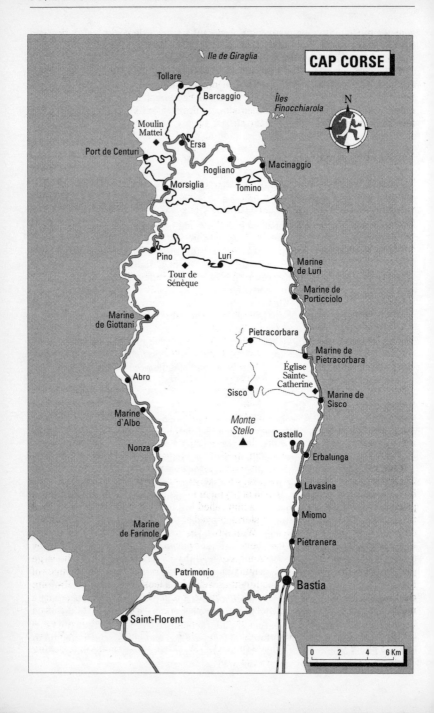

sent many Corsicans overseas, with Cap Corsins favouring South America and the Caribbean. Corsican colonies still exist in Venezuela and Jamaica – indeed, a former Venezuelan president was a Corsican.

Today, though wine continues to be a major export and nationalist politicians are promoting the exploitation of the indigenous cedrat fruit, from which a liqueur and jam are made locally, tourism has become the only way to make real money. So far, however, it has been slow to develop on the cape, and there are few spots where concrete spoils the view.

The eastern cape

The **eastern coast** of the cape progresses from tightly packed villas immediately outside Bastia to desolate *marines* such as **Pietracorbara** in the north, via fishing villages such as **Erbalunga** and **Porticciolo**. The D80, which follows the coast all the way around Cap Corse as far as Saint-Florent, is mostly built up within a short radius of Bastia (about the first 5km), so it's a good idea to leave the main road at the roundabout that's about a couple of kilometres out of town, taking the turn-off signposted as the Route de la Corniche. This loop bypasses the worst of the developed strip and gives a good panorama from the mountains.

San-Martino-di-Lota to Lavasina

Three kilometres along the corniche you pass through the terraced village of **SAN-MARTINO-DI-LOTA**, no longer a pristine place but giving a tremendous view, which on clear days takes in the islands of Monte Cristo and Elba. In the neighbouring hamlet of Canale there's a good **hotel**, *De la Corniche* (☎95 31 40 98; ②), which possesses a magnificent terrace shaded by chestnut trees.

The winding road rejoins the coast at **MIOMO**, a conspicuously wealthy village of posh villas and private beaches. By the small pebbly public beach stands the southernmost **Genoese tower** of the coast, an enormous squat construction with a ridged turreted top. Miomo's only hotel, *Les Sablettes* (☎95 33 26 13; ④), is a good place to **stay** if you don't feel like staying in Bastia. A huge pink turreted building opposite the *mairie* on the main road, the hotel has a terrace over the sea and a swimming pool.

LAVASINA, a further 3km up the coast, grew up around a sanctuary created in the sixteenth century by one Danesi, who was given a painting of the Virgin which he donated to the sanctuary in lieu of payment for some merchandise. It became a place of pilgrimage in 1675, when a nun called Marie-Agnès, having disembarked from a boat to take shelter from a storm, prayed at the sanctuary and was promptly cured of her paralysis of the legs. Within two years the **Église Notre-Dame-des-Graces** had been built to house the miraculous painting. An ugly rectangular grey tower, surmounted by a cumbersome statue of the Virgin, was added to the large pink building in the nineteenth century and effectively ruined the classical lines of the church. Inside, however, you might as well take a look at the famous **Madone de Lavasina**, which hangs above the great black and white altar. The painting, a melancholy work from the school of the Umbrian artist Perugino, is still believed to perform miracles and is the focus of a festival on September 8, involving a candlelit procession on the beach and a midnight Mass. The tiny *Hôtel les Roches*, on the right as you leave the village (☎95 33 26 57; ①), has cosy rooms overlooking the sea and serves authentic Corsican fare.

Erbalunga and around

Built along a rocky promontory 3km north of Lavasina, the small port of **ERBALUNGA** is the highlight of the east coast, with its aged, pale buildings stacked like crooked boxes behind a small harbour and ruined Genoese watch-tower. A little colony of French artists lived here in the 1920s, perhaps drawn by the fact that the ancestors of the poet Paul Valéry came from here, and the village has drawn a steady stream of admirers ever since. It gets a fair number of tourists throughout the year, and come summer it's transformed into a veritable cultural enclave, with concerts and arty events adding a spark to local nightlife.

A port since the time of the Phoenicians, Erbalunga was once a more important trading centre than Bastia or Ajaccio. With the increasing exportation of wine and olive oil, in the eleventh century it became the capital of an independent village state, ruled by the da Gentile family, who lived in the palazzo that dominates **place de Gaulle**. Its ascendancy came to an end in the 1550s, when long-running conflicts within the da Gentile camp finally broke the family's hold on this part of the cape, and in 1557 French troops destroyed the port, reducing the fifteenth-century tower to the ruined state it is in today.

Erbalunga is famous for the **Good Friday procession** known as the **Cerca** (The Search), which has evolved from an ancient fertility rite. Starting at Église Saint-Erasme, at the entrance to the village, a procession of hooded penitents covers a distance of fourteen kilometres, passing through the hamlets of Pozzo, Poretto and Silgaggia in the mountains and picking up people on the way. At nightfall, back in Erbalunga, the penitents form a spiral known as the *Granitola* (snail); candles held high, they move to place de Gaulle and the spiral unwinds, while a separate part of the procession forms the shape of the cross.

The village is closed to vehicles, but there's a **car park** on the left-hand side of the main road from Bastia, where the regular **bus** from place Saint-Nicolas stops. From here you walk down to the harbour through place de Gaulle, where the *mairie* and the palazzo Gentile stand side by side. In the harbour a couple of **bars** shaded by an enormous chestnut tree look out across the water to the tower. The one **hotel**, the *Castel-Brando*, is sited at the entrance to the square (☎95 33 98 05; ④); it's an elegant old stone-floored building, but it's closed in winter and doesn't have a restaurant. For a **restaurant** meal you have the choice of *Le Pirate*, right on the sea some thirty metres from place de Gaulle, which has been here for years and serves mainly fish, and *Chez Antoine*, directly overlooking the jetty, which serves basic but excellent fish dishes and regional food, such as pasta with wild boar.

CASTELLO

The thirteenth-century castle at **CASTELLO**, one of the many bases of the da Gentile family, stands 2km inland from Erbalunga, beyond the hamlet of Mausoleo. This ghostly village, dominated by the now ruined castle, was the scene of a family feud which lasted a hundred years and split the da Gentile family into two factions. The strife began in 1450, when the lady of the castle, known simply as *La Sposetta* (the little wife), began an affair with one Guelfuccio, cousin of her husband Vinciguerra da Gentile. On discovery of this deception Vinciguerra stabbed his errant wife to death, chased his cousin out of the castle and stormed off to settle with his brother in nearby Erbalunga. Here he built a new castle, which was wrecked in 1556 by the French, supported by members of

MONTE STELLO

The starting point for the climb up **Monte Stello** (1037m), the highest peak on Cap Corse, is the medieval hamlet of Pozzo, 3km from Erbalunga and 1km from Castello. In Pozzo's square a sign marked "Monte Stello 3h" points the way through the houses into the maquis, where the trail starts off clearly marked by arrows and daubs of blue paint. Behind the village you'll come to a stream which you cross and then scramble up the slope onto a wide terrace wall. From here there are fine views of the dark slopes rolling down to the sea, and the schist roofs of Pozzo and Poretto set amongst olive trees and blackberry bushes.

Ten minutes' walk up the slope you come to a deserted stone cottage, just beyond which you cross a stone wall, and then take the right track where the road forks. At the next fork continue bearing right and then, just before you reach another abandoned building, turn left. After thirty minutes you'll come to the meeting of four paths – bear left here, and follow the red painted arrows into the deep valley. Another fifteen minutes will bring you to a fork, where you continue along the higher track, which passes a bubbling spring – a good place to stop for a breather and a drink before the final ascent. The narrow path through the valley is marked by piles of stones, which are easy to lose sight of if you're not concentrating.

Another five minutes and you'll come to a marshy patch of scrub; here you head straight up the mountainside between two piles of stones set amid the undergrowth. Skirting to the left of a prominent rocky outcrop, you'll come to the **Col de Santa Maria**, where you get a breathtaking view over the cape to the gulf of Saint-Florent and beyond to the Désert des Agriates. As you cross this ridge the rocky sprawl of Monte Stello appears to the right. A few minutes down to the right you'll see white paint marks leading on towards the summit. After ten minutes, you'll come to a large rock with an arrow and "500m" painted on it, marking the final ascent – here you have a choice of the easier path to the left, or the steep climb which veers up to the right, again marked with white paint. At the top, after a total of about three hours' walking, you have a stupendous view of the cape and, if it's not too misty, south to the highest mountain peaks of Corsica, among them Monte Cinto, Monte Renoso, Monte Incudine and Rotondo.

the Castello branch of the da Gentile clan. Quick to retaliate, the Erbalunga side of the family, supported by the Genoese, launched an attack against Castello, an action resulting in the total devastation of the port when the French struck back the following year. *La Sposetta* is generally thought to haunt Castello – presumably she also drops in on the da Gentile family's house, built in 1602 at the entrance to the hamlet.

Fifteen minutes' walk south of the village along the road to Silgaggia you come to the well-preserved little chapel of **Notre-Dame-des-Neiges**, which dates from the tenth century and houses the oldest known **frescoes** in Corsica. Dating from 1386, they depict several saints, including Saint Christopher and Saint Catherine as well as a possible Saint George.

From Erbalunga to Tomino

Beyond Erbalunga the landscape takes on a more desolate aspect and the road gives an ever clearer view of the rocky coast. After 6km you reach **SISCO**, a *commune* made up of several hamlets scattered over the mountainside and the tiny seaside village of **Marine de Sisco**. This last comprises a small sandy beach and a cluster of restaurants and hotel, making it a pleasant stopover. If you decide to **stay** the best place is *Hôtel de la Marine*, the first hotel you come to on the right (☎95 35 21 04; ②), with terraced pavilions on the beach. *Camping Renajo*, off a small track leading into the mountains on the opposite side of the road (☎95 35 21 14), provides adequate **camping** facilities.

There are two churches in Sisco worth visiting. The most striking is **San Michele**, a beautiful Romanesque chapel which can be reached from Chioso, the commune's principal hamlet, 7km via the D32 which leads off from the coast road at the centre of the *marine*. Just beyond the large unremarkable church of Saint Martin, take the right-hand track signposted to San Michele, and after a couple of minutes you'll see a rocky track leading uphill on the left; you can leave the car here and climb the last 2km to San Michele. The elegant chapel, built in 1030 by Pisan masons, occupies a spectacular windswept hillside overlooking the Marine de Sisco, with Pietracorbara a misty ridge of buildings stretching to the north. On September 29 the Festival of Saint Michael brings pilgrims up from the surrounding hamlets to celebrate Mass here.

Back on the main coast road, the huge **Couvent de Santa-Catalina** stands on a hillside high above the corniche, about half a kilometre beyond Marine de Sisco. The convent is now an old people's home, but you can visit the church, which is reached by taking a left off the main road, along a hairpin bend which doubles back to the building. (Ignore the turning next to the large stone statue of Saint Catherine, some 200m before, which leads to a dead end.) Built in the twelfth century, the graceless church, overshadowed by an ugly tower, was enlarged in the fifteenth century, when the hulking buttresses were added and the entrance widened to receive the pilgrims who came to see its famous relics. Including a piece of the clay from which Adam was made, an almond from Paradise, and one of Enoch's fingers, the relics were enshrined here in the thirteenth century by fishermen who, caught in a storm off Cap Corse, vowed to bring their holy cargo to the first church they came across if they were saved. This happened to be Santa-Catalina; unfortunately, the relics are now kept in the *mairie* at Chioso and are not accessible to visitors. Perhaps the most impressive feature of the bare interior is the round crypt, dating from the 1200s and based – like nearly all round churches – on the Holy Sepulchre at Jerusalem.

Heading north, you'll soon come to **Pietracorbara**, where's there's a beach and a couple of pizzerias, but it's a less alluring spot for a picnic and a bathe than **PORTICIOLO**, a further 7km on. The village is attractively small and crumbling, with a tiny mooring for fishing boats jutting into the green sea and a white sandy beach which you're pretty much guaranteed to have to yourself.

At the little *marine* of **SANTA SEVERA**, 2km further, there's the opportunity to cut across the cape to visit Luri and the Tour de Sénèque (see p.59). The village also has a few hotels, but as it doesn't ooze character you're better off waiting until you get to Macinaggio. **Meria**, a collection of pastel-shaded cottages surrounding a well-preserved tower, lies 6km beyond, and then it's another 2km to the little *commune* of **TOMINO**, sited on a windy rocky spur 2km south of Macinaggio. A Christian centre in the sixth century and once a serious rival to commercial Rogliano (see p.56), producing an excellent muscat wine, the village today is virtually deserted, but the **view** is worth the steep climb. Following the un-signposted hairpin road, on foot or by car, which emerges on the left just before you enter the village of Macinaggio, you'll soon come to the crest of the hill, where a Baroque chapel and a Genoese tower face each other across the road before a scattering of houses. In the near distance you can see the Îles Finocchiarola and the Tuscan island of Capraia across the vast expanse of deep blue sea.

The northern cape

Macinaggio, northern terminus of the road along the east side of the cape, is also the largest settlement due north of Bastia, offering a spread of hotels and restaurants, as well as a fuel station. The only bus service to this somewhat isolated resort runs in summer from Bastia three times a week. The land between Macinaggio and **Barcaggio**, at the very tip of Corsica, forms part of a protected site with the **Îles Finocchiarola** and **Île de la Giraglia**, and is a good area to explore on foot, boasting some glorious **beaches**. Known as the "holy promontory" in Roman times because of its Christian settlements, the tip of the cape also has many ruined chapels, such as **Santa Maria** near Macinaggio. Inland, the eight hamlets of **Rogliano**, spectacularly spread out over the slopes 5km from Macinaggio, were for a few centuries the fief of the da Mare family, whose castles and towers lie scattered over the hills. On the western side of the northern tip, the chief focus of interest is **Centuri-Port**, where the colourful horseshoe-shaped harbour holds several hotels.

Macinaggio

A port since Roman times, well-sheltered **MACINAGGIO** was developed by the Genoese in 1620 for the export of olive oil and wine to the Italian peninsula, and in later years played its part in the wider history of the island. Pascal Paoli landed here in 1790 after his exile in England, whereupon he kissed the ground and uttered the words "O ma patrie, je t'ai quitté esclave, je te retrouve libre" (Oh my country, I left you as a slave, I rediscover you a free man) – a plaque commemorating the event adorns the wall above the ship chandlers. Napoléon also stopped here on his way to Bastia as he fled from the Paolists in 1793, and in 1869 the Empress Eugénie was forced by a storm to disembark here on her way back from the opening of the Suez Canal, before taking refuge in Rogliano – the road from Macinaggio to Rogliano has been called *Chemin de l'Impératrice* ever since. There's not much of an historic patina to the place nowadays, but with its boat-jammed marina, its line of colourful seafront awnings and its definitive end-of-the-world feel, Macinaggio has a certain appeal in itself. In addition, its proximity to some of the best beaches on Corsica make it irresistible.

The best **place to stay** is *Hôtel des Îles*, opposite the marina (☎95 35 43 02; ②), which also has a good restaurant. All the cosy rooms in this renovated old building overlook the port, but it does get noisy at night, being above the most popular bar in the place. Otherwise your best bet is *U Libecciu*, situated behind the marina, on the road that leads north off the D80 road to Rogliano (☎95 35 43 22; ③); it's a modern building with no view to speak of, but the rooms are spacious and the restaurant is excellent. *U Ricordu* on the south side of the road to Rogliano (☎95 35 40 20; ④) is along the same lines as the *U Libecciu*, and has a swimming pool.

As for **restaurants**, the *Pizzeria San Columbu*, at the end of the port facing out to sea, does a passable seafood pizza, or you can have a Corsican feast at *Les Îles*, which also does good fresh fish dishes. Diving enthusiasts should visit the **diving club** in the port (☎95 35 46 61).

BEACHES AROUND MACINAGGIO

The town beach is seaweed-ridden and dirty, but you can get to some stunning stretches of white sand and clear sea by following the track at the north end of the marina. The **Baie de Tamarone**, 2km along this stretch, has deep clear waters, making it a good place for diving and snorkelling. Just behind the beach the road forks, and if you follow the left-hand track for twenty minutes you'll come to the isolated Romanesque **Chapelle Santa-Maria**. Raised on the foundations of a sixth-century church, the building comprises a tenth-century chapel and a twelfth-century chapel merged into one, hence the two discrepant apses.

Three kilometres north of the chapel you come to **Plage Santa Maria**, a perfect arc of white sand overlooked by the huge **Tour Chiapelle**. Dramatically cleft in half and entirely surrounded by water, the ruined three-storied building was one of three built on the northern tip of the cape by the Genoese in the sixteenth century (the others are at Tollare and Barcaggio) as lookout posts against the increasingly troublesome Moorish pirates. As Macinaggio grew in importance, the towers began to be used also by health and customs officers, who controlled the maritime traffic with Genoa. Pascal Paoli established his garrison here in 1761, having been unsuccessful in his attempt to take Macinaggio, and contemplated building a rival port. Six years later, to undermine Genoa's position in the area, Paoli sent two hundred men under the command of Achille Murati to capture the neighbouring island of Capraia, which had belonged to Genoa since 1507. Murati's relatively easy victory marked the beginning of the downfall of the Genoese in Corsica.

CAPANDULA AND THE ÎLES FINOCCHIAROLA

The region between Plage Santa Maria and Barcaggio (see p.57) comprises the protected site of **CAPANDULA**, a bleak stretch of maquis-shrouded land which between March and June is a stop-off for migrating birds from North Africa. Hundreds of gulls and cormorants haunt the area, especially around the **Îles Finocchiorola**, a sprinkling of islets off the eastern corner of the cape, named after the wild fennel which grows in abundance over the rocks. Look out for the elusive **Audouin's gull**, with its distinctive red bills encircled by a black band. Only 2500 pairs still survive in the Mediterranean, and they are a protected species here. Other types you might expect to see are the more common **herring gull**, large with grey upperparts, black wingtips and a yellow bill; the black-headed **Mediterranean gull** and perhaps a **Manx shearwater** or **Cory's shearwater**. Though similar in appearance to gulls, these last two brown-backed species are distinguished by the way they glide low over the sea with straight, stiff wings.

The islets are a nature reserve, only visitable between March and August, and fires and camping are strictly forbidden. Boat excursions run in July and August from the marina in Macinaggio; tickets cost 50F. The round trip includes a stop on the largest islet so that enthusiasts can do a spot of birdwatching.

Rogliano

A cluster of hamlets scattered in a lush valley below Monte Poggio make up the *commune* of **ROGLIANO**, 7km along a series of hairpin bends from Macinaggio. The constituent hamlets – Bettolacce, Olivo, Magna, Soprana, Vignale, Sottana and Campiano – were the base of the da Mare lords from the twelfth to the sixteenth centuries, and the ruins of their convents, towers and castles are distributed amongst them.

The easternmost and largest hamlet, **Bettolacce**, is dominated by the privately owned **Tour Franceschi**, an enormous round tower in remarkable condition, and has a **post office** and two **hotels**. The *Auberge Sant'Agnellu* (☎95 35 40 59; closed winter; ②), opposite the pleasantly proportioned Église Sant'Agnellu, has large comfortable rooms with televisions and a magnificent restaurant terrace overlooking the valley. *Auberge di Magna* (☎95 35 44 98; ②), 300m from *Sant'Agnellu* and signposted down a lane, also affords a splendid view and serves delicious home cooking.

Isolated in the valley some 500m beneath Bettolacce stands the ruined sixteenth-century **Église Saint-Côme-et-Saint-Damien**, accessible via the path leading opposite *Auberge Sant'Agnellu*. A curious rectangular bell tower stands separated from the nave, which is the oldest part of the church. **Vignale**, the hamlet above Bettolacce, is dominated by the crumbling ruins of the **Castello di San Colombano**, from where there's a magnificent view across the valley to Macinaggio. The castle was built in the twelfth century and became known as "U Castelacciu" (the Bad Castle) in the sixteenth when Giacomo Santa da Mare abandoned the Genoese cause, switched his allegiances to Sampiero Corso and defected to the Franco-Turkish army. In 1553 the Genoese retaliated by destroying the castle, which was later restored then burnt down in 1947.

From here a track leads 300m to Olivo and the **Couvent Saint-Francois**, an imposing vine-covered building straight out of a Gothic romance. The convent and adjoining church, surmounted by a spindly clock tower, were built in 1520 by the Franciscans, who also restored them in 1711. They are now private property and closed to the public.

Barcaggio and around

To get to the very tip of Corsica, continue west along the D80 for about five kilometres (slowing down for goats on your way), until you reach **Ersa**, where the D253 twists off northwards to **BARCAGGIO**, giving breathtaking views of the Île de la Giraglia surrounded by pale green sea.

Barcaggio is tiny – just a jetty, a couple of restaurants and a dozen houses built from the greenish local schist – but the setting is sublime and the **beach** is one of the finest in Corsica. You can leave your vehicle in the village **car park** (also a park for camper vans), and from here a track leads to a superb unspoiled strand of white sand dunes lapped by a crystalline sea. The *La Giraglia* **hotel** (☎95 35 60 54; ④) has a fantastic location at the north end of the village overlooking the tiny harbour, though it's expensive for what it offers and doesn't accept credit cards. For a **meal** try *U Pescadore* on the jetty, where you're guaranteed fresh fish.

The northern extremity of Corsica is marked by the **ÎLE DE LA GIRAGLIA**, a green islet covered with wild leeks growing a metre high. Surmounted by a lighthouse, it also has a sixteenth-century Genoese tower and a pair of ruined chapels adorning its rocky slopes.

About 2km west of Barcaggio lies **TOLLARE**, a neglected little coastal village with a small beach. This place attracts sailing enthusiasts and there are always a few yachts moored in the bay. Windsurfers will also find facilities here.

Centuri

From Tollare you can drive south to complete a loop back at the D80, close to the turn-off for Barcaggio. If you continue west on the main road you'll go over the **Col de Serra** (365m); for a fantastic **view** of both sides of the cape, walk from the col up to **Moulin Mattei**, the round building with the coloured tiled roof on the hill above the road.

Once you've passed over the col you soon come to **CAMERA**, the first hamlet of the *commune* of **CENTURI**, where the bizarre cylindrical turrets of the **Chateau de Général Cipriani** peer from the woods beneath the road. The castle (closed to the public) was built in 1812 for one Count Leonetti Cipriani, a Tuscan soldier and friend of Napoléon. The smaller hamlet of **CANELLE**, overlooking Centuri-Port and accessible from Camera along the road heading north or on foot from the port, is renowned for its enormous fig trees, whose drooping branches overhang the houses and shadow the road.

When Boswell arrived here from England in 1765, the former Roman settlement of **CENTURI-PORT** was a tiny fishing village, recommended to him for its peaceful detachment from the dangerous turmoil of the rest of Corsica. Not much has changed since Boswell's time: Centuri-Port exudes tranquillity despite an influx of summer residents, several of them artists who come to paint the fishing boats in the slightly prettified harbour, where the grey stone wall is highlighted by the green serpentine roofs of the encircling cottages, restaurants and bars. The only drawback is that you'll find the small **beach** disappointingly muddy and not ideal for sunbathing.

PRACTICALITIES
Centuri-Port has more **hotels** than anywhere else on Cap Corse. The least expensive place, *Hôtel-Restaurant du Pêcheur* (☎95 35 64 47; ①), the yellow building in the harbour, is also the most pleasant and fills up quickly in the high season; its rooms are agreeably cool, with thick stone walls, and it has a popular **restaurant**. The *Vieux Moulin* (☎95 35 64 47; ③), which occupies a prime location behind the harbour on the right as you enter the village, has a marvellous terrace but the rooms are rather stuffy and the obligatory 150F menu is not up to much. *Hôtel La Jetée* (☎95 35 64 47; ③), at the far end of the jetty, is well situated and has a good fish restaurant, though the rooms are pretty ordinary. Otherwise you have *Hôtel A Marinara* (☎95 35 62 95; ②), a small welcoming hotel situated behind *du Pecheur*, also with a restaurant. For **campers** there's *Camping l'Isolettu*, 400m south (☎95 35 62 81), an uninviting option but unfortunately the only choice in the vicinity. Centuri-Port has a **supermarket** which sells newspapers, and a **bread van** comes at ten o'clock every morning and stops outside the *Vieux Moulin*.

The western cape

South of Centuri the corniche cuts through villages stacked up the cliffsides above small *marines* that are often masked from the road by rocky outcrops. At **Pino** you can take a detour inland to see the **Tour de Sénèque**, while farther south **Canari** offers another remarkable Romanesque church. Just a few kilometres north of Saint-Florent lies **Nonza**, perhaps the most spectacular of all the cape villages, perched on the edge of the cliffside above a black sandy beach.

Morsiglia to Canari
The change of scenery south of Centuri is striking and sudden: gentle green slopes give way to chalky cliffs that plunge down from the high corniche road, deep indents punctuate the coast and the sea is a dark peacock-feather blue.

After 6km the three towers of **MORSIGLIA** come into view: six of these enormous structures were originally built here to defend against Moorish pirates in the sixteenth century. A few kilometres farther lies the **Golfe d'Aliso**, a small cove where the sea has an incredible depth and colour, the red sand striking a dazzling contrast with the dark turquoise water. There's access to the shore from the road, although not much room to park.

A sense of the tropics pervades the air at **PINO**, some 2km south of here. Palm trees grow up the cliff, and the houses – many owned by emigrés returned from Venezuela – are coloured pale pink, orange and yellow and feature turreted roofs and verandas. You could stop in the village for a drink under the shade of the chestnuts and plane trees, or follow the steep road from just outside the village down to the *marine*, where a fifteenth-century **Franciscan convent** lies half-hidden amongst a jungle of bamboo. Although the outward appearance is grim, try to get inside for a look at the faded fifteenth-century frescoes above the entrance, featuring the Virgin flanked by saints Francis and Bernard. (If it's locked, ask for the key at Église Sainte-Marie in the centre of the village.)

Tour de Sénèque and Luri

A short distance to the north of Pino, a turn-off in the direction of Luri will take you winding through pine woods to the Col de Sainte-Lucie. If you take the steep turning on the right just before the col you'll soon come to an abandoned school above which looms the **Tour de Sénèque**. Set atop a pinnacle of black rock, the impressively forbidding tower was built in the fifteenth century by the da Mare family, on the spot where Seneca is said to have lived from 41 to 49 AD, having been exiled for offending Emperor Claudius and accused of seducing the emperor's niece. His rampant misconduct didn't stop here. Nettles are supposed to grow in such profusion around the base of the tower because during his exile Seneca reputedly once came down from his rock in an attempt to ravage the Corsican women, and was attacked with nettles as a result. Whilst here he wrote a few bitter verses about the place:

> *Oh Corsica whom rocks terrific bound*
> *Where nature spreads her wildest deserts round*
> *In vain revolving seasons cheer thy soil*
> *Nor ripening fruits, nor waving harvests smile.*

It's a thirty-minute climb through the brambles to the tower, and as you can't enter the building, you may as well just view it from down below.

Passing over the Col de Sainte-Lucie, you soon come to the *commune* of **LURI**, an unexceptional place surrounded by a delightful landscape of lemon trees and vineyards. At **PIAZZA**, Luri's central hamlet, you might take a look at **Église Saint-Pierre**. Dating from the seventeenth-century, it houses a late-sixteenth-century painting that represents the life of Saint Peter against a background showing the local castles in the fifteenth century – the one on the left is the Tour des Motti, a precursor of the Tour de Sénèque, and on the right is the Castello di San Colombano at Rogliano (see p.56).

Canari and around

South of Pino the high corniche road winds past rocky inlets for several kilometres through Barretali and **Marine de Giottani**, where there's a small pebbly beach. Some 5km farther and you'll come to **CANARI**, a large *commune* with a couple of notable churches.

Canari's chief hamlet, **MARINCA**, has the Romanesque **Santa-Maria-Assunta**. Right on the main road, it was built at the end of the twelfth century, and is attractive chiefly for the quirky sculpture that decorates the cornice beneath the roof – weird mask-like faces alongside strange beasts and stylized patterns. The gloomy Baroque **Église Saint-François**, formerly attached to a

Franciscan monastery, is situated a little way up the road in **PIEVE**. The high-light here is a fifteenth-century gilded **panel** of Saint Michael, on the left as you enter; a panel from the same altarpiece is set into the sacristy cupboard door. Also of interest is the sixteenth-century *Assumption of the Virgin* on the right of the nave, above the tomb of Vittoria da Gentile, who died in 1590 at a convent, no longer in existence, in Canari.

From here it's a gentle fifteen-minute walk along a marked path up to **EMISA** and the tiny fifteenth-century **Chapelle Sainte-Catherine**, which houses two faded panels from that period. Alternatively, you could descend to the tiny *marine* of Canari, where the *U Scogliu* **restaurant** serves the tastiest fish on Cap Corse.

South of Marinca, beyond a stretch of cliffs blighted grey by the disused road-side asbestos factory, you pass through **Marine d'Albo**, where you could make the six-kilometre inland diversion to see the tenth-century chapel at **Olcani**, half-ruined and half-hidden in the maquis. Otherwise, you're just a couple of kilometres from Nonza.

Nonza

Set high on a black rocky pinnacle dropping vertically into the sea, the village of **NONZA** is one of the highlights of the Cap Corse shoreline. The village was formerly the main stronghold of the da Gentile family, and the remains of the **fortress** are still standing on the furthest rocks on the overhanging cliff. Nonza has a shady square, behind which you twist your way through the houses and geraniums to reach the ruined fortress and the more impressive green Genoese **Tower** nearby. In 1768 the tower witnessed one of the greatest con-tricks in military history. The French, having succeeded in taking over all of Cap Corse, closed in on the Nonza garrison, which was under the command of one Captain Casella. Fearing that Casella's tenacity would lead them to their deaths, the Corsican troops absconded, leaving him to defend the tower single-handed. This he did, using a system of cables to maintain constant fire from a line of muskets and a single cannon, until the disheartened French offered a truce. Old Casella demanded that his army be allowed to parade out in dignity, and duly emerged alone, brandishing his pistol, to the amazement of the besieging army.

Nonza is also famous for **Saint Julia**, patron saint of Corsica, who was martyred here in the fifth century. The story goes that she had been sold into slavery at Carthage and was being taken by ship to Gaul when the slavers docked here. A pagan festival was in progress, and when Julia refused to participate she was crucified; the gruesome legend relates that her breasts were then cut off and thrown onto a stone, from which sprang two springs, now enshrined in a chapel by the beach. To get there follow the sign on the right-hand side of the road before you enter the square, which points to the **La fontaine de Sainte-Julie**, down by the rocks.

The semicircular black **beach**, a thick line of white surf bordering the dark sea, is thus coloured as a result of pollution from the asbestos mine up the coast. This may not inspire confidence, but from down here you do get the best view of the tower, which looks as if it's about to topple over into the sea.

You can **stay** in Nonza at *Auberge Patrizi* (☎95 37 82 16; ①), run from the big orange restaurant in the square. Made up of two village houses, the *Auberge* is an old-fashioned place where half-pension is obligatory, but the food is good and plentiful.

The Nebbio

Taking its name from the thick mists which sweep over the region, the **Nebbio** has for centuries been one of the most fertile parts of the island, producing honey, chestnuts and some of the island's finest wine. Officially the region includes the barren **Désert des Agriates** on its western edge, but essentially the Nebbio comprises the amphitheatre of rippled hills, vineyards and cultivated valleys that converge on Saint-Florent, a region nicknamed La Conca d'Oro (Golden Shell) by Pascal Paoli because it encompassed all the wealth of the region.

A bishopric until 1790, **Saint-Florent** is a chic coastal resort at the base of Cap Corse. It remains the Nebbio's chief town and best base, while villages such as **Olmeta-di-Tuda** and **Oletta**, being close to Bastia, are lively and well-populated places, especially in the summer when families move up to the cooler mountains from the city. The wine produced around **Patrimonio** rivals that of Sartène, and *caves* offering wine tastings are a feature of the whole region. The two unmissable historic sites in this part of the island are the Pisan church of **Santa Maria Assunta**, just outside Saint-Florent, and the diminutive **San Michele de Murato**, close to the chapels that are scattered in the valley between **Rapale** and **Santo-Pietro-di-Tenda**.

The only public transport serving Nebbio is the twice-daily bus that runs directly from Bastia to Saint-Florent.

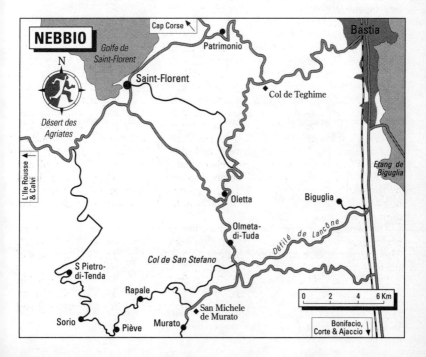

Saint-Florent

Viewed from across the bay, **SAINT-FLORENT** (San Fiorenzu) appears as a bright line against the black tidal wave of the Tenda hills, the pale ancient houses seeming to rise straight out of the sea, overlooked by a huge circular citadel. It's a relaxing town, blessed with a decent beach and a good number of restaurants, but the key to its success is the **Marina**, which by luring the yacht-owning classes has made Saint-Florent something of a low-key Saint Tropez. Yet for all the attentions of the rich and famous, the place remains relatively unspoilt for the time being, and its position next to the Désert des Agriates lends it a pleasant air of isolation.

In Roman times a town existed on the site where the Santa Maria Assunta stands today, a kilometre east of the present village. Few traces remain of the settlement that grew up there, which in the fifteenth century was eclipsed by the port that developed around the new Genoese citadel. Saint-Florent prospered as one of Genoa's strongholds, and was fought over by the Corsicans, the French and the Genoese in the mid-sixteenth century and again during Corsica's struggles for independence in 1769. It was from here that Paoli set off for London in 1796, never to return.

The town is tiny and you won't find a great deal to see, but there are lots of cafés to sit and do nothing in. **Place des Portes**, the centre of town life, has tables facing the sea in the shade of plane trees, and in the evening fills with strollers and nonchalant *boules* players. In rue du Centre, which runs west off the square, parallel to the seafront and marina, you'll find some restaurants, a few shops and a couple of wine-tasting places – be sure to sample the sweet, maquis-scented muscat made around here. To reach the **Citadel** you climb to the end of rue du Centre and pass through the large wire gate – it looks like private property, but is accessible to the public. Unique in Corsica for its circular shape, the citadel was built in 1439 for the Genoese governors but is now a run-down construction full of pigeons. It does, however, give a beautiful view of the hills of the Nebbio and the mountains of Cap Corse disappearing into mists up the coast. At sundown you should move back down to the seafront, when the rocks glow with a fiery light.

The nearest **beach**, plage de la Roya, is a windy stretch of sand and mud flats to the west of the village, fine for windsurfers but the sea is rather murky due to the sewage from the town. To get there cross the bridge to the south of place des Portes, taking a right through the car park. A better option is the nameless beach which lies a further 2km southwest along the main road inland – at the beach it turns into the D81. Here the sea is much clearer and you get a fantastic **view** of the town, with its dark backdrop of undulating mountains.

Practicalities

Buses run from Bastia to Saint-Florent twice daily (except Sun), leaving at 6am & 11am. They arrive in the village car park, from where a return bus departs at 8am & 2pm. The journey takes one hour. For **tourist information** go to the *Centre Administratif* (Mon–Fri 9am–noon & 2–6pm; ☎95 37 06 04), which is on the Bastia road, northeast of the village, next door to the *mairie*, about five minutes' walk from place des Portes. You'll find the **post office** on the same road a little further out; it doesn't charge commission on currency exchange, unlike the two **banks**, situated either side of the road on the north side of the square.

Les Halles de Saint-Florent, on the bridge, is a good **supermarket**, and is open on Sundays in the summer. There's a **pharmacy** two minutes up the small unmarked road that leads east off place des Portes towards the Santa Maria Assunta cathedral. You'll find a cluster of **telephones** in the marina car park in front of the square.

To explore the beaches off the Désert des Agriates, you can hire a **boat** from *Corse Plaisance*, on the bridge overlooking the marina (☎95 3719 28).

ACCOMMODATION

Saint-Florent is a popular resort and **hotels** fill up quickly, especially at the height of summer when prior booking is essential. *Hôtel-Restaurant du Pêcheur* on the quay (☎95 53 60 14; ①) is the cheapest, but the *Hôtel Europe* in place des Portes (☎95 37 00 33; ③) is the most attractive option – an old-fashioned place with elegant rooms in a prime location. *Hôtel du Centre*, opposite the *Europe* (☎95 37 00 68; ②), has tiny rooms but an equally good view. *L'Albinu*, situated at the turn-off for Nonza a kilometre out of town towards Bastia (☎95 30 15 55; ④), is a modern, well-equipped hotel open in the high season. Otherwise there's *Auberge U Liamone*, 500m out on the road to Bastia, next door to the *Elf* service station (☎95 30 12 81; ③), a comfortable modern hotel with balconies and bathrooms in every room. All but the *Hôtel Europe* are closed during winter.

A fair number of **campsites** are dotted about the coast, but these are two-star places which are packed in August and closed out of season. *Camping U Pezzu*, route de la Plage (☎95 37 01 65), is closest to town, 1km west on the small road which backs the beach. *Camping Kalliste,* 2km further on the same road (☎95 37 03 08), is clean and large, with its own beachside bar and restaurant.

EATING AND DRINKING

Saint-Florent is renowned for its crayfish (*langouste*) and red mullet, but be careful when choosing your **restaurant** – the tourist places displaying menus in every language tend to be mediocre. A reasonably priced place for excellent fish and Corsican specialities, such as stews and rich game dishes, is *Le Cabistan*, in the rue du Centre with a huge fish tank facing the street. More expensive is *La Marinuccia* at the far end of the same street, below the citadel, which serves the best fish in Saint-Florent and boasts a terrace jutting out into the sea. Otherwise *Pizzeria Citadel*, the fortress-shaped place just over the bridge south of the square, does very good pizzas and salads, served outside to the accompaniment of clanky organ music. *Pizzeria de la Place*, in the main square, is an inexpensive and jolly bistro-pizzeria, with seats out in the square.

The *Europe* is the most popular **café** in place des Portes. *Bar du Passage* opposite attracts a younger clientele, partly on account of its jukebox, but *Bar de Col d'Amphore*, on the north side, has stylish 1930s decor and is the place to pose in. If money's no object, you could slouch in the chairs of *Bar Athena* in the marina, where cocktails and ice creams are served at vast expense.

Around Saint-Florent

The area around Saint-Florent offers plenty of opportunities for short excursions: the cathedral of **Santa Maria Assunta** is only a fifteen-minute walk from the town centre; the **Tour de Mortella** also lies within walking distance of the town, as does the creepy **Dolmen of Monte Recincu**; and the wonderful beach of **Saleccia** can easily be reached by boat.

SANTA MARIA ASSUNTA

Situated in a lonely spot, a kilometre east of Saint-Florent on the original site of the Roman settlement of Nebbium, the church of **Santa Maria Assunta** – the so-called cathedral of the Nebbio – is a fine example of Pisan Romanesque architecture, rivalled only by La Canonica at Mariana, its exact contemporary (see p.48).

To reach it, follow the small road east off place des Portes. In summer the cathedral is left open all day, but in winter you have to ask for the key at the tourist office.

Deprived of its bell tower, which was knocked down in the nineteenth century, and set among pastures next door to a farmyard, the cathedral has a distinctly barn-like appearance. Built of warm yellow limestone, it's a superlatively elegant barn, though, and a close look soon reveals an unexpected wealth of harmonious detail: gracefully symmetrical blind arcades decorate the western facade, and at the entrance, twisting serpents and wild animals adorn the pilasters on each side of the door.

The interior, too, appears deceptively simple. Carved shells, foliage and animals adorn the capitals of the pillars dividing the nave where, immediately to the right, you'll see a glass case containing the mummified figure of **Saint Flor**, a Roman soldier martyred in the third century for his Christian beliefs. The soldier's remains were donated by Pope Clement XIV to the Bishop of the Nebbio in 1771, and a gilded wooden statue stands as a further commemoration in the apse. The spacious nave also holds the tomb of **General Antoine Gentili**, a supporter of Pascal Paoli during the struggles for independence.

THE DOLMEN OF MONTE RECINCU

A visit to the **Dolmen of Monte Recincu**, a large stone tomb in the maquis on the edge of the Désert des Agriates, makes a pleasant half-hour walk from Saint-Florent. To get there walk to the end of the beach – just beyond a left-hand track leads to the dolmen.

This megalithic tomb, made up of three roughly hewn stone slabs, is popularly known as the **Casa di u Lurcu**, meaning "house of the ogre", after a gigantic creature with the head of a man and a wolf-like body, which allegedly used to terrorize the locals by sucking the blood of their cattle. One day, so the legend goes, the people decided to strike back. Gauging the monster's shoe size from his footprints, they made him some huge boots which they filled with tar and left by his drinking place. Duly ensnared, the *Lurcu* tried to bribe the villagers with a special recipe for *brocciu*, a Corsican cheese, but the people suspected a trap and threw him into a ditch and buried him. Though it's not clear exactly when the stones were placed here, the legend dates them around 1500 BC.

TOUR DE MORTELLA

The ruined **Tour de Mortella**, isolated on the coast 7km west of Saint-Florent, is the most impressive piece of Genoese architecture hereabouts. Built around 1520 as an anti-piracy measure, the tower soon fell into disuse due to its inaccessibility, then was rediscovered two hundred years later by English soldiers. During the wars of independence the English made use of the tower and later used it as a model for the towers raised back home in preparation for Napoléon's expected invasion. Known as **Martello towers** in deference to this Corsican prototype, many of these forts still stand on the southern coast of England.

You reach the tower on foot by following the track which leads off from the end of the beach (past the left-turn to the dolmen). At first the track gently climbs past villas and houses before cutting through some woods; after half an hour you'll come to a gate with a sign reading "Anse de Fornali" – go through the gate and follow the path straight on to the sea, from where a narrow track leads along the rocks to the tower. If you don't relish the walk, you can get a good view of the tower from the boat to Saleccia beach (see below).

SALECCIA
About 6km further west along the coast of the Désert des Agriates, the **Plage de Saleccia** is one of the finest beaches on Corsica. A glistening stretch of silver sand lapped by translucent green sea, it's so photogenic it was used in the film *The Longest Day.* Hourly boats leave from the marina in the summer; otherwise you can only get to it via a rough track by jeep or motorbike. There's a basic campsite on the beach.

A tour of the Nebbio

The villages of the Nebbio can be visited in a slow day's drive from Saint-Florent, following a loop up to the Col de Teghime, then down through Oletta, past the Col de Santa Stefano, and onward to Murato, through Santo-Pietro-di-Tenda and back to Saint-Florent. If you're driving into the Nebbio from Bastia, you can join this loop at Col de Teghime or Col de Santa Stefano, the latter approached by the dramatic Défilé de Lancone; driving from Saint-Florent, you can shorten the circuit by taking the road straight up to Oletta. The Bastia–Saint-Florent bus follows the direct route over the Col de Teghime, not stopping along the way.

Patrimonio

As you leave Saint-Florent by the Bastia road, the first village you come to, after 6km, is **PATRIMONIO**, centre of the first Corsican wine region to gain *appelation controlée* status. Apart from the local muscat, which can be sampled in the village or at one of the *caves* along the route from Saint-Florent, Patrimonio's chief asset is the sixteenth-century **Église Saint-Martin**, occupying its own little hillock and visible for miles around. The colour of burnt sienna, it stands out vividly against the rich green vineyards, but the interior was effectively ruined in the nineteenth century, when an elaborately painted ceiling and overdone marble altar were installed. In a tiny garden close by stands a limestone **statue-menhir** known as *U Nativu*, a late megalithic piece dating from 800–900 BC. A carved T-shape on its front represents a breastbone, and two ears and a chin can also be made out.

Col de Teghime to Oletta

From Patrimonio the road climbs to **Col de Teghime** (548m), from where it's possible to see the coastlines of both sides of the cape when it's not covered in a pervasive fog. A stunning panorama of Saint-Florent and Patrimonio is laid out to the west, while to the east you'll see Bastia, with the glistening Étang de Biguglia stretching south. It's not unusual for the weather to be entirely different on the other side. For an even better view follow the Bastia road for another 1km and turn left onto the D338, which leads to the **Serra di Pigno**, a gentle climb of about 45 minutes – a massive television antenna marks the summit.

The road south of the Col de Teghime will bring you after 10km to **OLETTA**, where faded multicoloured houses are stacked haphazardly against each other up the hill, with vegetation springing from the cracks in the walls. The eighteenth-century **Église Saint-André**, at the edge of the village, has an ancient relief of the Creation embedded in its facade, a relic from the church which occupied the site in the twelfth century. Inside there's a graceful triptych dating from 1534 and portraying the Virgin and Child flanked by saints Andrew and Reparata. Those intent on seeing every last ancient structure in the Nebbio could detour to the ruined twelfth-century **Couvent Saint-Francois**, 2km from Oletta along the direct road down to Saint-Florent – the elegant bell tower marks it out from afar.

Olmeta-di-Tuda to Murato

If you continue along the D82 you come to the hamlet of **OLMETA-DI-TUDA**, which rises abruptly from the rocky slopes, with huge elm trees dominating the foreground and the distant peaks of Monte Astu creating a forbidding backdrop.

A further 3km along, the crossroads at the **Col de San Stefano** (349m) marks the entrance to the **Défilé de Lancone**, an exhilarating, precipitous descent that hits the main coast road 9km south of Bastia. Hewn out of the black rock, with nationalist graffiti adorning the rock faces at every lurching bend, the road winds far above the River Bevinco, from the bed of which the serpentine for the church of San Michele de Murato was quarried. The *Défilé* is a road to be treated with respect – numerous little shrines along the way testify to the fatal smashes that have occurred here.

If you continue along the D5 instead of taking the *Défilé*, you'll soon pass the Pisan church of **San Michele de Murato**, which sits gracefully on a grassy ledge high above the hazy mountainous landscapes of the Nebbio. Built around 1280, this late Romanesque building is notable for its asymmetrical patterning of dark green serpentine and off-white marble, a jazzy counterpoint to the simple lines of the single-naved church, though these were damaged in the late nineteenth century when the disproportionate bell tower was added. Outside, there's some sophisticated carving on the arches of the blind arcades and immediately beneath the roof, depicting gargoyles, wild beasts and human figures – look out for a relief on the north wall, showing an ashamed Eve reaching out to take the huge apple proffered by the serpent. Within the church you'll find less to catch the eye, though there's a faded fifteenth-century *Annunciation* frescoed on the arch of the apse. The church is always open to visitors.

The village of **MURATO**, a short distance beyond the church, has a good **restaurant**, *Le Monastère*, which serves delicious roast kid and lamb in maquis herbs.

On from Murato

To continue the Nebbio tour, backtrack to the D162, which hugs the side of the Tenda massif as it runs west, snaking through villages built precariously on the lip of a shadowy forested valley. At **RAPALE**, a tiny ancient hamlet with castle-like houses built of schist stone, you can see the Romanesque chapel of **San Cesareo**, a green and white ruin hidden in the woods above the village – it's a fifteen-minute walk.

Back on the main road another 2km will bring you to **PIEVE**. One kilometre before you reach the village, there's a **statue-menhir** set back from the right-hand side of the road behind a tiny chapel. Dating from 1000 BC, the megalith is worked in the green slate which – like serpentine – abounds in the area, a unique distinction. In front of the church in the heart of Pieve there are two more stone menhirs, dating from 2000 BC. From here it's worth making the three-kilometre trek along a mule track to the abandoned chapel of San Nicolao. This largely ruined tenth-century Romanesque building stands on a grassy plateau above the village. Its interest lies in the remains of the Tuscan stone sculpture decorated with geometric motifs which once adorned the chapel's pediments.

From Pieve the road twists through valleys along the River Aliso through Sorio and on to **SANTO-PIETRO-DI-TENDA**, an attractive red stone village spread out under the shadow of the Tenda massif. The village's main point of interest is the tall Baroque **Église Saint-Jean** joined by a bell tower to the contemporaneous Chapelle Sainte-Croix. The latter is closed to the public, but inside the larger church you'll find the most lavish decor in the Nebbio – elaborate trompe l'oeil painting on the walls and a gloomy seventeenth-century *Descent from the Cross* above the altar, which has a wooden tabernacle that displays some fine marquetry on its pedestal.

If you follow the road for 12km until it joins the D81, another 7km takes you to Saint-Florent.

The Désert des Agriates

Bordered by thirty-five kilometres of wild and rugged coastline, the **Désert des Agriates** is a vast area of uninhabited land, a rocky moonscape interspersed with clumps of cacti and maquis-shrouded hills. The desert's limits extend eastwards to Golfe de Saint-Florent, stretch west to the mouth of the Ostriconi River and down as far south as San Pietro di Tenda. It might appear inhospitable, yet the desert has a long agricultural history, as implied by its name – *agriates* means "cultivated fields". Every winter until the early years of this century, shepherds from the mountains of Niolo and Asco would move down with their flocks to the desert for the annual bartering of goats' and ewes' cheese which they would exchange for olive oil and wheat cultivated by the farmers on the Agriates. These farmers, most of whom lived on Cap Corse, were responsible for building the stone storage huts known as *pagliaghju*, about twenty groups of which still exist and are used by hunters for shelter.

In order to prevent foreign speculators from developing the area the entire desert, including the coastal stretch, has recently been designated by the government as a protected site. Wildlife, however, remains under threat, not least from trigger-happy hunters, although various ecologically sound projects are currently under discussion. These include plans to introduce controlled breeding of the Agriates' **wild boar**, the purest type on the island, due to the isolation of the area, but now endangered by illegal hunting. Other rare species such as the huge, bright orange and brown *Jason* butterfly are also under threat of extinction, largely due to the fires which increasingly devastate the maquis. The maquis harbours hundreds of rare birds, including bee-eaters, red-backed shrikes, and various species of warbler.

Practicalities

There's just one major road on the desert, the D81, which cuts across its south side and passes through the **Bocca di Vezzu** (312m), a mountain pass where fabulous views extend across to the Nebbio.

To encourage people to explore the Agriates, pathways are being built around the coast and also in some inland areas. At the moment, however, only some parts of the coast are accessible from inland, such as the area around Saleccia (see p.65) and Plage du Loto. The coastline shields some fine sandy coves which are easiest approached by boat from Saint-Florent (see p.63). The **Plage du Loto**, for example, is a sheltered rocky cove which makes a good bathing spot: to get there take the D81 from Saint-Florent and turn right at Casta, and from here 5km along a rough track will bring you to the beach.

For **information** about the area you should visit the *Syndicat Mixte Agriate*, in Santo-Pietro-di-Tenda (☎95 37 72 51 Mon–Fri 9am–noon & 2–4pm). Information is also available from the tourist office in Saint-Florent. If you feel like braving the wilds, there's a **campsite** at Saleccia, 10km from Saint-Florent. It's very basic, the only facilities being toilets and a couple of taps for washing.

travel details

Trains

Bastia to: Ajaccio (4 daily; 4hr); Algajola (2 daily; 3hr); Aregno-Plage (2 daily; 3hr 10min); Belgodere (2 daily; 3hr 15min); Biguglia (4 daily; 10min); Bocognano (4 daily; 3hr); Calanzana (2 daily; 2hr 45min); Calvi (2 daily; 3hr 30min); Casamozza (4 daily; 20min); Corte (4 daily; 2hr); Francardo (4 daily; 1hr 45min); Furiani (4 daily; 15min); L'Île Rousse (2 daily; 3hr 15min); Mezzana (2 daily 1hr 50min); Pietralba (2 daily; 2hr 45min); Ponte Novu (4 daily; 1hr 45min); Ponte-Leccia (4 daily; 1hr 30min); Sant'Ambrogio (2 daily; 3hr 20min); Ucciani (2 daily; 2hr); Venaco (4 daily; 2hr 15min); Vivario (4 daily; 3hr 15min); Vizzavona (4 daily; 3hr).

Buses

Bastia to: Ajaccio (2 daily; 3hr); Barretali (3 weekly in summer; 2hr); Calvi (1 daily; 3hr); Canari (2 weekly; 1hr 30min); Centuri (3 weekly in summer; 2hr) Corte (2 daily; 2hr); Erbalunga (6 daily; 20min); Macinaggio (3 weekly in summer; 2hr); Moriani (3 daily; 3hr 45min); La Marana (2 daily; 30min); Saint-Florent (2 daily; 45min); Porto-Vecchio (2 daily; 3hr); Solenzara (1 daily in summer; 2hr).

Ferries

For ferry details see page 39.

CHAPTER TWO

THE NORTHWEST

Much of Corsica's **northwest** is taken up by the **Balagne**, a region divided into Haute-Balagne – the coast between Calvi and L'Île Rousse, and its hinterland – and Balagne Déserte, the area south of Calvi. In the past the Haute-Balagne was the most fertile region of Corsica, famous for prolific production of honey, fruit and wine, but nowadays – though it has its patches of lushness – a stark brightness characterizes the fire-devastated landscapes of the interior, with acres of gnarled olive trees and wavy vestiges of dry stone walls intermittently breaking the pattern of pale orange rock. If you're approaching this region from the east the first glimpse of its coast is an arresting sight, the turquoise and white stripes of sea and sand making a vibrant contrast with the mottled land.

Calvi, the Balagne's largest town and Corsica's third largest port, is also one of the most attractive places in Corsica, with its medieval citadel rising majestically from a stark granite promontory. Six kilometres of sandy beach, backed by a dark ribbon of pines, ensures its popularity as a summer resort, the seasonal influx being served by numerous hotels and a string of campsites. Tourist development has got a little out of hand to the east of Calvi, where private marinas and expensive holiday villages occupy much of the Haute-Balagne coast, but the beaches are outstanding, none more so than at the former Genoese stronghold **Algajola**. A stunning white strand also forms the focal point of nearby **L'Île Rousse**, a beguilingly faded port built in the eighteenth century as a rival to Calvi.

The hinterland of Haute-Balagne is a glorious landscape, with thousands of abandoned olive trees swathing the rocky slopes and fortress villages such as **Sant'Antonino** and **Speloncato** cresting the hilltops, each one embellished with a Baroque bell tower. Many of these settlements are at the receiving end of government programmes aimed at reviving ancient industries and crafts, so you'll see functioning workshops in various places – indeed **Pigna** and **Feliceto** are practically run by their artisan communities. Southeast of the Haute-Balagne you come within the borders of the **Parc Naturel Régional** as you enter an expanse of forests and rivers called the **Vallée de la Tartagine**, superb walking territory.

South of Calvi the landscapes become increasingly extraordinary, and the isolated coastal retreat of **Galéria** is well placed for excursions into some outstanding terrain. Inland, there's the **Vallée du Fango**, whose dense forests track the river to the base of towering Cinto Massif, or the particularly popular **Cirque de Bonifato**, a ridge of jagged peaks encircling another forested valley. On the coast, another essential visit is to the spectacular reserve of **La Scandola**, an area of astonishing rocky landscapes where the balance of nature has been little disturbed for thousands of years.

La Scandola is accessible only by boat from Calvi or from **Porto**, a busy resort overshadowed by purplish crags at the centre of the stormy **Golfe de Porto**. On the gulf's south side are the **Calanche**, a jumble of ravines and crumbling pinnacles once described as "nature's nightmare in stone". Inland, the highest road in

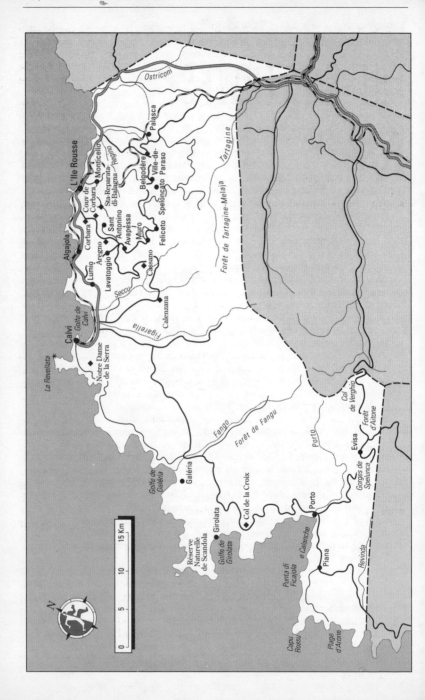

Corsica leads up to **Evisa**, a pleasant hiking base situated between the **Gorges de Spelunca** and the **Forêt d'Aitone**, the latter featuring the most stupendous specimens of Laricio pine and some of the best river-bathing on the island. Drive further and the landscape becomes more desolate in the approach to the **Col de Verghio**, a mountain pass marked by a mostly redundant ski station offering year-round accommodation.

The northwest has scarce public transport. Buses from Bastia and Ajaccio serve just the main towns, and a local **bus** serves the coast from Calvi to Porto from June to September. The **train**, operating all year round, follows the Haute-Balagne coast northeast of Calvi, moving inland beyond L'Île Rousse to Belgodère, before continuing on to Ponte-Leccia, which connects to Bastia and Ajaccio. (For details, see p.19.)

A brief history of the Balagne

Settled in antiquity by Phoenician and Etruscan traders, the Balagne was only fully exploited by the **Romans**, who began the cultivation of olives here in its fertile soil. Until the tenth century the Balagne was prey to relentless Saracen raids, but this came to an end with the arrival of the **Pisans**, who constructed forts all over the region to keep the marauders at bay. After the **Genoese** takeover in the thirteenth century, the citadels at Calvi and Algajola were built, and these new ports did a steady trade with Tuscany, the chief cargo being the local olive oil, which for hundreds of years enjoyed a reputation as the best in the Mediterranean. Under the Genoese, the region was divided into semi-autonomous cantons ruled by the local nobility or **Sgio**, many of whom were highly cultured men who had been educated in Italy – a remarkable contrast to the wild Sgio of Sartène (see p.147). Furthermore, although class divisions were as strong as elsewhere in Corsica, the peasants of the Balagne were distinguished by their versatility, with many working as tailors or cobblers as well as farmers, and by their greater independence from their lords, in that they were allowed their own flocks. The result of this comparatively enlightened rule was that the people of the Balagne remained loyal to Genoa well into the eighteenth century.

The Balagne reached its apogee in the nineteenth century, but decline set in when emigration began in the early twentieth century and the small oil mills in the depopulated villages could no longer compete with industrialized producers. It wasn't until the 1950s, when Calvi and L'Île Rousse became popular tourist spots, that the local economy began to pick up, and hotels and holiday complexes mushroomed along the Balagne coast. More recently, the new D8 road, linking Calvi to Bastia via Ponte-Leccia, has improved communications with the rest of the island, while maritime traffic and flights to mainland France have also increased in the last couple of years. A revival of the economy is being further boosted by a modern irrigation programme, by the stimulation of small-scale olive oil and wine production, and by the encouragement of handicrafts aimed at the tourist market.

ACCOMMODATION PRICES

Throughout this guide, hotel accommodation is graded on a scale from ① to ⑥. These numbers show the cost per night of the **least expensive double room in high season**, and correspond to the following prices:

① under F200	③ F300–400	⑤ F500–600
② F200–300	④ F400–500	⑥ over 600F

Calvi

Seen from the water, **CALVI** is a beautiful spectacle, with its three immense bastions topped by a crest of ochre buildings, sharply defined against a hazy backdrop of snow-capped mountains. Below the citadel, a finely drawn strip of red-roofed houses and spidery palm trees delineate the **Basse Ville**, with its yacht-crammed marina, from where the town beach sweeps in a graceful semi-circle around the bay. Add a perpetually mild climate and convivial atmosphere to this visual appeal, and you can see why Calvi has been attracting year-round tourists for quite a while.

A hang-out for European glitterati in the 1950s, when *Tao's* nightclub kept the tangos playing till dawn, Calvi now has the ambience of an old-fashioned English resort, the glamorous bars supplanted by souvenir shops and ice-cream stalls. However, summer nightlife is livelier than first impressions might suggest, especially during the third week in June, when the **jazz festival** fills the quiet streets of the **haute ville** with big names from the international scene. Calvi also has its fair share of more authentically Corsican customs, principally Easter's **Granitola** procession of hooded penitents, September's **Citadella in Festa**, when traditional Corsican musicians provide nightly entertainment, and the October 12 celebrations for **Christopher Columbus** day. Calvi is widely believed in Corsica to have been the birthplace of the great navigator, a dubious claim proclaimed through a plaque in the citadel and various statues scattered about town.

Buses from Calvi run daily throughout the year to Bastia, stopping at L'Île Rousse along the route. Ajaccio is more difficult to get to – you can either take a bus down to Porto (June–Sept only) and then another bus to the south, or take the **train** as far as Ponte-Leccia, picking up the Ajaccio rail connection here. Alagajola, Lumio, L'île Rousse and Belgodère are also served by train.

A brief history of Calvi

Calvi began as a fishing port on the site of the present-day *basse ville*, but like many of Corsica's coastal towns it was victim to relentless Vandal and Ostrogoth raids in the fifth century. Until the Pisans conquered the island in the tenth century there existed no more than a cluster of houses and fishing shacks on the site. It wasn't until the arrival of the Genoese that the town became a stronghold when, in 1268, **Giovaninello de Loreto**, a Corsican nobleman, built a huge citadel on the windswept rock overlooking the port and named it Calvi.

The republic of Genoa granted Calvi special privileges, such as freer trading rights and tax exemptions, in order to ensure the fidelity of the population who, in any case, were for the most part Genoese. This fidelity was tried in 1553 by a terrible combined siege of the Turks and French, earning Calvi its motto: *Civitas Calvis Semper Fidelis*. In 1758 Calvi refused to become part of independent Corsica, a stand for which it suffered in 1794, when Paoli made an alliance with the British. A fleet commanded by Nelson launched a brutal two-month attack, bombarding the walls from all sides and eventually forcing surrender. It was in this attack that Nelson lost his eye, and he left saying he hoped never to see the place again.

The nineteenth century saw a decline in Calvi's fortunes, as the Genoese merchants left and the French concentrated on developing Ajaccio and Bastia. One Victorian traveller describes it as "a frowning fort with cracked, tottering ruins, worn and wasted by the rain". Later Calvi became primarily a military base, used as a point for smuggling arms to the mainland in World War II, and home to the Foreign Legion since 1962 – you're bound to see legionnaires strolling up and down the marina and thronging the bars. Tourism, however, is now the essence of Calvi: the town became fashionable right after the war and has done good business as a holiday resort ever since.

FERRIES

SNCM ferries to and from Nice run five times per week in each direction in July and August, once a week in June, twice a week in September and very sporadically during the rest of the year. The journey takes about four hours and costs about 500F per vehicle, plus 200F per person. To make a reservation (essential in July) go to the Port de Commerce on quai Landry (☎95 65 01 38).

Corsica Ferries (☎95 65 10 84) operate boats to and from Genoa twice a week in July and August and once a week in June and September.

Arrival, information and accommodation

Sainte-Catherine **airport** lies 6km south of Calvi; the only public transport into town is by **taxi**, which shouldn't cost more than 50F. The train **station** is on avenue de la République, close to the marina, where you'll find the **tourist office** on quai Landry (May–Oct Mon–Fri 9am–noon & 2–6pm, Sat 9am–noon) – the staff are generally very helpful and will book rooms for a small fee. **Buses** from Bastia stop outside the station but those from Porto and Ajaccio use **place Christophe Colomb**, the large square at the top of the main street, **boulevard Wilson**, north of the station. **Ferries** come in at the Port de Commerce at the centre of the *basse ville*.

Accommodation is easy to find in Calvi except during the jazz festival. There are some excellent hotels, ranging from cheap *pensions* to more upmarket places. Those on a tight budget can choose between two **youth hostels** and several **campsites** within walking distance of the town.

Hotels

Balanea, 6 rue Clemenceau (☎95 65 00 45). Grand place at the centre of the marina, with lavish rooms and excellent views of the citadel and sea. Closed winter. ④.

Belvedère, place Christophe Colomb (☎95 65 01 25). Large, simple rooms, in a good location in between the citadel and *basse ville*. Open all year. ②.

Le Caravelle, l'Orée des Pins (☎95 65 01 21). Very pleasant hotel with own garden on the beach, about ten minutes' walk from the marina. Closed winter ④.

Du Centre, 14 rue Alsace-Lorrraine (☎95 65 02 01). Occupying the old police station in a small, pretty street near the church of Sainte-Marie-Majeure. Pleasant rooms overlooking a garden. Open all year. ②.

Christophe Colomb, place Christoph Colomb (☎95 65 06 04). Spacious rooms with expansive views across the bay. Closed winter. ③.

Grand Hotel, 3 bd Wilson (☎95 65 09 74). Old-fashioned luxury hotel in centre of town. Swish cocktail bar and restaurant. Closed winter. ③.

Le Kalliste, 1 av du Commandant Marche (☎95 65 09 81). Small dark rooms in the centre of town. Own restaurant. Closed winter. ②.

Laetitia, 5 rue Joffre (☎95 65 05 55). Very central, close to station and marina. Kindly *patronne* but only seven rooms, so often booked up. Closed winter. ①.

Meditérrannée, 45 av Napoléon (☎95 65 02 08). Clean comfortable rooms, 500m out of the centre along the D81 towards Porto. Closed winter. ③.

L'Onda, 5 av Christophe Colomb (☎95 65 35 00). Well-equipped modern block on the N197 to Bastia, overlooking the beach, 200m from the centre. Closed in winter. ③.

Hostels

Corsotel, 43 av de la République (☎95 65 33 72). Huge youth hostel in prime position opposite the station and facing the sea. Very clean rooms for up to six people, some with balconies. 100F per night, breakfast included.

Relais International de la Jeunesse, 4km from the centre of town on the Route de Pietra-Maggiore (☎95 65 14 16). Follow the N197 for 2km, turn right at the sign for Pietra-Maggiore, and the hostel – two little houses with dormitories looking out over the gulf – is in the village another 2km further on. 55F per night, breakfast included.

Campsites

Camping La Pinède, 1km east of Calvi between the beach and the N197 (☎95 65 17 00). Popular site in pine forest with bar, restaurant etc. April–Oct.

Camping-caravanning Bella Vista, 2km along the N197 from Calvi (☎95 65 11 76). A quiet and friendly site; to get to it, turn right at the sign to Pietra-Maggiore, and the campsite's another 1km along on the right-hand side. April–Oct.

International Camping, 1km along the N197 near *Prisunic* (☎95 65 01 75). Full of young Europeans drinking all night. Closed winter.

The Town

Social life in Calvi focuses on the restaurants and cafés of the **quai Landry**, a spacious seafront walkway linking the marina and the port. This is the best place to get the feel of the town, but as far as sights go, there's not a lot to the *basse ville*. At the far end of the quay, under the shadow of the citadel, stands the sturdy **Tour du Sel**, a medieval look-out post also once used to store imported salt. If you strike up through the narrow passageways off quai Landry, you'll come to rue Clemenceau, where restaurants and souvenir shops are packed into every available space. In a small square giving onto the street stands the impossingly white **Sainte-Marie-Majeure**, built in 1774, whose spindly bell tower rises elegantly above the cafés on the quay but whose interior contains nothing of interest. From the church's flank, a flight of steps connects with boulevard Wilson, a wide modern high street which rises to **place Christophe Colomb**, point of entry for the *haute ville* or Citadelle.

The Citadelle

At the foot of the steep cobbled ramp from place Christophe Colomb to the **Citadelle** you'll find a small **information office** (Mon–Sat 9am–noon & 2–6pm) where you can get a map of the upper town. Beyond the ancient gateway, with its inscription of the town's motto *Civitas Calvi Semper Fidelis*, you come immediately to the enormous **Caserne Sanpiero**, formerly the governor's palace. Built in the thirteenth century, when the great round tower was used as a dungeon, the castle was recently restored and is currently used for military purposes, and therefore closed to the public. The best way of seeing the rest of the citadel is to follow the **ramparts**, which connect three immense bastions. From each bastion the **views** across the sea, the Balagne and the Cinto massif are magnificent.

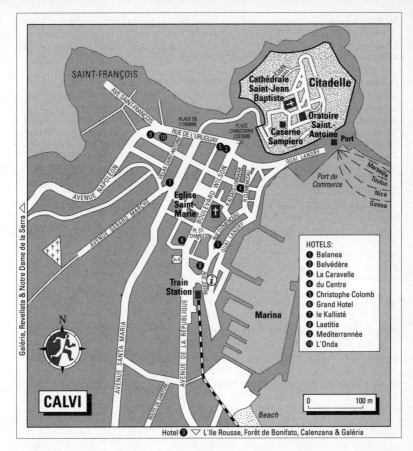

Hotel ❸ ▽ L'Ile Rousse, Forêt de Bonifato, Calenzana & Galéria

Within the walls the houses are tightly packed along tortuous stairways and narrow passages that converge on the diminutive **place d'Armes**. Dominating the square is the **Cathédrale Saint-Jean-Baptiste**, set at the highest point of the promontory and sitting uncomfortably amid the ramshackle buildings. This chunky ochre edifice was founded in the thirteenth century, but was partly destroyed during the Turkish siege of 1553 and then suffered extensive damage twelve years later, when the powder magazine in the governors' palace exploded. Rebuilt in Greek Cross form and surmounted by a black-tiled octagonal dome, the church became a cathedral in 1576, as the reconstruction was drawing to a close.

Inside, to the left of the entrance, are three elaborate alabaster **fonts** which date from 1568. Beside the ostentatious marble altar stands a finely carved eighteenth-century wooden **pulpit**, while beneath the dome lies the tomb of the **Baglioni** family, an illustrious Genoese clan who made their money from trade in the fourteenth century. In 1400 the hot-headed Bayon Baglioni is said to have saved the town from a treacherous pair who were plotting to hand Calvi over to the Aragonese. As he stabbed the traitors he screamed "libertà! libertà!", a cry that became part of the family name and eventually, by a circuitous line of descent, became the name of one of London's most famous stores, *Liberty*. If you look up, you'll see a line of theatre-like **boxes** screened by iron grilles under the roof of the cupola; built for the use of the noblewomen of the town, the grilles acted as protection from the commoners' gaze. In the apse there's a seventeenth-century wooden statue of John the Baptist, framed by a solemn triptych dated 1498 and attributed to the obscure Genoese painter Barbagelata. The church's great treasure, is the **Christ des Miracles**, which is housed in the chapel on the right of the choir; this crucifix was brandished at the marauding Turks during the 1553 siege, an act which reputedly saved the day.

To the north of place d'Armes, in rue de Fil, stands the shell of the building that Calvi believes was **Christopher Columbus's birthplace**, as the plaque on the wall states. The claim rides on pretty tenuous circumstantial evidence. Columbus's known date of birth coincides with the Genoese occupation of Calvi, at which time a weaving family by the name of Columbo lived in the town. Papers left by Columbus's son state that Christopher was the son of weavers, that he had two relations in the navy (there was indeed a Corsican sea captain named Columbo), who "came from the sea" (which could be interpreted as coming from the island of Corsica). What's more, Columbus is said to have taken Corsican dogs on his voyage, and he placed his first New World ports under the protection of popular Corsican saints. Believers claim that the Genoese deliberately burnt the town archives in 1580 and renamed the street, formerly rue Columbo, in order to cover up the truth. The house itself was destroyed by Nelson's army during the siege of 1794, but as recompense a statue was erected on May 20, 1992, the 500th anniversary of his "discovery" of America; his alleged birthday, October 12, is a now a public holiday in Calvi celebrated with fireworks and speeches.

On the east side of the citadel it's a quick walk along the ramparts to Maison Pacciola, where Napoleon spent a night in 1793. Close by, the **Oratoire Saint-Antoine** is an unremarkable building dating from the early sixteenth century, but look out for a graceful black slate **relief carving** above the door – the figure holding the piglet is Saint Anthony, patron saint of Calvi, and he's flanked by Saint John the Baptist and a kneeling Saint Francis. Heading downwards, the grand house on your left is the fifteenth-century Palais Giubega, once home of the bishops of Sagone.

The beach

Calvi's outstanding **beach** sweeps right round the bay from the end of quai Landry, but most of the first kilometre or so is owned by bars which rent out sun loungers for a hefty price. To avoid these follow the track behind the sand which will bring you to the start of a more secluded stretch. The sea might not be as sparklingly clear as at many other Corsican beaches, but it's warm, shallow and free of rocks.

Eating, drinking and nightlife

Eating is a major pastime in Calvi, where you'll find a wide selection of restaurants and snack bars catering for all tastes. **Fish restaurants** predominate in the marina, where – at a price – you can eat excellent seafood fresh from the bay and enjoy the quayside atmosphere. You'll find it's cheaper to eat in the inland streets of *basse ville*, whose stairways and cramped forecourts hide a host of buzzing **pizzerias** and **Corsican** restaurants.

Cafés, complete with raffia parasols, line the marina, becoming more expensive the nearer they are to the Tour de Sel. You'll find the best places are those nearest the beach, which also get the sun all day.

Calvi boasts a busy **nightlife**, with discos opening up all over town in the summer; the best of the marina's discos is *Le Calypso*, at the far end of quai Landry under the citadel (summer only). There's also a summer **open-air cinema** next to *Prisunic* on the RN197, a kilometre out of town towards L'Île Rousse, which screens new releases every night.

For food **shopping** the best place is the *alimentation* at the bottom of rue Clemenceau, or there's the big *Prisunic* (see above). The fruit and vegetable **market** is open every morning in the hall between rue Clemenceau and boulevard Wilson.

Cafés and bars

Bar au Mal Assis, opposite the cathedral in the citadel and popular with locals – drop in for a flavour of Calvese life.

Café des Marins, quai Landry. Looks like a huge boat inside, with portholes and a curvy bar. Best place for breakfast.

Café Rex, top of bd Wilson on the corner of place Christophe Colombe. Full of singing locals and people waiting for the bus.

Restaurants

L'Abri Côtier, on the *quai* but entrance on rue Joffre. Excellent fish, pizzas and Corsican specialities; has a terrace which looks out to sea. Closed in winter. Expensive.

U Casanu, 18 bd Wilson. Tasty and simple local dishes, inexpensive set menus and cosy little booths for the anti-social.

Chez Tao, rue Saint-Antoine, in the citadel. Legendary nightclub, now turned into a piano bar that serves excellent nouvelle cuisine and local fish dishes. Outstanding view of the bay. Expensive.

Pizzeria Le Corsaire, 12 av de la République, next to the youth hostel. Unremarkable pizzas, but the cheapest place to eat in Calvi.

Pizzeria La Galère, 6 rue des Anges. Unusual pasta dishes, such as tortelloni stuffed with aubergines and wild mushrooms. Trendy yet friendly. Moderate.

U Minellu, 3 bd Wilson. A friendly pizzeria with Corsican specialities at a moderate price.

Pizza/Pasta, 15 quai Landry. Cheap and crispy pizzas, good for a snack. Inexpensive.

Le San Carlu, place Saint-Charles, off rue Clemenceau. Fine seafood, excellent paella, and menus at various reasonable prices. Nice garden terrace.

Le Santa-Maria, next to the church of Ste-Marie-Majeure, rue Clemenceau. Good-value four-course tourist menus. One of the few places you can eat *stifatu*, a local dish combining different meats rolled up. Inexpensive and always busy.

Le Semiramis, av Paul-Doumer. Delicious fish dishes and couscous, famous desserts. Expensive.

Festivals and events

Calvi's earliest **festival** in the calendar is the **Granitola**, which takes place on Good Friday. *Granitola* means "snail" in Corsican, and the festival gets its name from the way the procession of hooded penitents winds and unwinds itself through the streets. Starting at 9pm in the *basse ville*, the line of penitents, barefoot and carrying simple wooden crosses, makes its way up to the citadel accompanied by an eerie chanting from the onlooking crowd. The annual **festival du jazz** occurs in the third week in June; most acts are free in the day with spontaneous jam sessions taking place all over town, but you have to buy tickets for the more formal evening performances. Then there's the **Cassano** olive festival on the third weekend of July, when everyone dons olive branches and parades around the citadel. **Citadella in Festa** on the second Sunday in August is a lively celebration of Corsican culture with conferences, exhibitions of local crafts and musical shows and concerts. In late September the three-day **Rencontres Polyphoniques** gathers singers and musicians from abroad, as well as the best Corsican names who perform nightly in the Église Saint-Jean-Baptiste.

Around Calvi

Even without your own vehicle, you can take in some interesting sights around the outskirts of Calvi. For an unrivalled view of the town you should walk, drive or ride to the **Chapelle de Notre-Dame-de-la-Serra**, sited high on a cliff overlooking the town. An easier walk goes along the **Punta della Revellata**, the rocky peninsula that shelters Calvi to the west. If you don't fancy a walk, there are the hourly boat trips from Calvi marina to the **Grottes des Veaux Marins**, a cluster of spectacular sea caves located behind the peninsula.

Punta della Revellata

To get to the **Punta della Revellata** follow the Ajaccio road from place Christophe Colomb for about 1500m, where a signposted path veers off to the right, snaking its way to the lighthouse at the very end of the peninsula. The walk takes about half an hour from the road, an easy-going ramble through russet-toned boulders, and the reward is an outstanding **view** that takes in the citadel of Calvi and the distant west coast of Cap Corse.

Chapelle de Notre-Dame-de-la-Serra

The **Chapelle de Notre-Dame-de-la-Serra**, situated high above Calvi to the south, is reached by following the Ajaccio road for 3km, then taking the steep left turn which ascends the cliff – the chapel lies 1km ahead, set amidst bulbous clusters of pale pink granite. Built in the 1860s over the site of a fifteenth-century sanctuary, the building boasts a fine parchment painting of the Immaculate Conception, but it's essentially the **view** that draws the visitors – the great bastions of Calvi emerging abruptly below, the sea dashing against the rocks of the Punta della Revellata, and the tree-spattered valley of Calenzana spreading to the east. To the left of the building a rather treacherous footpath leads down to Calvi, coming out onto the D81 road 3km from the town centre.

Grotte des Veaux Marins

Several companies in the marina advertise boat excursions to the **Grottes des Veaux Marins**, nearby sea caves which were inhabited by a seal colony up until the 1960s, hence the name, meaning simply "seals" cave. The highlight of the trip is a great cavern in which flickering sunlight glitters on the many-hued granite to ghostly effect. Expect to pay about 100F for a three-hour ride there and back.

Listings

Airport enquiries ☎95 65 20 09.

Banks All the main banks are on bd Wilson.

Bike rental *Location Ambrosini*, place Bel Ombra; heading out of town towards Porto, on the right just beyond place Christophe Colomb (☎95 65 02 13).

Bus information *Agence de Beaux Voyages*, place de la Porteuse d'Eau (☎95 65 11 35).

Currency exchange *Bureau de change,* place de la Porteuse d'Eau at the bottom of bd Wilson (open June–Sept 9am–noon, 3–7pm).

Car rental *Aloha*, at the airport (☎95 65 28 08); *Avis*, 6 av de la République (☎95 65 06 74); *Europcar*, at airport (☎95 65 10 19); *Garage Luigi*, at the airport (☎95 65 15 31).

Pharmacy *Guerini*, 17 bd Wilson; *Pharmacie de la Plage*, 4 rue Joffre.

Police Av de la République (☎95 65 33 30).

Post office At the lower end of bd Wilson.

Train station av de la République (enquiries ☎ 95 65 00 61).

Taxis At the airport and place de la Porteuse d'Eau (☎95 65 03 10).

Travel agents *Agence les Beaux Voyages*, Résidence Le Vieux Chalet, place de la Porteuse (☎95 65 11 35); *Corsica Touring*, route de l'Aéroport d'Eau, right opposite the airport (☎95 65 20 70); *Agence Corse Voyage*, 6 bd Wilson (☎95 65 00 47).

Watersports *Le Blockos*, on the beach by the car park at the far side of the marina (☎95 65 11 20). Windsurfing, waterskiing, paragliding etc.

The Haute-Balagne coast

The Haute-Balagne coast may have been exploited in recent decades, with private resorts such as the Marine de Davia springing up, but there are many unspoilt places to spend a pleasant few days in this corner of the northwest. East of Calvi the N197 cuts inland through superbly located **Lumio**, a terraced village with an exceptional Romanesque church. By far the least expensive place to stay in the area is **Algajola**, a small relaxing village graced with a golden half-moon beach, a few kilometres further along the same road. Some four kilometres north of here the rather overrated and overrun town of **L'Île Rousse** provides a good base for the outstanding beaches of **Lozari** and **Rindara**.

At various points along the coast road you can turn off to visit the Haute-Balagne hill towns, the pick of which are covered in the section beginning on p.85.

Lumio and Algajola

Stacked up a sun-drenched hillside facing the gulf of Calvi, **LUMIO** was in ancient times the centre of a sun-worshipping cult, and was known to the Romans as Ortis Culis or "where the sun rises". One kilometre before you reach the village it's worth stopping to take a look at the pale granite **Chapelle San-Pietro**, situated on the left-hand side of the main road amidst a monumental cemetery. Founded in the eleventh century and rebuilt in the eighteenth, it retains some of its original Romanesque features, notably the palm-shaped capitals and geometric windows at the eastern end of the apse. The most outstanding feature, however, is the pair of grinning **lions** jutting from the facade above the door; it's thought they were originally intended to support a porch.

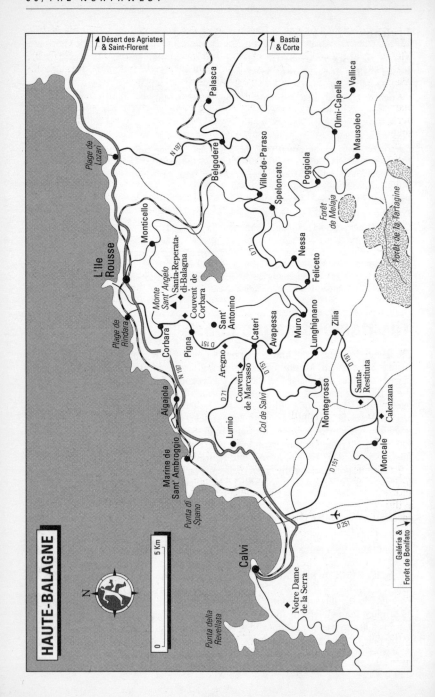

Désert des Agriates
& Saint-Florent

Bastia
& Corte

Palasca

Plage de Lozari

N 197

Belgodere

Ville-de-Paraso

Speloncato

Poggiola

Olmi-Capella

Vallica

Mausoleo

Monticello

L'Ile
Rousse

Forêt de Melaja

Forêt de la Tartagine

Santa-Reperata-
di-Balagna

Monte
Sant' Angelo

Couvent de
Corbara

Nessa

Feliceto

D 71

Plage de
Rindara

Corbara

Pigna

Sant'
Antonino

Cateri

Avapessa

Muro

Lunghignano

Zilia

D 151

Aregno

Couvent
de Marcasso

D 71

Col de Salvi

D 151

Santa-
Restituta

Algaiola

N 197

Lumio

Montegrosso

Calenzana

Marine de
Sant' Ambroggio

D 151

Moncale

Punta di
Spano

D 251

Galéria &
Forêt de Bonifato

Calvi

Notre Dame
de la Serra

Punta della
Revellata

HAUTE-BALAGNE

5 Km

N

0

Even if you don't intend to stay in Lumio, it's worth getting out of the N197's traffic for a gaze across the sea and the Balagne mountains. Excellent views are offered by both the village's **hotels**: the *Bellevue*, in the centre (☎95 60 72 07; ③), or the more modest *Chez Charles*, a little further down the main road through the village (☎95 60 78 19; ②). Both have good restaurants as well.

Prized by locals for its good surfing, **ALGAJOLA** is only a minute from the main road yet has an immediately striking off-the-beaten-track appeal. Hotels here don't tend to get crowded, and the old courtyard of the sandy-hued citadel, sheltering a gaggle of restaurants and bars, has a relaxing atmosphere that perfectly augments the attraction of the golden sands.

Because of its exposed situation, Algajola suffered the frequent attentions of hostile forces: in 1643, for example, the Turks devastated the Genoese citadel, and in the 1790s Nelson assailed the town as a preliminary to the great Calvi siege. Despite such setbacks, Algajola did a steady trade in oysters and olive oil, and continued to be a major port in this part of the coast until L'Île Rousse developed towards the close of the eighteenth century. The village's status was temporarily revived early this century, when hotels were built over the old port and it became something of a smart resort. However, decline set in after World War II, with the growing attractions offered by Calvi and L'Île Rousse.

Algajola consists of just one street, which begins alongside the beach, Aregno-Plage, and leads up to the **Citadelle**. Beyond the gates, the dominant building is the **Castello**, raised on its small promontory in the thirteenth century then heavily restored in the seventeenth century, when the fortifications were added after the Turkish attack. For a hundred years it served as the Genoese lieutenant governor's residence – until the middle of the eighteenth century. It is still an administrative building, so closed to the public. However, you can walk around the ramparts behind the castle, from where a path leads back down to the beach.

Practicalities

Virtually every **hotel** in Algajola overlooks the sea, although none can claim to be anything special. *L'Ésquinade*, next door to the **post office** right by the citadel gates (☎95 60 70 19; ①), is the low-budget choice, with breakfast included in the very reasonable price. There's no restaurant and the bar closes at 8pm, but rooms are adequately clean and all have en-suite bathrooms. The *Saint-Joseph*, at the entrance to the village coming from Calvi (☎95 60 73 90; ③), is more upmarket, affording an impressive sea view and comfortable rooms. A more luxurious set-up is the *Hôtel-Restaurant L'Ondine*, on the beach (☎95 60 70 02; ⑤), which has a garden, a swimming pool and of course commands a panoramic view of the rocks. At *Le Beau Rivage*, next door (☎95 60 73 99; ③), you get the same view at a more reasonable price. **Campers** can stay at *Camping de la Plage*, at the north end of the beach (☎95 60 71 76).

For **food**, *L'Ondine* has the most adventurous chef – he's into black pasta, trout stuffed with *brocciu* and similarly inventive dishes. *Le Beau Rivage* restaurant is slightly more expensive, but the fish is very good. On the citadel's only square, *Pizzeria U Furnellu* does decent pizzas and cheap Corsican dishes, but for a livelier atmosphere you could try *Cantarettu City*, situated off the main road, 500m east of the village. Decorated like an American ranch, it serves charcoal-grilled steaks and suchlike, and stays open till around midnight in the summer.

L'Île Rousse

Developed by Pascal Paoli in the 1760s as a "gallows to hang Calvi", the port of **L'ÎLE ROUSSE** (Isula Rossa) simply doesn't convince as a Corsican town, its palm trees, neat flower gardens and colossal pink seafront hotel creating an atmosphere that has more in common with the French Riviera. Yet for all its artificiality, the place has become unbearably popular in recent years, receiving more ferries and packing in more tourists than Calvi, even though it's a smaller port. The town has a certain swanky cachet: there are plenty of smart shops, and if you're in Corsica to pose on the beach, this is the place for you.

Pascal Paoli had great plans for his new town, which was laid out from scratch in 1758. He needed a port to export the olive oil produced in the Balagne region, and Calvi obstinately continued to be held by the Genoese. Originally the place was to be called Paolina, but the *Rubica Rocega* (Red Rocks) label had stuck from Roman times and L'Île Rousse it became. A large part of the new port was built on a regular grid system, featuring lines of straight parallel streets quite at odds with the higgledy-piggledy nature of most Corsican villages and towns. Thanks to the busy trading of wine and oil, it soon began to prosper and, two and a half centuries later, still thrives as a successful port. These days, however, the main traffic consists of holidaymakers. That the only town intended to be a Corsican success story makes its living from tourism as a classic French-style resort adds an ironic twist to Paoli's dream.

L'Île Rousse is easily accessible by bus from Bastia and Calvi, and the train stops here on the Calvi–to–Ponte-Leccia line.

FERRIES

Ferries between L'Île Rousse and mainland France depart from the Port de Commerce, 1km north of the centre. There are daily five-hour crossings in July and August, to either Marseille, Nice or occasionally Toulon, but it's essential to book well in advance. Tickets, which cost about 280F per passenger plus 300F for a car, can be bought either from *Mariani*, place Paoli (☎95 60 11 29), or from the *gare maritime* (☎95 60 09 56).

Arrival, information and accommodation

The **train station** is on route du Port, 500m south of where the ferries arrive. The Bastia–Calvi bus stops just south of place Paoli in the town's main thoroughfare, avenue Piccioni. The **tourist office**, on the south side of place Paoli (June–Sept daily 9am–noon & 2–7pm; ☎95 60 04 35) charges for hotel and restaurant lists, but details of ferries and bus timetables are free.

Such a long season (May–Oct) means that L'Île Rousse fills up early in the year and it can be difficult to find a **hotel**, so be prepared to hunt around. Most places are modern buildings, more functional than personable.

HOTELS
L'Amiral, 5 bd de la Mer (☎95 60 28 05). Proximity to the beach is the main attraction here; has a bar terrace but no restaurant. Open March–Oct. ②.

Cala di l'Oru, 6 bd de Fogata (☎95 60 14 75). Large plain building with spacious rooms but indifferent staff. Open all year. ③.

Chalet de la Gare, on route du Port opposite the station (☎95 60 12 05). Tiny whitewashed vine-covered place with the cheapest rooms in town. March–Oct. ①.

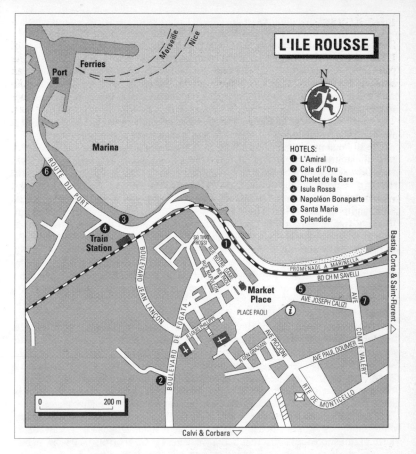

Calvi & Corbara ▽

Isula Rossa, on route du Port next door to the station (☎95 60 33 02). Useful if you can't get into the nearby *Chalet de la Gare*. Small, tiled rooms, with own bathrooms. April–Oct. ③.

Napoléon Bonaparte, 3 place Paoli (☎95 60 06 09). Garish converted *palazzo* which for years was the only luxury hotel on the island; it still has a certain old-fashioned appeal. April–Oct. ⑤.

Santa Maria, in the port (☎95 60 13 49). Hardly an attractive locale, but this is one of the larger low-budget places. Rooms are adequate. Open all year. ②.

Splendide, 4 rue Comte Valéry (☎95 60 00 24). Thirties-style building with new swimming pool; a lively place to stay. Open March–Aug. ③.

The town

All roads in L'Île Rousse lead to **place Paoli**, a shady square that's open to the sea and has as its focal point a fountain surmounted by a bust of "U Babbu di u Patria" (Grandfather of the Nation), one of many local tributes to Pascal Paoli. There's a Frenchified covered market at the entrance to the square, while on the west side rises the grim facade of Église de l'Immaculée Conception, currently under large-scale restoration. Most **banks** are on place Paoli, although the **post**

office is situated five minutes to the east in rue Monticello. There's a huge **pharmacy** on the corner of avenue Piccioni, L'Île Rousse's main shopping street, where a large **bookshop** sells foreign newspapers and books on Corsica.

From place Paoli, the three parallel streets of the old town run north to square Tino Rossi, where the Hôtel de Ville, in Paoli's time a military headquarters, displays the Corsican flag. Opposite stands a **Tower** dating from before Paoli's time, but a plaque commemorating the Corsican hero has been recently placed up on the wall.

To reach the **Île de la Pietra**, the islet that gives the town its name, continue north, passing the station on your left. Once over the causeway connecting the islet to the mainland, you can walk through the crumbling mass of red granite as far as the lighthouse at the far end, from where the **view** of the town is spectacular, especially at sundown, when you get the full effect of the red glow of the rocks. Heading back along the promenade, **A Marinella**, which follows the seafront behind the town beach, a ten-minute walk will bring you to the **Aquarium**, the main sight in the town. The Musée Océanographique (April–Oct Mon–Fri 10.30am–1pm & 2–7pm; 35F), situated at the north end of the beach, publicizes itself as the "Grotte aux Requins", although the only members of the shark family on display are some timid dogfish. Nonetheless, the guided tour of tanks full of lobsters, conger eels, rays, octopuses and scores of other aquatic species is interesting, especially at feeding time, which can be a hair-raising experience. The owner, Pierre Pernod, knows everything there is to know about fish behaviour.

The beaches

Apart from the town beach, the most popular beach hereabouts is **Plage de Rindara**, a fantastic duned strand with deep pale-green translucent water, 4km southwest of L'Île Rousse. A track signposted "Roc e Mare" leads from the main road to the beach's scruffy campsite and a fee-charging car park – but you can park for free across the rail line in the field which backs onto the beach, although it's forbidden to park on the dunes. A **snack bar** serves refreshments for the crowds in the high season, but outside August you can usually rely on relative peace.

The equally spectacular **Plage de Lozari**, a long semicircular sweep of pure white sand, lies 7km northeast of town. A decent road signposted "Lozari" leads down to the shore and a discreet holiday village, *De Lozari* (☎95 60 08 74), which offers upmarket accommodation and attracts big crowds in summer.

Eating and drinking

Tourism has taken its toll here, hence the abundance of mediocre **eating places** in the town. A few restaurants do stand out, however, some catering for the fussy French *continentaux* with classic gourmet menus, and other Corsican places serving superb fresh seafood.

The best cafés are found in place Paoli along the southern side – *Café des Platanes* is especially popular with tourists and locals alike.

California, place Paoli. American-style snack bar. Inexpensive.

Chez Paco, rue Paoli. Tasty Spanish food and spicy fish dishes. Young hang-out. Inexpensive.

Le Grand Bleu, rue Napoléon. Brash decor but excellent food, mainly French fish dishes such as sea bass with fennel. Expensive.

Le Grillon, av Paul Doumer. Popular French grill; *Steak au Roquefort* a dream. Expensive.

L'Île d'Or, place Paoli. Bustling basic bistro, in a prime location for watching the *boules* players. Moderate.

La Jonque, rue Paoli. Trendy, compact place serving Vietnamese food at reasonable prices.
A Merenda, rue Napoleon. One of the town's few Corsican places. Wholesome soups and stews, as well as fresh fish. Moderate.

Inland Haute-Balagne

Many of these fortress villages of inland Haute-Balagne are nearly a thousand years old, having developed from the time of the Pisan occupation, when **Romanesque churches** such as Église San Trinita at Aregno and Église Santa Restituta at Calenzana were built. The rash of Baroque churches in the region emerged in the prosperous years under the Genoese, and some of them, such as the church at Corbara, warrant a visit for the sheer flamboyance of their decoration, even if Baroque isn't your thing.

A recent government redevelopment programme for the Balagne has meant the regeneration of certain traditional practices, including the production of olive oil using old presses. Young people are being encouraged to settle in the villages by the introduction of special grants for artisans willing to live and work here, and several places have their own musical and crafts societies – the tourist offices in Calvi or L'Île Rousse can give you information on summer concerts in Pigna and Begodère.

Buses are nonexistent here, but the train stops at Belgodère which has some hotel accommodation and makes a good base if you want to stay in the region. There are more hotels at Speloncato and Feliceto.

Calenzana

Overshadowed by the great bulk of Monte Grosso and encircled by a belt of olive trees, the village of **CALENZANA** is set at the heart of some of the most fertile land on the island. Historically an economic rival to Calvi, it's still a thriving agricultural centre, renowned for its wine, honey and the village speciality, a little dry cake blessed with the tongue-twisting name of *cusgiulelli*. There's a less pacific side to Calenzana as well. In the eighteenth century it was known as a refuge for Paoli's freedom fighters, who weren't welcome in the Genoese stronghold of Calvi, and this century it gained a reputation for harbouring French gangsters and pimps – with Marseille a quick hop across the water, many high-ranking gangsters retired here in the 1960s.

Lying close to the borders of the national park, Calenzana provides the point of departure for the **GR20 hike** (see box), which crosses Corsica's mountain ridge and finishes in Porto-Vecchio. It's also the starting point for the shorter **Tra Mare e Monti** walk, which traverses a section of the national park as far as Cargèse, so ramblers are very much part of the scenery.

The lively core of the village, **place de l'Hôtel de Ville**, is a pleasant tree-lined square overlooking the gulf of Calvi. Close by, the heavily Baroque **Église Saint-Blaise** boasts a resplendent interior, its centrepiece a marble altar dated 1767. The adjacent bell tower, built in the 1870s, overlooks the **Cimetière des Allemands**, burial place of 500 Prussian mercenaries hired by the Genoese to quell an uprising in 1732. Not having any artillery, the victorious villagers used anything they could as makeshift weapons, even hurling beehives from their windows to frighten off the attackers.

THE GR20 AND TRA MARE E MONTI

The **GR20** covers the 140km between Calenzana and Conca near Porto-Vecchio in southern Corsica, and despite its hardships it's a very popular hike, with as many as a thousand walkers doing it at any one time – though many people cut the walk in half by starting at the Col de Vizzavona, reached by the N193. It should only be attempted by those with sound experience of mountain-hiking, and it's essential to be prepared for sudden variations in climatic conditions. In some particularly hazardous parts of the route the GR20 becomes more of a climb than a walk, with stanchions, cables and ladders driven into the rock as essential aids.

Practicable from mid-June until November, the GR20 is divided into fifteen stages of six to eight hours, each clearly marked by red and white paint flashes and starting and finishing at a mountain **refuge**. Booking isn't possible for these basic and often unstaffed huts, and meals are not available at them, so you need to stock up en route, either in the villages or at the main passes of Col de Vergio, Col de Vizzavona, Col de Bavella and Col de Verde, which have stores selling basic provisions – the first three also have restaurants.

Camping wild is forbidden in the Parc Naturel. An alternative to the refuges is to take farmhouse accommodation in *gites d'étapes* along the way, but you have to book these in advance. You can get current details from the main office of the **Parc Naturel Régional de la Corse** in rue Fiorella, Ajaccio (☎95 21 56 54), or enquire at the *mairie* in Calenzana, which has a subsidiary office (☎95 62 76 66).

Both these offices supply detailed information on the GR20 and on the easier **Tra Mare e Monti** walk, which is waymarked in orange paint from Calenzana to Cargèse, via Galéria, Porto and Evisa. Views are tremendous across the mountains and sea and the walk can be attempted all year round, although the best seasons are spring and autumn. Ten stages of four to six hours make up the journey, and the situation regarding accommodation is the same as for the GR20.

There are only two **hotels** in Calenzana: the *Monte Grosso*, in rue du Fond (☎95 62 70 15; ②), is favoured by the hiking crowd and offers a decent half-board arrangement; the *Bel Horizon*, in place de l'Église (☎95 62 71 72; ①), is far more basic.

Église Santa-Restituta

One of the most important places of pilgrimage in Corsica, **Église Santa-Restituta**, is set beside a shady grove of olive trees to the north of Calenzana, about 1500m along the D151. Dedicated to the martyred Saint Restitude, who in 303 AD, during the reign of Diocletian, was decapitated in Calvi for her Christian beliefs, the Romanesque church has been rebuilt many times but retains its attractive eleventh-century single nave. In the crypt you can see the fourth-century **sarcophagus** of the martyr. Discovered 1951, it's a magnificent marble tomb, decorated with a figure of Christ and strikingly human faces adorning each end. The sarcophagus was originally covered by a thirteenth-century cenotaph decorated with **frescoes** depicting Saint Restitude and her fate against a tableau of Calvi, which are displayed nearby. The key to the church is kept by the *mairie* in Calenzana.

Cassano to Catteri

The next main stop along the D151 is **CASSANO**, which boasts a unique village square in the form of a star and has an outstanding sixteenth-century triptych in its **Église de l'Annonciation**.

Fountains, arcaded houses and ancient streets characterize the village of **MONTEMAGGIORE**, which occupies a rocky pinnacle 3km north of Cassano. **Église Saint-Augustin**, in the main square, has some interesting seventeenth-century paintings and an impressive **organ** dating from the 1700s, but can't compete with the view from **A Cima**, the rocky outcrop at the eastern end of the village – from here you can see the ruins of the old village of Montemaggiore and right across to Calvi.

The Romanesque church of **San Raniero**, one of the Balagne's most enchanting buildings, is best approached by the rough track that begins 2km along the D151 from Montemaggiore. Constructed by Pisan stone workers in the eleventh and twelfth centuries, the church has an intricate multicoloured facade, topped by two heads flanking a little cross. Inside, three hideous sculpted faces look out from the cylindrical stone font.

Winding onwards along a high ridge, after 3km the road crosses the **Col de Salvi** (509m), from where the seaward view is superb. Another 2km and you need to turn left along the D71 to get to **CATTERI**, which lies by the crossroads of the principal routes of the Balagne. Tiny streets with overgrown balconies surround the requisite Baroque church, **Église de l'Assomption,** a seventeenth-century edifice dedicated to the martyr Saint Bernin, whose tomb is the principal feature inside. The hamlet of **San Cesariu**, below the village, is worth visiting for a look at its Romanesque sanctuary, while 1km west of the village lies the oldest functioning Franciscan convent in Corsica, the **Couvent de Marcasso** dating from 1621. The church houses some interesting wooden saints, and it's possible to stay here as well (☎95 61 70 21).

Catteri is a cheese-making centre, and an excellent **restaurant** called *La Lateria*, on the left as you leave the village, makes the most of the local produce, serving such specialities as *fiadone,* a delicious cheesy cake; the terrace affords a beautiful view over the Calenzana valley. *Chez Jean*, in the centre of the village, also does good, inexpensive local specialities. You can stay at *Hôtel U San Dume* (☎95 61 79 31; ②), 200m along the road towards Lavatoggio.

Moving on from Catteri you have three possible routes: the D71 down to the sea, passing through **Lavatoggio** (which offers a brilliant view from the terrace of its church); the D151 north towards Sant'Antonino and Aregno; or the D71 south to Muro, Feliceto and Speloncato (see p.90).

Sant'Antonino to Monticello

The hazy silhouette of the oldest inhabited village in Corsica, **SANT'ANTONINO**, is visible for miles around, its crest of orange buildings merging with the arid granite. Sant'Antonino was occupied in the ninth century when the Savelli counts ruled from the now-ruined castle. You can't drive up into Sant'Antonino, but there is a **car park** by the church on the left-hand side of the D413, just below the village. This church houses an **organ**, dating from 1777. Built on a circular plan, the village's vaulted streets and sinuous passageways make it an appealing place to explore, and the platform to the left of the village entrance offers an unrivalled 360° view of the Balagne.

Aregno

A kilometre further down the D151 lies **AREGNO**, an orange-growing village which emerges from a blanket of orchards, with olive, orange and lemon trees carpeting the slopes down to the sea. The chief attraction here is the graceful Romanesque **Église de la Trinité et San Giovanni**, which like San Michele de Murato is constructed of chequered green, white and ochre stone, but dates from the twelfth century. The triple-decker facade is a fascinating diversity of stonework: an arch above the door is framed by two primitive figures; over these is a blind arcade decorated with geometric patterns and fantastic creatures; and right at the top there's a window surmounted by a couple of intertwined snakes and a crouching man holding his foot. Inside there are some arresting frescoes: on the left are the four Doctors of the Church, painted in 1458, and on the right is Saint Michael, from 1449.

Pigna

The tiny village of **PIGNA**, a compact cluster of orange roofs set beneath the road 2km from Aregno, is home to one of the most successful restoration projects in the region. Combining the practical refurbishment of buildings with a revival of popular culture, the project's achievements so far include the building of a new *mairie* out of earth, and the transformation of an old goats' shed into a lively theatre. Several artisans' workshops (open to the public from around 4pm to 9pm in summer) are good for browsing, with various craftworks for sale, including pottery and traditional wood carvings.

The village follows an architectural plan typical of the Balagne, known as *a Chjapatta* (hedgehog), whereby the streets branch out from the centre like spines. Pretty piazza d'Olmu and piazza Piazzarella provide glorious views of the sea, but your first visit will probably be to the central **Église de l'Immaculée Conception**, built in the eighteenth century on a Romanesque base. Surrounded by a staircase and surmounted by a squat cupola, the church houses a magnificent **organ** that was restored in 1991 by local craftsmen.

In the summer the nearby open-air theatre hosts concerts, often incorporating performances of the ancient Moorish dance, the *Moresca*. Pigna is especially lively throughout June and July when the **Festivoce** and **Paese in Festa** festivals provide forums for long nights of traditional *paghjella* singing. Concerts run by *E Voce di U Comune*, an association of artists and musicians dedicated to the promotion of Corsican literature, singing and art, are also held at the *Casa Musicale*, an old house which has been turned into a kind of musical inn at the edge of the village. Its **restaurant** serves distinctive Corsican specialities, such as *Cabrettu a l'Istrettu*, a kind of spicy kid stew.

Couvent de Corbara and Corbara

One kilometre down the road from Pigna stands the little chapel of **Notre Dame de Latio**, which houses a beautiful painting of the Virgin dated 1002. Opposite, a steep road leads up to the austere **Couvent de Corbara**, attractively framed by olive trees at the foot of Monte Sant'Angelo (see below). Founded as an orphanage in 1430, it was transformed into a Franciscan convent in 1456, badly damaged during the revolution of the 1750s, abandoned soon after, then restored in 1857 by the Dominicans. During World War I the place was used as a prisoner-of-war camp. The Dominicans returned in 1927, and the place is still used as a spiritual retreat. Inside the adjoining white church, of which the oldest part is the eighteenth-century **choir**, you can see the **tombs** of the Savelli family (see below) bearing the family arms, depicting two lions holding a rose. A mule track behind the convent leads to the summit of **Monte Sant'Angelo** (560m), a stiff one-hour walk that requires proper boots. From the top you can see for miles across the Balagne and over the Désert des Agriates to the west coast of Cap Corse – on extremely clear days, it's possible to see the Alps. You can descend either by the same route, or south to Sant'Antonino or east to Santa-Reparata-di-Balagna.

Fanning out over the Colline de Monte Guido, 2km beyond the convent road and 2km inland from the coast road, **CORBARA** is a strange mixture – a quintessential Balagne town with a distinctly Moorish appearance, thanks to its bleached flat-roofed houses and narrow vaulted passageways. Capital of the Balagne before the Genoese took over and founded the citadel at Calvi, Corbara boasts the largest of the Balagne parish churches, the **Église de l'Annonciation**, a glitzy Baroque edifice built in 1685. Inside, the most overblown feature is the enormous swirling main altar flanked by two cloud-borne angels, which was constructed from Carrara marble brought over in the 1750s. The painted panels and carved furniture in the sacristy date from the fifteenth century and are relics of the church that occupied this site before the present structure.

Two doors down from the church stands the **Maison des Turcs**, a grand house which bears the arms of the Franceschini, the family who owned the village from the ninth to the nineteenth centuries. The house was built in memory of Davia Franceschini, who was carried off by slavers in 1798, then married the Moroccan sultan, only to die of plague the following year.

Occupying a rocky pinnacle below the village, the craggy ruin of **U Forte** was once seat of the Savelli clan, the former overlords of this region. Founded in 1292 by Aldruvando, a vassal who had rebelled against Count Arrigho Savelli, the castle was completed in 1375 by Savelli's son, Mannone Savelli de Guido. When the castle was dismantled by the Genoese in the early sixteenth century, following a battle between the feudal lords and the republic, Savelli de Guido's descendants restored the nearby **Castel de Guido**, a fort founded in 816 by Guido de Sabelli, who was made Count of the Balagne by the pope after a victory against the Saracens. Here the Savellis ruled in an uneasy coexistence with the Genoese for two hundred years. Then in 1798 this castle too was wrecked, on the orders of a political adversary of the Savelli family, one of whom was Paoli's chief administrator for the new town of L'Île Rousse.

Santa-Reparata-di-Balagna and Monticello

From Corbara you can head back inland by the D263, which climbs up the side of the Regino valley for 3km before reaching **SANTA-REPARATA-DI-BALAGNA**, a terraced village of ancient crumbling buildings and arcaded streets that give you spectacular glimpses of the sea. The best viewpoint is the terrace of **Santa Reparata** in the principal hamlet of Busca, from where L'Île Rousse occupies the foreground against a magnificent crest of mountains. The church was built over a Pisan chapel and retains the eleventh-century apse, though the facade dates from 1590.

Four kilometres higher up the D263 lies **MONTICELLO**, fief of the great warlord Giudice della Rocca, whose thirteenth-century **Castel d'Ortica** sits on a rocky hillock to the north of the village, surrounded by a belt of olive trees. In the centre of the village, the sole sight is the imposing **Maison Malaspina**, formerly owned by descendants of Pascal Paoli's sister, and yet another house in which Napoléon once spent a few days.

You can **stay** at *A Pasturella* on route de Monticello, 5km from L'Île Rousse and 1km north of Monticello (☎95 60 05 65; ②).

Catteri to Belgodère

To the south of Catteri the D71 swings through a region that's received a lot of government money to attempt to reverse the effects of the Balagne's recent dramatic depopulation. Smaller-scale initiatives are in place too, as you'll see at **AVAPESSA**, whose ancient water-driven mill produces an olive oil that you can sample at *L'Alivu*, a restaurant set up by a community of young people trying to revive the local economy. New *gîtes* have also been opened in the vicinity – the *mairie* in the village square has full details (☎95 61 74 10).

The next village along the route is **MURO**, once a hive of artisans, black-smiths, silkweavers and carters. Nowadays Muro is part of the programme to revive old industries in the region, and the two olive oil mills which straddle the river have been set working again.

The village's three churches provide further evidence of the former prosperity of this once thriving community. An elegant bell tower and an imposing facade decorated wth statues distinguish the eighteenth-century **Église de l'Annonciation**, on the right as you enter the village. Inside, the usual profusion of marble surrounds a **Crucifix des Miracles** dating from 1730. The church opposite, **Santa Croce**, is much older, dating from the fourteenth century, and even more ancient is nearby **San Giovanni**, a partly ruined eleventh-century church, one of the oldest in Corsica.

Glass and olive oil are the chief products at **FELICETO**, a village scattered over the banks of the River Regino, 2km east of Muro. The village is also famous for the purity of its water – a couple of sources 200m west of the village provide a refreshing halt along the way. The inevitable Baroque church is **Église Saint-Nicolas**, its crypt holding the lavish tombs of the local bigwigs; the next-door **Chapelle Saint-Roch** has a beautiful seventeenth-century wooden statue of Saint Roch in a chapel beside the altar. If you're in the mood for a brisk walk, you could clamber up to the building known as the **Falconaghja** (Eagle's Nest), an hour's climb along the footpath on the left as you leave the village heading north. A mayor of the village constructed it in the last century so he could keep an eye on his citizens with a telescope; later it became a hideout for passing outlaws, hence the alternative name *Maison des Bandits*.

In the village centre you'll find one of the few **hotels** in these parts, the *Mare e Monti* (☎95 61 73 06; ②), occupying a fifteenth-century building with huge rooms and thick stone walls. Feliceto also boasts a fine **restaurant**, *U Mulinu* (June–Sept; ☎95 61 73 23), a restored oil mill at the eastern end of the village; it's known throughout the Balagne for its excellent game and *charcuterie*, so book ahead.

Named after the caves and cavities that riddle the rocky prominence on which it sits, **SPELONCATO**, 6km from Feliceto, is one of the most appealing Balagne villages. The ruins of an eleventh-century fortress dominate the village from the north, while the core of the place is the delightfully compact market square, **place de la Libération**. Opposite its lively café stands the massive *Hôtel Spelunca* (☎95 61 50 38; ②), former residence of Cardinal Savelli, an eighteenth-century papal minister whose corruption earned him the nickname *Il Cane Corso* (the Corsican dog). The village church, **Saint-Michel**, just to north of the square, has an unusual nineteenth-century organ, the work of a local sculptor, and some elaborate wooden tabernacles.

At **VILLE-DI-PARASO**, set in a profusion of olives, eucalyptus, parasol palms and cedars 1km from Speloncato, you might want to stop at **Église San Simone**, which is connected to a superb clock tower and contains the monumental tombs of the Fillippi and Malaspina dynasties. The adjacent building has been transformed into a gallery which shows contemporary exhibitions of local artists.

BELGODÈRE, 12km northeast of Ville de Paraso, lies at the junction of the main inland routes and provides a possible base for the beaches around L'Île Rousse (see p.84), of which it has a splendid view. The main Calvi–Ponte Leccia train stops here. You can **stay** at *Hôtel Niobel* in the centre of the village (☎95 61 34 00; ②), a small intimate hotel with a good local restaurant. There are a couple of churches in the main square to have a look at: **Église Saint-Thomas** dates from the sixteenth century and houses a magnificent painted panel of the Virgin and Child; the neighbouring **Oratoire de la Madonuccia** harbours Corsica's oldest statue of the Madonna, placed here in 1387 to seal a reconciliation between Speloncato and the rival villages of San Columbano. Once you've checked them out, you could walk up to **Château Malaspina**, a nineteenth-century fort, accessible by a stone stairway 500m along the road to Speloncato.

Quite a lively spot by Balagne standards, Belgodère hosts two music festivals: the Festival de Musique Classique de Lozari in April and Rencontres Musicales Aostu in Musica in August.

Vallée de la Tartagine

The **Vallée de la Tartagine** is a spectacularly isolated part of the Balagne, enclosed by Monte Grosso (1938m) and Monte Padro (2393m), the northernmost high peaks of Corsica's mountainous spine. Rising in the cirque of Monte Corona, just to the south of Monte Grosso, the River Tartagine hurtles from west to east, fed on its northern flank by tributaries whose ravines are overlooked by four high-altitude villages. The easiest approach to this awesome region is the D63, which begins about 500m south of Speloncato, climbs up a high open route and then plunges south, coming to a dead-end in the base of the valley, in an area of densely forested land, featuring evergreen oaks and maritime and Laricio pines.

The first place you'll come to along this route is **PIOGGIOLA**, a crown of yellow buildings nestling in a fold of chestnut trees at 1000m – which makes it one of the highest villages in Corsica. You can **stay** here in the ten-roomed *Auberge l'Aghjola* (☎95 61 90 48; ③), situated on the left as you leave the village. Its terrace juts out over the mountainside and the food is excellent, with locally shot game and other mountain specialities providing the staple fare.

Beyond Pioggiola the road divides, one branch of the D963 descending to the region's principal village, **OLMI-CAPELLA**, a cluster of sharp red roofs and mellow stone overlooking the Tartagine. Carry on 3km further east and you'll come to **VALLICA**, a sleepy place swamped in greenery and overshadowed by Monte Padro on the other side of the valley. You may want to visit the tiny **museum** in the *mairie* (June–Sept Mon–Sat 10am–noon & 2–5pm), which exhibits traditional farm implements and various ancient tools uncovered in the region.

The other branch of the D963 descends to a junction for the ancient village of **MAUSOLEO**, the last of the Tartagine quartet, which boasts a fifteenth-century church containing an olive-wood statue of John the Baptist. Past the Mausoleo turning, the D963 twists through the spectacular gorges of the River Melaja to the banks of the Tartagine, terminating at the *maison forestière* and the **Fôret de la Tartagine-Melaja**. If you want just a taste of the forest, you can follow various short marked paths from here; the two principal major hikes are detailed overleaf.

WALKS IN THE TARTAGINE

The route to the **Col de la Tartagine** (1852m) is a reasonably difficult hike of 15km (4hr 30min) over rocky terrain, providing breathtaking mountain vistas through the trees. Cross the river at the *maison forestière* and take the waymarked forest trail to the left, turning right shortly afterwards and following the south side of the river for some distance above the valley bed until you come to a small waterfall. A track on the north side of the Tartagine stream follows the water for 100m before it comes to a wide track and a sign for "Tartagine Col" points west. Follow this track, ascending gradually for 500m before crossing the Balininu stream; then a short scramble through the maquis in a north-northwest direction will bring you back to the Tartagine stream. Climbing up on the west side of the stream you eventually arrive at a steep zigzag trail up a rocky spur. The track quickly peters out, but 100m up on the right you can pick up a faint track leading southwest which takes you up to the col.

The **Col de l'Ondella** (1845m) lies 10km southwest of the *maison forestière* and is a good five-hour hike. Follow the same route as for the Col de la Tartagine until you reach the Balininu stream, then veer left, following the orange paint flashes which mark the trail. Then it's a straightforward hike to the top.

South of Calvi

From Calvi, two routes run south down to **Galéria**, a tiny resort sited about 25km down the coast. If speed is your main concern, the inland D251/D51 is the better option, a well-maintained road which cuts through the **Balagne Déserte**, an uninhabited region of deep red rocks and shiny green maquis. The D51 separates from the D251 about 10km out of Calvi at **Suare**, from where the latter road continues to the **Cirque de Bonifato**, a luscious forest of Laricio pines and evergreen oaks bordering some of the highest mountains in Corsica. The alternative route to Galéria is the D81, a hair-raising corniche that's bordered by gigantic boulders and looks down on a rock-strewn deep purple sea. This road meets the D51 at the Cinque Arcate bridge, where a right turn brings you to Galéria and a left leads to the **Vallée du Fango**, one of the least traversed areas of Corsica, worth visiting for its dramatic combination of deep green forests and barren ground scattered with great orange rocks. To the southwest of Galéria stretches a peninsula whose tip is protected as the **Réserve Naturel de Scandola**, a wildlife-rich seascape that can be viewed only by boat.

Cirque de Bonifato

An immense basin of forested land encircled by a ring of orange crags, the **Cirque de Bonifato** is a thirty-kilometre drive along the D251 southeast of Calvi, plus a further 8km on foot. The adjacent forests of Calenzana and Bonifato are magnificent hiking terrain, and the best place to start exploring them is the *maison forestière*, a foresters' hut located in the heart of the woodland where the road ends. If you just want to take a look around, leave the car in the nearby car park and retrace your approach as far as the **Chaos de Bocca Rezza**, a viewing point on the north side of the road, less than a kilometre away. From here you can see across the forest as far as the immense granite pinnacles that enclose the cirque to the east. If you're going to tackle anything more ambitious, you'll probably want to check into the large **auberge** by the car park; catering mainly for ramblers and backpackers, it does obligatory half-board accommodation at an excellent price (☎95 63 72 10; ②).

The most obvious walk is the one up to **Spasimata** (1190m), a row of disused dry stone huts in the core of the cirque, marking the spot where shepherds once rested on their journey down to Calenzana. It's a relatively easy-going five-hour hike from the *auberge*, initially following the forest trail which skirts the nearby waterfall and then tracks the River Figarella, which courses through great hollowed-out slabs of pink granite. After thirty minutes you'll come to the confluence of the rivers Melaja and Figarella, from where a path marked with red and white paint ascends to Spasimata, a route that crosses several streams and intersects with the **GR20** mountain trail at the top. Here you'll find the *réfuge du Carozzu*, the only refuge in the vicinity.

Galéria

Isolated at the edge of a scalded landscape of deep red rocks and straggly eucalyptus trees, **GALÉRIA** was a malaria-ridden village as recently as the 1930s, but has now turned its unusual location to profit, becoming a popular summer resort and sailing centre. Its handful of hotels and restaurants back onto a jetty and surround a small semicircle of sand, while 500m north out of the village lies Plage de Riciniccia, a vast red-shingled cove that's been adopted by nudists.

Galéria's **tourist office** is at *Maison a Torra*, a hut located 4km away from the village, at the junction of the D81 and D351 by the Cinque Arcate bridge (June–Sept daily 9am–noon & 2–6pm; ☎95 62 02 27). The office carries useful information for ramblers, including a list of mountain *Gîtes d'Étapes*. The **bus** stops at this junction twice daily, at 10am coming from Porto and 3pm from Calvi. If you're reliant on the bus, you may want to stay here at the *Hôtel Cinque Arcate* (April–Oct; ☎95 62 02 54; ③). There are also couple of hotels 1km east of here, in the lower Fango valley (see below).

For **accommodation** in Galéria, the *Filosorma* (☎95 62 00 02; ②) is a modern place, with large, balconied rooms and a good restaurant, at the entrance to the village. *Auberge Galeris*, set back from the road behind the *Filosorma* (☎95 62 02 89; ①), is very simple, clean and comfortable with views of the sea. The small and cosy *L'Auberge* (☎95 62 00 15; ①) offers excellent home cooking. **Campers** tend to camp wild behind the Riciniccia beach, as *Camping Idéal* at the eastern end of the beach is rather expensive and unpleasant. The very best **restaurant** is the *Loup de Mer* overlooking the jetty, for fish fresh from the bay.

There's a track to Girolata from Galéria, a walk best started early in the morning before the sun becomes too hot – the maquis holds the heat and it's very exposed. The five-hour trek is part of the *Tra Mare e Monti* walk (see p.86).

Vallée du Fango

The road into the **Vallée du Fango** follows the Fango River for 15km as far as the base of the Paglia Orba mountain. A forest of pines, chestnuts, beeches and eucalyptus carpets the valley slopes, offering excellent picnic spots and walking possibilities. A couple of villages scattered over the slopes of the valley do little to disperse the desolate feel of the place, and few people venture up the mountain unless it's for trout fishing or hunting, for which the area is renowned.

About 1km from the Cinque Arcate bridge, the D81 along the river becomes the D351 for 13km as far as Barghiana. At this wild junction there are two **hotels**, the *Fango* (☎95 62 01 92; ②) and *A Farera* (☎95 62 01 87; ①), the only places to stay in the valley, also useful if Galéria is overcrowded. The shark's fin of Paglia Orba, visible for most of the onward drive, can be seen to especially good effect 6km along the road from the junction at **Tuarelli**, where a fifteen-minute walk down a track to the left of the road leads to a bridge over the Fango.

To get into the thick of the forest, however, continue a further kilometre along the D351. There, on the right of the road, a track penetrates a kilometre and a half into the woodland, ending at the **Maison Forestière de Pirio**, where the only information available is a large map showing the principal footpaths.

Back on the main road, you'll soon come to the turning for the village of **MANSO**, dispersed over the mountainside. A terrace at the entrance to the village affords a glorious view over the valley: a low screen of olive trees strung across the base of Paglia Orba and Capo Tafonato looming up to the southeast. After Manso the D351 road deteriorates as it comes to an end amidst the chestnut trees at the hamlet of **Barghiana**. A two-kilometre walk up to the **Pont de la Rocce**, a bridge over a tributary of the Fango River, leads off to the right, from which point there's a breathtaking panorama of Capo Rosso and Capo Tafonato, belonging to the Cinto massif (see p.187).

Réserve Naturel de Scandola (Scandula)

The **Réserve Naturel de Scandola** takes its name from the wooden tiles (*scandule*) that cover many of the island's mountain houses, but the area's rooflike rock formations are only part of its amazing geological repertoire. Its stacked slabs, towering pinnacles and gnarled claw-like outcrops were formed by volcanic eruptions 250 million years ago, and subsequent erosion has fashioned shadowy caves, grottoes and gashes in the rock. Scandola's colours are as remarkable as the shapes, the hues varying from the charcoal grey of granite to the incandescent rusty purple of porphyry.

The headland and its surrounding water were declared a nature reserve in 1975, so **wildlife** is as varied here as anywhere in Corsica. Dolphins thrive in the area, which also supports more than 450 types of seaweed and some remarkable fish, such as the grouper, a species more commonly found in the Caribbean. Colonies of gulls and cormorants inhabit the cliffs, and you might see the odd **peregrine falcon**. These prey on the **blue rock thrushes** which build their nests on the bare rock pinnacles. **Ospreys**, extremely rare in the Mediterranean, are also found here. There used to be only seven pairs but careful conservation has increased the number to twenty-one. Rare plants native to Corsica grow freely, such as the sea daffodil *Pancratium maritimus* and the *Senecio cineraria* with its distinctive furry silver leaves.

Scandola can be viewed only by boat, which for tourists means taking one of the daily **excursions** from Calvi and Porto. These leave from Calvi at 9am and Porto at 9.15am and 2.30pm (April–Oct), the first two stopping for two hours at Girolata (see below) and returning in the late afternoon. The later boat from Porto only stops for 45 minutes. It's a fascinating journey, well worth the 250F – but it's a good idea to take a picnic, as the restaurants at Girolata are extremely pricey.

Starting the round trip from Calvi, the first port of call is the **Baie d'Elbu**, where the rocks stand out magnificently red against a deep blue sea. Two kilometres south of here lies the **Punta Palazzu**, so-called because of the soaring rocky towers that spring from the sea like a giant palace. Over the course of the last thousand years or so the seaweed here has formed a thick white band around the base of the cliffs just above the surface of the water – a rare phenomenon that provides invaluable information about the changing sea level.

Beyond this point the boat weaves through the narrow straits by **Île de Gargalo**, an islet created from volcanic lava where the most westerly point on Corsica is marked by a lighthouse. Excursion boats from Calvi and Porto stop for two hours (the later boat from Porto stops for 45 minutes) at Girolata before turning round.

Girolata

Connected by a mere mule track to the rest of the island, and dwarfed by the plunging maquis-shrouded slopes, the tiny fishing haven of **GIROLATA** has a dreamlike quality that's highlighted by the vivid red of the surrounding rocks. For hundreds of years the few inhabitants lived a reclusive life, living from fishing and hardly communicating with the rest of the island. In 1530 the notorious corsair Dragut was taken prisoner at Girolata by the Genoese general Andrea Doria, who captured nine galleys. Dragut paid the men and returned eleven years later to get his revenge by razing Girolata to the ground. A short stretch of stony beach and a few houses are overlooked by a stately **watchtower**, built later in the seventeenth century in the form of a small castle by the Genoese, and set high on the hills above the beach. Nowadays, the hamlet has just fifteen year-round inhabitants, who make most of their money from a couple of expensive restaurants and bars that cash in on the daily boat trips. There are no hotels, but *La Cabane du Berger* (☎95 20 16 98; ②), in the village above a good restaurant, is a reasonable *gîte d'étape*.

The Golfe de Porto

The coast of the **Golfe de Porto** is one of Corsica's classic landscapes, famed for the corroded beauty of its crimson granite cliffs. Niched into the furthest indent of this gulf, the resort of **Porto** presents a scene that is similarly emblematic of the island's finest qualities: on the flank of the village an imposing tower overlooks a stark crescent of shingle beach, while in the background a band of eucalyptus shimmers against thunderous red granite crags that turn slowly black at sunset. North of Porto, a cliff road zigzags up to the **Col de la Croix**, offering breathtaking glimpses of the gulf round every corner. Highlight of the southern gulf are the **Calanche**, twelve kilometres of dizzying pinnacles and ravines, ideally explored from a boat or on foot. A couple of fantastically located hotels overlooking the Calanche make the village of **Piana** a tempting alternative to Porto as a base, and two outstanding beaches – Anse de Ficajola and Plage d'Arone – lie close at hand.

A bus serves the coastal route from Calvi to Porto; the bus from Ajaccio to Porto takes in the Calanche, but for visiting the above beaches, you really need your own transport.

Porto

The overwhelming proximity of the mountains, combined with the pervasive euca-lyptus and spicy scent of the maquis, give **PORTO** a uniquely intense, loaded atmosphere that makes it one of the most interesting places to stay on the west coast. Except for a watchtower built here by the Genoese in the second half of the sixteenth century, the site was only built upon with the onset of tourism since the 1950s. The location, hemmed in by steep mountain slopes, precludes overdevelop-ment, as hotels can spread only a little way up the road and along the short quay. At the same time Porto is so small that it can become claustrophobic in July and August, when overcrowding – thanks to predominantly German tourists – is no joke. Off-season, the place becomes eerily deserted, so you'd do well to choose your time carefully – the best months are probably May, June and September.

An avenue bordered by eucalyptus, route de la Marine, links the two parts of the resort. A strip of shops and hotels a kilometre from the sea makes up the actual village of Porto, but the main focus of activity is the small **marina**, located at the avenue's end. In the nineteenth century Porto was used for exporting Laricio pines from the inland forests, and the route de la Marine was built to accommodate the great carts that used to haul the timber down from the moun-tains. Clustered around the great red rock, a nucleus of hotels and restaurants vye for the best view of the tower, while the rest of the buildings are crammed into what little space remains.

It's about a fifteen-minute walk from the marina up to the **Genoese Tower**, a square chimney-shaped structure that was cracked by an explosion in the seven-teenth century, when the tower was used as an arsenal. An awe-inspiring view of the crashing sea and maquis-shrouded mountains make it worth the short climb, and when the restorers have finished you'll be able to go inside.

The **beach** consists of a pebbly cove south beyond the shoulder of the massive rock supporting the tower. To reach it from the marina, follow the little road that skirts the rock, cross the wooden bridge which spans the River Porto on your left, then walk through the car park under the trees. Although it's rather exposed, and the sea very deep, the great crags overshadowing the shore give the place a vivid edge.

Practicalities

The **bus** from Calvi stops a little way north of the village, but leaves for the return journey from the marina; Ajaccio is served by minibus, arriving in and leaving from the marina. A **post office**, **bank** and **tourist office** (June–Sept Mon–Fri 10am–noon & 2–6pm) are all in the village. Information about **boat** excursions to Scandola and the Calanche, plus tickets, are available from *Boutique Anthony* in the marina (May–Oct Mon–Fri 9am–noon & 2–6pm), a far more helpful place than the tourist office; you can also change money here and buy tickets for the minibus which runs daily to Ajaccio in summer. For information on **diving** in the Porto area, contact the headquarters of the diving club (☎95 26 10 29) in the village of Ota (see p.101).

As for **hotels**, the most expensive places are found in the village, whilst the lower-budget hotels are gathered by the sea. The larger hotels cut their prices dramatically in September in order to entice the straggling tourists. The nearest campsites are just a bit farther inland from the village. All the places listed below are marked on our map of Porto.

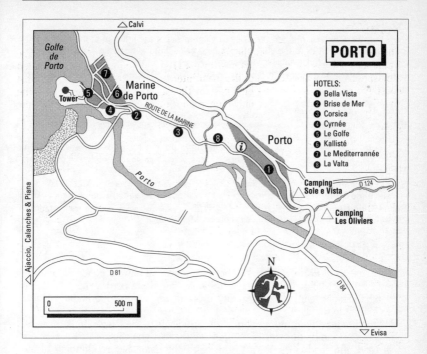

Pizzerias and standard hotel **restaurants** make up the bulk of eating places in Porto, with prices generally increasing the nearer you get to the tower. You can buy food at one of two **supermarkets** in the village, and you'll find a general store which opens daily beneath the archway overlooking the wooden bridge.

HOTELS

Bella Vista, in the village, three doors down from the bank (☎95 26 11 08). The best of a string of similar hotels in the village. Rooms are dark but well furnished and the balconies command an outstanding view of the mountains. September discounts. ④.

Brise de Mer, on left as you approach tower from the village (☎95 26 10 28). A large old-fashioned place, with very friendly service and a good restaurant. ③.

Corsica, in a eucalyptus grove between the village and the marina (☎95 26 10 89). Has a large swimming pool, and benefits from the shade of the eucalyptus trees. September discounts. ③.

Cyrnée, the first hotel opposite bridge (☎95 26 12 40). Simple rooms, popular restaurant. ②.

Le Golfe, at the base of the rock in the marina (☎95 26 13 33). Small and cosy; every room has a balcony with a sea view. The small restaurant on the ground floor serves good breakfasts, omelettes, steaks and snacks. ②.

Kallisté, the marina (☎95 26 10 30). Despite its ugly exterior, this place is the most comfortable hotel in the area, with spacious rooms and a popular bar. ④.

Le Méditerrannée, the marina (☎95 26 10 27). Large flashy hotel, every room has a bathroom; half-board only in summer. Closed winter. ④.

La Valta, in the village next door to the supermarket (☎95 26 12 81). A long-established family-targeted place. September discounts. ③.

CAMPSITES

Camping les Oliviers, high on the slopes 1500m inland at the junction of the road to Ota junction (☎95 26 14 49). At the edge of a ravine overlooking the torrential River Porto; very crowded in summer, but a fantastic location.

Camping Sole e Vista, close to *Les Oliviers* (☎95 26 15 71). A less expensive but equally well-situated site.

BARS AND RESTAURANTS

Brise de Mer, see above. Hearty home cooking; good local specialities such as roast lamb in maquis herbs. Inexpensive.

Le Moulin, just beyond the village at the junction of the Calvi and Evisa roads. Excellent French food and some tasty regional dishes such as *sanglier en daube*, a rich wild boar stew. Moderate.

Soleil Couchant, at the foot of the tower. Don't be put off by the green umbrellas, fake foliage and disco lights; this place serves excellent pizzas and there's often a queue. Expensive.

Bar le Tour Genoise, right opposite the tower. Serves snacks in the bar but the restaurant does a lot of fresh fish and basic Corsican cuisine. Moderate.

The northern gulf

The D81 north of Porto, a thirty-kilometre sequence of hairpin bends around the base of Monte Manganello, provides breathtaking views across the gulf to the glowing Calanche and the opportunity to swim or dive at a sprinkling of tiny coves along the way.

About 5km into the route, an abrupt left turn leads to the **Plage de Bussaglia**, the longest strand on this side of the gulf and the first you can get to. Back on the main road, the road curls down to the cliff edge again before climbing to the village of **Partinello**, set on the side of the mountain under folds of green woodland. A left along the D324 here takes you down to the popular **Plage de Caspio**, a red sandy cove, backed by a bar. The sun disappears behind the cliff in the afternoon in summer, so you need to arrive early if you want to catch some rays.

A more enticing cove along this stretch is the **Plage de Gratelle**, located just north of Caspio, but accessible via a narrow signposted road at a point where the road widens about 10km on from Partinello. The deep translucent sea and the view of the Calanche from this beach make it extremely popular.

A short distance beyond the Gratelle turning, **Col de la Croix** has a strategically placed drinks hut from which to relish the view westwards towards Scandola and southwards to the chaos of the Calanche. **Col de Parmarella**, a further 10km north, gives more glorious vistas across the Scandola headland and distant forests.

The southern gulf

South of Porto the D81 passes through the Piana forest before entering the spectacularly eroded terrain of the **Calanche**. The village of **Piana**, 12km along the route, has this area's concentration of cafés, restaurants and hotels and lies within easy reach of **Capo Rosso**, which marks the southern extremity of the Golfo de Porto, and **Capo d'Orto**, a small mountain set in the Piana forest. On the seaward side of Piana, the panoramic **Route de Ficajola** connects with the D824, a refreshingly smooth road leading to **Plage d'Arone**, the finest beach in the vicinity. The **bus** from Porto to Ajaccio stops at Piana twice daily – otherwise there's no public transport.

The Calanche

The UNESCO-protected site of the **Calanche** takes its name from *calanca*, the Corsican word for creek or inlet (in French, *calanque*), but the outstanding characteristics of the Calanche are the vivid orange and pink rock masses and pinnacles which crumble into the dark blue sea. Liable to unusual patterns of erosion, these tormented rock formations and porphyry needles, some of which reach 300m above the sea, were described by Maupassant as a "nightmarish menagerie petrified by the will of an extravagant god", and have long been traditionally associated with different animals and figures, of which the most famous is the **Tête de Chien** at the north end of the stretch of cliffs. Other figures and creatures conjured up include a Moor's head, a monocled bishop, a bear and a tortoise.

One way to see the fantastic cliffs of the Calanche is by boat from Porto; excursions leave daily in summer, cost 100F and last about an hour. Alternatively, to see the best of this landscape you could drive along the corniche road which weaves through the granite archways on its way to Piana. Eight kilometres along the road from Porto, the *Roches Bleues*, once a restaurant but now abandoned, is a convenient landmark and place to park for **walkers**.

CALANCHE WALKS

Four routes, varying from easy to strenuous, can be followed in the environs of the *Roches Bleues*. Coming from Porto, 1km before you reach the building, a marked trail leads off for the short **Château Fort** walk, which provides the best views of the cliffs. A car park on the right-hand side of the road indicates the beginning, and an easy forty minutes brings you to a massive rock formation resembling a ruined fort.

The **corniche** walk lasts about fifty minutes and starts on a well-worn track, east off the road directly in front of the *Roches Bleues* before the bridge. The track, signposted "Corniche", climbs in a loop around to the main road, coming out a few kilometres down from where you started.

For a more demanding three-hour ramble, another path, beyond the corniche track and signposted "Châtaigneraie", follows a pleasant shady trail through the **chestnut forest**, indicated by painted marks all the way.

A shorter walk of an hour begins by the little chapel half a kilometre south of the *Roches Bleues*, west off the road where two lay-bys provide parking. A mule track marked by blue paint leads off to the north of the road. Initially a steep ascent passes between two massive rocks, then follows the coast for an hour, affording fabulous views over the gulf, before the track regains the road.

Piana

For some reason **PIANA** has suffered little from its prime location overlooking the Calanche. Retaining its sleepy village atmosphere, it comprises a cluster of pink houses around an eighteenth-century church, plus just a few hotels and restaurants. If you want to **stay** here, head straight for *Hôtel les Roches Rouges* (☎95 27 81 81; ②), at the entrance to the village on the Porto side; built in the 1930s, it has huge rooms (make sure you get one facing the water) and a restaurant terrace that juts out over the cliffs, affording a magnificent view of the Calanche and the sea. A cheaper alternative is *Hôtel Continental* (☎95 27 82 02; ①), on the right as you leave Piana; it's an old house with high wooden ceilings and a leafy garden. The *Mare e Monti* (☎95 27 82 14; closed winter; ③), in the same direction, on the left next to a petrol station, also offers fine views.

The ten-kilometre walk from Piana east to **Capo d'Orto** should take between five and six hours, providing you're in good shape and have the right footwear for the rocky terrain. The track begins 2km north of Piana. Follow the D81 half way, then take the little road on the right just before the bridge. After another 1km this stops at a fork where you can leave the car. Take the right-hand track of the fork and continue alongside the river. After 3km the track gives way to a path marked with flashes of orange paint which ascends east through a pine wood. The orange paint ends at the mountain pass of **Foce d'Orto**, a huge gap between giant mounds of rock, two hours into the walk. For Capo d'Orto head north along the left path which soon peters out and the way to the summit becomes marked by stone cairns. A corridor of rock overgrown with scrub leads up to a plateau, from which point it's an easy scramble to the top and a truly glorious view.

AROUND PIANA

If you've only got time for a very short trip from Piana, just head 2km south of the village along the D81 to the **Col de Lava**, a famed viewing platform for the gulf. Rather more rewarding, though, is the **route de Ficajola** (D624), a short steep road which loops down to the shore from the central junction in Piana. Stunning views of the gulf make it a lovely drive in itself, and ten minutes' walk away from the road's end, accessible via a stone stairway, there's the bonus of the **Anse de Ficajola**, a small cove of red rocks and limpid sea.

Best of all, though, is the drive along the D824, which leaves the route de Ficajola a short way outside Piana. About 6km along the road, there's the option of a walk along the marked trail to the **Tour de Turghiu**, a Genoese watchtower occupying the extremity of **Capu Rossu**, the finger of red rocky land that marks the southern boundary of the Golfe de Porto. It's a dramatic sight from afar, its sharp point dwarfed by a great toothlike spur, and the view at the end is even more remarkable, extending south to Cargèse and north as far as the Golfe de Girolata. The walk takes about four hours, and is hard going on the final stretch.

Continue along the D824 for another 6km and you'll reach another exceptional beach, **Plage d'Arone**. This strand of white sand and clear sea is far removed from the crowds, and has a discreet **restaurant** serving excellent Corsican food.

Inland from Porto

East of Porto the D84 climbs 40km to the Col de Verghio, cutting through maquis and forest as it approaches the crags of the remote mountainous interior. The great feature of this part of the island is the breathtaking **Spelunca gorge**, which can be approached either by the D84 or along the smaller D124, via the attractive village of **Ota**, the administrative centre for the area. From there you can walk through the gorge and past its elegant Genoese bridges, but if you want to stay in the gorge region, the hike is best tackled from **Evisa**, a mountain resort situated a few kilometres up the D84. Evisa is also well placed for a visit to the lofty **Forêt d'Aitone**, which borders the route to the dizzying **Col de Verghio**, the highest point in Corsica that's traversable by road.

For those without transport the Ajaccio–Porto bus passes through Ota, but Evisa can only be approached by bus from Ajaccio along the inland route. These are the only buses there are in the region.

The Gorges de Spelunca

Spanning the two kilometres between the villages of Ota and Evisa, the **Gorges de Spelunca** is a formidable sight, its bare orange granite walls, a thousand metres deep in places, plunging into the foaming green torrent created by the confluence of the rivers Porto, Tavulella, Onca, Campi and Aitone. The sunlight, ricocheting across the rock walls, creates a sinister effect that's heightened by the dark jagged needles of the encircling peaks. It's scarcely surprising that local legend has it that the gorge was hewn by the devil in a terrible rage.

The most dramatic part of the gorge can be seen from the road, which hugs the edge for much of its length, but the best way to see it is on foot from Ota or Evisa.

Ota

Isolated on a verdant ledge 5km east of Porto, **OTA** is dominated by **Capo d'Ota**, a colossal dome of a mountain that appears so close to the village that it's said the local monks used to tether the huge overhanging rock at its summit with hemp to prevent it falling on the villagers. You'll find a large **post office** and a few **restaurants** here, as well as the *Funtana al'Ora* **campsite**, 1km east of the village towards Evisa (☎95 26 15 48), deep in the countryside and close to the river.

Evisa

EVISA's bright orange roofs emerge against a lush background of chestnut forests about 10km from Ota, on the eastern edge of the gorge. Situated 830m above sea level, the village caters well for hikers and makes a pleasant stop for a taste of mountain life – the food is particularly good up here, and the atmosphere buzzes in summer.

The best place to **stay** is the cosy, rambling *Hôtel du Centre* (☎95 26 20 92; July–Sept; ②) opposite the statue in the centre of the village; the attached **restaurant** serves wholesome Corsican specialities. *Hôtel l'Aitone*, at the north exit to

---

WALKS FROM EVISA

An enjoyable short walk from Evisa runs down to the local **chestnut wood** beneath the village. About 250m west of the village a stone gateway leads into the wood, from where you soon emerge into a field of bracken. The view here embraces the Golfe de Porto, the Spelunca gorge and Ota. This is a good walk to do at sunset, when the colours can be amazingly vivid.

The five-kilometre **walk from Evisa to Ota** is basically easy-going, although from Ota you may well prefer to hitch back to Evisa rather than climb back up through the gorge. Follow the road west of the village as far as the cemetery, where a steep path marked "Ota–Evisa" descends into the gorge, through maquis interspersed with pines. Already you'll be able to see Ota, with the pink crags behind it. Continue through the mossy trees, past precipitous walls of bald grey rock, until you hit the river, and then follow it. About 45min from Evisa, the Genoese **Pont de Zaglia** appears, a row of alders leaning across its cobbled walkway – a good place for a swim. Carry on for 2km and you will come out at the D124; past the two road bridges known as the Ponts d'Ota, carry on for 100m, then take the track on the left of the D124, following the orange paint marks. After 400m you'll rejoin the river, and another 800m will bring you to the **Ponte Vecchio** or **Pont de Pianella**, a perfectly restored Genoese bridge at the confluence of the Onca and the Porto, and another good bathing spot. Cross the bridge and turn left through the gate, carrying on along the river past two blades of rock, and climb up the hill into Ota.

the village (☎95 26 20 04; ②), is a large country hotel with comfortable rooms, a swimming pool, and a reputation for gastronomic prowess. Otherwise it's possible to rent a *gîte* for a couple of nights: ask at the building on the left next to the former *Hôtel Belvedère* by the church – they rent small apartments with glorious views across the valley (☎95 35 21 36). *Camping Paisolu d'Aitone* (☎95 26 20 39), 1km east of the village, is a smart all-year **campsite**. For a **drink**, your only option is the *Modern Bar*, by the fountain, where you can hang out with the locals on the shady terrace.

Forêt d'Aitone

Thousands of soaring Laricio pines, some of them as much as fifty metres tall, make the **Forêt d'Aitone** the most beautiful forest in Corsica. Incorporating the mountainous Fôret de Lindinosa, it reaches 1391m at its highest point – the **Col de Salto** – and extends over ten square kilometres between Evisa and the Col de Verghio. Well-worn tourist paths cross the forest at various points, but human disturbance is not yet great enough to upset the balance of local **wildlife**, even if the Aitone foxes have become quite tame owing to visitors feeding them. Wild boar and stoats thrive here, while high up in the remoter parts of Lindinosa, mouflon are sometimes seen. Birds sighted in the forest include eagles, sparrowhawks and goshawks, and if you're lucky you may spot a Corsican nuthatch, an unique species distinguished by a black crown and a white stripe over the eye. The most exotic creature to haunt these parts is a rare, large and savage cat known as a **Ghjattu Volpe** – literally "fox-cat". A recent haul of illegal game from Corsica was uncovered by French customs, amongst which one of these cats was discovered. However, sightings of the creature in the wild are extremely rare.

You can park 7km along the road from Evisa by the **Maison Forestière d'Aitone**, the forest headquarters and information centre (June–Sept 9am–noon & 2–6pm), and a starting-off point for walks in the area. In this part of the forest grow the oldest Laricio pines in Corsica, some of them clocking up five hundred years. Fine-grained, strong and very resistant to weathering, the Laricio was highly valued for ships' masts and furniture. Throughout the latter half of the nineteenth century forests all over Corsica were regularly decimated, as the island has the very best specimens of this species, which only grows in forests higher than 1000m.

One of the most popular short walks goes to the **Belvedère**, a great projecting rock 5km north of Evisa. To reach it follow the signposted track leading into the forest, from beside a wide lay-by on the left-hand side of the road. The magnificent **view** across the valley takes in the rivers Aitone and Porto, rushing between high walls of copper-tinted rocks down to the Spelunca gorge.

Another well-trekked route leads to the multiple **Cascades de la Valla Scarpa**, where the crystalline waters of the Aitone crash into a pool hollowed out by the falls. It's just fifteen minutes' walk from the *maison forestière*, signposted "Piscines/les Cascades", and thus it does become overcrowded in summer – though you don't have to walk much farther along the river to find more tranquil spots for a picnic and a swim.

If you want to reach the higher slopes, an hour's walk from the *maison forestière* will bring you to the **Col de Salto**, and a further three hours' heavy climbing along the same rocky track will bring you to **Col de Felce**, for a fantas-

THEODORE POLI: ROI DES MONTAGNES

Theodore Poli was twenty in 1817, at a time when the French administration was conscripting young men all over the island in an attempt to curb banditry. A brigadier from Poli's village of Guagno, in an act of spite, neglected to inform Poli that he was due for national service, thereby making him a deserter – an offence on which the French were especially harsh. Poli shot the man in revenge and, in true outlaw tradition, took to the maquis, where his confederation of some 150 bandits soon elected him "Roi des Montagnes". A bandit constitution was drawn up, whereby Poli was named Theodore II, after the Theodore I who had briefly ruled Corsica some sixty years earlier. Hiding out in the Aitone forest, Theodore and his gang proceeded to terrorize the neighbourhood, imposing a heavy "tax" on the rich and the clergy, while exempting the poor. Becoming ever more ambitious, these self-styled champions of the downtrodden poor whipped up anti-French feeling wherever they could, raiding the gendarmeries for arms and even gunning down the local executioner of Bastia when he refused to participate in anti-French demonstrations. In 1827 the Roi des Montagne's rule came to an abrupt end – lured into a forest glade by a beautiful woman, he was shot dead by one of his many enemies.

tic vista of the Golfe de Porto. For the more ambitious, the **Col de Cuccavera** – above the tree line at 1500m – can be attained by cutting north before the Col de Felce, striking right up the mountainside. Once you're this far up, you can make out hazy distant views of the Gorges d'Asco (see p.184).

Just 4km beyond the *maison forestière*, the **Col de Verghio** (1477m) borders the remote district of the Niolo and marks the limit of the Fôret de Valdo-Niello (see p.188). The *Castellacciu* hotel (☎95 26 20 09; ②), a rather grim building, doubles as a basic ski station, but these days there's rarely enough snow to keep it in use. The road is extremely rocky along the last stretch up to the building, where a café is usually open from May until September.

travel details

Trains

Algajola to: Ajaccio (2 daily; 3hr 40min); Bastia (2 daily; 3hr); Belgodère (2 daily; 40min); Corte (2 daily; 2hr 10min); L'Île Rousse (2 daily; 10min); Lumio (2 daily; 12min); Palasca (2 daily; 40min); Ville de Paraso (2 daily; 30min).

Calvi to: Ajaccio (2 daily; 4hr); Algajola (2 daily; 20min); Bastia (2 daily; 3hr 30min); Belgodère (2 daily; 1hr); Corte (2 daily; 2hr 30min); L'Île Rousse (2 daily; 30min); Lumio (2 daily; 10min); Palasca (2 daily; 1hr); Ponte Leccia (2 daily; 40min); Ville de Paraso (2 daily; 50min).

L'Île Rousse to: Ajaccio (2 daily; 3hr 25min); Algajola (2 daily; 10min); Bastia (2 daily; 3hr); Belgodère (2 daily; 30min); Corte (2 daily; 3hr); Lumio (2 daily; 25min); Palasca (2 daily; 30min);

Ponte Leccia (2 daily; 1hr 10min); Ville de Paraso (2 daily; 15min).

Buses

Calvi to: Bastia (1 daily; 3hr); Calenzana (2 daily; 20min); Galéria (1 daily; 1hr 20min); Porto (1 daily; 2hr 30min) Saint-Florent (1 daily; 3hr).

Evisa to: Ajaccio (3 daily; 1hr 30min).

Galéria to: Calvi (1 daily; 1hr 15min); Porto (1 daily; 1hr 15min).

Porto to: Ajaccio (2 daily; 2hr); Calvi (1 daily; 2hr 30min); Cargèse (2 daily; 1hr); Piana (2 daily; 20min); Ota (2 daily; 10min).

Ferries

For ferry details see pp.73 & 82.

CHAPTER THREE

THE AJACCIO REGION

Ajaccio is Corsica's largest town, capital of the *département* of Corse-du-Sud and seat of the island's Assemblée Regionale, yet the image it immediately projects is that of the classic French Mediterranean resort, with its palm trees, street cafés and yacht-filled marina. Modern blocks are stacked up behind the town, but they do little to diminish the visual impact of its warm yellow-toned buildings and majestic citadel, set in a magnificent bay and framed by a shadowy mountain range. Unlike Bastia, Ajaccio makes most of its money from tourism, a fact partly attributable to its own attractions, partly to its proximity to the west coast's wonderful beaches, and partly to its having been the birthplace of **Napoléon Bonaparte**. The prime Napoleonic sites – the Maison Bonaparte and the Salon Napoléonien – are not, however, the best of Ajaccio's cultural assets: that distinction goes to the **Musée Fesch**, which boasts France's most important collection of Italian paintings outside the Louvre.

The **Golfe d'Ajaccio**, an ethereal vista of mist-shrouded mountains by day, is transformed at night into a completely different but equally evocative scene by the lights of the bay's sprawling tourist developments. Flung out at the northern tip of the gulf, beyond the hotels, the islets known as the **Îles Sanguinaires** are perhaps the most popular excursion from the town, rivalled by **Porticcio** on the gulf's southern shore, a trendy outpost for weekending Ajacciens. Of greater appeal to most visitors are the secluded beaches that punctuate this side of the bay as **Capo di Muro**, ideal targets for a picnic and a swim.

Inland from Ajaccio, the craggy **Gorges du Prunelli** edge the river as far as **Bastelica**, birthplace of Corsican freedom fighter Sampiero Corso but an uninspiring village which owes its popularity to the nearby ski station on Plateau d'Èse. North of Ajaccio lies the **Cinarca**, a region of gently sloping vineyards whose produce you can sample in pleasant villages such as Sari d'Orcino and Casaglione. Adjoining the Cinarca is the vast **Golfe de Sagone**, where long stretches of sand have incited a build-up of hotels at the tired resorts of Tiuccia and Sagone, both of which are eclipsed by the enchanting village of **Cargèse**, sited high on a cliff at the northern extremity of the gulf. East of here the sombre town of **Vico** provides a base for excursions into some of the remoter mountain areas, the lovely **Gorges de Liamone** and the rocky region around **Orto** being two of the least-visited areas in the interior of the island.

ACCOMMODATION PRICES

Throughout this guide, hotel accommodation is graded on a scale from ① to ⑥. These numbers show the cost per night of the **least expensive double room in high season**, and correspond to the following prices:

① under F200	③ F300–400	⑤ F500–600
② F200–300	④ F400–500	⑥ over 600F

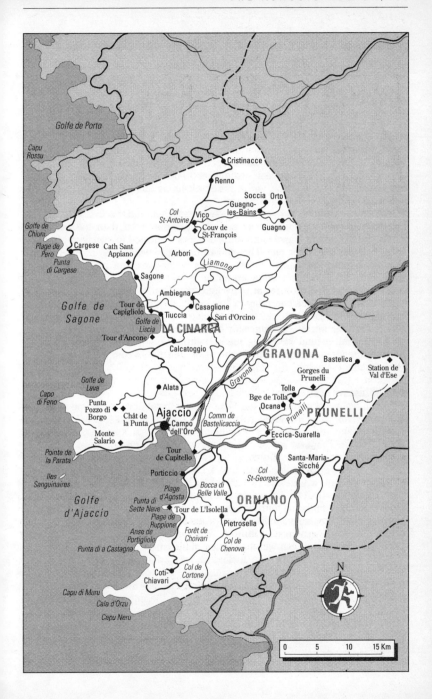

Apart from the train line to Bastia and a few long-distance bus connections, public transport in this region is confined to a few shuttle services past the holiday complexes of the Golfe d'Ajaccio.

Ajaccio

Edward Lear claimed that on a wet day it would be hard to find so dull a place as **AJACCIO** (Aiacciu), a harsh judgement with an element of justice. The town has none of Bastia's sense of purpose and can seem to lack a definitive identity of its own, as if French domination has sapped its energy. On the other hand, it's a relaxed and good-looking place, with an exceptionally mild climate, a wealth of cafés, restaurants and shops, and a more welcoming attitude to tourists than you might encounter elsewhere in Corsica.

Napoléon gave Ajaccio international fame, but though the self-designated Cité Impériale is littered with statues and street names related to the Bonaparte family, you'll find the Napoleonic cult has a less dedicated following in his home town than you might imagine. The emperor is still considered by many Ajacciens as a self-serving Frenchman rather than as a Corsican, and from time to time their disapproval is expressed in a dramatic gesture – such as painting his statue yellow, as happened a couple of years ago. Napoléon's impact on the townscape of his birthplace wasn't enormous either. Spacious squares and boulevards were laid out during Ajaccio's brief spell as island capital, but Napoléon's efforts did little to alter the intrinsic provinciality of the place, and Ajaccio remains memorable for the things that have long made it attractive – its battered old town, the pervasive scents of maquis and fresh coffee, and the encompassing view of its glorious bay.

A brief history of Ajaccio

Although it's an attractive idea that Ajax once stopped here, the name of Ajaccio in fact derives from the Roman **Adjaccium** ("place of rest"), a winter stop-off point for shepherds descending from the mountains to stock up on goods and sell their produce. This first settlement, to the north of the present town in the area called Castelvecchio, was destroyed by the Saracens in the tenth century, and modern Ajaccio grew up around the citadel that was founded in 1492 by the **Bank of Saint George**, a Genoese military organization that handled the administration of Corsica. Built to intimidate the local nobility, who had been launching regular assaults on the oppressive Genoese, the citadel was packed with Ligurian immigrants and remained off-limits to Corsican settlers for half a century.

In 1553, the Corsican patriot Sampiero Corso took control of the citadel, having sided with the French, but within six years the former rulers had returned, inaugurating a period of expansion fuelled in part by an influx of people fleeing Moorish raids on the surrounding countryside. The town's population rose from 1200 to 5000 between 1584 and 1666, a period that saw the reinforcement of the citadel, the construction of a new cathedral and the improvement of the **port**, which by 1627 was doing better trade than Bastia, at that time a far more important military and political centre. Nonetheless, the infertility of the immediate hinterland kept many Ajacciens in extreme poverty and made the town reliant on imports of Genoese olive oil and wheat, while trading restrictions imposed on the town's merchants fostered resentment among the rising bourgeoisie.

Yet when Pascal Paoli launched his first campaign for an independent republic in 1739, the Ajacciens stayed faithful to their Genoese masters. In 1796, however, the **French** finally prevailed, and the ramparts were demolished on the orders of Napoléon. In its new role as capital of Corsica, Ajaccio expanded more rapidly than ever before and maintained its economic momentum right through the nineteenth century, largely due to the success of the wine trade. Since World War II – when Ajaccio, a centre for resistance fighters, was the first Corsican town to be liberated – the tourist industry has become the most important income provider, yet Ajaccio continues to suffer from the malaise that afflicts the rest of the island, with many young people emigrating to France as soon as they leave school. It is the determination to reverse this trend that lies behind the success in elections to the Assemblée Regionale of **Corsica Nazione**, a union of politicians committed to the development of Corsica's economy and to the planning of future independence from France.

Arrival, information and accommodation

Ajaccio's **airport**, Campo dell'Oro, is 6km south of town; three buses per hour provide a shuttle service into the centre, stopping on cours Napoléon, the main street. Other buses go to the **bus station** next to the port de Commerce, a five-minute walk from the centre. **Ferries** also come in here, but the **train station** lies almost a kilometre east along boulevard Sampiero, a continuation of the port's quai l'Herminier. There are two free **car parks** flanking quai l'Herminier, close to the **tourist office** (May–Oct Mon–Fri 9am–noon & 2–6pm, Sat 9am–noon; ☎95 21 40 87) on the ground floor of the Hôtel de Ville.

For **accommodation** you'll find a dearth of cheap hotels, and a fair amount of moderate to upmarket places. All those listed are open all year round, unless specified otherwise.

Hotels

Arcade, 115 cours Napoléon (☎95 20 43 09). Modern, comfortable place with lots of rooms, 1km from town centre . ③.

Bella Vista, 20 bd Lantivy (☎95 21 07 97). Large, rather imposing place offering views of the gulf. ②.

Bonaparte, 1 rue Etienne Conti (☎95 21 44 19). Tiny rooms but friendly service. Handy for the restaurants behind the market. Closed Nov–March. ②.

Colomba, 8 av de Paris (☎95 21 12 66). Cheapest place in Ajaccio but only three rooms. Very central, opposite place de Gaulle. Third-floor reception. ①.

Le Dauphin, 11 bd Sampiero (☎95 21 12 94). Clean, impersonal place near the port. Bar downstairs straight out of a French *policier*, complete with jukebox, pinball machine and old men sipping *pastis* under a cloud of Gauloise smoke. ②.

Fesch, 7 rue Cardinal Fesch (☎95 21 50 52). The most appealing hotel in Ajaccio with sheepskin furnishings and medieval-style decor designed by Corsicada, a group of local artisans. ③.

Du Golfe, 6 bd du Roi Jerôme (☎95 21 47 64). Balconies overlooking the bay; televisions in every room; modern decor. ④.

Idéal, 97 cours Napoléon (☎95 22 17 51). Central but pretty ordinary. ③.

Kallysté, 51 cours Napoléon (☎95 51 34 45). Hotel with an international atmosphere. Rooms accommodate up to four people; also rents studios with kitchenettes and TVs. Proprietor speaks English. ③.

Marengo, 12 bd Madame Mère (☎95 21 34 45). West of centre, off bd Albert Premier. Pleasant, small hotel away from the city bustle. ③.

Napoléon, 4 rue Lorenzo Vero (☎95 21 80 40). Very plush hotel, 500m east of town centre. ⑤.

Du Palais, 5 av Beverini (☎95 23 36 42). Off cours Napoléon. Basic, dingy but central. ②.

San Carlu, 8 bd Danielle Casanova (☎95 21 13 84). Recently renovated hotel opposite the citadel, close to the beach, with own parking facilities. ③.

The Town

The core of the old town holds the most interest in Ajaccio: a cluster of ancient streets spreading north and south of **place Foch**, which opens out to the sea front by the port and the marina. Nearby **place de Gaulle** outside the old town forms the town centre, and is the source of the main thoroughfare, **cours Napoléon**, which extends parallel to the sea almost 2km to the northeast. West of place de Gaulle stretches the modern part of town fronted by the beach, overlooked at its northern end by the citadel.

Around place de Gaulle and the new town
Place de Gaulle – otherwise known as place du Diamant, after the Diamanti family who once owned much of the property in Ajaccio – is the most useful point of orientation, even if it's not much to look at, being just a windy concrete platform surrounded by a shopping complex. The only noteworthy thing on the square is the huge **bronze statue** of Napoléon at the southern end: nicknamed *l'Encrier* (the Inkstand), this pompous lump was commissioned by Napoléon III in 1865, and shows Napoléon in Roman attire, surrounded by his four brothers on horseback.

The only museum in this part of town, **A Bandera** (May–Sept Mon–Sat 10am–noon & 3–7pm; Oct–April Wed 2–6pm, Thurs & Fri 10am–noon & 2–6pm; 20F), is a short way north of the square, in rue Général Levie, behind the prefecture. Though underfunded and a bit scruffy, this small military museum has an unusually wide range and includes some fascinating stuff, most of it explained in an English guide that can be borrowed from the desk when you buy your ticket. Room one is devoted to prehistoric times, with a model of a Bronze Age settlement or *castellu* alongside bronze daggers and pottery fragments; the more interesting second room deals with the Moorish raids, displaying beautiful ivory-handled stilettos and several pictures of flamboyantly dressed corsairs. Among them is the notorious Dragut, a Moorish pirate who allied himself with the French during the campaign of 1553 when Sampiero Corso recaptured Corsica

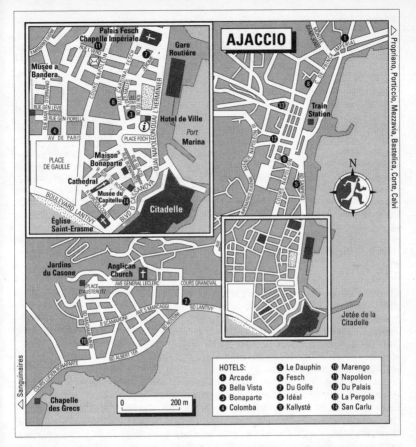

Map key:

HOTELS:

1. Arcade
2. Bella Vista
3. Bonaparte
4. Colomba
5. Le Dauphin
6. Fesch
7. Du Golfe
8. Idéal
9. Kallysté
10. Marengo
11. Napoléon
12. Du Palais
13. La Pergola
14. San Carlu

from the Genoese. The Wars of Independence are covered in room three, featuring statutes drafted by Pascal Paoli and Sir Gilbert Elliot during the Anglo-Corsican alliance of 1794–96. The last room has a section on World War II and the Corsican resistance, though the highlights are the press cutting and photos presenting the island's **bandits** as genial, popular, local heroes and showing notorious figures such as Spada hobnobbing with aristocratic ladies in forest glades.

Devotees of Napoléon should take a stroll a kilometre up cours Grandval, the wide street rising west of place de Gaulle and ending in a square, the **Jardins du Casone**, where gaudily spectacular *son et lumière* shows take place in summer. On the way you'll pass the **Assemblée Nationale**, an enormous yellow Art Deco building fronted by a jungle of palms and a couple of police vans. An impressive **monument** to Napoléon dominates the square – a replica of the statue at Napoléon's burial place, Les Invalides in Paris, standing atop a huge pedestal inscribed with the names of his battles. Behind the monument lies a graffiti-bedaubed **cave** where Napoléon is supposed to have frolicked as a child.

Place Foch

Once the site of the town's medieval gate, **place Foch** lies at the heart of old Ajaccio. A delightfully shady square sloping down to the sea and lined with cafés and restaurants, it gets its local name – place des Palmiers – from the double row of huge palms bordering the central strip. Dominating the top end, a fountain of four marble lions provides a mount for the inevitable statue of Napoléon, this one by Ajaccien sculptor Maglioli. A humbler effigy occupies a niche high on the nearest wall – a figurine of Ajaccio's patron saint, **La Madonnuccia**, her base bearing the text *Poseurunt me custodem* (they have made me their guardian). The image dates from 1656, a year in which Ajaccio's local council, fearful of infection from plague-struck Genoa, placed the town under the guardianship of the Madonna in a ceremony which took place on this spot. Ajaccio was saved on this occasion and again in 1745, when *La Madonnuccia* was paraded around the ramparts to dispel the Anglo-Sardinian fleet that was bombarding the city – whereupon the enemy beat a miraculous speedy retreat. If you're here on March 18 you can witness Ajaccio's big event, the **Fête de la Miséricorde**, which involves conveying the statue through the old town as a prelude to a big party and firework display.

Taking up the northern end of place Foch, the **Hôtel de Ville**, with its prison-like wooden doors and barred windows, was built in 1826. The first-floor **Salon Napoléonien** (Tues–Sat 10am–noon & 2–4pm; 5F) consists of two rooms that are really only for dedicated Napoléon fans. A replica of the ex-emperor's **death mask** takes pride of place in a chamber bedecked with velvet, crystal chandeliers and a solemn array of Bonaparte family portraits and busts. Next door, the smaller medal room has a batch of minor relics – a fragment from Napoléon's coffin and part of his dressing case – plus a model of the ship that brought him back from Saint Helena, and a picture of the house where he died.

South of place Foch

An archway on the south side of place Foch, standing on the former dividing line between the poor district around the port and the bourgeoisie's territory, gives access to **rue Napoléon**, the main route through the latter quarter. Built on the promontory rising to the citadel, the secluded streets in this part of town – with their dusty buildings, gambling dens and busy workshops lit by flashes of sea or sky at the end of the alleys – retain more of a sense of the old Ajaccio than anywhere else. Of the families who lived here in the eighteenth century, one of the most eminent was the **Pozzo di Borgo** clan, whose house still stands at 17 rue Bonaparte, its facade adorned by trompe l'oeil frescoes. Carlo Andrea Pozzo di Borgo was a distant cousin and childhood friend of Napoléon, but was later to become one of his bitterest enemies. A supporter of Paoli, he was elected to the Corsican legislature and became president of the Council of State under the short-lived Anglo-Corsican rule of 1794–96. Described as "a man of talent, an intriguer", Pozzo wasn't content with this domestic position and in 1803 he became the ambassador to Russia, later befriending Wellington, with whom he fought at Waterloo. He went on to become a favourite at the English court, where Queen Victoria referred to him affectionately as "Old Pozzo".

MAISON BONAPARTE

Napoléon Bonaparte was born in the colossal **Maison Bonaparte** (May–Sept Mon 2–6pm, Tues–Sat 9am–noon & 2–6pm, Sun 9am–noon; Oct–April Mon 2–6pm, Tues–Sat 10am–noon & 2–5pm, Sun 10am–noon; 20F), on place Letizia, just off the west side of rue Napoléon. The Bonaparte family first appeared in the chronicles of Ajaccio in the fifteenth century, when they lived in a house that was demolished in 1555 by the French attack on the citadel. This later residence, acquired piecemeal over the years, passed to Napoléon's father Carlo in the 1760s and here he lived, with his wife Letizia and their family, until his death. Soon after, in May 1793, Letizia and her children were driven from the house by Paoli's partisans, who stripped the place down to the floorboards. Requisitioned by the English in 1794, Maison Bonaparte became an arsenal and a lodging house for

NAPOLÉON AND CORSICA

"M. de Choisel once said that if Corsica could be pushed under the sea with a trident it should be done. He was quite right. It is nothing but an excrescence." This sentiment, expressed by Napoléon to one of the generals who had followed him into exile on St Helena, encapsulates his bitterness about his birthplace. Corsica's opinion of its most famous citizen can be equally uncomplimentary.

The year of **Napoléon's birth**, 1769, was a crucial one in the history of Corsica, for this was the year the French took over the island from the Genoese. They made a thorough job of it, crushing Paoli's troops at Ponte Nuovo and driving the Corsican leader into exile. Napoléon's father **Carlo**, a close associate of Paoli, fled the scene of the battle with his pregnant wife in order to escape the victorious French army. But Carlo's subsequent behaviour was quite different from that of his former leader – he came to terms with the French, becoming a representative of the newly styled Corsican nobility in the National Assembly, and using his contacts with the French governor to get a free education for his children.

At the age of nine Napoléon was awarded a scholarship to the Brienne military academy, an institution specially founded to teach the sons of the French nobility the responsibilities of their status. The French were anxious to impress their values on the potential leaders of a now dependent territory, and with Napoléon they certainly appear to have succeeded. Give or take a rebellious gesture or two, this son of a Corsican Italian-speaking household used his time well, leaving Brienne to enter the exclusive École Militaire in Paris. At the age of sixteen he was commissioned into the artillery. When he was twenty the Revolution broke out in Paris and the scene was set for a remarkable career.

Always an ambitious opportunist, he obtained leave from his regiment, **returned to Ajaccio**, joined the local Jacobin club and – with his eye on a colonelship in the Corsican militia – promoted enthusiastically the interests of the Revolution. However, things did not quite work out as he had planned, for Pascal Paoli had also returned to Corsica.

Carlo Bonaparte had died some years before, and Napoléon – though not the eldest son – was effectively the head of a family that had formerly given Paoli strong support. Having spent the last twenty years in London, Paoli was pro-English and had developed a profound distaste of revolutionary excesses (it was his determination to keep the guillotine out of Corsica that, as much as anything else, led him into the later failed experiment of union with Britain). Napoléon's French allegiance and his Jacobin views antagonized the older man, and his military conduct didn't enhance his standing at all. Elected second-in-command of the volunteer militia, Napoléon was involved in an unsuccessful attempt to wrest control of the citadel from Royalist sympathizers. He thus took much of the blame when, in reprisal for the killing of one of the militiamen, several people were gunned down in Ajaccio, an incident which engendered eight days of civil war. In June 1793 Napoléon and his family were chased back to the mainland by the Paolists.

Napoléon promptly renounced any special allegiance he had ever felt for Corsica. He Gallicized the spelling of his name, preferring Napoléon to his baptismal Napoleone. And although he was later to speak with nostalgia about the scents of the Corsican countryside, and to regret he did not build a grand house there, he put the city of his birth fourth on the list of places he would like to be buried.

English officers, amongst whom was Hudson Lowe, later Napoléon's jailer on Saint Helena. Though Letizia later paid for its restoration with an indemnity given to those Corsicans who had suffered at the hands of the English, her heart wasn't in the job – she left for the second and last time in 1799, the year Napoléon stayed here on his return from Egypt. Owned by the state since 1923, the house now bears few traces of the Bonaparte family's existence.

The visit begins on the second floor, but before you go up look out for the wooden sedan chair in the hallway – Letizia was carried back from church on it when the prenatal Napoléon started giving her contractions, and it's one of the very few original pieces of furniture left in the house.

Upstairs an endless display of portraits, miniatures, weapons, letters and documents gives the impression of having been formed by gathering together anything that was remotely connected with the family and unwanted by anyone else. Amongst the highlights of the first room are a few maps of Corsica dating from the eighteenth century, some deadly "vendetta" daggers and two handsome pairs of pistols belonging to Napoléon's father. The next-door Alcove Room was, according to tradition, occupied by Napoléon in 1799 when he stayed here for the last time, while in the third room you can see the sofa upon which the future emperor first saw the light of day on August 15, 1769. Adjoining the heavily restored long gallery is a tiny room known as the Trapdoor Room, whence Letizia and her children made their getaway from the marauding Paolists.

THE CATHEDRAL AND SAINT-ERASME

Napoléon was baptized in 1771 in the **Cathedral**, around the corner from Maison Bonaparte in rue Forcioli Conti. Generally known as *A Madonuccia*, the cathedral was built in 1582 on a much smaller scale than originally intended due to lack of funds – an apology for its diminutive size is inscribed in a plaque inside, on the wall to the left as you enter. The interior is interesting chiefly for a few Napoléonic connections: to the right of the door stands the font where he was dipped at the age of 23 months; Napoléon's dying words are inscribed in a plaque adorning a pillar on the left; and his sister, Elisa Baciochi, donated the great marble altar in 1811. Before you go, take a look in the chapel to the left of the altar, which houses a gloomy Delacroix painting of the Virgin.

Further down the same road stands **Saint-Erasme**, a Jesuit chapel built in 1617, then dedicated to the town's fishermen in 1815. Should you find it open, you can see inside some model ships, a statue of Saint Erasmus and a pair of wooden Christs.

MUSÉE CAPITELLU AND THE CITADELLE

A left turn at the eastern end of rue Forcioli-Conti brings you onto boulevard Danielle Casanova. Here, opposite the citadel, an elaborately carved capital marks the entrance to **Musée Capitellu** (May–Oct Mon–Wed 9am–noon & 2–6pm; 20F), a tiny museum mainly given over to offering a picture of domestic life in nineteenth-century Ajaccio. The house belonged to a wealthy Ajaccien family, the Baciochi, who were related to Napoléon through his sister's marriage, though he doesn't figure at all here.

Watercolour landscapes of Corsica line the walls of the first room, which also contains a marble *Madonuccia* whose head was cut off with a sabre during the French Revolution. Busts of Sampiero Corso, a common adornment of smart nineteenth-century households, are dotted about the second room, with some elegant copies of figures of Venus from Herculaneum. The glass display cases hold the most fascinating exhibits, however, including a rare edition of the first history of Corsica, written by Agostino Giustiniani, a bishop of the Nebbio who drowned in 1536, and the 1796 *Code Corse*, a list of laws set out by Louis XV for the newly occupied Corsica. The last room contains a bronze bust of a chubby-cheeked Pascal Paoli, and a striking painting titled *Sunrise over Bavella*, attributed to Turner's nephew.

Opposite the museum the restored **Citadelle**, a hexagonal fortress and tower stuck out on a wide promontory into the sea, is occupied by the military and usually closed to the public. Founded in the 1490s, the fort wasn't completed until the occupation of Ajaccio by Sampiero Corso and the powerful Marshall Thermes in 1553–58. The building overlooks the town beach, **Plage Saint-Francois**, a short curve of yellow sand which faces the expansive mountain-ringed bay. Several flights of steps lead down to the beach from boulevard Danielle Casanova.

To get a better view of the town, follow the waterfront back to the marina and walk to the end of the **Jetée de la Citadelle**, which juts into the sea under the shadow of the fortress.

North of place Foch

The dark narrow streets backing onto the port to the north of place Foch are Ajaccio's traditional trading ground. The main **market** takes place every morning on boulevard du roi Jerôme, an essential part of Ajaccien life which shouldn't be missed – the stalls overflow with local cheeses and *charcuterie*, and in the mornings the cafés opposite are the liveliest in town.

Behind the market the principal road leading north is **rue Cardinal Fesch**, a delightful meandering street lined with boutiques, cafés and restaurants. Halfway along the street, set back from the road behind iron gates, stands the **Palais Fesch**, home of Ajaccio's best gallery, the recently refurbished **Musée Fesch** (Mon–Fri 9am–noon & 2–6pm, Sat 9am–noon; 25F).

Cardinal Joseph Fesch, whose image in bronze presides over the courtyard, was Napoléon's step-uncle and Bishop of Lyons, a lucrative position from which he invested in large numbers of paintings, many of them looted by the French armies in Holland, Italy and Germany. A highly cultured man with an eye for a bargain, he bequeathed a thousand paintings to Ajaccio on the condition that an Academy of Arts was created in the town. His wishes were contested by Napoléon's brother Joseph, who turned a quick profit by dispersing much of the collection on the art market. Luckily for Ajaccio, however, Renaissance art was less highly regarded in those days than in later years, so many of the more valuable works remained here.

On the first floor there's an exhibition of contemporary local artists, and the second floor is devoted to seventeenth-century French and Spanish masters, Poussin among them. But it's on the third and fourth floors that you'll find the **Italian paintings** which are the chief attraction. Raphael is represented by a *Virgin and Child*, Titian by *Man Holding a Glove,* a picture charged with latent menace, and Paolo Veronese by the erotic *Leda and the Swan*. In another room, Bellini's *Virgin and Child* is rather overshadowed by an infinitely graceful treatment of the same subject by Botticelli, an early work which on its own makes the visit worthwhile.

On the top floor, huge brightly restored battle scenes form the principal exhibition, while in the basement there are loads of Napoleonic memorabilia from the first and second empires, amongst which a glittering array of gold coins holds irresistible appeal.

You'll need a separate ticket for the **Chapelle Impériale** (same hours; 10F), which stands across the courtyard from the museum. With its gloomy monochrome interior the chapel itself is unremarkable; the interest lies in the crypt which holds various members of the Bonaparte family. It was the cardinal's dying wish that all the Bonaparte family be brought together under one roof, so the chapel was built in 1857, and the bodies subsequently brought in – as recently as 1951 Charles Bonaparte was re-buried here, alongside Letizia, Cardinal Fesch and half a dozen other Bonapartes.

Lucien Bonaparte laid the first stone of the **Bibliotheque Municipale** opposite, which contains a huge collection of books on Corsica – so if you fancy doing a bit of reading up, this is the place.

Eating, drinking and nightlife

Restaurants in Ajaccio vary from basic bistros to trendy pizzerias and pricey fish restaurants, the majority of which are found in the old town. Most places compensate for unadventurous menus by an appealing location, with tables set out on the pavements in the thick of city life. **Bars** and **cafés** jostle for pavement space all over town but especially along cours Napoléon, which is generally lined with young people checking out the promenaders, and on place de Gaulle, where old-fashioned cafés and *salons du thé* offer a more sedate scene. If you fancy sipping with a view of the bay, you can go to one of the flashy cocktail bars that line the seafront beyond the citadel on boulevard Lantivy, but not surprisingly you pay a lot more for the privilege.

What **nightlife** there is in Ajaccio consists chiefly of eating and drinking, although there are two cinemas and a few trashy **discos** to cater for the tourists and the more adventurous Ajacciens. *A l'Aghjia*, 13 chemin de Biancarello, north of cours Napoléon, does occasional Corsican shows and plays.

Snacks, bars and cafés

Le Canebière, 69 cours Napoléon, opposite *Kallysté* hotel. Smart, untouristy bar, at the quiet end of the street, away from shopping crowds.

A Cantina, 18 bd du Roi Jerôme. Unpretentious place opposite the port, serving simple Corsican snacks such as *charcuterie* sandwiches and salads, as well as steaks and pasta.

Chjiami e Rispondi, 5 rue Docteur Versini. Candlelit nationalist bar; nightly Corsican cabaret and singing.

Café du Flore, 45 rue Fesch. Relaxing; good breakfasts and a young crowd.

La Grisbi, top of rue Stephanopoli, off cours Napoléon. Small and intimate; a favourite with shopping Ajacciens.

Nord Sud, 12 place de Gaulle. Elegant Art Nouveau *salon du thé*.

Bar Rade, 1 place Foch. Popular local café overlooking the boats which gets the sun in the morning.

Royal, 4 cours Napoléon. Central spot for posing.

Safari, 18 bd Lantivy. Enormous cocktail bar backing onto the beach; an evening hang-out.

Snack bar de la Jetée, Jetée de la Citadelle. Very busy bar overlooking the marina. Hamburgers and chips.

Snack La Serre, 91 cours Napoléon. Popular place, serving good-value bistro dishes and snacks.

Restaurants

Abri des Flots, 2 place Foch. Touristy, with a 1960s interior, but a good place for lunch. Mostly fish and pasta with the odd speciality of the region thrown in. Inexpensive.

L'Amor Piattu, 8 place de Gaulle. A Corsican restaurant serving refined local dishes, such as an excellent fish soup. Closed Mon. Expensive.

Le Boccaccio, 20 rue Roi de Rome. Good variety of Italian meat and pasta dishes. Moderate.

Au Bec Fin, 3 bd du Roi Jerôme. Mostly seafood but also standard French brasserie cuisine. Moderate.

Chez Vlody, 6 rue Roi de Rome. Spicy Creole food and excellent salads. Open late. Expensive.

Chez Paolo, 8 rue Roi de Rome. Lively pizzeria which does the best pizzas in town. Tables on the pavement. Moderate.

Da Mamma, passage Guingette, off bd du Roi Jerôme. Good Corsican food: roast wild boar, *canneloni al brocciu* and the like. Moderate.

L'Échoppe, 3 rue des Trois Martyrs. Very French Greek taverna. Moderate.

Le Maroukesh, 14 rue Fesch, next door to Palais Fesch. Arab cuisine in compact, bright surroundings. Does takeaways. Moderate.

Pizzeria Napoli, 3 rue Bonaparte. Tasty pizzas and regional specialities such as roast kid and Corsican lasagne. Lively place and open very late. Moderate.

A Pignata, 15 bd du Roi Jerôme. Easy-going restaurant where you can get *marcassin* (baby wild boar) in season. Also does unusual pasta dishes and illegal Eau de Vie. Moderate.

Le Point U, 30 rue Fesch. Reputedly Ajaccio's best restaurant. Serves renowned *aziminu* (Corsican fish soup) and gourmet French food. Closed Sun. Expensive.

A Spurtella, 4 rue de l'Assomption, off cours Napoléon. Basic and traditional Corsican fare. Inexpensive.

Cinemas

Empire, 18 cours Napoléon. Thirties'-style mainstream cinema.

Laetitia, 48 cours Napoléon, opposite the post office. Small place screening art house films.

Discos and clubs

Casino, 5 bd Lantivy. Flashy Europop disco. Expensive.

A Cassetta, 4 av Sebastiani. Corsican nightclub with traditional singing as well as modern music.

Pennies, 13 rue Bonaparte. Popular nightclub hidden in the old town. Good music.

Listings

Airlines *Air France*, 1 bd du Roi Jerôme (☎95 29 45 45); *Air Inter*, the airport (☎95 21 63 06).
Airport enquiries ☎95 21 07 07.
Banks All the main banks are on place de Gaulle or on cours Napoléon.
Bike rental *Leandri*, 4 rue Jean Pandolphi (☎95 76 01 49).
Bookshops *Librairie la Marge*, 7 rue Emanuelle Arène, has the best selection of books about Corsica.
Bus information ☎95 21 06 30.
Car rental *Aloha*, at the airport (☎95 20 52 00); *Avis*, 3 place de Gaulle (☎95 21 01 86); *Hertz*, 8 cours Grandval (☎95 21 70 94); *Europcar*, 16 cours Grandval (☎95 21 05 49).
Hospital *Centre Hospitalier*, av Impératrice Eugénie (☎95 29 90 90).
Laundry Bottom of rue Maréchal Ornano off cours Grandval.
Pharmacies Lots of pharmacies on place Foch and cours Napoléon.
Police 2 cours Napoléon (☎95 23 20 36).

Post office 8 cours Napoléon.
Sports facilities Swimming pool and tennis courts halfway along cours Grandval.
Taxis Taxi rank on the north side of place de Gaulle (☎95 21 00 87).
Telephones Booths in place de Gaulle.
Travel agents *Nouvelles Frontières*, 14 place Foch (☎95 20 13 69); *Ollandini*, 3 place de Gaulle (☎95 20 52 00); *Corsica vacances*, 13 rue Maréchal Ornano (☎95 21 43 39).

Around Ajaccio

The maquis-carpeted ridge of hills north of Ajaccio, known as **Les Crêtes**, holds a few interesting possibilities for a half-day excursion, provided you have your own transport. Chief of these is the **Punta di Pozzo di Borgo**, which provides an excellent view of Ajaccio and its bay and is reached by a road that takes you close to **Les Millelli**, the country residence owned, but seldom visited by, the Bonapartes. Walkers can take the gentle stroll west of town to **Monte Salario** to see the **Fontaine de Salario**, or chance the more strenuous ascent up the pink granite masses of the **Rochers des Gozzi**, a landmark in the Gravona valley northeast of town.

Les Millelli and Punta di Pozzo di Borgo

Situated 5km northwest of Ajaccio, off the D61, **Les Millelli** (9am–noon & 2–6pm; open all year, closed Tues; 5F) came into the Bonaparte family in 1797, but was used rarely. In 1793, before it came into the family, Letizia was forced to hide out here on her way to the Tour du Capitello in her flight from the Paolists, and Napoléon stayed here with Murat in 1799 on his return from Egypt – but that's about the extent of its relevance. Nonetheless it's a firmly established stage on the Napoleonic trail. It's a stolid, plain, eighteenth-century house whose real attraction is the surrounding terraced olive grove with its fine views of the gulf. Inside there's just a small and dreary ethnographical museum.

If, instead of taking the turn to Les Millelli, you go 6km farther along the D61 you'll come to the Col de Pruno, where a left turn along a narrow twisting road will bring you after another 6km to the **Punta di Pozzo di Borgo** and its ruined **chateau**. Built by the Pozzo di Borgo family in 1886, the chateau was constructed with materials provided by the demolition of the Tuileries in 1871 and is the exact reproduction of one of the pavilions of that palace – an inscription on the wall states that it was built to preserve a precious souvenir of the home country. In the nineteenth century the Pozzo di Borgo family still owned everything round here, but virtually nothing remained of their native village, which was razed by pirates in 1594; a tower on the track up to the Punta is the sole remnant. From the terrace of the chateau you get fine **views** of the gulfs of Sagone and Ajaccio, and of Monte d'Oro and Renoso to the east.

La Fontaine de Salario

It's a five-kilometre walk or drive from Ajaccio, or a ride on the #7 bus from place de Gaulle, to the **Fontaine de Salario** (or Funta Salamandra), a spring on a three-hundred-metre hill at the base of Monte Salario. Named after the salamanders that once crawled all over this part of the country, the spring offers another magnificent view of the Golfe d'Ajaccio. From here a trail leads up to **Monte Salario**, a half-hour walk, and from the summit a rocky trail known as the Chemin de la Serra leads directly back down to town.

The Rochers des Gozzi

A solid pink-tinted clump of bare rock rising from the dense maquis and culti-vated fields and vineyards northeast of Ajaccio, the **Rochers des Gozzi** provides the Ajaccio area's finest panorama of the mountains and the sea. The ten-kilometre hike should take about two and a half hours from the village of **Appietto**, 20 km from Ajaccio. From Ajaccio take the **bus** to Listincone (16km), which drops you off in the village, just by the signposted turn-off for Appietto, another 4km up a narrow road. Drivers can take the car as far as Appietto.

The track to the summit begins by Appietto's cemetery, leading initially to the church standing on the facing ridge, continuing as a goat track to the top of the ridge. Following the crest of the ridge, the track cuts through the maquis. After about 4km from the church you'll come to a fence which you can cross by means of a large boulder. Some 300m farther, climb the crumbling stone wall which runs down the ridge, then continue to the right of this wall for a few metres before you reach a rocky platform, which affords tantalizing vistas and a place to catch your breath. Heading along the right-hand branch of the path which skirts the hillside from the platform, you'll come to a faint trail which crosses the ridge over some difficult ground – follow it for 1km to another fork. Either branch will do, and you'll soon reach a trickle of a stream by a precipice facing a derelict stone building. You need to take care from now on, as you walk along the wall and scramble down into the easily visible gap which cuts across the neck of the Rochers. After a stiff climb of 485m, with deep ravines dropping on either side, you'll reach the top.

The Golfe d'Ajaccio

The liveliest spot along the southern arm of the Golfe d'Ajaccio – known as **La Rive Sud** – is **Porticcio**, the largest and most established resort along this stretch. Once a hang-out for the rich and famous, the place nowadays has lost its elitist appeal and gets swamped by watersports enthusiasts and weekenders from Ajaccio as soon as summer sets in. Quieter spots are found south of Porticcio, where the coast is less developed and the scent of the maquis takes over, the shrubland clearing at intervals to reveal superb sandy beaches such as **Plage de Verghia** and **Portigliolo**. Genoese watchtowers again feature on every headland, the most prominent being the **Tour de la Castagna** and the enormous construc-tion on **Capo di Muro**, the southernmost point of the gulf. An alternative to the coast road is the inland route from Pisciatella, crossing a series of lovely moun-tain passes surrounded by maquis and dense woodland, through the belvedere village of **Coti-Chiavari** and then down to Capo di Muro.

West of Ajaccio the **Route des Sanguinaires** (as the D111 is known) hugs the coast for 12km, passing a succession of tourist developments and sandy beaches before coming to an end at the northern tip of the gulf, the **Punta della Parata**. This headland faces the cluster of crumbling red granite islets called the **Îles Sanguinaires**, a miniature archipelago ideally seen from the sea. If you're not lucky enough to have your own boat, you can hire a little motorboat or opt for an **excursion** from Ajaccio marina, though you'll have to contend with a banal running commentary; the trip costs about 100F and lasts two hours, stopping for an hour at the largest island, Mezzo Mare. Although the **beaches** along this stretch don't rate as highly as the more secluded strands of the southern gulf, they are more accessible to those without a vehicle. Regular **buses** from place de Gaulle follow the route: buses #1 and #2 go as far as Ajaccio's cemetery, whereas #5 will take you all the way to Punta della Parata, stopping at **Barbicaja**, **Scudo** and **Terre Sacré**.

The southern gulf

Following the main road along the N193 south of Ajaccio for 8km will bring you to the junction with the D55, which follows the Rive Sud as far as Port de Chiavari, some 40km from town. A minor road continues to Punta de la Castagna. Buses along the coast depart hourly from Ajaccio's *gare routière* for Plage de Ricanto, near the airport, with hourly buses in summer going as far as Plage de Ruppione.

To reach the inland route along the southern gulf, you need to follow the N196 from Ajaccio to the airport in the direction of Porticcio, until you reach Pisciatella, where you switch to the D302. There are no buses along this route.

La Rive Sud

Four kilometres before Porticcio, the massive **Tour du Capitello** appears at the end of a short track which leads off to the right of the road across the bridge. The tower's cracks were the result of a famous siege in 1793, when Napoléon and fifty men from the French fleet were stranded waiting for backup in preparation for an attack on Ajaccio. With only one cannon to protect them from the army of Corsican patriots, they were holed up for three days. This was also the scene of Napoléon's reunion in 1793 with his mother and Cardinal Fesch, who sought refuge here after being chased out of town by Paolists before their flight to Toulon (see p.111).

PORTICCIO village basically comprises a loop of modern hotels and shops dominated by a huge shopping complex – however, the **beach** is fabulous, a wide sandy stretch commanding a great view of the gulf. Come summer the place is overwhelmed by Ajacciens in a constant stream of cars, but on the other hand there's the compensation of the lively nightlife, as the cinemas and discos get cranked up for the holidaymakers.

A small **tourist office** (daily May–June & July 8.30am–noon & 3–6.30pm; Aug 8am–noon & 3–9pm) in the shopping complex can be helpful for finding somewhere to stay. Much of the **accommodation** is aimed at rich *sportif* types, but rooms are well priced at *Hôtel de Porticcio* (☎95 25 05 77; ③) at the crossroads in the centre of the village; breakfast is included in the price, rooms are light and airy, and the hotel has its own tennis courts. Otherwise you can try *Isolella* (☎95 25 41 36; ②), 500m to the south of the village, a smaller place with balconied rooms. If you fancy splashing out go to *Le Maquis* (☎95 25 05 55; ⑤), set in a secluded cove 2km south of Porticcio and done up like a Palladian villa. For **campers** there's *Mare e Machja* (☎95 25 10 58), an open, pleasant site situated deep in the maquis up a track opposite the tourist office; the site has its own pool and pizzeria. *Camping Prunelli* (☎95 25 19 23) and *Camping Benista* (☎95 25 19 30) are other alternatives, both 1km north of the village, on opposite sides of the Ajaccio road.

Pizzeria l'Ostaria, south of the centre on the main street, is the cheapest **eating** place around and boasts a terrace with a view. Another popular joint is the very Corsican *Crêperie Marie* on the road to Ajaccio, which does inexpensive and tasty *crêpes* of every description.

BEACHES SOUTH OF PORTICCIO

South of Porticcio the D55 narrows in its progress along the coast, a high bank of maquis screening expensive villas and private beaches from the passing cars. Some 5km along you'll come to **Plage d'Agosta**, a popular, wide, sandy beach sheltered in the south by the Punta di Sette Nave, a narrow, rocky headland crowned by the Tour de l'Isolella. A couple of hotels here are worth checking out: *Agosta Plage* (☎95 25 46 76; ②) overlooks the beach, while *L'Isolella* (☎95 25 56 89; ③) has a good restaurant.

By far the finest beach along this stretch and a less frenetic spot than Plage d'Agosta lies 2km to the south at **Plage de Ruppione**, a half-moon-shaped cove – perfect for sheltered swimming and snorkelling. Campers can stay here at the well-sited *Camping le Sud* (☎95 25 40 51), one of the less expensive campsites along this coast.

From here onwards the coast becomes gloriously rural, with folds of woodland backing onto tapering rocky headlands and golden coves. At **PORT DE CHIAVARI**, some 5km south of Ruppione, the beautiful **Plage de Verghia** has a makeshift bar and a **campsite**, *La Vallée* (☎95 25 44 66), set back from the main road close to the beach. At this point the D55 narrows and turns sharply inland towards Côti-Chiavari. The road ahead deteriorates on the approach to the **Anse de Portigliolo**, a delightful, almost circular sandy cove overlooked by the *Celine* hotel (☎95 25 43 78; ②), the only base for this part of the coast. Beyond here the road climbs and crumbles as it gets nearer to the **Tour de la Castagna**, a great Genoese tower on the promontory jutting into the gulf. Camping wild is possible beyond the Punta di a Castagna.

A WALK IN THE FORÊT DE CHIAVARI

From the Plage de Verghia it's a gentle climb into the **Forêt de Chiavari**, a dense mass of eucalyptus, maquis, oaks and cork trees shrouding the slopes above the beach. The more or less circular walk described below should take about three hours, covering a distance of 16km.

Just before the D55 veers inland a wide forest track signposted "Forêt Domaniale de Chiavari" strikes up through the trees. Pass the picnic tables and ignore the first track to the right, taking instead the right track at a junction 500m ahead. After 2km you'll pass a graveyard; 200m beyond here, continue straight at the junction where the path broadens into an avenue of eucalyptus trees. You will hit the D55 after another 1km; at this point you re-enter the forest along the track above the road, heading back in the direction you came, then pass through a fence, snatching views of Ajaccio and the gulf through the trees. After another 3km a break in vegetation affords views over the Port de Chiavari, with the Punta di Sette Nave to the north. Great rocks piercing the maquis-shrouded hills characterize the surrounding landscape. Heads towards the open valley, crossing the stream twice before you reach the ruins of a penitentiary hidden amongst the trees. Once used to house convicts serving sentences of hard labour (many of them buried in the overgrown graveyard), it's now a shell of ghostly passageways and dark cellars.

Behind the building take the left fork downwards, past a drinking fountain, then left at the next fork. The track narrows in its descent to the coast but provides expansive views over the bay. After 6km cross a stone wall and you'll soon reach an intersection; carry on straight, skirting round the wood of gnarled eucalyptus. Ignore the right fork and carry on until a junction, where you must bear left down the track through vines and lavender-carpeted ground. You'll hit the D55 by Ruppione beach, 5km north of where you began.

The inland route

Some 10km from Pisciatella, the **Col de Bellevalle** (522m) opens out with views of Ajaccio and the Sanguinaires laid out to the west. The right fork here will take you more directly to the Chiavari forest, but to get the most out of the landscape, take the left fork, in the direction of Bisinao. This latter road twists through a dark rocky gorge, giving a great view of the Punta di Sette Nave, before reaching the **Col d'Aja Bastiano** (638m). At this point the D55 cuts south up a gentle gradient amidst heavy scrubland of broom, mimosa, gorse and wild thyme, a mixture known as the *maquis dense*. Some 4km ahead, the **Col de Chenova** (629m) offers more expansive views, then the continuation of the D55 will bring you into the eucalyptus-lined route shouldering the **Forêt de Chiavari**.

The **Col de Cortone** (523m) lies towards the southern edge of the forest, and from here it's a short way to **CÔTI-CHIAVARI**, a pretty orange stone village overlooking the Golfe d'Ajaccio. You can **stay** here at the *Hôtel Belvédère*, a family house at the north end of the village (☎95 27 10 32; ②); it does excellent home cooking, served on a terrace overlooking the sea, and has a loyal following – so make sure you book ahead if you want to stay. Several people rent out apartments and rooms in the village; the *Belvédère* can point you in the right direction.

North of the village a road favoured by practising rally drivers hairpins down to Port de Chiavari, while the D55 continues deeper into the headland. About 4km along the D55, a narrow track leading off to the right will take you almost as far as **Capo di Muro**, where a watchtower marks the southern limit of the Golfe d'Ajaccio. There's a good **beach** here called **Cala d'Orzu**, accessible along one of four rocky paths which branch off the track as it peters out. In summer you should try the **restaurant** on the beach, *Chez Francis*, which serves fresh fish from the gulf.

Route des Sanguinaires

The first landmark along the coast north of Ajaccio, the **Chapelle des Grecs**, lies 3km along the route. Built in 1632 by Artilio Pozzo di Borgo, it was allocated for the use of the Greeks in 1733, who settled in Ajaccio after being driven out of their small colony at Paomia by Corsican rebels (see p.125) and forced to take refuge here.

The beaches start beyond the cemetery, starting about 1km along at **Barbicaja**, a usually crowded sandy stretch providing adequate swimming. **Marinella**, another 2km on, is the next beach and the most popular, backed by bars and restaurants. About 4km further, **Terre Sacré** gets its name from the metre-high stone urn, containing the ashes of soldiers killed in World War I, that stands on the beach. This stretch is quieter and an excellent restaurant, the *Auberge du Terre Sacré*, backs onto the sand. **Cala Lunga** is the last strand which leads up to **Punta della Parata**, the narrow, rocky headland that was once connected to the Îles Sanguinaires. Tremendous views of the gulf make it worth the twenty-minute clamber up to the **Tour de la Parata**, a tall Genoese construction built in the sixteenth century to ward off Moorish pirates.

Îles Sanguinaires

Composed of four humps of red granite, the **Îles Sanguinaires** might be named after Sagone or after *Sagonarri* (black blood), from the colour they turn at sunset. A protected site, the islands harbour large colonies of gulls, and it's forbidden to pick flowers or take eggs from the land.

WALK TO CAPO DI FENO FROM PUNTA DELLA PARATA

A good way to see the westernmost point of the Golfe de Sagone is to do the walk north of Parata along the coast as far as **Capo di Feno**, a route that also has the attraction of giving access to some fine beaches. The distance of 15km should take about four hours; it's an easy walk but there is quite thick maquis to plough through, so you'll need strong shoes and covered legs.

Start by the restaurant that faces the tower, from where a broad path leads into the maquis, skirting round a deep cove with a rifle range to your right. Follow the track uphill, passing through a fence before you reach a wider path where you should go left. Cross a low ridge, passing another rocky inlet below: a track on the left goes down to the sea, the broader path going on to Capo di Feno, which emerges ahead after a few metres. Continue along the coast for about 2km, when you'll start to descend through thick maquis, emerging onto a track above the white sandy cove at **Capigliolo**. Beyond the next cove a clear path leads to the **Anse de Minaccia**, a nudist beach. Pass the bar and after 1km you'll see a fence blocking the way: Go under it, following the path through more scrub onto another track. After another 1km you'll come to a glade shaded by pines and mimosa. Pass a house and fork left, continuing as far as a T-junction and a fence. Go through the gate or climb over and continue straight until you join the main trail to Capo di Feno. Follow the descent into a secluded cove before picking up the trail again at the end of the beach, where a view of Capo di Feno emerges with a Genoese watchtower crowning the promontory.

The largest islet, called **Mezzo Mare** (or Grande Sanguinaire) is topped by a lighthouse, where Alphonse Daudet was inspired to write one of his *Lettres de Mon Moulin*, in which he waxed lyrical about the islet's "reddish and fierce aspect". Tufts of gorse, a ruined tower and crashing surf give the place a dramatic air, which is perhaps why Joseph Bonaparte wanted to be buried here, although his wish wasn't carried out.

The Cinarca

Contained within mountains approaching 1000m high to the north and south, the **Cinarca** forms the hinterland to the Golfe de Sagone north of Ajaccio. Once the seat of the powerful Cinarchesi, a family of corrupt self-titled nobles who ruled the country in the thirteenth century, the region is today renowned for its *appellation controlée* wine, produced near the banks of the River Liscia, in a cluster of sleepy villages along the **Route des Vins**. A tour of the Cinarca can easily be made in about two hours, passing through **Calcatoggio** en route to the chief village of the region, **Sari d'Orcino**, an appealing little place set deep in the verdant countryside, continuing through the villages of **Casaglione** and **Ambiegna** before returning to the coast road.

The villages

Just 2km from the main D81, just over 20km north of Ajaccio, **CALCATOGGIO**'s bleached houses rise from a jungle of vineyards and orchards, creating a scene that's typical of the Cinarca. The terraced hillside location gives a pleasant view of the azure Golfe de la Liscia, and there are more marvellous views if you continue for about 1km beyond the village and then turn right along the D101, descending to the sinuous corniche of the lush Liscia valley.

Passing through Sant'Andrea d'Orcino and Canelle, two villages nestled close together amidst vines and fig trees, the road threads its way up to **SARI D'ORCINO**, a village composed of two hamlets stacked up the slopes of Punta San Damiano. In the second, Acqua in Giu, the parish church's terrace gives a panorama of the whole of the Cinarca, its green carpet of fruit trees sliced by the river, which you can see flowing into the Golfe de la Liscia. Just beyond the village, you can stop and **taste wine** at the *Clos d'Alzeto*, owned by Pascal Albertini (☎95 52 24 67).

North of Sari d'Orcino the D1 skirts a high rocky wall for 3km as far as **AMBIEGNA**, an elegant village bordering the Liamone valley and a soaring pine wood. Head south from here along the D25 for 3km to **CASAGLIONE**, an ancient cluster of silvery stone buildings grouped around a church which houses a painting of the Crucifixion dated 1505. From here it's a gentle meander back down to the coast.

GIUDICE DELLA CINARCA

The medieval **Cinarchesi**, a loose association of feudal lords, many of them distantly related, controlled wide tracts of the wilder southern half of Corsica, maintaining an especially tight grip on the Cinarca region. The most famous of these chieftains was Sinucello della Rocca, better known as **Giudice della Cinarca**, described by fifteenth-century historian Giovanni della Grossa as "one of the most extraordinary men who has ever existed on the island".

Born in Olmeto in 1219, Giudice began his career allied to the Genoese, but he refused to give up his feudal rights and become a vassal to the republic. Constantly battling against the rival Cinarchesi from his base in the castle of Istria, he managed to gain effective control of the whole of the south of the island before the Genoese had him chased out of Corsica. Thereupon Giudice took up the Pisan cause, distinguishing himself at the battle of Meloria in 1284, the naval engagement that was Pisa's downfall. After that he returned to the mountain fastnesses of Corsica to resume his war on Genoa and his neighbouring warlords.

It was during this period that Giudice (meaning "judge" or "governor") set himself up as a figure of public authority, arbitrating vendettas, forcing the rich to pay high taxes, and punishing wrongdoers and enemies with extreme brutality – blinding his adversaries was a favoured tactic. He consolidated his position by allowing a greater degree of freedom to the burgeoning peasant bourgeoisie than was accorded by other Cinarchesi tyrants, and married off his six daughters to local counts to ensure the continuation of his power. In 1289 and 1290 the Genoese launched two massive and unsuccessful attempts to overthrow Giudice, who by this time was nearly blinded by venereal disease, yet he was only captured when betrayed by one of his many illegitimate sons. Thrown into a common prison, he died in 1307.

The Golfe de Sagone

Long stretches of sandy beach characterize Corsica's largest gulf, the **Golfe de Sagone**, which stretches forty kilometres from Capo di Feno up to the Punta di Cargèse. The gulf lacks the wild allure of much of the west coast, with new holiday villages, bungalows and campsites springing into existence every year, but on the plus side there's a glut of bargain accommodation in the high season, and the resorts make acceptable bases for a few days if you have your own transport. Tucked into the **Golfe de la Liscia** at the easternmost indent of the gulf, the resort of **Tiuccia** is the most sheltered spot, with a fine golden **beach** close by. North of here, **Sagone** thrives as a centre for scuba diving and watersports, but it can't match the appeal of **Cargèse**, a lovely and increasingly chic clifftop village at the northern tip of the bay.

Tiuccia and Sagone

Once the D81 hits the coast, the first concentration of hotels and campsites can be found at **TIUCCIA**, some 25km north of Ajaccio at the northern end of the Golfe de la Liscia, a half-moon bay set within the Golfe de Sagone. Consisting chiefly of a line of modern buildings bordering the main road, Tiuccia has a trio of minor historic sights – two seventeenth-century Genoese watchtowers and the ruined **Castello di Capraja**, seat of Giudice della Cinarca – but its strong point is the **Plage de la Liscia**, a broad golden strand which lies 500m to the south.

Tourist information is handled by *Hôtel Cinarca* on the main street (☎95 52 21 39; ③), where the rooms afford a good view of the bay. You'll find the least expensive bed at *Les Flots Bleus* (☎95 52 21 65; ②), just south of the centre, a comfortable hotel with a garden sloping down to the sea. Other options include *Chez André* (☎95 52 21 12; ④), 200m north of the above, which has a huge terrace and restaurant, and *Le Beau Rivage* at the centre of the village (☎95 52 21 09; ②). **Buses** from Ajaccio stop next to the **campsite** by the main road just outside the village.

The next significant place along this stretch is **SAGONE**, formerly a bishopric and important fishing port until marauding Saracens destroyed the town in the sixteenth century. The only evidence of Sagone's past glory is the cathedral of **Sant'Appiano**, a crumbling ruin dating from the twelfth century sited a kilometre north of the village.

The village itself is a string of tired-looking hotels and restaurants, slightly redeemed by the **Plage du Liamone**, a long sandy beach to the north of the resort. Despite its minimal charm, Sagone gets pretty crowded in the high season, principally on account of the watersports facilities offered along the beach. The **tourist office**, in *Immeubles les Mimosas* at the centre of the village, can help you find somewhere to stay. *La Marine*, on the left of the road to Ajaccio, just beyond the village (☎95 28 00 09; ②), has a terrace jutting into the sea which gives it the edge on other **hotels** in the vicinity. *Hôtel Cyrnos*, next door to *Immeubles les Mimosas* (☎95 28 00 01; ③), is functional but nothing special – it is, however, the base for the *Centre Subaquatique* (☎95 28 00 01). Otherwise there's *A Rena d'Oru* (☎95 28 00 09; ③), 1km south of town on the quieter beach at Esigna, or *Funtanella*, 2km along the road to Cargèse (☎95 28 02 49; ③), which is shady and secluded but doesn't have a restaurant. The best **campsite** in the area, *Camping Sagone* (☎95 28 03 44), lies 3km inland on the road to Vico; offering riding, tennis and underwater fishing, it's not too expensive and the people are friendly.

Eating in Sagone isn't recommended; instead try *Chez Diane* on Plage d'Orcino, 1km south at Esigna, for an outstanding meal of superior Corsican and Mediterranean food – excellent value with menus at 95F.

Cargèse

Sitting high above a deep blue bay on a cliff scattered with olive trees, **CARGÈSE** (Carghjese) oozes a lazy charm that attracts hundreds of well-heeled summer residents to its pretty white houses and hotels, giving the place an air of an exclusive holiday resort. The full-time locals, many of them descendants of Greek refugees from the Peloponnese in the seventeenth century (see box opposite), seem to accept this inundation and the proximity of a Club Med complex with generous nonchalance, but the best time to visit is September, when Cargèse empties and you can enjoy its distinctive qualities in peace.

Two **churches** stand on separate hummocks at the heart of the village, one Catholic and one Orthodox, a reminder of the old antagonism between the two cultures. The **Greek** church, the more interesting of the two, is a large granite neo-Gothic edifice built in 1852 to replace a church that had become too small for the congregation. Inside, the outstanding feature is the **iconostasis**, a gift from a monastery in Rome, decorated with **icons** brought over from Greece with the original settlers in the late seventeenth century – the graceful *Virgin and Child* is thought to date from as far back as the twelfth century. The icons are currently being restored by a team of European fresco painters who are also working on new frescoes for the walls, giving the church a rather too vibrant look.

Built for the minority Corsican families in 1828, the **Catholic church** is one the latest examples of Baroque in Corsica and has a trompe l'oeil ceiling that can't really compete with the view from the church's terrace.

You can swim off the rocks beneath the hotel *Bel Mare* (see below), if you climb down the cliff through the gate just past the hotel. The nearest beach, **Plage de Pero**, is 2km north of Cargèse – walk up to the junction with the Piana road and take the left fork down to the sea. Overlooked by a Genoese tower, this white stretch of sand is the best beach in the area, and has a couple of bars. **Plage du Chiuni**, a further 2km along the same road, is much busier thanks to its windsurfing facilities and the presence of Club Med. A more secluded spot lies a kilometre south of the village at **Plage du Monachi**; this small, sandy cove is reached by climbing down the track at the side of the road past the little chapel on the cliff side.

Practicalities

There's an unusually helpful **tourist office** (Mon–Fri 9am–noon & 3–6pm) on rue Docteur-Dragacci which can provide you with a map of the area and will help you find accommodation; it also sells tickets for the **boat trips** up to the Calanches (see p.99), leaving at 9am daily in summer and costing about 150F for the day.

All the best **hotels** are located within minutes of the centre, with the budget places at the top end of the village. *Hôtel de France* (☎95 26 41 07; ①), the large white building on the northern edge of the village, offers discounts in the autumn, while the *Continental*, on the left as you descend into the main square (☎95 26 42 24; ①), looks a bit dark but is comfortable enough. Slightly more expensive, the *Bel Mare*, about two minutes' walk along the road to Ajaccio (☎95 26 40 13; ②), is an old-fashioned place full of character with a wide terrace bar extending over the cliff; all the rooms have balconies but try and get one in the annexe, where views of the sea are breathtaking. Otherwise there's *La Cyrnée* in the main square (☎95 26 40 03; ②), and opposite the *Bel Mare* there's *La Spelunca* (☎95 26 40 12; ③), a modern block with big rooms overlooking the bay. If you'd rather be by the beach, try the *Thalassa* on Plage de Pero (☎95 26 40 08; ④), an intimate little place with friendly owners. There is also a **campsite** on Plage de Pero.

There are a fair number of **restaurants** scattered about the village, as well as the standard pizzerias. *A Volta*, next to the Catholic church, offers an interesting menu, serving game and stuffed pasta on a spectacular terrace jutting out over the sea. The bizarre *Restaurant/Bar Le Select* in rue Dragacci is worth a visit for its fairy lights and accordion music; the food is mainly inexpensive French bistro food, plus pizzas until they run out of dough in the early evening. Down in the marina, *Chez Antoine* does a good *bouillabaisse* and other fish dishes; it's more expensive than the previous places but well worth the cost. For a **drink** go no further than the main square, where you can watch all the action from *Bar Des Amis*, which has a pool table, or *Bar Chantilly*, which commands the best vantage point.

Change money at the **post office**, set back from the road in the main square, rather than in the banks on the Piana road. **Buses** for Ajaccio and Porto stop outside the building every day at 2pm.

THE GREEKS OF CARGÈSE

A thousand **Greek settlers** originally landed on Corsica in 1676, after a deal was struck between the Genoese and the citizens of Zitylos in the Turkish-occupied southern Peloponnese. As part of a Genoese plan to weaken Corsican resistance by colonizing the island with different nationalities, the deal involved the payment of a large sum of money in return for guaranteed protection from any hostile Corsicans who may object to their presence. The Greeks were allowed to maintain their own customs, including their Orthodox religion (although they had to recognize the supremacy of the pope), but were forced to Italianize their surnames: thus Papadakis and Dragakis became Papadacci and Dragacci, two prominent names in the village today.

The first settlement was 4km northeast of Cargèse at a place they called **Paomia**. Within a year they had built five hamlets, proving so successful as farmers that they began to incur the wrath of the locals, who resented Genoa's patronage. Peace came to an abrupt end in 1729, when Paomia was ransacked by Corsican patriots enraged by the Greeks' refusal to take up arms against their Genoese benefactors. After much bloodshed, the Greeks were forced to take refuge in Ajaccio, where they remained for forty years until the arrival of the French brought temporary peace to the island.

Their deliverance came in the form of a **Count Marbeuf**, an ambitious French nobleman who in 1773 attempted to integrate the communities by forming a united regiment of Greeks and Corsicans, and offered the Greeks Cargèse as compensation for the loss of Paomia. Unfortunately, the building of 120 family houses and a castle for Marbeuf again provoked the locals, who in the same year descended from the hills to burn the castle and drive the Greeks into hiding in the towers of Plage de Pero. In 1793 the Greeks were attacked once more; their village was burnt to the ground and they had to flee to Ajaccio. Four years later, only two-thirds chose to return. Gradually the Corsicans came to join them in their reconstructed village, marking the beginning of an uneasy coexistence which, largely through intermarriage, eventually led to integration. In the nineteenth century the Corsicans built their own church, after which the Greeks built one opposite and adopted some Catholic rites, as a gesture towards integration.

There are still three hundred Greek families in Cargèse, well assimilated into the Corsican way of life but still observing the Greek liturgy and conducting weddings in the traditional Greek style, with the bride and groom crowned with vine leaves and olive branches. Also distinctively Greek are the festival of Saint Spiridion on December 12, when fireworks light up the village, and the Easter Monday blessing of the village, when all the women dress in black, the lights in the village are extinguished and the villagers form a candlelit procession to the church.

Vico and around

Vico, a dismal outpost in one of the remoter parts of Corsica, lies crouched in the mountains 15km northeast of Sagone. Although there's not much to recommend the place itself, its single hotel is an ideal base for drives into the surrounding granite peaks. Close by you can visit the **Couvent Saint Francois** on the way to the beautifully wild **Gorges du Liamone**, which extend to the south of the village. To the north the **Col de Sevi** provides unrivalled views across the mountains, or you can strike eastwards and visit the thermal springs at **Guagno-le-Bains**. Intrepid drivers can venture further up this way to the dramatically situated hamlets of **Soccia** and **Orto**, perched on a ledge in front of the crags of Monte Sant'Eliseo.

The only public transport in this region is the daily **bus** from Ajaccio to Evisa (see p.130) via Vico and the Col de Sevi.

Vico and the Gorges du Liamone

Dominated by the dome of La Sposata, **VICO** lies at a crossroads amidst a high wooded valley, remaining invisible until the final approach. It's a place with a tough ambience that's heightened by the tall dark houses and cold mountain air, but it does have the only **hotel** hereabouts, *U Paradisu*, on the outskirts of town along the road to Arbori (☎95 26 61 62; ②). Its rooms are spartan, but it does good Corsican mountain food.

For two hundred years Vico was the residence of the bishops of Sagone after their settlement was destroyed by the Saracens in the tenth century. It went on to become the seat of the da Leca clan, a Cinarchesi family who ruled the district in the fifteenth century. One day in 1456 twenty-three members of this rebel family were put to death by the Genoese governor Spinola, who had their throats cut out on the slopes east of town, where they were left to die a lonely death. Gian' Paolo da Leca escaped this massacre and in 1481 founded the only surviving remnant of Vico's past – **Couvent Saint-Francois**, a great white building encircled by vivid green woods and gardens 1km along the road to Arbori. The seventeenth-century church (daily 2–6pm) is worth a look chiefly for the carved **chestnut furniture** in the sacristy and the fifteenth-century wooden figure of Christ above the altar, thought to be the oldest in Corsica.

South of the convent the D1 follows the River Liamone for 7km through the **Gorges du Liamone**, a gloriously remote landscape of sweeping valleys shrouded in chestnut trees, framed by shadowy ridges covered in patches of deep maquis. Wild pigs roam the route as far as **ARBORI**, an exquisite village of russet buildings strung out on a ledge jutting into the valley. Unless you want to continue down to the Cinarca, this is a good point to turn back.

Col de Sevi

Aside from the obvious draw of the mountain views, a drive up to the **Col de Sevi** gives you an unadulterated taste of the rural Corsican way of life. By regaining the D70 north of Vico, you'll start the ascent along a high maquis-clad ridge. A detour 5km along will bring you to the apple-growing village of **RENNO**, spectacularly set amidst swathes of orchards and chestnut trees – be sure to taste the marvellous pippins that are sold in summer along the roadside. At first sight solely populated by pigs and chickens, the village hosts the annual **Saint-Roch** fair (August 16–18), a traditional country jamboree which involves selling livestock, honey and chestnut-related products, as well as the usual pastis-imbibing.

Back on the D70 it's not far up to the **Col de Sevi** (1110m), the pass which links the Liamone basin with the Porto valley. From up here there's a tremendous **vista**, but for an even better view of the Golfe de Porto you can walk up to a spot called **L'Incinosa**, an easy-going two-hour stroll there and back – just follow the path to the right of the road for 4km along the ridge until you reach the top.

After the Col de Sevi, the road continues to rise for 1km before descending into the valley on the approach to Evisa.

Guagno-les-Bains, Soccia and Orto

A tedious winding route east of Vico passes goat enclosures and muddy green countryside before coming to **GUAGNO-LES-BAINS**, 12km along the D23. A couple of hot springs were first exploited here in the eighteenth century, when illustrious personages such as Pascal Paoli made the trip by mule to take a thermal bath. The spa reopened quite recently and is open from May to October.

Just beyond Guagno-les-Bains, a left turn up the unsignposted D123 to Poggiolo and a left again will bring you to **SOCCIA**, where the *U Paese* (☎95 28 31 92; ②) provides half-board **accommodation** for hikers attempting the Lac de Creno. Perched on a high mountain shelf across the valley, **ORTO** is also only accessible from Poggiolo, from where a pitted track squirms up to the village. The attraction here is the forbidding proximity of Monte Sant'Elisio. Only masochists would take the road from Guagno-les-Bains to Guagno, 9km to the east.

The Gorges du Prunelli

A drive up through the **Gorges du Prunelli** provides an easy but immensely varied excursion inland from Ajaccio, as the landscapes change dramatically from gardens and orchards to the bare jagged granite of the gorges themselves. Two roads climb the opposite flanks of the valley for 20km before converging on the run-up to **Bastelica**, a mountain village equipped with restaurants and hotels and providing access to the ski station on **Plateau d'Èse**. The road on the north side of the valley, the D3, passes through the villages of **Bastelicaccia** and **Ocana** on its way to the dam at **Tolla**, where the road becomes increasingly hair-raising. To view the gorges from the other side, you can descend from Bastelica along the D27 via the **Col de Crichetto** and the attractive village of **Cauro**. The first route affords the best views, while the second is more easily negotiable by car; no public transport reaches these parts.

Bastelicaccia to Tolla

Fully cultivated since the nineteenth century in order to feed the growing population of Ajaccio, the plain around **BASTELICACCIA** has an air of cornucopian opulence, with its overflowing orchards of orange and lemon trees mingled with flower gardens and deep maquis. This is among the most pleasant places to stay within a short radius of Ajaccio, and one of the best local hotels is *L'Orangeraie* (☎95 20 00 09; ③), situated 1km beyond the village amidst an orchard and a garden of palms; in addition to rooms, you can rent studios here by the night or the week. Another good place is *Le Vieux Chêne*, 2km up the D303 in the hamlet of Boccacina (☎95 20 00 13; ③), a modern place where all rooms have terraces in a garden overlooking the Golfe d'Ajaccio. *Les Amandiers*, on the main road past the village on the right (☎95 20 02 18; ③), just before the *Orangeraie*, offers seclusion in a sea of eucalyptus and bougainvillea.

Beyond Bastelicaccia the road threads through the maquis alongside the River Prunelli, past hordes of roaming wild pigs. Some 10km along you'll come to **OCANA**, a tiny village set in a small valley beneath a belt of fig trees, olive trees and cactus. Here they make *brocciu*, a milky cheese you'll find on sale in the market in Ajaccio – hence the abundant herds of ewes.

Beyond Ocana the scenery undergoes a dramatic change, as high rock walls and pointed granite teeth begin to emerge from the greenery. After 2km you'll see **TOLLA**, a pretty village strung out on a ridge overlooking an immense reservoir of the **Lac de Tolla**. Trees abound; a bank of apple, walnut and chestnut orchards overhangs the valley in the approach to Tolla. Before you reach the village you can stop at the **Col de Mercuju** (716m) dominated by two great pyramids of rock rising from the circular hollow of the gorges. At the col a Corsican **restaurant**, *Chez Baptiste*, is set back from the road and overlooks the gorges. Opposite the restaurant a path leads down to a platform above the dam, affording an impressive view across the lake.

Tolla itself is a lively place in summer, popular with Ajacciens who, returning to visit the family home, flock to the open-air pizzeria at the entrance to the village on the left. Unless you know someone, the only place to stay is a well-placed **campsite** down by the lake, *A Selva* (☎95 27 00 28), which also offers tasty Corsican cooking.

Once past Tolla the landscape continues to be wild – rocky walls strewn with high maquis border the road, overlooked by the ragged crest of Punta di Forca d'Olmu to the south. After the roads converge it's only a short ascent of 4km up to Bastelica.

Bastelica and Plateau d'Èse

Set at 800m on the lower slopes of Monte Renoso, **BASTELICA** is a stark and unusually unprepossessing spot with a few rows of cold granite houses and an ugly modern church. It attracts a fair number of visitors, however, partly because it's close to the **Val d'Èse** ski station, and partly because it is the birthplace of Sampiero Corso (see box opposite), whose statue, dating from the 1890s, stands in the village centre. To visit the spot where Sampiero was born, walk up the road north of the church into the adjoining hamlet of Dominicacci. The original house was burnt down by the Genoese in 1554. The facade of its replacement (1855) is adorned with an inscription that extolls "the most Corsican of Corsicans, a famous hero amongst the innumerable heroes that love of the country, superb mother of male virtues, has nursed in these mountains and torrents".

Bastelica has a couple of **hotels** open in summer, both situated a little out of town: *U Castagnettu*, past Sampiero's birthplace 1km north of the church (☎95 28 70 71; ②), and *Chez Paul*, 200m further along the same road (☎95 28 46 78; ③), which also rents small apartments and boasts an excellent restaurant. *Le Sampiero*, a large modern building 500m on the road to Plateau d'Èse, is open in winter and caters mainly for skiers (☎95 28 71 99; ③). The *U Pullonu* pizzeria, 50m east of the church, past the statue, is a good place to have lunch.

The narrow D27a south of Bastelica offers astounding views of the mountains as it rises to **Plateau d'Èse** and the basic Val D'Èse **ski station**, 10km from Bastelica at the end of the road.

SAMPIERO CORSO

"The most Corsican of Corsicans", **Sampiero Corso** was born into a peasant family in 1498 and first took up arms in 1517, when he entered the service of the Medici as a mercenary – a career followed by many of his poorer compatriots. Gaining himself a reputation for audicious ambition – he is said to have put forward a plan to assassinate Charles V in 1536 – he arrived in France in the company of Catherine de'Medici, and went on to distinguish himself in several campaigns, becoming renowned as the most valiant captain in the French army. At Perpignan in 1543 he saved the life of the future Henry II, husband of Catherine de' Medici, thereby ensuring his promotion in 1547 to colonel of the Corsican infantry. He returned to Corsica a proud and popular figure, and promptly married a young noblewoman named Vannina d'Ornano. The match was not approved by her brothers, who saw their inheritance about to slip from their fingers – and their enmity was to have dire consequences.

Around this time the Genoese, suspicious of Sampiero's prestige, decided to lock him up for a spell, accusing him of having plotted an uprising against the republic. Their action engendered a hatred of Genoa which Sampiero was to hold for the rest of his days. It was the French declaration of war against Genoa in 1553, and their attempt to "liberate" Corsica from the despotic republic, which established Sampiero's legendary status. Setting out with Marshal Thermes and an expeditionary force of 7000 mercenaries, amongst them a Turkish contingent led by the notorious Dragut, he managed a rapid takeover of Bastia, Ajaccio and Corte. Bonifacio and Calvi weren't such an easy proposition, however, being populated primarily by Ligurian settlers and thus more firmly entrenched as Genoese strongholds. Long and relentless sieges ensued, with Turkish ships ruthlessly bombarding the towns in a prelude to massacre and pillage.

The subsequent Genoese alliance with the Spanish resulted in Sampiero's return to the continent in 1557, and two years later the treaty of Cateau-Cambresis gave Corsica back to Genoa. Sampiero passionately wanted independence for Corsica, but could not command the backing of France after murdering his wife in Aix-en-Provence, suspecting her of infidelity and collusion with the Genoese. Escaping with some of her fortune, he returned to Corsica in 1564 to organize another revolt. Quickly he took over much of the island's interior but failed to take the ports, and enthusiasm for his cause soon diminished, a process doubtless hastened by the 2000-ducat price the Genoese put on his head. In 1567 Sampiero was decapitated in an ambush near Bastelica, a murder engineered by the Ornano brothers, who had never forgotten their grudge. His head was impaled on the town gate of Ajaccio, a warning to would-be rebels that ensured his martyr's status.

Bastelica to Cauro

On the way back down the main D27, there's the option of turning off the road 4km south of Bastelica to follow a parallel road which gives a stunning view of the gorges. If you're in a sturdy vehicle, you could take the rough mountain track that branches off just before this junction at the **Col de Menta** (762m) and that runs parallel to the D27, merging with it at the **Col de Cricheto**. This route offers even better views of the crags, but it should only be attempted by sturdy vehicles. The D27 is bordered by the **Forêt de Pineta**; a carpet of laricio pines, chestnut and beech trees makes a good place to have a picnic. From the *maison forestière*, 3km along the same road, it's a ten-minute marked walk to the **Pont de Zipitoli**, a single arc of Genoese stone spanning the River Èse.

After regaining the D27 at the **Col de Marcuggio** (670m), you descend through an increasingly pastoral terrain of verdant vineyards interspersed by fields and folds of woodland. About 6km along from the col, just before the hamlet of Radicale, a bridge on a sharp left bend marks the start of a fifteen-minute trail to the **Cascade de Sant'Alberto**, a high waterfall hidden amidst the forest. **CAURO**, a pleasant but unremarkable village at the junction of the D27 and N169, has a good **hotel** – *Sampiero*, in the centre opposite the post office (☎95 28 44 84; ②). Buses from Ajaccio to Bonifacio pass through here daily before crossing the Col Saint-Georges, 7km south of here.

From Cauro it's an easy detour to **SANTA MARIA SICCHÉ**, birthplace of Sampiero's wife Vannina d'Ornano. The village is situated 9km south along the N196, at a junction with the inland route to Zicavo (see p.198). Vannina's house is a fifteenth-century tower, situated 500m south of the village centre along the road to Cardo Torgia, while the sombre ruin of **Palazzo Sampiero**, the house Sampiero built in 1554, dominates the nearby hamlet of Vico d'Ornano.

travel details

Trains

Ajaccio to: Bastia (4 daily; 4hr); Bocognano (4 daily; 45min); Calvi (2 daily; 3hr 30min); Corte (4 daily; 2hr); L'Ile Rousse (2 daily; 3hr); Ponte-Leccia (4 daily; 2hr 30min); Vizzavona (4 daily; 1hr); Venaco (4 daily; 1hr 30min).

Buses

Ajaccio to: Bastia (2 daily; 3hr); Bonifacio (2 daily; 3hr); Cargèse (2 daily; 1 hr); Corte (2 daily; 2hr); Evisa (3 daily; 1hr 30min); Levie (1 daily; 1hr 45min); Porticcio (hourly; 20min); Porto (2 daily; 1hr 45min); Porto-Vecchio (2 daily; 3hr 30min); Propriano (2 daily; 2hr); Sagone (3 daily; 50 min);

Sartène (2 daily; 2hr 20min); Sainte-Lucie-de-Tallano (1 daily; 1hr 30min); Tiuccia (3 daily; 30min); Vico (3 daily; 1hr); Vizzavona (2 daily; 1hr); Zonza (1 daily; 2hr).

Cargèse to: Ajaccio (2 daily; 1hr); Piana (2 daily; 20min) Porto (2 daily; 30min); Sagone (2 daily; 30min); Tiuccia (2 daily; 40min).

Porticcio to: Ajaccio (hourly; 20min).

Sagone to: Ajaccio (3 daily; 50min); Cargèse (3 daily; 30min); Piana (3 daily 1hr); Porto (3 daily; 1hr 30min); Tiuccia (3 daily; 15min).

Ferries

For ferry details see p.107.

CHAPTER FOUR

THE SOUTH

For the sheer variety of its landscapes, **the south** of Corsica is the most stunning part of the island, its coast of white sands and translucent turquoise sea hemming scrubland deserts, huge granite peaks, mountainous forests of Laricio pine, limestone plateaux, and slopes covered by orchards and vineyards. The hinterland is rich in mystery too, with ancient monuments and menhirs lurking in the woodlands of the southwest. This region also has its share of unspoiled traditional villages, with two of the best, **Sollacaro** and **Olmeto**, lying close to the primitive statues mustered at **Filitosa**, the most important prehistoric site in Corsica.

For a visit to Filitosa you could stay at **Porto Pollo**, a delightful seaside village at the northern end of the vast **Golfe de Valinco**. Alternatively, there's **Propriano**, a livelier modern port in the centre of the bay, offering the widest choice of hotels, shops and restaurants in the area. From here you could also explore the southern section of the Golfe de Valinco, where there's a secluded sandy beach at **Campomoro**, or roam into the island's richest wine-producing country, taking in **Fozzano** and the splendid Romanesque church of **Santa-Maria-Figaniella**. A bit deeper inland, the region of **Alta Rocca** has an abundance of historic villages and prehistoric sites – the architecture of **Sainte-Lucie-de-Tallano** pays testimony to the wealth of the area's former overlords, the della Rocca family, while a visit to the Bronze Age ruins of the **Pianu di Levie** is an essential complement to the Filitosa trip. In the heart of Alta Rocca, the village of **Zonza** stands on the threshold of the south's major natural attraction, the sublime granite "needles" of **Bavella**.

Moving southwest, **Sartène** is in many ways the ultimate Corsican town, its history saturated with stories of vendetta and its stark, fortified buildings redolent of the harshness of life in the not so distant past. South of Sartène, a wild landscape of thick maquis and parched rock makes an appropriate background for the **megaliths of Cauria** and **Alignement de Palaggiu**, Corsica's largest arrays of prehistoric standing stones.

Marking the southern extremity of Corsica, **Bonifacio** is one of the most dramatically sited towns in the whole Mediterranean, its old quarter sitting atop vertiginous white cliffs and almost severed from the mainland by a deep natural harbour. It's a popular holiday centre for the island's wealthier tourists, as is **Porto-Vecchio**, an ugly town that's close to some superb beaches and to the majestic forest scenery of the **Massif de l'Ospedale**.

The area is reasonably served by **public transport**, with buses running twice daily from Ajaccio to Bonifacio via Propriano and Sartène, and four times daily from Bonifacio to Porto-Vecchio. Daily buses also pass through the mountains from the west coast as far as Zonza, but for Bavella and for all the prehistoric sites you will need your own vehicle. The *micheline*, Corsica's idiosyncratic train, doesn't reach as far south as this, although there are plans for a line in the future.

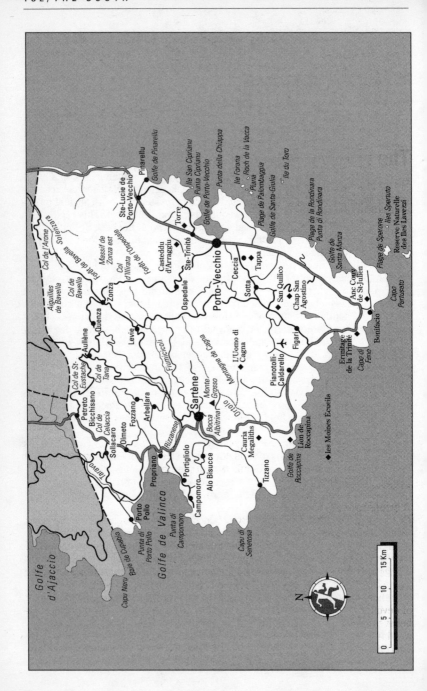

The Filitosa region

Set deep in the countryside of the fertile Vallée du Taravo, **Filitosa** is one of the most important prehistoric sites in the western Mediterranean, a wonderful array of statue-menhirs and prehistoric structures. Situated some 40km south of Ajaccio and 17km north of Propriano, the site lies within easy reach of **Sollacaro** and **Olmeto**, two attractive inland villages, and of the tiny village resort of **Porto Pollo**, the only coastal base on the north side of the Golfe de Valinco.

Filitosa

Eight thousand years of history are encapsulated by the extraordinary **STATION PRÉHISTORIQUE DE FILITOSA** (March–Oct daily 8am–7.30pm; 15F). Little is known about the peoples who inhabited this spot, a fact that gives an added element of mystery to Filitosa's statue-menhirs, which glare amid intensely green meadows, patches of wild orchid and gnarled olive trees, a scene little changed since their creation. The site remained undiscovered until one Charles-Antoine Cesari came upon the ruins on his farmland in the late 1940s. He and Roger Grosjean, who was to become head of the centre for archeological research in Sartène, set about a full-scale excavation, discovering some menhirs lying face down in the maquis, others broken at waist level inside what is now known as the central monument. When the digging was completed the menhirs were set into lines, and the site was opened to the public in 1954.

There's no public transport to this site, but **organized trips** leave once a day from Ajaccio (May–Sept; 100F for full day) and Propriano (June–Sept; 50F for half day).

A brief history of Filitosa

Filitosa was occupied from 6000 BC when it was settled by **neolithic** farming people who lived here in rock shelters until the arrival of **megalithic** navigators from the East in about 3500 BC. These invaders were the creators of the menhirs, the earliest of which were possibly phallic symbols worshipped by an ancient fertility cult. Later statues display stylized human features, making them quite distinct from nearly all other European menhirs of the megalithic period – such as those at Stonehenge and Avebury – which would seem to have been abstract expressions of devotion to a godhead rather than tributes to humankind. Most archeologists believe that the representational menhirs were memorials to dead chieftains and warriors. Grosjean, however, maintained that they were portraits of enemy **Torréens**, who – most people agree – arrived in the Golfe de Porto-Vecchio from the eastern Mediterranean around 1700 BC. As they settled, these people built

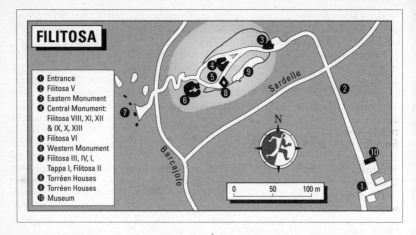

conical structures known as *torri* (towers) all over the south of Corsica. Again, no one is absolutely certain of their function, but it's generally agreed that the smaller of these beehive-like towers are likely to have been used as places of worship to some divinity, but traces of ashes and bones in the vicinity also suggest these could have been where the Torréens burnt or buried their dead. The larger *torri*, not spacious enough for human habitation, are thought to have served as stores for weapons or food, or perhaps as refuges or lookout towers.

When the Torréens conquered Filitosa around 1300 BC, they destroyed most of the menhirs, incorporating the broken stones into the area of dry-stone walling surrounding the site's two *torri*. Around the towers, the remains of which are the central and western monuments, they constructed a village of cyclopean stone shacks – a complex known as a *casteddu*. As such *casteddi* became more numerous their inhabitants were forced into attacking neighbouring settlements in order to protect their land and livestock. Grosjean believed that competition between the *casteddi* forced Torréen expeditions to migrate to northern Sardinia, which would explain the existence on that island of *nuraghi*, larger and more technically advanced versions of *torri*. A rival theory, however, suggests that the Torréens were in fact indigenous Corsicans who simply acquired their technical expertise from the Sardinian *nuraghi* builders.

The site

Vehicles can be left in the small **car park** in the hamlet of Filitosa, where you pay the entrance fee; from here it's a fifteen-minute walk to the site, which includes a **café**, a small **museum** (best seen after the site) and a workshop producing reproduction prehistoric ceramics.

Filitosa V looms up on the right before you cross the stream. The largest statue-menhir on the island, it's an imposing sight, with clearly defined facial features and a sword and dagger outlined on the body. Beyond a sharp left turn lies the oppidum or central monument, its entrance marked by the **eastern platform**, thought to have been a lookout post. The cavelike structure sculpted out of the rock is the only evidence of neolithic occupation and is generally agreed to have been a burial mound.

Straight ahead, the Torréen **central monument** comprises a scattered group of menhirs on a circular walled mound, surmounted by a dome and entered by a corridor of stone slabs and lintels. Nobody is sure of its exact function.

Nearby **Filitosa XIII** and **Filitosa IX**, implacable lumps of granite with long noses and round chins, are the most impressive menhirs on the site – indeed Grosjean considered Filitosa IX to be the finest of all western Mediterranean megalithic statues. Filitosa XIII, the last menhir to be discovered here (the Torréens had built it into the base of the central monument), is typical of the figures carved just before the Torréen invasion, with its vertical dagger carved in relief – **Filitosa VII** also has a clearly sculpted sword and shield. **Filitosa VI**, from the same period, is remarkable for its facial detail. On the eastern side of the central monument stand some vestigial Torréen houses, where fragments of **ceramics** dating from 5500 BC were discovered; they represent the most ancient finds on the site, and some of them are displayed in the museum.

The **western monument**, a two-roomed structure built underneath another walled mound, is thought to have been some form of Torréen religious building. Beyond here a meadow sweeps towards the River Barcajolo, on the other side of which five statue-menhirs are arranged in a wide semicircle beneath a thousand-year-old olive tree. A bank separates them from the **quarry** from which the megalithic sculptors hewed the stone for the menhirs – a granite block is marked ready for cutting.

In the **museum**, the major item is the formidable **Scalsa Murta**, a huge menhir dating from around 1400 BC and discovered at Olmeto. Like other statue-menhirs of this period, this one has two indents in the back of its head, which are thought to indicate that these figures would have been adorned with headdresses like the horn that's been attached to Scalsa Murta. Other notable exhibits are **Filitosa XII**, which has a hand and a foot carved into the stone, and **Trappa II**, a strikingly archaic face. Explanatory notes and photographs around the walls trace the progression of the excavations.

Filitosa to Olmeto

East of Filitosa, the D57 threads through hilly hedged-in pastures for about 8km before the village of **SOLLACARO** (Suddacaru) rises into view. A compact, reddish-toned gathering of houses, the village boasts the distinction of having been the setting for the first meeting of James Boswell and Pascal Paoli on October 21, 1765 (see box overleaf) – a plaque opposite the post office commemorates the occasion.

Soon after Sollacaro you'll hit the main road from Ajaccio at the **Col de Celaccia** (583m), where a right turn brings you down to **OLMETO**, situated about 5km to the south. With its grandstand view over Propriano, Olmeto was once a favourite spot with amateur sketchers such as Edward Lear, and it remains a captivating place, close to the coast but far enough from Propriano to retain a village atmosphere that's heightened by the lofty mellow buildings and lazy café life. **Colomba Carabelli**, the heroine of Merimée's novel *Colomba* (see p.141), died here in 1861, aged 96, in the forbidding mansion facing the *mairie*. Her reputation still attracts a few admirers, but what brings the tourists here today are the incredible views from the village's two streets, which are linked by steep stairways, with the foundations of the houses vanishing into a valley whose olive groves once sustained the local economy.

BOSWELL IN CORSICA

Dr Johnson's biographer courted men of genius as assiduously as he pursued women, and one of his early conquests was the Corsican patriot **Pascal Paoli**. In 1765, at the age of 25, **James Boswell** contrived to make the acquaintance of the great French philosopher Rousseau in Switzerland. The Corsicans, struggling to formalize their independence, had asked the author of the *Social Contract* to give them a new set of laws. In certain circles Corsica had something of the appeal that Greece was to offer Byron's generation sixty years later, and Boswell promptly suggested that Rousseau make him his ambassador to the Corsicans. He duly received a letter of introduction which he was able to present to Paoli the following year.

The meeting was a far more nervous occasion for Boswell than his encounter with the philosopher. "I had stood in the presence of many a prince but I never had such a trial as in the presence of Paoli", he wrote. "For ten minutes we walked backwards and forwards through the room hardly saying a word, while he looked at me with a steadfast, keen and penetrating eye, as if he searched my very soul." A student of physiognomy, Paoli also feared an attempt on his life, so the close scrutiny was scarcely surprising, and it didn't hinder the development of a friendship that was to hold throughout Paoli's later exile in London.

The success of Boswell's book about his visit, *An account of Corsica – the Journal of a Tour to that island and Memoirs of Pascal Paoli*, helped launch his social and literary career in London, and commemorated a passion that endured throughout his life. In 1769, the year of the book's publication, he attended the first annual celebration of Shakespeare's birthday in Stratford-on-Avon, an event organized by the actor David Garrick. Boswell appeared at the celebrations dressed in the Corsican national costume and wearing in his hat a card that read "Corsica Boswell".

Just before you enter the village, you'll notice the ruined **Castello della Rocca** on an isolated rocky peak. This inaccessible castle was inhabited in the fourteenth century by Arrigo della Rocca, the fiery great-grandson of Giudice della Cinarca (see p.122). Exiled to Spain in 1362, Arrigo enlisted the support of the King of Aragon and returned to Corsica ten years later, intent on taking over the whole island. He virtually succeeded, with only Calvi and Bonifacio holding out against him, and as Count of Corsica ruled the island for four years until his death at Vizzavona in 1401, poisoned by one of his own vassals.

The **hotel** *L'Aiglon* (☎95 74 62 95; ②), in the centre of the village, is bright and welcoming with a decent restaurant. The other place for a **meal** is *La Source* in the main street opposite *L'Aiglon*, which offers good, inexpensive Corsican food.

Porto Pollo

From Filitosa it's a short drive down to the bridge across the River Taravo, then on to the seafront village of **PORTO POLLO** (Porti Poddu). Despite its long popularity with holidaymakers, this place is still an attractive spot in summer, mainly due to the sublime view of the Golfe de Valinco and the long stretch of golden sand which fronts the village. A peaceful, sheltered harbour has moorings for yachts, and a few fishermen still venture out, providing the restaurants with fresh *langoustine* from the gulf.

Hotels dominate the only road, behind the beach. Of these *Kalliste* (☎95 74 01 88; ③), right in the centre of the village, is the best place to stay, with the distinction of being owned by a descendant of Pascal Paoli. The restaurant serves excellent fresh fish. Otherwise try the equally central *L'Éscale* (☎95 74 01 54; ②), a modern building with a terrace on the beach. *Le Golfe* (☎95 21 64 45; ③), the white building at the end of the beach, tends to get booked up by regular guests and its basic rooms are overpriced, but it does have a good seafood restaurant. **Campers** have *Camping Alfonsi*, at the entrance to the village (☎95 74 01 80), which has a good pizzeria.

You can rent surfing and windsurfing equipment at the *Centre Nautique de Porto Pollo* at the entrance to the village, though the best windsurfing beach is the beautiful half-moon **Baie de Cupabia**, northwest of Porto Pollo – take the D155 in the direction of Serra di Ferro, then turn left along the D155a about 4km from Porto Pollo. In the other direction there's the **Plage de Taravo**, a fabulous, wide, sandy stretch just 1500m east of the village, but with no facilities other than a makeshift bar.

Propriano and around

Tucked into the narrowest part of the Golfe de Valinco, the small port of **Propriano** has most of the area's hotels and campsites, and is handy for some good beaches as well as for the menhirs at Filitosa and the historic town of Sartène. The attractions of the minimally developed southern Golfe de Valinco culminate in **Campomoro**, an enchanting fishing village set behind a glorious long beach, while **Fozzano**, a pretty village renowned for a particularly virulent vendetta, provides an easy inland excursion, taking in some pastoral landscapes along the way.

Public transport serving Propriano consists of a twice-daily bus from Ajaccio to Bonifacio and Port-Vecchio. For Campomoro and Fozzano you'll need your own transport, however.

Propriano

Bracketed by the promontory of Scogliu Lungu, the fine natural harbour of **PROPRIANO** (Prupria) was exploited by the ancient Greeks, Carthaginians and Romans, but became a prime target for pirate raids and by the eighteenth century had been largely destroyed. The port, developed at the beginning of this century, now handles **ferries** to the French mainland and Sardinia, but still has an unfinished appearance. This is due in part to terrorist bombs; the post office, a symbol of the French administration and especially targetted for its isolated position here, has had to be rebuilt three times over the last ten years after nationalist attacks.

This is also notorious gangster territory – the newspapers are forever reporting shootings in Propriano – but the occasional eruption of violence doesn't seem to deter the tourists who come for the beaches, the sailing and watersports facilities, and the comparatively flourishing nightlife. Even if you're just passing through, this resort provides useful amenities (supermarkets, for example) at the midway point between Ajaccio and Bonifacio.

For the nearest **beach** head 1km north of town to the **Plage de Baracci**, a long sheltered stretch of sand which spans the narrowest part of the gulf. Just 3km further, the D157 branches off to the left and continues along the coast, which is built up with hotels and package tour holiday blocks until **Olmeto Plage**, 10km west, where an abundance of campsites are on offer (see p.139). You can only reach this last by car.

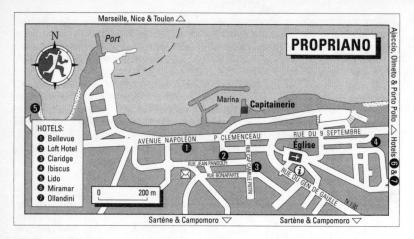

Practicalities

Ferries dock just five minutes' walk from where the **bus** stops at the top of rue du Général de Gaulle, the town's main street, which runs at right angles to the water. The **tourist office** at no. 17 (Mon–Fri 9am–noon & 2–6.30pm; Sat 9am–noon) issues a very useful leaflet which includes a plan of the town and lists of hotels and restaurants. For **accommodation** there's a reasonable choice of hotels in the centre of town but if you have a car and the means, you could try the more alluring places along the coast. Cafés and restaurants are concentrated along the marina's avenue Napoléon.

Propriano also boasts a rare self-service **laundry** (*Laverie Automatique*) opposite the Port de Commerce on avenue Napoléon. Diving equipment can be rented from *Valinco Plongée* in the marina (☎95 76 21 03).

FERRIES

Ferries depart from the Port de Commerce for Marseille and Toulon from the last week of March to the end of September. There's also an all-year service to Porto Torres in Sardinia.

SNCM, quai l'Herminier (☎95 76 04 36). To Marseille (March–May 1 weekly, June to mid-July 1 weekly, mid-July to Aug 5 weekly, Sept 4 weekly); Toulon (March–May 1 monthly, June to mid-July 1 weekly, mid-July to Aug 5 weekly, Sept 4 weekly). Prices start at around 300F per passenger, plus another 500F for a car. Daytime crossings take 9hr 30min, overnight 12hr.

Compagnie Meridionale de Navigation, quai l'Herminier (☎95 76 04 36). To Sardinia: twice weekly. The 5hr crossing costs 200F per passenger, 250F for a car.

HOTELS

Abartello, Olmeto Plage, 10km west of Propriano (☎95 74 04 73). Huge modern complex right on the beach. Also rents out chalets. ②.

Belle Vue, avenue Napoléon (☎95 76 01 86). Overlooking the marina halfway down avenue Napoléon, this is the cheapest central hotel; all rooms have balconies with a view of the gulf and are cheerfully decorated; downstairs there's a lively crêperie frequented by the locals. ①.

Claridge, rue Bonaparte (☎95 76 05 74). Ugly and a bit dingy, but it does have a lot of rooms. ③.

Ibiscus, 2 rue Tomasini (☎95 76 01 56). Modern and inoffensive hotel. ③.

Le Lido, at the southern end of Plage de Baracci, 3km from Propriano (☎95 76 06 37). A stunning seaside situation and a good restaurant. ④.

Loft Hotel, rue Jean Paul Pandolphi (☎95 76 17 48). Hi-tech building directly behind the port, and owned by a friendly wine merchant; bright clean rooms. ②.

Miramar, route de La Corniche (a continuation of route de Baracci), 5km towards Ajaccio (☎95 76 13 14). If you feel like splashing out, this is the place to go for, a splendid luxury hotel with a huge swimming pool and sauna. ⑤.

Ollandini, 2km along the route de Baracci to Ajaccio (☎95 76 05 10). Has a private beach and commands a good view. ②.

HOSTEL AND CAMPSITES

Propriano's **youth hostel**, 3km from Propriano on the route to Ajaccio (☎95 76 19 48), is open all year but gets overrun by German school parties. **Campers** are well provided for in the area: for the best facilities try *Listinco*, 3km north along route de Baracci and with a swimming pool (☎95 76 19 17), or the cheaper *Corsica*, 4km towards Ajaccio, 1km beyond the hostel (☎95 76 00 57). At Plage d'Olmeta the best site is *U libecciu* (☎95 74 01 28), the first place on the beach coming from Propriano, or you could try *Chez Antoine* (☎95 76 06 06) in Marinca d'Olmeto, north of the beach.

RESTAURANTS

Le Cabanon, rue des Pêcheurs. Excellent fish restaurant at the south end of the marina towards the port. Also serves pasta with some unusual sauces, such as prawns and coconut.

L'Hippocampe, rue Pandolphi. Tucked away behind the port, this is the best place for fresh fish at reasonable prices, with a quick turnover and a lively atmosphere.

U Paisanu, on the marina. Good-value tourist-oriented place, with the added advantage of a sea view.

Resto Nicoli, at the far end of rue Napoléon. Just about the cheapest place to eat; excellent omelettes for a pittance.

U Tavonu, rue Capitaine Pietri. Bright and cosy tourist restaurant, serving inexpensive Corsican dishes as well as pizzas.

BARS AND NIGHTLIFE

Best of the **bars** are those ranged opposite the port on avenue Napoléon, the most pleasant being those closest to the marina. Otherwise, you can mix with the local gangsters at the *Shanghai* on rue Général de Gaulle, whose owner sports a gold chain and spats. He also owns *Le Midnight*, Propriano's hot night spot, which puts on a cabaret every night – it's on the steps in rue Bonaparte, behind the *Shanghai*. The **theatre** in the sports complex 1km along the road to Sartène puts on concerts, plays and films in the summer.

The southern Golfe de Valinco

Separating from the Sartène road at the Rena Bianca bridge, 2km south of Propriano, the D121 winds down the coast, shouldering some gentle cliffs and deep green maquis which sets off the intensely blue sea. Some 7km along the route you'll come to **Portigliolo**, an exceptionally white and quiet curve of sand with a shady campsite, *Lecci e Murta* (☎95 76 02 67). Five kilometres beyond, at the hamlet of Belvedère, at the top of the cliff before you descend to Campomoro, there are two more campsites on the crest of the hill, *La Vallée* (☎95 74 21 20) and *Les Roseaux* (☎95 74 20 52), which are less crowded than the site by the beach.

A cluster of sturdy old buildings and a tiny chapel make up **CAMPOMORO**, a fishing village enjoying a tranquil isolation amongst the eucalyptus trees at the foot of the cliff. The main attraction is the beach, a golden mile of sand and pellucid sea, overlooked by an immense Genoese tower which dominates the headland. The village basically consists of one road, which follows the beach to the right and left of the junction by the post office, at the entrance to the village. Turn right and you come to the mooring for fishing boats where the main road comes to a dead end; a small road leads off to the right for the chapel and the village shop. The left-hand road from the junction follows the beach, at the end of which a fairly stiff twenty-minute climb takes you to the **tower** (summer 9am–7pm; free), a stunning lookout point.

You may have trouble finding a place to stay in July and August, as Campomoro possesses only two **hotels** and one **campsite**. *Le Ressac*, about 100m behind the chapel (June–Sept; ☎95 74 22 25; ③), is a friendly family concern where the rooms afford excellent views across the bay, but it only does half board. *Le Campomoro* (☎95 74 20 89; ④), overlooking the beach about 500m from the post office towards the tower, is more expensive and less welcoming, but the rooms are adequate if rather sparsely furnished. A possible alternative is Madame Carbini who rents **rooms** overlooking the beach, but you will need to reserve these in advance (☎95 74 20 69). *Bar des Amis*, opposite the beach near the chapel, will also rent out rooms, but don't expect luxury. *Camping Peretto* (☎95 74 20 52), on the left at the entrance to the village, is a basic **campsite** but fine if you like to sleep with the sea lapping your tent.

During the day there's a **snack bar** set up on the beach, where you can get the usual fast food as well as fresh salads and local *charcuterie*. For a bite in the evening, the **restaurant** of *Le Ressac* is your best bet, or you could try the pizzeria on the beach (open July & Aug only), which also has fresh fish from the gulf. Campomoro has two food **shops**: one is about five minutes' walk from the post office in the tower direction, and is open daily in summer until 8pm; the other is behind the chapel and has more erratic opening hours, closing for at least four hours in the afternoon.

Fozzano

East of Propriano, the north flank of the Alta Rocca region (see opposite) is scattered with stony old villages, of which the best known is **FOZZANO**, something of a tourist attraction as the hotbed of vendetta. Its notoriety dates from the early eighteenth century, when the whole village became politically divided over the Corsican uprising against the Genoese, the lower village lining up behind the Carabelli and Bartoli families, the upper behind the Durazzo and Paoli clans. **Colomba Bartoli**, born a Carabelli, was a driving force within her faction, a striking example of the role played by women in Corsican vendettas – mothers of murdered men would sew a piece of bloody clothing onto their grandsons as an emblem of the vengeance which had to be done, and devised songs ridiculing men who failed to avenge their murdered kin.

In 1830 tension in Fozzano intensified after a quarrel outside the church culminated in three murders, with two victims coming from the Carabelli clan. When, a year later, a confrontation led to the death of another Carabelli, Colomba plotted an ambush in the maquis to murder three of the enemy. The plan backfired and resulted in the murder of her son as well – the result of the mayhem was that Fozzano was thrown into a state of siege, with houses barricaded and children kept from school. When **Prosper Merimée** came here in 1839, he talked to the ageing but fiercely rancorous Colomba, who had become something of a celebrity – Flaubert also paid homage to her. The Merimée novel that came out of their encounter, *Colomba*, made the gang leader famous throughout France as a youthful, cold-hearted and beautiful heroine, a character rather different from the brutal and ugly reality.

The exceptionally high granite buildings and steep narrow streets are dominated by two towers: the fourteenth-century **Torra Vecchia**, on the left as you come from Arbellara, was the heavily fortified home of the Carabelli; **Torra Nova**, a Genoese construction built in 1548, was home to the Durazzo faction. It's possible to get inside the Torra Nova by asking for the key at the *mairie* in the main street, and at night the tower is dramatically lit.

At the edge of the village south of Torra Nova you'll find **Colomba's house** – the upstairs balcony is supposed to be where she heard the fatal gunshots far below in the maquis. Believing it to be only her enemies who had died, she gloated to the passing Durazzo "there's fresh meat for you down there", and received the retort that there was some for her too. The tombs of Colomba and her murdered son, Francescu, are in the nearby chapel.

There's nowhere to stay up here, but Fozzano has an excellent **restaurant**, *U Pitraghju*, which serves Corsican food and pizzas, with a terrace on the hillside.

Over the valley, some 2km away, the hamlet of **SANTA-MARIA-FIGANIELLA** boasts a twelfth-century church that's as pure an example of Romanesque as you'll find, with especially beautiful arcading under the roof and some fine carving on the door. The bell tower, set apart from the main body of the church, dates from a later period.

Alta Rocca and Bavella

A region of evocative prehistoric sites, delightful villages and stark mountain peaks, **Alta Rocca** also contains some of the most fertile parts of Corsica – **Vallée du Rizzanese**, in the south of the region, is cultivated with orchards and the most prolific vineyards on the island. In the upper part of the Rizzanese valley the highlight is **Sainte-Lucie-de-Tallano**, an outstandingly attractive village, while high in the valley of the Fiumiccicoli tributary lies **Levie**, where you can see a Bronze Age settlement and medieval castle. Many of the Alta Rocca villages have hotels, with the majority concentrated at **Zonza**, thanks to its proximity to the magnificent **Bavella**, whose granite needles and dense forests form one of the most celebrated Corsican landscapes.

If you're approaching Alta Rocca from Propriano, you can either follow the D19/119/69 from the village up to Aullène, or head south from Propriano along the N196, then turn onto the D69, which switches to the west bank of the Rizzanese River, leaving the D268 to continue to Saint-Lucie. The approach from the other side of Corsica, via the Ospedale route, is covered on p.166. A twice-daily **bus** runs from Ajaccio through Bicchisano, Sainte-Lucie-de-Tallano and Levie on its way to Zonza and Bavella, but there's no bus to Aullène.

Propriano to Carbini

The first diversion along the N196/D69 route from Propriano – the **Spin a Cavallu** bridge – comes 3km after the junction with the N196, and is reached by a track from the parking space down to the river. This elegant Pisan stone arch, beautifully set off by a background of rippling vineyards and olive trees, has survived intact since the thirteenth century, and provides room for two horses to pass – its name means "horseback bridge".

Sainte-Lucie-de-Tallano

Perched high above the Vallée du Rizzanese, the exquisite village of **SAINTE-LUCIE-DE-TALLANO** has been wealthy since Rinuccio della Rocca made it his stronghold. An eminent patron of the arts as well as a fearsome warlord, Rinuccio donated many works of art to the parish church in between his desperate attempts to oust the Genoese in the first decade of the sixteenth century. Graceful balconied houses remain as a legacy of the illustrious families who once resided here, while the prosperity of many present-day residents is attested by the Porsches lined up outside the church. Some of the money comes from gangsterism, but there are two more legitimate sources of income: locally produced **Fiumiccicoli** wine, and an extremely rare rock called *diorite orbiculaire*, which is quarried close by.

A wide street sweeps through the village in a loop, widening out in the centre to form the **place des Monuments aux Morts**, whose terrace gives a glorious view of vineyards and verdant hills that is interrupted by the prominent red roof of Chapelle Saint-Jean-Baptiste, a few kilometres to the south. The base of the monument incorporates the local diorite, a greyish-blue stone with concentric rings of black and white, like a leopard's pelt. Portable pieces of this strange stone can be bought for about 100F from Madame Renucci, next door to *Hotel Léandri* (see below). The anonymous **Église Paroissiale** has precursors going back to Roman times, but was many times rebuilt until its seventeenth-century Baroque incarnation. Inside there's a marble font in the form of a hand, dating from the 1490s and bearing the della Rocca arms, but the real treasure is the finely worked marble bas relief of the **Virgin and Child**, commissioned by Rinuccio della Rocca in 1498 – it's attached to a column on the left inside the church entrance. The church's late fifteenth-century *Crucifixion*, attributed to the Catalan painter known as the Master of Castel Sardo, is now locked away in the *mairie* next door, where you can ask to see it.

Behind the church stands the **Maison Forte**, a huge, impenetrable, grey granite house built to shelter the population in times of danger. For a good view of the village you could walk the five minutes north to the **Couvent Saint-Francois**, founded by Rinuccio in 1492 and set squarely on a plateau overlooking the village.

Sainte-Lucie has one **hotel**, the *Leandri*, on the main street south of the place des Monuments aux Morts (☎95 78 80 82; ①), a creakingly inviting establishment lined with the portraits of the Leandri family. For a **meal** there's *Pizzeria Santa Anna*, next to the monument, which pulls people from miles around, the attraction being the terrace as much as the food. The villlage **bar**, *Sporting*, may appear dismal on the outside but inside it's a typical example of a Corsican village café, lively with card games and pinball machines.

Levie (Livia) and the Pianu di Levie

In the eighteenth century **LEVIE** was the capital of Alta Rocca, its Genoese families prospering from the fertile countryside and presiding over a village more populous than Sartène. Today the village is rather dull, its main attraction being the proximity of the **Pianu di Levie** (see below), whose prehistoric sites provide much of the substance of the **Musée Archaeologique** (June–Sept Mon–Fri 10am–noon & 3–7pm; Oct–May Mon–Fri 10am–noon; 10F), underneath the *mairie* off the main street. The two most interesting exhibits, however, are the so-called *Dame de Bonifacio*, discovered near Bonifacio and dated around 6570 BC, making it the oldest human skeleton found in Corsica, and a beautiful ivory statue of Christ by a pupil of Donatello, given to Levie in the 1580s by Pope Sixtus V.

In the summer a small **tourist office** (Mon–Fri 9am–noon & 3–6pm) opens in the centre of the village on rue Sorba. A good place for a hearty meal is *La Pergola* on the same street – it serves plain home cooking and will make *charcuterie* sandwiches on request.

THE PIANU DI LEVIE

The most interesting prehistoric site on Corsica after Filitosa, the **Pianu di Levie** (June to mid-Sept daily 9am–8pm; 20F) is reached by taking the signposted track to the left of the road, 1km west of Levie. A further 2km will bring you to a field where you can park and buy your ticket – you get a ninety-minute cassette-guided tour of the site for no extra charge.

A fifteen-minute walk brings you to the **Casteddu di Cucuruzzu**, the remains of a Torréen habitation dating from 1400 BC. Emerging from a dense oak wood and integrated into the chaos of eroded granite boulders, this is the best example of a *casteddu* in Corsica. Dominated by a circular *torre* and surrounded by a thick high wall, the complex was inhabited by Bronze-Age artisans and farmers, who lived in the chambers surrounding the *torre* and in dry stone shacks close by. The *casteddu* is entered by a steep and narrow stairway. Storerooms are ranged on the right, opposite a series of chambers with openings above to let the light in and the smoke out. Straight ahead, the *torre* has retained its vaulted roof of wide granite slabs, below which stones jutting out sideways from the walls suggest the existence of another floor. Stone tools, bronze belt links and domestic utensils, found in the course of excavations here, all point to the tower's having a functional rather than religious purpose.

Another twenty minutes through oak woodland brings you to **Capula**, a site occupied from the Bronze Age until 1259, when its so-called **castle**, an impressive circular monument, was partly destroyed. Just below the entrance stands a headless menhir, and other pieces of Bronze and Iron Age stonework are incorporated into the monument, mixed with hundreds of small granite bricks from the medieval period. About 200m beyond the castle stands **Chapelle San Lorenzu**, a tiny thirteenth-century Romanesque building extensively restored this century.

Carbini

South of Levie, the D59 runs 8km through a twisting valley to **CARBINI**, whose isolated bell tower heads a straight road lined with lime trees and low cottages. Adjacent to the tower, which is all that remains of the church of Saint Quilico, stands **San Giovanni**, built in the first half of the twelfth century and decorated with elegant early Romanesque arcading. In 1354, in the aftermath of the Black

Death, this stately building saw the birth of a sect called the **Giovannali**, a bizarre Franciscan offshoot whose religious meetings were rumoured to end with orgies – their doctrine of the equal division of property extended to the sharing of wives as well as all wordly goods. Despite persecution the Giovannali spread throughout the east of Corsica until, in 1362, Urban V dispatched an expedition that resulted in the massacre of a hundred people here. The village then had to be repopulated by families from Sartène.

Aullène and around

Aullène, lying at a crossroads of four main inland routes, is most easily approached from Propriano by following the D69 across the Rizzanese or by taking the D19 directly out of Propriano, a route that becomes the D69, then meanders north through the verdant **Vallée du Coscione**. From Aullène you loop back to Propriano via the **Col de Saint-Eustache** and **Petreto-Bicchisano**, or alternatively head east for the mountains to **Quenza**, in the direction of Zonza.

Aullène
Lush vegetation characterizes the region around the dispersed village of **AULLÈNE** (Auddé), whose inhabitants relied for centuries on the surrounding chestnut woods for survival. Set midway between the east and west coasts, Aullène might make a pleasant upland stop – its long-established *De la Poste* **hotel** (☎95 78 61 21; ②) boasts a fine restaurant. If you're just passing through, pause at the seventeenth-century **church**; its pulpit displays wooden carvings portraying pirate raids and is supported by twisting sea monsters emerging from a Moor's head.

Aullène to Petreto-Bicchisano
Striking westwards out of Aullène along the D420, a looping road rises through a spectacular rocky landscape, with enormous boulders dominating the road as far as the **Col de la Tana** (975m), situated some 7km along. Beyond this pass a high narrow road hugs the mountainside above a belt of pinewood and overshadowed by the pink granite bulk of the Punta di Taccaluccjia. At the Col de Saint-Eustache (995m), a further 3km, the view extends north over the mountains to the Vallée du Taravo, its mass of greenery swamping the slopes.

A further 10km will bring you to **PETRETO-BICCHISANO**, an imposing sixteenth-century village made up of two hamlets. The church at Petreto is worth a look for its wooden statues representing Saint Francis of Assisi, Saint Claire and the Immaculate Conception, while Bicchisano has a small **hotel** and **restaurant**, *De France* (☎95 24 30 55; ②).

Aullène to Quenza
Southeast of Aullène, the D420 passes through two particularly pretty villages, Serra-di-Scopamena and Sorbollano, before reaching **QUENZA**. Set on a granite eminence smothered in pines and chestnut groves, with Bavella as a spiky backdrop, Quenza has a spectacular location and a fine Romanesque church, **Santa Maria**, which stands at the entrance to the village. Dating from 1000, it's built on a single nave plan with an oven-shaped apse, and retains some traces of its original frescoes. The church next door has a wooden pulpit supported by a couple of dragons and a Moorish head, as well as a curious fifteenth-century multicoloured wooden panel of the Virgin and Child, in a chapel to the left of the altar.

AN ALTA ROCCA WALK

A circular **walk from Quenza through Zonza** is a relatively easy hike of about four and a half hours, with opportunities for swimming in the river along the way. About 600m from the eastern exit from the village, the path to Zonza is signposted to the right. Heading into the wood the path veers right, then follows a small stream for 200m. Leaving the stream, you pass through more woodland for about another 3km until you reach a wall, where you bear right through a pine plantation and again cross a stream. At a clearing in a hollow the footpath crosses a ravine, then a stream again and heads up into some chestnut trees. Turn left as you enter the trees and then almost immediately right onto a wider footpath which leads to the road, 1km from Zonza. At Zonza take the main road south, then after 1km a track leads right between two walls and crosses a stream. A few metres on, strike to the right along the path marked Quenza, until you reach a junction where you turn right and the path begins the climb back to the village. A further 2km will bring you to another junction, but continue straight ahead, following the stream. Half an hour's straightforward climbing through wooded rocky terrain will bring you back into Quenza, coming out in the south of the village.

Quenza's **hotel**, the *Sole e Monti* (☎95 78 62 53; ③), is just past the centre along the road to Zonza – it's a large, attractive, old building, with good food. You can get a less expensive room at the *Chez Pierrot* bar from M. Milanini (☎95 78 63 21), who also rents out apartments in the area. Quenza's well-equipped **campsite**, *I Muntagnoli Corsi* (☎95 78 64 05), 1km along the road to Zonza, has an excellent Tahitian cook and offers organized mountain biking, rambling and riding. Horse-riding can be arranged at *Chez Pierrot*, and information about cross-country skiing on the plateau du Coscione, north of here, can be obtained at *Centre Ecole de fond du Coscione* (☎95 78 64 79), 500m along the road to Coscione. If you just fancy a **swim**, take the road signposted to Jallica opposite the square in front of the church, and after 200m turn left onto the footpath, which will bring you to the deliciously clear Codi stream.

Zonza and the route de Bavella

One of the main tourist centres of Alta Rocca, **Zonza** lies at a junction of roads to Levie, Ospedale, Quenza and Bavella. The route north is perhaps the most dramatic road in all Corsica, crossing **Col de Bavella**, passing through the forests of Zonza, Bavella and Tova, affording sublime views of the **Aiguilles de Bavella** and descending steeply to the coast from **Col de Larone**, alongside the sparkling River Solenzara.

Zonza

Unassuming **ZONZA** is transformed in summer when, as the gateway to Bavella, this austere granite village receives its influx of summer visitors. A cluster of **hotels**, all with more than decent restaurants, cater for the hordes. *La Terrasse* (☎95 78 67 69; ①), situated up a ramp behind the main street, is an excellent place, offering large comfortable rooms with a view of the valley and an enticing menu of wild boar and seasonal specialities. *Le Tourisme*, to the north of the village, set back on the west side of the Quenza road (☎95 78 67 72; ②), is a smarter option, with a cosy restaurant that's renowned throughout this area. Otherwise there's *L'Aiglon* (☎95 78 67 79; ②), in the village centre on the main road to Ospedale, an adequate alternative if the former places are booked up.

The **office** for Parc Naturel Régional is situated 500m north of the village (May–Sept daily 9am–noon & 3–5pm; ☎95 78 66 58).

Route de Bavella

North of Zonza, the D268 penetrates the **Forêt de Zonza**, a dense expanse of pine and chestnut trees, as it rises steadily to a pizzeria and the *Auberge du Col* (☎95 67 89 09; ②), on the final approach to the **Col de Bavella** (1218m). A towering statue of Notre-Dame-des-Neiges marks the pass itself, which has a bleak and blasted look, the flattened pines crouched from the wind, their jagged branches sharply black against the green-hued granite peaks. An amazing panorama of peaks and forests surrounds the col: to the northwest the serrated granite ridge of the Cirque de Gio Agostino is dwarfed by the pink pinnacles of the **Aiguilles de Bavella**; behind soars Monte Incudine; and the east is dominated by the ruddy shades of Punta Tafonata and the distant sea. A cluster of huts just beyond the col was built in the early nineteenth century for the inhabitants of the eastern plain to take refuge from the suffocating summer heat of the lowlands.

From this point it's a steep descent through what's left of the **Forêt de Bavella**, which suffered a devastating fire in 1960 but still features some huge Laricio pines. The winding road offers numerous breathtaking glimpses of the Aiguilles de Bavella, whose granite pinnacles are roamed by the rare mouflon, although you'd be lucky to spot one. About 10km from the Col de Bavella you'll come to the **Col de l'Arone** (608m), which offers stunning vistas of the mountains and the **Forêt de Tova** in the north.

WALKS FROM THE AUBERGE DU COL

A waymarked variant of the GR20 trail gives you an 80-minute walk around the Col de Bavella. Begin by following the GR20, leading to the right of the *Auberge du Col* and clearly marked with red and white paint; after 1500m leave the GR20 and ascend a path, this time indicated by red paint flashes, that runs alongside the river and after 3km leads to a stream. Continue up the left bank for a short stretch until you reach a grassy platform scattered with twisted pines. From here there's a **view** of the Aiguilles de Bavella and both the east and west coast of Corsica. Descend by the right-hand path along the larger slope down to the chapel, from which a path leads down to the *auberge* again.

A two-hour walk from the *auberge* goes to the Trou de la Bombe, a circular opening that pierces the Paliri crest of peaks. From the auberge follow the GR20 for 300m, then take the first path to the right, signposted "Col de Velaco". The track rises through a wood as far as a ridge where a path follows the line of the crest, the Trou de la Bombe emerging to the right of the Calanca Murata mountain. Another hour's walk (4km) will take you to the Col de Velaco (1483m), dominated by the red granite peaks of Pointe de Velaco. Take the same path back.

Sartène

A "town peopled by demons" is how German chronicler Gregorovius described **SARTÈNE** (Sarté) in the nineteenth century, and the town hasn't shaken off its hostile image. Located near the coast and therefore vulnerable to foreign invaders, Sartène was persistently attacked by pirates in the Middle Ages, and from the twelfth to the sixteenth centuries became the seat of the ferocious **Sgio** (from *signori*), feudal lords who preferred to implement justice without interference from the island's rulers and thus turned Sartène into an asylum for refugees from the law of the state. A bloody vendetta in the nineteenth century sealed the town's reputation and left a legacy of tall, grim fortress houses. An insular outlook continues to this day, and outsiders can be put off by the implacable ambience of the place and by the heavy presence of wealthy-looking Godfather types. On the other hand it's a smart, clean town, noticeably better groomed than many small Corsican towns, its principal income coming from Sartène **wine** – the best on the island.

Despite its turbulent history, the town doesn't offer many diversions once you've explored the enclosed **vieille ville** and paid a visit to the **Musée de Préhistoire Corse**. The only time of year Sartène teems with tourists is at Easter for **U Catenacciu**, a highly charged Good Friday procession (see p.150) that packs the town's one central hotel with onlookers.

A brief history of Sartène

Sartène was formed when, in the tenth century, the inhabitants of this region's agglomeration of hamlets were forced to congregate in one place by Turkish raids. In the twelfth century the **della Rocca** family held sway over the area with the consent of its Pisan governors, but as the Genoese took over in the thirteenth century, Sartène became a centre of discontent. The laws which gave Genoa a monopoly on Corsica's trade were anathema to the local nobility, the **Sgio**, who continued to resist the Genoese until the final stand of Rinuccio della Rocca, who was defeated after a long struggle in 1502.

It was not until early in the sixteenth century that Sartène became a Genoese administrative centre, and even then their tenure was deeply troubled. In 1565 Sampiero Corso's army destroyed the town after a 35-day siege, then the Genoese took it back, only to lose it again in 1583 to **Hassan Pasha**, the mad king of Algiers, who ransacked the town and abducted four hundred of its inhabitants, a third of the population. Thereafter Sartène remained faithful to Genoa, so much so that Paoli had a struggle to win Sartène to his cause in the fight for a Corsican republic.

The nineteenth century saw the re-emergence of the Sgio: recognized as members of the nobility by the French monarchy, the Sgio prospered under privileges granted by Napoléon III, and whereas other parts of Corsica suffered depopulation and decline, the Sgio oversaw the development of a wine industry that still underpins the local economy. Today as the *sous-prefecture* of southern Corsica, Sartène is the region's second town after Ajaccio.

The town

Place Porta – its official name, place de la Libération, has never caught on – forms Sartène's nucleus. Once the arena for bloody quarrels, it's now a well-kept square opening onto a wide terrace which overlooks the rippling green valley of the Rizzanese – the cafés at the edge of the terrace have the best view. Somnolent by day, place Porta comes alive for the early evening *passeggiata*, when it gets cramped with a mixture of hunters, aristocrats and smart young people.

Flanking the south side of place Porta is **Église Sainte-Marie**, built in the 1760s but completely restored to a smooth granitic appearance. The chief interest here is historical – it was in this church that the warring families of nineteenth-century Sartène were forced to make their peace, though the truce often lasted only until they got outside again. Inside the church you can see the weighty

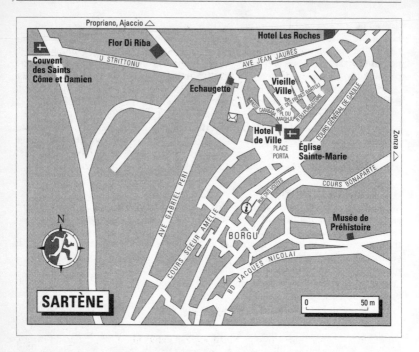

wooden cross and chain which are used in the Catenacciu procession (see p.150), but otherwise the only notable feature is the Baroque altar, a present from the town's Franciscan monastery, no longer in existence.

Formerly the palace for the Genoese governor, the nearby **Hôtel de Ville** serves as an archway into the Santa Anna district of the *vieille ville*; the building isn't open to the public and its archives have been closed since the 1880s, due to the endemic corruption of local politics, it's said.

THE VIEILLE VILLE
A flight of steps to the left of the Hôtel de Ville leads to the ruined **echauguette**, a small lookout tower which is all that remains of the town's twelfth-century ramparts. This apart, the best of the **vieille ville** is to be found behind the Hôtel de Ville in the **Santa Anna** district, a labyrinth of contricted passageways and ancient fortress-like houses that rarely give any signs of life. Featuring few windows and often linked to their neighbours by balconies, these houses are entered by first-floor doors which would have been approached by ladders – dilapidated staircases have replaced these necessary measures against unwelcome intruders. The main "road" across Santa Anna is rue Frère Bartoli, to the left of which are the strangest of all the vaulted passageways, where outcrops of rock block the paths between the ancient buildings. Just to the west of the Hôtel de Ville, signposted off the tiny **place Maggiore**, you'll find the **impasse Caraba**, a remarkable architectural puzzle of a passageway cut through the awkwardly stacked houses. A few steps away, at the western edge of the town, **place Angelo Maria Chiappe** offers a magnificent view of the Golfe du Valinco.

VENDETTA IN THE VIEILLE VILLE

In the villages of nineteenth-century Corsica it was common for blood feuds to start over something as trivial as the theft of a goat, but Sartène's vendetta had its roots in a political dispute between the rich **Roccaserra** family of Santa Anna – supporters of the Bourbons – and the anti-monarchist Ortoli family of the poorer Borgo district. In 1830, on the occasion of the overthrow of the Bourbons in France, a group of Ortolis and their cohorts marched through Santa Anna to provoke the mayor, a royalist Roccaserra. In the ensuing fight Sebastien Pietri, a leading light in the Roccaserra clan, was killed and five of his comrades were wounded, which provoked an invasion of the town by a thousand Roccaserra allies from the mountains. The scene was witnessed by French chronicler A.C. Pasquin Valéry, who wrote, "The French are powerless against the nature, manners and passions of the Corsicans." After a series of violent confrontations in the maquis, where many members of both factions were killed, a mediator was brought in, a peace treaty drawn up and in 1834, at a Mass in Église Sainte-Marie, the survivors of the vendetta were forced to swear to live in peace. Even then, street corners were guarded and windows bricked up, the feud only relaxing on the election of Napoléon III in 1848, when the children of the families were allowed to dance together at the celebrations.

MUSÉE DE PRÉHISTOIRE CORSE

Set in a shady garden a short distance east of place Porta, the **Musée de Préhistoire Corse** (Mon–Fri 9am–noon & 2–6pm; 25F) is Corsica's centre for archeological research and is packed with findings from digs throughout the island, dating mostly from 6000 to 500 BC. Beyond the entrance hall, where a chart traces the history of human habitation in Corsica, **room one** contains Neolithic exhibits, mainly pottery fragments, and covers the early development of agriculture, fishing and hunting. More sophisticated items are found in **room two**, where finely carved arrow heads and tools of polished obsidian are presented alongside more accomplished fragments of decorated ceramics, gold jewellery and statuettes, as well as a pile of human bones deformed by fire, discovered near Bonifacio.

Next door, in **room four**, a model of Cucuruzzu (see p.143) gives a good idea of what a Bronze Age settlement looked like, while specimens of functional Torréen pottery contrast with the more elaborate examples in the previous section. Two **statue-menhirs**, one of them coloured red as it would have been during the megalithic era, stand opposite cases containing colourful **bracelets** from the Iron Age, a period also represented by weaponry and decorated pottery. Painted ceramics from the thirteenth to the sixteenth centuries complete the museum.

COUVENT DE SAN DAMIANO

A ten-minute walk along the road to Bonifacio will take you to the **Couvent de San Damiano**, the building in which the Catenacciu penitent spends the night before the procession, when he has to be guarded from curious outsiders by police. One of the last of the old-style bandits, a formidable character called **Muzarettu**, died here in the 1940s at the age of ninety, having been given refuge by the monks. Cast out from his village for killing a nephew who had slapped his face, Muzarettu took to the maquis, then proceeded to terrorize the neighbourhood from his cave hideout near Propriano, where he hosted wild parties for the fishermen who brought him food and drink. A few more murders along the way kept him outlawed for many years, but as an old man he developed cancer and came to this convent to die; repenting his sins right at the very end, he was visited by the chief of police on his deathbed.

U CATENACCIU

Sartène's Good Friday ceremony of **U Catenacciu**, generally considered to be the most ancient ritual in Corsica, is a frighteningly authentic imitation of Christ's walk to Golgotha, despite a touch of exploitation in recent years. The nocturnal procession through candlelit streets is headed by the **Grand Pénitent** or Pénitent Rouge: dressed in a scarlet hooded robe which covers his face, he carries a heavy wooden cross and is chained on the ankle – *u catenacciu* means "chained one". In former times the penitent was usually a bandit whose identity was officially known only to the priest. Nowadays Grand Pénitent is still anonymous and there's a waiting list of twelve years to take part, which means that some of the penitents are very old men. If the Grand Pénitent is too frail to shoulder the cross alone, he's helped out by the **Pénitent Blanc**, who follows behind, representing Simon of Cyrena. Behind him comes a troop of **Pénitents Noirs** bearing the statue of Christ on a bier. Accompanied by the continuous unearthly chanting of an ancient Corsican prayer, *Perdonu miu Diu*, the penitents pass slowly from Église Sainte-Marie through the streets of the *vieille ville*, ending up three hours later in place Porta, where they receive benediction at midnight.

In the past it was a dangerous event, as the penitents were often known murderers at whom onlookers would fling stones – though this was one time of year when a truce was observed between sworn enemies, so nobody got killed. It's still a rough affair, with a lot of rough and tumble to get the best view among the throng of tourists, and shots are often fired into the air at the end of the ceremony, by which time excitement is running high.

The convent is now home to a brotherhood of Belgian monks and is out of bounds to the public, but there's a fine view of the valley from the outside.

Practicalities

If you're arriving in Sartène by **bus** you'll be dropped at the top of rue Général de Gaulle. Just south of here, across place Porta, you'll find a tiny **tourist office** at 6 rue Borgo (summer Mon–Fri 9am–noon & 2–6.30pm). Drivers can park in rue Général de Gaulle and walk up into town.

The only **hotel** in Sartène itself *Les Roches*, on rue Jean Jaurès, a large family-run place on the west side of the *vieille ville* (☎95 77 07 61; ②); it commands panoramic views of the Vallé du Rizzanese and has a restaurant that serves copious amounts of hearty Corsican food, such as *daube Sartenaise* (a rich stew) and *cuvet de sanglier* (roast wild boar). At *Le Jardin des Orangers*, 1km west of town along the road to Propriano (☎95 77 02 72; ③), you can rent studios and rooms set in a delightful garden. You could otherwise try *Fior di Riba*, 500m further along the same road (☎95 77 01 80; ③), or *Villa Piana*, 4km along the Bonifacio road (☎95 77 07 04; ④), a more upmarket place overlooking the Golfe de Valinco. The nearest **campsite** lies 5km along the D69 to Castagna (☎95 77 11 58) – it offers a free bus service to and from Sartène.

As for **restaurants**, *U Catenacciu* on rue Capitaine Benedetti, south of place Porta, serves pizzas and reasonably priced Corsican food in summer, while Sartène's young people hang out in *Pizza Porta* on cours Soeur Amélie. *Crêperie Santa Anna* in rue Frère Bartoli serves up a good herby *crêpe du maquis*, and at 27 rue des Vôutes, the understated *Ghjuvan Micheli* offers good-value 65F menus of *cuisine familiale*. *La Sirenata*, on rue Général de Gaulle, also has reasonable Corsican food and hosts a cabaret of traditional guitar music every night.

Bars cluster round place Porta, where *Au Bien Assis* has the best views across the valley, but its cocktails are extortionate. *Bar Idéal* has friendly owners, *du Central* charges less for drinks and *Bar des Amis* attracts the hunting fraternity.

Around Sartène

You get captivating views of Sartène and the Golfe de Valinco by driving along the D50 southeast of Sartène, descending into the Ortolo valley before reaching the tiny hamlet of **MOLA**. This nest of reddish houses lurks in the shadow of the **Uomo di Cagna**, a gigantic globular rock perched on top of the mountain which dominates the landscape of the Sartenais district south of Sartène.

West of Sartène, the prehistoric monument of **Alo Bisucce** is reached by a lovely road that leads eventually to Campomoro (see p.140). To get there take the N196 south as far as the Col de l'Albitrina, branching right towards Tizzano and then soon after veering along a sudden, unsignposted right turning which worms around the hillside in the direction of Grossa. After about 4km the unsignposted site emerges as a mound on the left-hand side of the road. Neolithic settlers occupied this rocky peak around 1700 BC, before the arrival of the Torréens, building a double wall of cyclopean boulders surmounted by a structure measuring 8m across and centring on a hearth. East of here lies a rough platform, probably used for surveying the surrounding countryside for possible attackers.

Southwest Corsica: the megalithic sites

Sparsely populated today, the rolling hills and deep maquis of the southwestern corner of Corsica is a land rich in prehistoric sites. The **megaliths of Cauria**, standing in ghostly isolation 10km southwest from Sartène, comprise the **Dolmen de Fontanaccia**, the best-preserved dolmen on Corsica, and the nearby alignments of **Stantari** and **Renaggiu**, an impressive congregation of statue-menhirs. More than 250 menhirs can be seen northwest of Cauria at **Palaggiu**, another rewardingly remote site. Equally wild is the coast hereabouts, with deep clefts and coves providing some excellent spots for diving and secluded swimming. Closest to the ancient sites is the miniature port of **Tizzano**, while further east there's the beautiful white cove of **Roccapina** and then the village of **Pianotolli-Caldarello**, set on the deserted plain inland from the narrow **Baie de Figari**.

There's no public transport in this region except the twice-daily **bus** from Ajaccio to Bonifacio.

The megaliths of Cauria

To reach the **Cauria** megalithic site you need to turn off the N196 about 2km outside Sartène, at the Col de l'Albitrina (291m), taking the D48 towards Tizzano. Four kilometres along this road a left turning brings you onto a winding road through vineyards, until eventually the **Dolmen de Fontanaccia** comes into view on the horizon, isolated in a clearing amidst a sea of maquis. A blue sign at the parking space indicates the track to the dolmen, a fifteen-minute walk away.

Known to the locals as the *Stazzona del Diavolu* (the Devil's Forge), a name that does justice to its enigmatic power, the Dolmen de Fontanaccia is in fact a burial chamber from the second phase of the megalithic era, around 2000 BC. This period was marked by a change in burial customs – whereas bodies had previously been buried in stone coffins in the ground, they were now placed above, in a mound of earth enclosed in a stone chamber. What you see today is the great stone table, comprising six huge granite blocks nearly 2m high topped by a stone slab, that has remained once the earth rotted away.

The twenty "standing men" of the **Alignement de Stantari**, 200m to the east of the dolmen, date from the same period. All are featureless except two which have roughly sculpted eyes and noses, with diagonal swords on their backs and sockets in their heads where horns would probably have been attached.

Across a couple of fields to the south you'll find the **Alignement de Renaggiu**, a gathering of forty menhirs standing in rows amid a small shadowy copse, set against the enormous granite outcrop of Punta di Cauria. Some of the menhirs have fallen, but all face north to south, a fact that seems to rule out any connection with a sun-related cult.

Palaggiu and Tizzano

For the **Alignement de Palaggiu**, the largest concentration of menhirs in Corsica, you regain the D48 and continue southwards, keeping your eyes peeled for a clearing that emerges to the right of the roadside about 3km south of the junction for Cauria. Pass through the gate here (there are no signposts) and head in a straight line to get to the menhirs. The 258 menhirs, stretching in straight lines across the countryside like a battleground of soldiers, include three statue-menhirs with carved weapons and facial features – they are amidst the first line you come to. Dating from around 1800 BC, the statues give few clues as to their function, but it's a reasonable supposition that proximity to the sea was important – Grosjean's theory is that the statues were some sort of magical deterrent to invaders.

TIZZANO (Tizza), at the end of the road about 3km south of Palaggiu, is a secluded little marina tucked into a sheltered inlet. The village consists of a couple of ancient buildings and a chic terraced **café** set on the rocks overlooking the yacht moorings. Just south of the village, the glorious **beach** of white sand and limpid sea draws increasing numbers of tourists every year, but some equally enticing little coves can be found in the area if you're prepared to do a bit of scrambling over the rocks northwest of the beach. There's no hotel here but there is a campsite.

The road to Bonifacio

South of Sartène, the N196 undulates through a strange landscape of gentle barren hills and vivid blue sea, dominated by the Uomo di Cagna. Once the road hits the coast, about 25km along, the huge roseate rock of the **Lion de Roccapina** comes into view, part of high, crumbling, granite cliffs that shelter the **Golfe de Roccapina**. To get to its superb beach, look out for the right-hand turning at Asinaja, signposted "Camping Roccapina" – the road is accessible to vehicles but extremely rocky, so you may want to walk the 3km to the sea. Shallow bathing and sublimely soft white sand ensure the cove's popularity, and the beach has recently been made a protected site, hence the fence safeguarding the dunes.

Back on the main road the first sign of civilization for miles comes at PIANOTOLLI-CALDARELLO, the largest – indeed practically the only – village between Sartène and Bonifacio. Two hamlets make up the village, and their names tell you everything about the locale: Pianotolli, the northern half, is derived from the word for "plain", and Caldarello, 500m to the south, means "extreme heat". Amidst the chaos of rocks by the side of the road as you leave

Caldarello, you'll see an **oriu**, one of many such cave houses found scattered about this part of the island. Hollowed out of a detached rock, sometimes with a masonry doorway and usually with a high slanting roof, these *orii* are thought to have been prehistoric dwellings, and were more recently used to store grain and hay and as shelters for shepherds. However, as their floors are of rock, no archeological evidence has been unearthed in these structures to shed any light on their prehistoric significance.

A Genoese tower guards the **Baie de Figari**, 2km south of Caldarello, where a deep narrow gulf provides moorings for yachts, its appeal enhanced by the strange backdrop of the Montagne de Cagna.

Bonifacio

BONIFACIO (Bonifaziu) enjoys a superbly isolated situation at Corsica's southernmost point, a narrow peninsula of dazzling white limestone creating a town site unlike any other on the island. The **haute ville**, a maze of tortuous streets, rises seamlessly out of sheer cliffs that have been hollowed at their base by the buffeting waves, while on the landward side the deep cleft between the peninsula and the mainland forms a pefect natural harbour. A haven for boats for centuries, this harbour is nowadays a marina that attracts yachts from all around the Med, with a plethora of hotels and restaurants to cater for the thousands of summer visitors.

Separated from the rest of the island by an expanse of maquis, Bonifacio has maintained a certain temperamental detachment from Corsica, and is distinctly more Italian than French in atmosphere. It has its own dialect based on Ligurian Italian, a legacy from the days when it was practically an independent Genoese town. The old town retains Renaissance features found only here, and with Sardinia just a stone's throw away, much of the property in the area is owned by upper-echelon Italians.

Such a place has its drawbacks: exorbitant prices, crowds in August, and a commercial cynicism that's atypical of Corsica as a whole. However, it's perhaps the island's best-looking maritime town, and you'll find Bonifacio boasts a lively nightlife, culminating in the **Rencontres Méditérranéennes** music festival at the beginning of September. Bringing together performers from as far afield as Turkey and Egypt, the festival spices up an already cosmopoiitan ambience.

A brief history of Bonifacio

It could be that Bonifacio's first documented appearance is as the town of the cannibalistic Laestrygonians in the **Odyssey**; Homer's description of an "excellent harbour, closed in on all sides by an unbroken ring of precipitous cliffs, with two bold headlands facing each other at the mouth so as to leave only a narrow channel in between" fits the port well. The unploughed land which Odysseus comes across inland of the harbour could be a reference to the plain beyond the Bonifacio promontory, and it's also possible that the Neolithic tribes that once lived in this area were the barbaric attackers of Odysseus's crew.

In Roman times there was a village on this site, but the town really came into being in 828 when **Count Bonifacio of Tuscany** built a castle on the peninsula. Like other towns on the Corsican coast, this one suffered continuous pirate raids, but its key position in the Mediterranean made various powers covet the port. In

1187 Pisa and **Genoa** were disputing the town, which eventually fell to the Genoese, who then proceeded to massacre the local population and replace them with Ligurian families to whom they offered exemption from tax and customs duty in Genoese ports. Two hundred and fifty families duly settled here and soon the town had developed into a mini-republic with its own constitution and laws, governed by elected magistrates called *Anziani*.

In 1420 **Alfonso V** of Aragon set his sights on Corsica, and for five months his fleet blockaded the port, hoping to starve the Bonifaciens into submission. Every citizen joined in the defence of the citadel, with clergymen, women and children flinging wooden beams, rocks and blinding chalk dust down on the attackers – they even tried to demoralize the enemy by pelting them with cheese, an action masterminded by one Marguerita Bobbia, whose ingenuity is commemorated by a street named after her in the old town. Eventually Genoese warships sailed into the port just as the townspeople were about to surrender, but it was a last show of bravado from the starving Bonifaciens which broke the resolve of the Aragonese. Donning the uniforms of their dead soldiers, the women processed around the citadel to create the illusion of a large army, and at this their attackers lost heart and decamped.

Another celebrated siege occurred in 1554, when the town was recovering from an outbreak of plague which had claimed two-thirds of the population. **Henri II** of France arrived with the Turkish fleet, led by the fearsome corsair Dragut. The town held on through eighteen days and nights of cannon fire, and then a member of the eminent Cattacciolo family was despatched to Genoa to raise help. He was seized on his return by the Turks, who forced him to carry a forged letter refusing them the assistance of the republic, a ploy that brought about Bonifacio's surrender. The invaders pillaged the town, which was then rescued by Sampiero Corso. There followed a brief period of French rule, which came to an end when the Treaty of Cateau-Cambresis returned Corsica to Genoa in 1559.

Thereafter the Genoese port enjoyed relative prosperity until the late eighteenth century, when the French gained control of the island. No longer permitted their special autonomy, the merchants moved away and the town suffered a commercial decline that was really only reversed with the advent of tourism. Fishing, however, still brings in some income for a few Bonifaciens.

Arrival, information and accommodation

Arriving by plane, you'll land at **Figari** airport, 17km north of Bonifacio. There's no bus service from here so you'll have to take a taxi into town – around 200F. If arriving by **bus** you will be dropped at the car park by the **marina**, close to most of the hotels. Drivers can either park here or head straight up avenue Général de Gaulle to the *haute ville*. This is where you'll find the **tourist office** (May–Oct Mon–Fri 9am–noon & 2–6pm, Sat 9am–noon), in rue des Deux Moulins, opposite the *Genovese* hotel. The most they will give you is a map of the town and a list of hotels.

Finding a **place to stay** can be a chore, as Bonifacio's hotels are quickly booked up in the high season, so if you want to stay centrally make sure you ring in advance. You'll find the least expensive accommodation a little outside the marina on the road to Ajaccio, while **campsites** abound on the road to Porto-Vecchio.

Hotels

La Caravelle, 37 quai Comparetti (☎95 73 00 03). Stylish olde worlde place with an excellent restaurant in a prime location. ④.

Des Étrangers, 4 av Sylvère Bohn (☎95 73 00 03). On the road to Ajaccio just past the port, this is the cheapest place in the south, gathering an interesting mix of travellers who compensate for the dull decor. Closed winter. ①.

Le Genovese, la Citadelle (☎95 73 00 03). Deluxe hotel overlooking the port. Swimming pool and a fantastic view of the cliffs. ⑤.

Centre Nautique, the marina (☎95 73 02 11). Plain but chic, and full of yachties. ③.

Du Roy d'Aragon, 13 quai Comparetti (☎95 73 03 99). New, well-appointed hotel. ④.

Le Royal, rue Fred Scamaroni (☎95 73 03 65). Above a modern bar in the *haute ville*. Bright, clean place with views of the citadel and the sea. ④.

Les Voyageurs, 15 quai Comparetti (☎95 73 00 46). Small but adequate rooms with a good view of the port; a backpackers' favourite. Popular restaurant with terrace. ①.

Campsites

L'Araguina, av Sylvère Bohn, opposite the service station near *Hotel des Étrangers* (☎95 73 02 96). Closest place to town, gets overcrowded.

U Farniente, Pertamina, 3km along the road to Porto-Vecchio. (☎95 73 05 47). Very flash, all mod cons – essential to book in summer.

Campo di Liccia, opposite *U Farniente* (☎95 73 03 09). Well shaded and large, so you're guaranteed a place.

U Pian del Fosse, route de Santa Manza, 7km out of Bonifacio along the D58 (☎95 73 14 40). Very basic but cheaper than the rest.

FERRIES TO SARDINIA

Ferries for Santa-Teresa-di-Gallura leave from the port at the far southern end of the marina. The *Navarma* company operates ten daily crossings between July 1 and September 4, reduced to four from May 18 to June 30 and September 5 to October 1, with none for the rest of the year. The 1hr crossing costs 70F per passenger, plus 180F per car. You can get tickets from *Agence Gazano*, Port de Bonifacio (☎95 73 00 29).

The Town

Apart from the cafés, hotels and restaurants of **quai Comparetti**, the only attraction in the lower town is the marina's **Aquarium** (daily 10am–6pm; 15F), where the blue lobsters are the star attractions. At the far end lies the port where ferries leave for Sardinia, and in between, a cluster of restaurants and shops lies at the foot of **Montée Rastello**, the steps up to the *haute ville*.

Haute ville

Many of the houses of the **haute ville** are bordered by enormous battlements which, like the houses themselves, have been rebuilt many times – the most significant modifications were made by the French during their brief period of occupation following the 1554 siege, after they had reduced the town walls to rubble. Remnants of cannonshot-peppered buildings still scatter the *haute ville*, especially around the **Bosco** area at the tip of the promontory, where the barbed wire fences round the military facility and the rubbish flying about in the wind all add to the war-torn appearance. The *haute ville* has been sparsely populated since

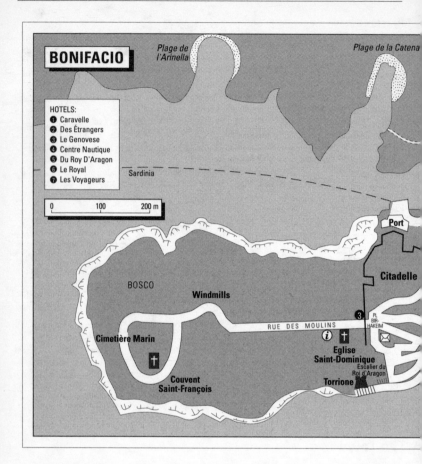

HOTELS:
1 Caravelle
2 Des Étrangers
3 Le Genovese
4 Centre Nautique
5 Du Roy D'Aragon
6 Le Royal
7 Les Voyageurs

the Genoese merchants moved out in the eighteenth century, and the precariousness of many of its buildings is no enticement to settle – on the southeast side the houses have no surrounding wall to protect them, and in 1966 one house fell into the sea, killing two people. Since then various plans have been put forward to reinforce the cliff, but the state of the buildings is still a great problem.

From the top of the Montée Rastello steps you can cross avenue Général de Gaulle to **Montée Saint Roch**, which gives a stunning view of the white limestone cliffs and the huge lump of fallen rockface called the **Grain de Sable**. At the **Chapelle Saint-Roch**, built on the spot where the last plague victim died in 1528, more steps lead down to the tiny beach of Sutta Rocca, which is mainly frequented by divers.

At the top of the Montée Saint Roch steps stands the drawbridge of the great **Porte des Gênes**, once the only entrance to the *haute ville*. Through the gate, in place d'Armes, you can see the **Bastion de l'Étendard** (daily 9am–noon, 2–6pm; 10F), sole remnant of the fortifications destroyed during the siege of 1554. A few

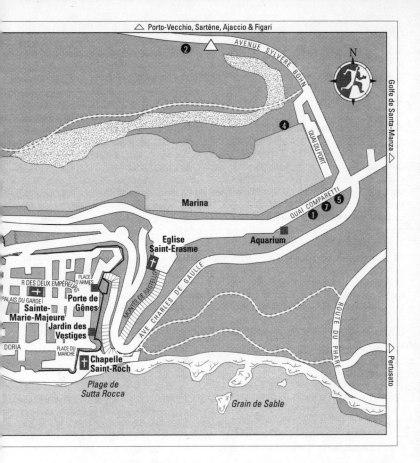

paces further lies **rue des deux Empereurs**, where at no. 22 you'll see the flamboyant marble escutcheon of the Cattacciolo family, one of many such adornments on the houses of this quarter. In 1541 the emperor Charles V, having been caught in Bonifacio by a storm, stayed in this house as a guest of Filippo Cattacciolo; after the departure of his illustrious visitor, Cattacciolo shot the horse he had loaned to him, on the grounds that nobody else was worthy to ride the poor beast after it had supported the ruler of half the known world. Opposite stands the house in which Napoléon resided for eight months in 1793.

Cutting across to rue Palais du Garde brings you to **Église Sainte-Marie-Majeure**, originally Romanesque but restored in the eighteenth century, though the richly sculpted belfry dates from the fourteenth century. The facade is hidden by a **loggia** where the Genoese municipal officers used to dispense justice in the days of the republic. If you look up you can see buttresses connecting the houses in the adjoining streets to the roof of the church – these were vital not just as support but also for draining rainwater into a huge cistern underneath the porch, which provided the town with water in times of siege and during the dry summers. This church's treasure, a relic of the **True Cross** said to have been brought to Bonifacio by Saint Helena, the mother of Constantine, was saved from a shipwreck in the Straits of Bonifacio; for centuries after, the citizens would take the relic to the edge of the cliff and pray for calm seas whenever storms raged. The relic is kept in the sacristy, along with an ivory cask containing relics of Saint Boniface, and you'll only be able to get a glimpse if you can find someone to open the room for you. In the main body of the church the highlight is the marble **tabernacle** to the left of the door; decorated with carvings of Christ supported by eight cherubs, it's thought to have been created by a north Italian sculptor towards the end of the fourteeeth century. The holy water stoup below it is a third-century **sarcophagus**, the sole Roman item in town.

Nearby **rue du Palais de Garde** is one of the handsomest streets in Bonifacio, with its closed arcades and double-arched windows separated by curiously stunted columns. The oldest houses along here did not originally have doors; the inhabitants used to climb up a ladder which they would pull up behind them to prevent a surprise attack, while the ground floor was used as a stable and grain store.

The **Jardin des Véstiges**, just a couple of minutes southeast of rue du Palais de Garde, is a good place to stop for a drink overlooking the white cliffs on both sides. South of here, rue Doria leads towards the Bosco (see below); at the end of this road a left down rue des Pachas will bring you to the **Torrione**, a 35-metre-high lookout post built in 1195 on the site of Count Bonifacio's castle. Descending the cliff from here, the **Escalier du Roi d'Aragon**'s 187 steps were said to have been built in one night by the Aragonese in an attempt to gain the town in 1420, but in fact they had already been in existence for some time and were used by the people to fetch water from a well.

THE BOSCO

To the west of the tower lies the **Bosco**, a quarter named after the wood that used to stand here in the tenth century. In those days a community of hermits dwelt here, but nowadays the limestone plateau is open and desolate. The only sign of life comes from the military training camp where young Corsicans sweat out their national service. The entrance to the Bosco is marked by **Église Saint-Dominique**, a rare example of Corsican Gothic architecture – it was built in 1270, most probably by the Templars, and later handed over to the Dominicans.

Beyond the church, rue des Moulins leads on to the ruins of three mills dating from 1283, two of them decrepit, the third restored. Behind them stands a memorial to the 750 people who died when a troop ship named *Sémillante* ran aground here in 1855, on its way to the Crimea, one of the many disasters wreaked by the straits.

The tip of the plateau is occupied by the **Cimetière Marin**, its white crosses standing out sharply against the deep blue of the sea. Open until sundown, the cemetery is a fascinating place to explore, with its flamboyant mausoleums displaying a jumble of architectural ornamentations: stuccoed facades, Gothic arches, classical columns, even flashing lights. Next to the cemetery stands the **Couvent Saint Francois**, allegedly founded after Saint Francis sought shelter in a nearby cave – the story goes that the convent was the town's apology to the holy man, over whom a local maid had nearly poured a bucket of slops. Immediately to the south, the **Esplanade Saint-Francois** commands breathtaking views across the bay to Sardinia.

Eating, drinking and nightlife

Eating possibilities in Bonifacio might seem unlimited, but it's best to avoid the chintzy restaurants in the marina, few of which merit their exorbitant prices – the places in the *haute ville* are less pretentious. The **bars** and **cafés** on quai Comparetti are the social focus for much of the day and in the evening, but the main nightspot is the *Agora* disco on avenue de Carotola in the *haute ville* – it normally costs 100F to get in, but you can sometimes get free tickets on the marina.

Restaurants

Agora, 2 av de Carotola (same place as the disco, downstairs). Excellent pizzas, steaks and fish; wonderful location overlooking the sea. Moderate.

Chez Jules La Stella d'Oro, 23 rue Doria, near Église Saint-Jean Baptiste. Very expensive but does delicious Corsican specialities, mainly fish.

Le Guêpier, 7 rue Fred Scamaroni. Basic and inexpensive Corsican specialities.

La Main à la Pâtes, 1 place Bonaparte. Expensive fresh pasta; view of cliffs and marina.

Pizza Grill de la Poste, rue Fred Scamaroni. Very popular pizza joint.

Royal, 1 av de Carotola. Best fish in town. Expensive.

Le Tiki, 3 rue de Palais du Garde. The cheapest place in town for snacks, salads and pasta. 55F menus.

Bars

L'Amphore, 16 quai Comparetti. Pool table and a youngish crowd.

Central, 4 rue Fred Scamaroni. Everyone comes here for a nightcap.

L'Émeraude, 5 quai Comparetti. Shady relaxing bar close to aquarium. Draught beer and ice creams.

Laetitia, 12 quai Comparetti. Good place for breakfast.

Listings

Airport *Figari*, 17km north of town, off the D859 road. (☎95 71 00 22).

Bank *Societé Générale*, 2 rue Saint Erasme, at the foot of the steps to *haute ville*.

Bookshop *La Presse*, 19 rue Fred Scamaroni.

Car rental *Avis*, 20 quai Comparetti (☎95 73 01 28); *Hertz*, 3 quai du Commerce (☎95 73 02 47); *Europcar*, by the Esso garage on the way into town coming from Sartène (☎95 73 10 99).

Hospital 1 route de Santa Manza, at the entrance to town (☎95 73 95 75).

Laundry *Laverie automatique*, northeast side of the port, next to bar *L'Escale*.

Pharmacy 17 quai Comparetti.

Police Route de Santa Manza (☎95 73 00 17).

Post Office 1 rue Saint Dominique, opposite the tourist office.

Travel agent Ollandini, 17 quai Comparetti (☎95 73 01 28).

Around Bonifacio

Some marvellous beaches lie to the northeast of Bonifacio, especially in the silvery **Golfe de Santa Manza** and at the extraordinary **Plage de la Rondinara**, an almost circular cove midway between Bonifacio and Porto-Vecchio. Other enjoyable excursions include the **Grottes Marins**, a beautiful set of sea caves west of the town, the **Ermitage de la Trinité**, which affords impressive views of Bonifacio from the west, **Capo Pertusato**, which marks the southernmost point of Corsica, and the nature reserve of the **Îles Lavezzi**.

Beaches

The nearest accessible beach is **Plage de la Catena,** a kilometre to the west – a track just before *Camping L'Araguina* (see p.155) leads down to it. It's small and picturesque, but gets a lot of flotsam. For the best local beaches head northeast along the D58, where about 3km along there's a junction for a trio of beaches: the popular **Plage de Pianterella**, the dullest of the three; the adjacent **Plage de Sperone**, an excellent diving spot facing the islands of Cavallo and Lavezzi; and **Cala Lunga**, a lengthy stretch of sand, if not sparklingly clean. Further along the D58, a second right-hand turn leads to the hamlet of Gurgazu, on the southern edge of the **Golfe de Santa Manza**.

Stretching to the right is the **Plage de Santa Manza**, a narrow silver strip backed by a rough road where you can park your car. A better proposition is **Plage de Maora**, a wider beach with cleaner sand and a makeshift bar – reached by taking a left at the junction of the D60 and D58. The third beach of the gulf, **Plage de Balistra**, situated by a marshy lagoon, is less pleasant and not accessible from here; to get to it you need to follow the N198 north of Bonifacio for 12km, then take a right down a dirt track for 4km to the sea.

To reach the **Plage de la Rondinara** take the N198 north for about 10km, until a turning signposted "Camping Rondinara" appears suddenly to the right – the track to the sea is strewn with boulders, so you may prefer to walk the 3km. Sheltered by the Punta di Rondinara and backed by dunes, the small beach is a favourite with nudists.

Grottes Marins

Boat trips to the **Grottes Marins** are advertised all over the marina, all costing roughly 50F for a 45-minute trip. The largest of the three sea caves, the **Grotte du Sdragonatu**, is worth the money on its own – it's a magnificent grotto where the water takes on an extraordinary luminosity and the rocks glitter indigo and gold. Most excursions also take in the Bonifacio cliffs, giving an awe-inspiring view of the town.

Ermitage de la Trinité

The **Ermitage de la Trinité**, 7km west of Bonifacio, off the N196, stands on a site that has been inhabited since prehistoric times and was a hermitage right at the beginning of the Christianization of the island. Heavily restored in the thirteenth century, the whitewashed convent sits beside a terrace of olive trees,. a backdrop of gigantic boulders lending it a bizarre quality. There's a fine view of Bonifacio from here, and an even better one if you follow the track to the left before you reach the building and walk up to the **Mont de la Trinité**, about 25 minutes' gentle climbing.

Capo Pertusato

The deeply scored limestone cliffs southeast of Bonifacio culminate in the wide headland of **Capo Pertusato** (Pierced Cape), a steepish climb of about 45 minutes, preferably attempted in the cooler evening air. Leaving town along the

D58, almost immediately bear right along the D260, a narrow road hugging the cliff side as far as the **Phare du Pertusato**, the lighthouse at the edge of the point. (Driving is very dangerous, as there's no room for passing and no barriers at the side of the road.) At the end of the walk you'll be rewarded by an incredible seascape embracing Sardinia, the crested islands of Lavezzi and Cavallo, and Bonifacio itself, just discernible to the west.

Îles Lavezzi

The **Îles Lavezzi**, part of the archipelago to the east of the straits of Bonifacio, can be seen on a boat trip from the marina (2 daily in summer; 3hr; 80F). Having passed the Grain de Sable, the Phare du Pertusato and the heavily guarded private island of Cavallo, the boat moors at the main island of **Lavezzi**, beside a graveyard containing the bodies of the *Sémillante* shipwreck of 1855 – the victims are also commemorated by a stone pyramid on the western tip of the isle. Classified as a nature reserve since 1982, the island is home to several rare species of **wild flower**, such as the yellow horned poppy, the white sea daffodil and the stonecrop, distinguished by its fleshy red leaves beneath heads of small blue flowers. The boat stops here for an hour, and there's a small beach where you can swim.

The Porto-Vecchio region

Corsica's highest concentration of tourists is found in the area around **Porto-Vecchio**, a small town that seems entirely populated by Italians in summer. Spectacular beaches lie to the south of town, with **Palombaggia** the most popular and **Golfe de Santa Giulia** coming a close second, while to the north, the deep inlet of the **Golfe de Porto-Vecchio** boasts some luscious pine-backed strands. Continuing north, the bays of **San Ciprianu** and **Pinarellu** form a prelude to the **Cote des Nacres**, a chain of sandy beaches stretching towards the eastern plain.

Most people make at least one trip to one of the many **prehistoric sites** dotted around Porto-Vecchio – north to the Bronze Age settlements of **Torre** and the **Casteddu d'Araggiu**, or south to the monuments at **Ceccia** and **Tappa**. To get right away from the sultry coast, you could head inland up to the cool, scented **Forêt de l'Ospedale**, one of the highlights of southern Corsica.

There is no public transport to any of the beaches, but buses run from Bastia to Porto-Veccio, where you can get a connection to Bonifacio.

Porto-Vecchio

Set on a hill above a deep and beautiful gulf, surrounded by gigantic outcrops of pink granite, **PORTO-VECCHIO** was rated by James Boswell as one of "the most distinguished harbours in Europe". Yet it's a place that's never realized its potential, owing its success as a tourist attraction more to its proximity to some fine beaches than to its own character. Once rife with malaria, it still has a rather insalubrious atmosphere, with its approaches ruined by a confusing network of roads and its centre marred by constant building. Nonetheless, if you treat it purely as a base for some serious beach-work, Porto-Vecchio is worth a couple of days of anyone's time.

It was founded in 1539 as a second Genoese stronghold on the east coast, Bastia being well established in the north. The location was perfect; close to the unexploited and fertile plain, the site benefited from secure high land and a sheltered gulf. Unfortunately the Genoese hadn't counted on the mosquito problem, and within months malaria had wiped out the first Ligurian settlers. Sampiero Corso occupied the port for a brief period in 1564, having failed to take Ajaccio, but Genoa got it back a few months later, and things began to take off soon after, mainly thanks to the cork industry, which was thriving until this century. Today a third of Corsica's wine is exported from here, but most revenue comes from the rich tourists who flock inexplicably to the town each year, spending a fortune in Porto-Vecchio's flashy clothes shops.

Around the centre of town there's not much to see, apart from the well-preserved **fortress** and the small grid of ancient streets backing onto the main **place de la République**. East of the square you can't miss the **Porte Génoise**, which frames a delightful expanse of sea and through which you'll find the quickest route down to the modern **marina**, lined with cafés and hotels.

Practicalities

Buses from Bastia, Bonifacio and Ajaccio arrive at the marina. From here it's ten minutes' walk northeast to place de l'Hôtel de Ville, site of the modern and efficient **tourist office** (May–Sept Mon–Sat 9am–1pm & 4–8pm; Sun 10am–noon & 5–7pm), just west of place de la République. **Accommodation** is easy to come by except in high summer, and it's worth spending a bit extra for a place in the marina. If you're camping there's ample choice of **campsites** along the roads to Bastia and Ospedale, with many more in the Golfe de Porto-Vecchio.

Most **eating places** tend to be substandard tourist traps, but there are a couple of decent addresses where you can get fresh fish and seafood down at the marina, and **pizzerias** and **pasta** places are found all over the centre. **Cafés** line place de la République and cours Napoléon, which runs along the east side of the square – *Au Bon Coin*, facing the church, is the nicest and least expensive. Porto-Vecchio's bars are nothing special, many of them being unwelcoming gambling joints.

FERRIES

Car and passenger services from Porto-Vecchio to Marseille and Livorno operate from July to September, with none during the rest of the year.

SNCM, Port de Commerce (☎95 70 06 03). To Marseille (July & Aug 3 weekly; first 3 weeks in Sept 2 weekly). The 14hr overnight crossing costs 300F per passenger, 400F per car.

Navarma, Port de Commerce (☎95 31 46 29). To Livorno (July & Aug 1 daily; 2 in first week of Sept). The 7hr 30min crossing costs 200F per passenger, 400F per car.

HOTELS

Cala Verde, la Poretta, route de Marina di Fiori, 3km north of town along the route de Bastia (☎95 70 11 55). Classy place with a private beach, but no restaurant. ⑤.

Goeland, port de Plaisance (☎95 70 14 15). Pleasant hotel in an excellent location in the marina; large rooms, convivial atmosphere. ④.

Halzer, 12 rue Jean Jaurès (☎95 70 05 93). Central hotel but with no outstanding features. ②.

Mistral, 5 rue Toussaint Culioli (☎95 70 08 53). Comfortable place slightly removed from the noisy centre of town. ②.

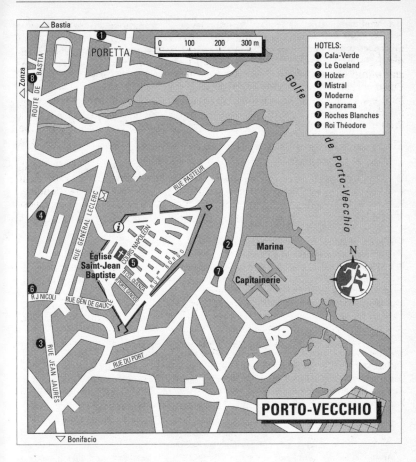

Modern'hotel, 3 cours Napoléon (☎95 70 06 36). A large, old building; noisy and popular with backpackers. ②.

Panorama, 12 rue Jean Nicoli (☎95 70 07 96). Simple family-run place with parking spaces; cheapest place in town. ①.

Roches Blanches, port de Plaisance (☎95 70 06 96). Well-placed hotel with rooms overlooking the sea. ④.

Roi Théodore, route de Bastia, 500m north of Porto-Vecchio (☎95 70 14 94). A splendid yet tranquil hideaway boasting an excellent restaurant and a swimming pool. ⑤.

CAMPSITES

Les Amis de la Nature, Araggio (☎95 70 21 57). Basic site set in a pine wood, 4km north of town.

Arutoli, route de l'Ospedale (☎95 70 12 73). Large, well-equipped site located 2km northwest of town along the D368. Enormous swimming pool makes it a good option.

Îlots d'Or, Trinité de Porto-Vecchio, 5km north of town along the Bastia road (☎95 70 01 30). Very upmarket site with swimming pool and many more facilities.

La Rondinara, on the tiny beach of the same name (☎95 70 43 15). Scruffy place with café in a lovely location.

Mulinacciu, Lecci de Porto-Vecchio (☎95 71 47 48). Popular and agreeably shady place by the river, 5km north of Porto-Vecchio along the RN198.

U Puntonu, Sainte-Lucie de Porto-Vecchio, 15km north along the Bastia road (☎95 71 42 75). Smart place with swimming pool and restaurant.

RESTAURANTS

Le Baladin, rue Général Leclerc. Expensive French joint serving excellent fresh fish and other gourmet delights.

Bistrot du Port, port de Plaisance. Sailors' hang-out serving omelettes and steaks as well as good Corsican food. Moderate.

U Borgu, rue Borgo, parallel to cours Napoléon in the old town. Cheap and cheerful Corsican place with a terrace and view over the hillside.

U Casteddu, rue Leandri, just south of place de la République. Standard pizzeria with a wood oven; also does good salads and pasta.

Le Donjon, rue S. Casalonga. Good cheap place for lunch, tucked away in a back street in the old town. Decent 65F menus.

Crêperie Jackony, rue J. Pietri, south of place de la République. Tasty crêpes with Corsican fillings such as wild boar and *brocciu*. Moderate.

La Marine, port de Plaisance. Best fish and seafood delicacies in town. Expensive.

Les Milles Pâtes, 4 rue Général de Gaulle. Popular with locals; offers wide variety of fresh pasta at average prices.

Le Tourisme, place de la République. Cheapest place in town; snacks and basic tourist fare.

DA MARE A MARE

The **Da Mare a Mare** is an arduous walk across the mountains, beginning 10km directly inland from Porto-Vecchio and ending 6km northeast of Propriano – a distance of about 60km which is usually done as a six-day hike, with hikers staying in a combination of *gîtes d'étapes* and hotels along the way. The special hiking **information** office just north of the tourist office (May–Sept 9am–noon, 3–6pm; ☎95 70 50 78) provides a list of accommodation which it's best to book in advance.

Marked with splashes of orange paint, the hike begins at a spot called **Alzu di Gallina**. To get there from Porto-Vecchio, take the D159 west in the direction of Muratello for 2km until you reach a junction. Turn right here, following the signpost to Nota, and after 1km you'll come to a small stone bridge over the Bala River. Cross over to pick up the trail.

The hike divides easily into six daily ten-kilometre stages. The first follows a steep route ascending as high as 1020m, leading to Ospedale and Cartalavone, where there's a *gîte d'étape* run by M. Monti (☎95 70 00 39). On the second day the hike descends to Carbini and on to Levie, which has a restaurant and a *gîte* run by M. Maestratti (☎95 78 41 62). Stage three takes you through the Forêt de Zonza and round to Quenza where the only accommodation is the *Sole e Monte* (☎95 78 62 53; ②), a smartish country hotel with restaurant. From here on the countryside becomes more desolate, and for a whole day the track traverses the maquis up to Serra-di-Scopamena, where you'll find the third *gîte* of the walk (☎95 78 64 90). On the fifth day the walk takes you through oak and chestnut forests to Sainte-Lucie-de-Tallano, where *Hotel Leandri* provides simple, old-fashioned accommodation with good home cooking (☎95 78 80 82; ②). The last day begins by crossing the gentle hills of the Vallée du Rizzanese until you reach the tiny hamlet of Burgo. Although the hike officially ends here, for somewhere to stay you'll need to carry on to Propriano.

The coast around Porto-Vecchio

Much of the coast of the **Golfe de Porto-Vecchio** and its environs is characterized by ugly development, bombed-out building sites and acres of dismal swampland, yet some of the finest beaches on Corsica are found around here.

Heading **south of Porto-Vecchio** along the main N198, take the turning signposted "Palombaggia" about 1km along and you'll find yourself on a narrow road
leading to the hamlet of **Picovaggia**. Here you can veer left for the headland
marking the southern limit of the Golfe de Porto-Vecchio, the **Punta di a
Chiappa**, or keep going 3km south to the **Plage de Palombaggia**, a golden
semicircle of sand edged by short twisted pines that are punctuated by fantastically shaped red rocks. This might be the most beautiful beach in Corsica if it
were not for the crowds, which pour onto the beach in such numbers that a
wattle fence has had to be erected to protect the dunes. A few kilometres further
along the same road takes you to the **Golfe de Santa Giulia**, a sweeping sandy
bay backed by a lagoon. Despite the presence of several holiday villages and facilities for windsurfing and other watersports, crowds are less of a problem here.

North of Porto-Vecchio the first beach lies some 4km along the D468, a
small bay within the Golfe de Porto-Vecchio called the **Baie de Stagnolu**, one of
the cleaner strands in these parts. Avoid the next one, **Plage de Cala Rossa**, as
this is bordered by ugly swampland and blackened by fires from bomb-struck
villas – head instead for the **Baie de San Ciprianu**, a half-moon bay of reddish
sand with an unobtrusive development. About 7km by road from here comes the
best beach of this stretch – **Golfe de Pinarellu** features a fine sandy beach, a
Genoese watchtower, smaller crowds and a good hotel, *du Golfe* (☎95 71 40 70;
③), which rents studios on the beach by the night or the week.

Beyond here, north of the village of **Sainte-Lucie-de-Porto-Vecchio**, the
Côte des Nacres covers the distance from Favone to Solenzara. The beaches at
the **Anse de Favone** and **Canella** are pretty average sandy stretches, but they
gain immensely from the backdrop of towering crags behind.

The prehistoric sites

Torréen settlements are concentrated south of a line running from Ajaccio to
Solenzara, with the majority located around Porto-Vecchio. The most fully
preserved example is **Torre** itself, situated not far to the north of Porto-Vecchio.
Nearby **Casteddu d'Araggiu**, another Bronze Age settlement set higher on the
mountain slopes above the gulf, is also worth a visit, and to complete the prehistoric tour, you can go south of Porto-Vecchio to visit the sites of **Ceccia** and
Tappa, also impressive legacies of the Torréen civilization.

Torre and the Casteddu d'Araggiu

Just follow the N198 north of Porto-Vecchio for 8km to reach **Torre**, which stands
on its own a little way from the main road on the right-hand side. Built against a
massive granite rock and covered in broad stone slabs, the semicircular construction is an impressive if small-scale Torréen structure (see p.134), possibly used as
a crematorium.

The **Casteddu d'Araggiu** lies on the other side of the main road, about 2km
up the D759; from the site's car park it's about half-an-hour's well-signposted walk

through maquis and scrubby woodland. Built in 2000 BC and inhabited by a community that lived by farming and hunting, the *casteddu* consists of a complex of chambers built into a massive circular wall. The site is entered via a ten-metre-long corridor covered in stone slabs. Immediately to the left you'll see a small triangular-shaped building, in the centre of which would have been a clay fireplace, a forerunner of the *zidda* (hearth) found in traditional Corsican households. Continuing in a clockwise direction you come to the *torre* itself, comprising a central chamber of which only the foundations remain. Past the tower, the next chamber – measuring 10m across – also has the remains of a fireplace, and a little further on it's possible to make out a well built into the thick walls, beyond which stands another small hut with fireplace.

Ceccia and Tappa

The **Ceccia** site lies about 5km southwest of Porto Vecchio along the D859, a twenty-minute walk from the village of the same name. Set on a conspicuous spur, this isolated tower was raised around 1350 BC, possibly for scanning the surrounding countryside for invaders, or for cult purposes. Unlike other Torréen sites, no traces of dwellings remain here.

About 1km west of Ceccia along the D853 you'll find the **Tappa** *casteddu* signposted to the south of the road, opposite an abandoned farm building. Set on a granite mound about ten minutes' walk away, the site lies on private property and is approached on foot, passing through the gate and following the direction indicated.

The surrounding wall is considered to be more recent than the rest of the *casteddu*, which was developed in a half-millennium prior to 1000 BC. A large *torre* at the southern end of the site consists of several small rooms around a central chamber. A ramp leads up to the main structure, which is entered by a narrow corridor, inside which another ramp winds up to a second level. The excavation of various clay pots, pounding implements and grindstones here has led archeologists to propose that this building was used for milling as well as storage.

Massif de l'Ospedale

Broadly covering the hinterland of the Golfe de Porto-Vecchio, limited in the northwest by the Massif de Bavella and in the southwest by the Montagne de Cagna, the **Massif de l'Ospedale** is a forested upland characterized by enormous granite boulders emerging from the deep greenery. Attractions up here include a magnificent beech forest, the **Forêt de l'Ospedale**, and an impressive artificial **lake**, ideal as a picnic spot.

Leaving Porto-Vecchio by the D368 northwest of town, a twisty drive of 15km up the slopes will soon get you to **Ospedale**, a village that has long been used as a summer resort by the inhabitants of Porto-Vecchio. Plumb in the middle of the forest, within a backdrop of massive clumps of granite, it provides fine views through the trees across L'Alta Rocca and over the Golfe de Porto-Vecchio in the other direction, but has few facilities.

Most people pass through and head for the **lake**, which emerges a couple of kilometres up the road. A shimmering blue expanse, backed by lines of spindly black trees which seem to grow from the water, the lake is surrounded by forest trails that are marked in every direction. A particularly enjoyable walk goes to the **Piscia di Gallo** (Piss of the Cockerel) waterfall, a two-hour ramble that provides plenty of opportunities to stop and bathe. The route begins about 1km past the dam on the right-hand side of the road, beyond the large parking area. From here the trail meanders through the pines and the maquis and crosses two streams before veering to the right. When you reach an opening in the pines, follow the stream for about 1km, keeping it on your right, and listen out for the sound of the waterfall about to come into view. Some 50m high, it's an impressive sight, plummeting between giant rocks into a swirling green pool.

North of the lake lies the **Forêt de Barocaggio-Marghèse**, a magnificent pine forest dominated by the pyramidal **Punta di u Diamante** (1227m); just past here the road crosses the **Col d'Illirata** (991m), 25km from Porto-Vecchio and 15km south of Zonza (see p.145).

travel details

Buses

Bonifacio to: Ajaccio (2 daily; 3hr); Olmeto (2 daily; 1hr 30min); (Porto-Vecchio; 2 daily; 30min); Propriano (2 daily; 1hr 15min); Roccapina (2 daily; 30min); Sartène (2 daily; 1hr).

Levie to: Ajaccio (2 daily; 3hr); Bavella (2 daily; 1hr); Sainte-Lucie-de-Tallano (2 daily; 30min); Zonza (2 daily; 30min).

Olmeto to: Ajaccio (2 daily; 1hr 30min); Bonifacio (2 daily; 1hr 30min); Porto-Vecchio (2 daily; 2hr); Propriano (2 daily; 20min); Roccapina (2 daily; 1hr); Sartène (2 daily; 40min).

Pianotolli-Caldarello to: Ajaccio (2 daily; 2hr 45min); Bonifacio (2 daily; 30min); Olmeto (2 daily; 2hr); Propriano (2 daily; 1hr); Porto-Vecchio (2 daily; 1hr 15min); Roccapina (2 daily; 15min); Sartène (2 daily; 45min).

Porto-Vecchio to: Ajaccio (2 daily; 3hr 20min); Bastia (2 daily; 2hr 30min); Bonifacio (4 daily; 30min); Olmeto (2 daily; 2hr); Propriano (2 daily; 1hr 30min); Roccapina (2 daily; 1hr); Sartène (2 daily; 1hr 20min).

Propriano to: Ajaccio (2 daily; 2hr); Bonifacio (2 daily; 1hr); Olmeto (2 daily; 20min); Porto-Vecchio (2 daily; 1hr 30min); Roccapina (2 daily; 40min); Sartène (2 daily; 20min).

Roccapina to: Ajaccio (2 daily; 2hr 30min); Bonifacio (2 daily; 30min); Olmeto (2 daily; 1hr); Porto-Vecchio (2 daily; 1hr); Propriano (2 daily; 40min); Sartène (2 daily; 30min).

Sainte-Lucie-de-Tallano to: Ajaccio (2 daily; 2hr 30min); Bavella (2 daily; 1hr); Levie (2 daily; 30min); Zonza (2 daily; 1hr).

Sartène to: Ajaccio (2 daily; 2hr 20min); Bonifacio (2 daily; 1hr); Olmeto (2 daily; 40min); Porto-Vecchio (2 daily; 1hr 20min); Propriano (2 daily; 20min); Roccapina (2 daily; 30min).

Zonza to: Ajaccio (2 daily; 3hr); Bavella (2 daily; 30min); Levie (2 daily; 30min); Sainte-Lucie-de-Tallano (2 daily; 1hr).

Ferries

For ferry services see p.155 & 162.

CHAPTER FIVE

EASTERN CORSICA

E astern Corsica may not match the intimidating scenery found elsewhere on the island, but it does have its attractions, not the least of which is one hundred kilometres of **sandy beach**, where scattered resorts offer some of the best-value accommodation on the island and make good bases for discovering the more challenging upland landscapes. **Solenzara**, for example, is one of the more alluring small seaside towns, and lies within striking distance of the fabulous Col de Bavella. North of here, beyond the rather tired resort of **Ghisonaccia**, you move into the **eastern plain**, an area of malaria-ridden swamps until the Americans sprayed the area with DDT after World War II. Now supporting acres of orchards and vineyards, this patchwork of fields is punctuated by shimmering lagoons, of which the **Étang d'Urbino** and **Étang de Diane** are the largest, supplying plentiful oysters and seafood for the local restaurants. Set on a rise between these lagoons is the Roman capital of **Aléria**, which has a compelling museum, a decent beach close by, and a few hotels straddling the main road.

Inland, you could drive up to the terraced villages of the **Fiumorbo** region for a grand view of the plain, or venture into the craggy gorges and precarious villages of the **Vallée du Tavignano** and the **Bozio**, either as a diversion on the drive to or from Bastia or as a route into the core of the island. To the north of here, the verdant **Castagniccia** is a fascinating region to explore, its tunnelled roads twisting past waterfalls and through an enormous forest of chestnut trees that's peppered with the highest concentration of highland villages in Corsica. A bed around here can be found at **Cervione**, the largest village in these parts, or **Piedicroce**, an old village fantastically located on the slopes of Monte San Petrone. North of the Castagniccia lies the **Casinca**, a more compact region of delightful villages such as **Vescovato** and **Venzolasca**, which could feasibly be seen on a day excursion from Bastia.

Transport around the east isn't too bad; a bus passes along the coast stopping at Solenzara, Ghisonaccia and Aléria on its way between Bastia and Porto-Vecchio, but there's no service into the Fiumorbo and Tavignano valleys. For the Castagniccia you'll need a car, although the *micheline* train does pass through Casamozza, from where you can hitch into the region.

ACCOMMODATION PRICES

Throughout this guide, hotel accommodation is graded on a scale from ① to ⑥. These numbers show the cost per night of the **least expensive double room in high season**, and correspond to the following prices:

① under F200   ③ F300–400   ⑤ F500–600
② F200–300   ④ F400–500   ⑥ over 600F

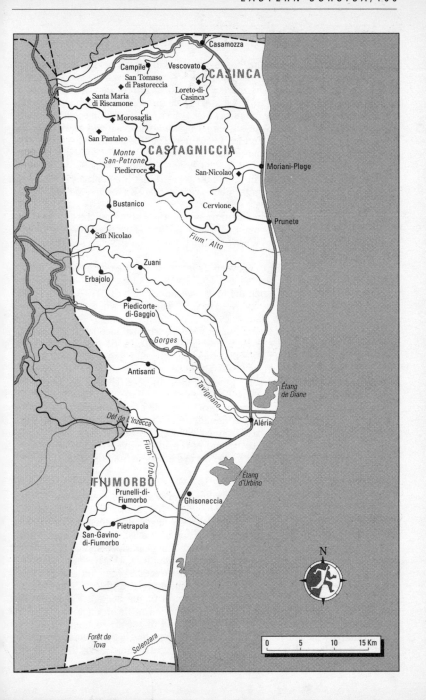

Solenzara, Ghisonaccia and Fiumorbo

SOLENZARA might not be the most scintillating of coastal resorts but its strip of hedge-fringed shops and busy marina give it a pleasantly lived-in look, and it does have a good clean beach. There are a few offbeat **hotels** here as well: try the *Mare e Festa* (☎95 57 42 91; ③), a pink Art Deco place on the beach at the southern end of the village, or the *Maquis et Mer* (☎95 57 40 07; ③) on the main street, a huge old-fashioned place with a solemn Corsican restaurant and a swish bar. *La Solenzara* (☎95 57 42 18; ②), on the beach north of *Maquis et Mer*, is an alternative, and the **tourist office**, on the main street opposite the *Prisunic* supermarket in the centre (May–Sept Mon–Sat 9am–noon & 2–6pm; ☎95 57 43 75), can provide additional addresses in the unlikely event that these places are booked up. For those spending the night under canvas there's *Camping de la Côte des Nacres*, 500m south of Solenzara on the beach.

A major reason for being in Solenzara is that it lies at the junction of the route de Bavella (see p.146), and you only have to go 500m for an invigorating plunge into the green torrent of the River Solenzara, which the Bavella road (the D268) follows for some distance.

The one sizeable village between Solenzara and Aléria is dusty, dismal **GHISONACCIA**, whose pejorative "accia" suffix (meaning "bad") seems just as applicable today as it was when the town was a malarial bog. That said, the place has enjoyed a certain prosperity ever since the late 1950s, when *pieds noirs* from Algeria were brought in to plant vineyards, and still has a healthy economy based on the wine and fruit processing that provide its principal income. If you have to stay here, make for the *De la Poste* (☎95 56 00 41; ②) in the main street on the corner of the Ghisoni road; otherwise there's the small *Franceschini* on the other side of the road, 200m north (☎95 56 06 39; ①), which tends to get swamped by boys doing their national service at the nearby army base. The **beach**, 4km to the east, is an acceptable strand.

Making your way north, you could turn off for the **Étang d'Urbino**, one of the half-dozen lagoons that break the monotony of the plain. Accessible via a dirt track, 10km along the main road from Ghisonaccia, this is a delightfully peaceful spot, fringed by reed beds. At the end of the track a pleasant inn, the *Ferme-auberge d'Urbino* (☎95 56 13 28; ③), serves oysters fresh from the lake.

Fiumorbo

The little-explored region of **Fiumorbo** (or Fium'orbo) has been renowned for the independent spirit of its inhabitants ever since 1769, when a group of shepherds who had refused to ascribe to French laws were struck down in an ambush along the road to Corte. Thirty years later a coalition of royalist, Paolist and pro-British Corsican exiles organized another anti-French rebellion which spread as far as the Sartenais before it was crushed by the French authorities. This tradition continued into the early nineteenth century, when an insurrection broke out and five thousand troops hired by Louis XVIII's government were unable to suppress the hordes of mountain people who seized control of the region. Eventually the ringleaders were either gunned down or deported to the French mainland by General Morand, who was nevertheless obliged to accede to them an area of coastal land. By the end of the century the Fiumorbo had become notorious bandit country, ruled by outlaws who terrorized the villages, untouched by the police, but today this is one of the quietest, most untroubled parts of Corsica.

The region is reached by taking the D244 west off the main road 2km south of Ghisonaccia, then turning onto the D145, a route that takes you into the valley of the **River Albatesco**, a tributary of the River Fiumorbo ("troubled waters") and location of the chief villages of the region. Once on the D145, you have a choice of taking the amazingly contorted sideroad up to **Serra-di-Fium'orbo**, which gives a fantastic view of the coastal plain, or continuing to **Pietrapola**, whose thermal baths attract hopeful people throughout the year. The baths are attached to the *Établissement Thermal*, a modern hotel dominating the village (☎95 56 70 03; ③).

Beyond here the road forms a loop round the northern flank of the valley, twisting through San-Gavino-di-Fium'orbo, Isolaccia-di-Fium'orbo and the especially attractive **PRUNELLI-DI-FIUM'ORBO**, approached from the west along an avenue of oak trees and pines. The entire length of the village street gives a panoramic view of the plain, although the best vantage point is from outside the church. You can **stay** up here at *Santa Susini* (☎95 56 02 29; ①), a huge villa hotel in the centre of the village. There are no restaurants.

Aléria

Built on the estuary at the mouth of the River Tavignano, **ALÉRIA** was the capital of the Corsican province during the Roman era, remaining the east coast's principal town and port right up until the eighteenth century. Little is left of the historic town except the **Roman ruins** and the Genoese fortress, which stands high against a background of chequered fields and green vineyards. A sizeable proportion of the local population are employed in farming oysters and mussels in the neighbouring **Étang de Diane**, formerly the Roman harbour and now an excellent place for a swim. (During his exile on Elba, Napóleon kept in contact with his homeland by ordering boatloads of oysters from the lagoon.) To the south, a strip of modern buildings straddling the main road makes up the modern town, but it's the village set on the hilltop just west of here which holds most interest.

A brief history of Aléria

This area was first settled in 564 BC by a colony of Greek Phocaeans who had been chased from their land by the Persian invasion. Calling their new port Alalia, these Greeks initiated the island's trade routes around the Mediterranean, selling the copper and lead they mined from the land and the wheat, olives and grapes they farmed here. In 535 BC they managed to survive a battle with the Carthaginians, but were left considerably weakened as a colony. Eventually fleeing to the mainland, the Phocaeans established a new capital at Massiglia (Marseille), retaining Alalia as a trading link between their colonies in southern Italy, Greece, Carthage and Spain.

In 259 BC the Romans arrived and conquered what was left of the port, which was by that time controlled by Carthaginians. It wasn't until around 80 BC, however, that they built up a naval base here, calling the town Aleria and re-establishing its importance in this part of the Mediterranean. As the only town of significant size, Aleria was named administrative capital of the province, before long boasting a population of some thirty thousand. Under the orders of the emperor Augustus a fleet was harboured in the Étang de Diane and public buildings were constructed here, including baths, a forum and a triumphal arch, the remains of which are visible today. Light industries also flourished during this

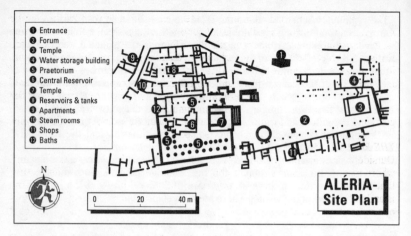

ALÉRIA-
Site Plan

① Entrance
② Forum
③ Temple
④ Water storage building
⑤ Praetorium
⑥ Central Reservoir
⑦ Temple
⑧ Reservoirs & tanks
⑨ Apartments
⑩ Steam rooms
⑪ Shops
⑫ Baths

N

0   20   40 m

period as Aleria developed into a thriving crafts centre, producing jewellery, ceramics and clothes. Honey and wax were also marketed here, and seafood from the Étang de Diane found a ready trade with the continent.

Aleria's Roman days came to an end in 410 AD when the city was struck by a fire which destroyed buildings and people alike. Malaria epidemics put paid to many of the survivors and the town was wiped out by Vandals later that century. Aleria was revived by the Genoese in the thirteenth century and was the seat of a bishopric for two hundred years. A fort was constructed in the sixteenth century, and when Theodor von Neuhof was received here in 1736 this was still one of the principal ports on the east coast.

The Musée Jerôme Carcopino and ancient Aleria

Your best plan is to begin your visit with the **Musée Jerôme Carcopino** (May–Sept Mon–Fri 8am–noon & 2–7pm; Oct–April 9am–noon & 2–6pm; 10F), which is housed in **Fort Matra**. Recently removed to three interconnected rooms on the first floor of the fort, the museum is crammed with some remarkable finds from the Roman site, among which ceramics, metal objects and jewellery form the bulk of the exhibits.

The **first room** contains magnificent evidence of ancient Aleria's importance as a trading port. Hellenic and Punic coins, rings and belt links are ranged alongside elaborate oil lamps decorated with Christian symbols, amphorae and some fragments of water pipes. An enormous **Attic plate**, depicting a red elephant against a black background, takes up one display case, with various glazed dishes using the same painting method ranged beneath. The highlight of this first room is a second-century marble **bust** of Jupiter Ammon, which was discovered near the forum. Opposite are more red and black ceramics, dating from around 450 BC; among them are two remarkable drinking vessels or **rhytons**, one representing the head of a mule, the other the head of a dog.

Finely worked Etruscan bronzes fill the **second room**, with some graceful statues providing the main attraction. You can also see jewellery from the fourth to the second century BC and objects discovered in the tombs of ancient Aleria, one of which, uncovered in 1966, revealed a priceless collection of elegantly curved, exquisitely made Greek swords, lances and daggers from the fifth century BC.

The highlight of the **third room** is an Attic **vase** adorned with twisting erotic figures thought to date from 480 BC, attributed to master artist Panaitios and one of the museum's most treasured exhibits. There are also painted earthenware Etruscan goblets and more remarkable ceramics, many in perfect condition. Most notable is a wide-mouthed drinking vessel, decorated with images of Dionysus dancing with a nymph and two satyrs. Iron weapons and hundreds of finely painted cups called "craters", one featuring a picture of Hercules and the Lion and another representing Dionysus, this time overseeing the grape harvest, complete the exhibition, along with a reconstruction of a fourth-century BC tomb.

THE ROMAN SITE

Outside it's a stone's throw to the **Roman site** (closes 30min before museum), where most of the excavation was done as recently as the 1950s, despite the fact that Merimée noticed signs of the Roman settlement during his survey of the island in 1830. Most of the site still lies beneath ground and is undergoing continuous excavation, but the balneum (bathhouse), the base of Augustus' triumphal arch, the foundations of the forum and traces of shops have been unearthed. The proximity of the sea, the strong scent of wild tarragon and the arresting view of snow-capped mountains and Fort Matra give a much-needed boost to the atmospherics.

First discovered was the **arch**, which formed the entrance to the governor's residence – the praetorium – on the western edge of the **forum**. In the adjacent **balneum**, a network of reservoirs and cisterns, the **caldarium** bears traces of the underground pipes that would have heated the room, and a patterned mosaic floor is visible inside the neighbouring chamber. To the north of the site lie the foundation walls of a large house, while at the eastern end of the forum the foundations of the **temple** can be seen, and at its northern edge, over a row of column stumps, are the foundations of the apse of an early Christian church.

Some traces of the Greek settlement, comprising the remains of an acropolis, have been discovered further to the east. It's believed that the main part of the town would have extended from the present site over to this acropolis and down to the Tavignano estuary. The port was located to the east of the main road, where the remnants of a second-century bathhouse have been found.

L'Étang de Diane

A saltwater lagoon, the **Étang de Diane** lies just north of the town. To get there you either take the narrow N200 at the Cateraggio crossroads, which will bring you to the beach and an oyster farm, or follow the main road north of Aléria for 4km until you reach a turning on the right, signposted "Terra Vecchia". A narrow dirt track leads down to the banks of the lagoon, a glittering stretch of water with a lookout tower marking the northeastern edge. The best places to swim are from the sandy eastern banks, which also make a pleasant picnic spot.

Practicalities

If you decide to stay, there are a few **hotels** worth checking out: *Les Orangers* (☎95 57 00 31; ③) is the best place, situated 50m north of the Cateraggio crossroads in the centre of the modern part; *l'Atrachjata* (☎95 57 03 93; ②), a little further north, does good **meals** and provides adequate accommodation; *L'Empereur*, a big chalet-style building a little further up from *Les Orangers* (☎95 57 02 13; ②), is clean and comfortable. For budgeting travellers *le Petit Bosquet*

(☎95 57 02 16; ①), 500m south of the Cateraggio crossroads, on the east side of the road, is an ordinary motel providing a decent bed.

Those with a passion for oysters can sample them fresh from the lagoon at *L'Auberge le Chalet*, 100m north of the crossroads, which also serves other excellent seafood dishes.

Vallée du Tavignano

Inland from Aléria, the **Vallée du Tavignano** forms an exhilarating approach to Corte, its craggy gorges and dark rocky slopes dotted with red-roofed villages adhering to the slopes. The N200, which tracks the river all the way to Corte, is the quickest route, but if you're in no hurry you could take the upland road through the savage country of the **Bozio**, on the north flank of the valley. If, however, you've only got time for a quick detour on your way across the eastern plain, you might drive up to the village of **Antisanti**, which overlooks the plain and Corsica's mountainous spine from the south side of the valley.

Antisanti

Located at an altitude of 700m, 15km west of Aléria, the rocky grey outpost of **ANTISANTI** offers views that more than reward anyone making the effort to get to it along the tortuous D43. In the twelfth century the village was an important stop-off point for merchants travelling between Corte and the coast. Resisting Pascal Paoli's revolution, the town was burnt down in 1753. Today it consists of only one street, but there's a café from which, on a clear day, you can see all the main peaks of Corsica, the craggy needles of Bavella and Incudine rising to the south, Monte d'Oro to the west, while eastwards the islands of Elba, Capraia and Monte Cristo can be made out way beyond the plain.

The gorge route

Following the River Tavignano, one of the island's principal rivers, the main N200 road from Aléria to Corte (around 60km) provides a direct scenic route into the heart of the island. The road meanders across the plain for about 10km until, past the hamlet of **Buggione**, it begins an ascent into the mountainous country of the interior, narrowing in the approach to a magnificent gorge a further 10km onwards. Slicing through the denuded schist walls of the valley, the road affords occasional glimpses of hilltop villages to the south, and after the same distance again you emerge from the gorge at the sparse hamlet of **Volta**, where a triple-arched Genoese bridge takes you across the river. Visible on the right bank is a tenth-century Romanesque chapel dedicated to John the Baptist, a tiny edifice built of patterned stones alternating with plain blocks of granite, now used as a shepherds' shelter.

From here on it's an easier road along the southern flank of the river; to the north you can make out the flinty villages of the Bozio, ridged high on the distant valley slopes.

The Bozio

Tucked between the Tavignano gorge and the Castagniccia, the **Bozio** is a grimly mountainous terrain, its maquis littered with Romanesque churches and sombre villages which were hotbeds of Corsican nationalism in the eighteenth century.

There are two routes through this region from Aléria: the D14, which leaves the N200 about 12km from town; or the D16/D116, which begins 5km north of Aléria, crossing the plain before rising to the north side of the Cursiglièse valley.

If you take the former road, the landscape becomes really wild at **PIEDICORTE-DI-GAGGIO**, a protruberance of red roofs above the bleak rock, with a central square that gives you a panorama of the eastern plain plus a hazy view of the giant peaks. The village church boasts an eighteenth-century facade and a huge clock tower, and the base of the building incorporates carved twelfth-century remnants. About 4km beyond lies **Altiani**, where the houses are attached to a spur amidst great blocks of granite, and from here it's another 9km of switch-back road to **ERBAJOLO**, which offers a fantastic view of the Tavignano valley and of Monte d'Oro and Monte Renoso. From here you can take a walk to the remote Pisan chapel of **San Martino**, a gentle thirty-minute walk along a mule track through the maquis from the church in the centre of the village. A further twenty minutes from San Martino lies the ruined hamlet of **Casella**, another spectacular belvedere.

The alternative route becomes increasingly tortuous once you've joined the D116, winding through the flinty semi-derelict villages of **Tallone** and **Zuani** on its way to the **Col de San Cervone** (899m), where you'll get a fine view across the Tavignano in one direction and towards the distant sea in the other. Beyond here you could make a loop down to Erbajolo (see above) or continue to **ALANDO**, the birthplace of Sambucuccio d'Alando, a legendary fourteenth-century rebel. Leader of a popular movement against the region's despotic nobility, he is credited with the invention of the "Temps du Commun", an organization which from 1359 to 1362 united villages all over Corsica under one administrative body of elected magistrates.

From Alando you can head north through the stark hills as far as **BUSTANICO**, the village said to be the source of the War of Independence. It began in 1729 when an old man named Casone sparked off a local rebellion against the Genoese, after a tax collector threatened to carry off all his possessions. Outraged at such injustice, fellow villagers rose up in his defence, triggering riots and raids all over eastern Corsica, culminating in the sack of Bastia in 1730. The village church has a graceful wooden figure of Christ, sculpted by a local craftsman in the eighteenth century.

If you head west along the D441 you'll soon come to **SERMANO**, famous for *A Paghjella* singing (see p.187), which if you're lucky you can hear at the Pisan chapel of **San Nicolao**. The chapel is fifteen minutes' walk from the church in the centre of the village, and is decorated with naive fifteenth-century frescoes of Christ, the Virgin, the Apostles and saints.

The Castagniccia

The **Castagniccia** covers a hundred square kilometres, extending south of the River Golo as far as the Bozio, and westwards just beyond the shadowy crest of Monte San Petrone. The region gets its name from its dense forests of chestnut or *castagna*, which were first cultivated here by the Genoese in the fifteenth century and became the key to the local economy, providing not only fuel and furniture timber but an important source of nourishment. Up until the late eighteenth century, when the French took control, this was the richest and most populated part of Corsica, but the region is now characterized by abandoned hamlets, derelict houses and redundant **sechoirs**, double-floored structures in which chestnuts were dried before being ground into the flour which used to sustain the population through hard winters. As well as providing sustenance, the chestnut flour was bartered for olive oil from other regions, while the wood was used for heating the houses, for furniture and for devotional carving – the work of the Castagniccia's skilled craftsmen can be seen in its numerous Romanesque and Baroque chapels. In the eighteenth century the arms industry thrived here as well, and its products found a ready market during the Corsican Revolution, when the Castagniccia was a bastion of support for Pascal Paoli, a native of **Morosaglia**.

Exploring the Castagniccia requires a vehicle and some caution: although there's a larger concentration of roads here than anywhere else on Corsica, routes are extremely tortuous and narrow, with the added hazard of roaming wild pigs. Daily trains from Bastia stop in Casamozza and Ponte Leccia, but unless you're prepared to walk or hitch this isn't much help for exploring the area. Furthermore, hotels and restaurants are to be found only at La Porta, Piedicroce and Cervione – though you could always stay on the coast at Moriani Plage and see the Castagniccia on a day's tour. You have a choice of routes into the region: from the east coast you can penetrate the forest from either Prunete or Moriani Plage; from the north strike in from Casamozza; while from the west it's a short drive from Ponte Leccia to Morosaglia.

Moriani Plage to Cervione

One of a string of virtually indistinguishable resorts which sprawl up the coast north of Aléria, **MORIANI PLAGE** offers a reasonable beach and lots of accommodation, so it makes as good a base as any for a Castagniccia foray. The budget **hotels** are *U Centru* (☎95 38 41 83; ①), a homely motel on the main road at the heart of the "village", and *Le Corsica* (☎95 38 50 05; ①), a sturdy old building right on the junction of the coast road and the inland D34 – the latter tends to attract backpackers, but there's plenty of space. *L'Abri des Flots* (☎95 38 40 76; ②), 100m north of the junction, right by the beach, is a clean modern place with a shady garden restaurant. At the top end of the market there's *Domaine de Soliciana* (☎95 38 50 15; ④), on the main road 1km south of the junction with the D34, a pleasant complex with a vast pine-shaded swimming pool shielded from the road.

About 2km along the D34, the village of **SAN NICOLAO** emerges, signalled by the prominent bell tower of its church, which boasts some colourful trompe l'oeil painting from the eighteenth century. If you feel like staying, *L'Île d'Or* (☎95 38 51 16; open June–Sept; ②) is a characterful hotel in an old village house with eight rooms but no restaurant. From here it's 5km south to the largest, busiest and most welcoming village of the Castagniccia, **CERVIONE**, whose houses tower over a sloping medieval square, from where archways lead off into the surrounding streets. Flanking the south side of the square is one of the first Baroque churches on Corsica, the **Cathédrale Saint-Erasme**, founded in 1578 by Saint Alexander Sauli, who was ordained bishop of Aléria in 1570 and soon transferred the bishopric to Cervione to escape the malaria-ridden swampland of the plain. Little remains of the old cathedral, which was restored in the nineteenth century, but the impressive black and white marble floor gives the place some appeal. Opposite the church stands the bishop's palace, once the residence of King Theodor (see box on p.178); its ethnographical **museum** (May–Sept Tues–Sat 9am–noon & 2–6pm; 5F) exhibits various rocks and farm implements.

There's one **hotel** in Cervione, the *Saint-Alexandre* (☎95 38 10 83; ②), to the north of the village square; it's a huge, underfurnished old place, but authentically Corsican. You can **eat** at the lively *U Casone* pizzeria, through an archway off the square, while for drinking there's a good **bar** next door to the church.

The elegant Romanesque chapel of **Santa Cristina** is a forty-minute walk from Cervione – take the road down towards Prunete for about 600m, then a signpost shows the way. Marvellous **frescoes** dating from 1473 decorate the twin apses (you'll find the key on a ledge above the door) – on the left side Christ is depicted with the Virgin, Saint Christina and a kneeling monk, on the right Christ is surrounded by the symbols of the Evangelists, and over the arch between them the Crucifixion is portrayed. A more ambitious three-hour walk into the mountains starts from the west of the village: follow the signs to Notre-Dame de la Scobiccia, a tiny Romanesque chapel about 2km up the slope, from where a mule track wends up into the maquis to the **Punta Nevera**, a rocky eminence overlooking much of the Castagniccia.

Cervione to Carcheto

South of Cervione, after about 12km of tormented roads comes **Valle d'Alesani**, from where it's a short detour up the D217 to the **Couvent d'Alesani** where King Theodor was crowned. The Franciscan monastery is mostly a ruin, but its church holds a beautiful fifteenth-century Sienese painting known as the *Virgin and the Cherry*. Back on the main road it's not long before you reach **FELCE**, where the Baroque church is decorated with simple yet arresting frescoes – on the ceiling you'll see the artist, palette in hand, floating among the clouds. Also of interest is the **tabernacle** above the altar, carved by a penitent bandit.

THEODOR VON NEUHOF

Scorned by Corsican historian Chanoine Casanova as an "operetta king", **Theodor von Neuhof** was crowned King of Corsica on April 15, 1736, a unique title he was to hold for just eight months.

Theodor was an ambitious nobleman with a very colourful past. Brought up in the court of France where he was page to the duchess d'Orléans, mother of the Prince Regent, he travelled around England, Holland and Spain, killed his best friend in a duel, and acquired a fortune through some rather dubious financial speculations. Captured by Moors in Tunis in the early 1730s and put into slavery in Algiers, he managed to bribe his way to freedom, and was soon sending word to a group of Corsican exiles in Livorno that he would provide them with aid in return for the crown of their troubled island. Impressed by his royal connections and fancy talk, and desperate for money and arms, the Corsicans agreed. Soon after, Theodor landed at Aléria, decked out in full Turkish regalia with a retinue of French, Italian and Moorish attendants, and was taken in state to the Couvent d'Alesani to be crowned King Theodor I of Corsica. His powers were severely constrained – a council of 24 men was appointed to advise him, and he was answerable to a Corsican parliament – but Theodor had plenty of opportunities for kingly behaviour. Living it up at the bishop's palace in Cervione, he distributed titles among the wealthier Corsicans, made increasingly exaggerated promises of arms for the liberation of his people, and organized a few ineffectual sieges and pointless military manoeuvres against the Genoese.

Mistrust amongst his ministers increased as the emptiness of his promises became obvious, and in November 1736 the king was forced to flee the island via Solenzara, disguised as a priest. Theodor didn't give up entirely on the Corsicans, however – in 1739 he returned with a small fleet but was deterred from landing by the French. Eventually Theodor returned to England, where he died in 1756 having accumulated massive debts. A plaque in London's Soho Square commemorates him: "Fate poured its lessons on his living head, bestowed a kingdom and denied him bread."

Another few windy kilometres takes you to **CARCHETO**, set amidst an ocean of chestnut trees and giving a good view of Piedicroce across the valley. Carcheto's **Église Sainte-Marguerite**, set by a wood on the edge of the hamlet, is an eighteenth-century edifice packed with examples of local work – luridly painted stucco covers the walls, portraying scenes from the Crucifixion, with an alabaster statue of the Virgin and Child providing a restrained counterpoint. Unfortunately the church is often locked, in which case you have to pick up the key from the *Refuge* hotel in Piedicroce (see below). Outside the church, a sign for "La Fontaine" directs walkers through the wood to a glistening waterfall which cascades through an opening in the trees – a fine spot for a dip.

Piedicroce and around

A cluster of villages belonging to the commune of Orezza lies to the north of Carcheto. The principal village in these parts is **PIEDICROCE**, a magnificent fifteenth-century hamlet that has the sole hotel in the area, *Le Refuge* (☎95 35 82 65; ②). The hotel does excellent Corsican food, especially Castagniccia specialities such as chestnut fritters served with *brocciu* cheese. Piedicroce's **Église-Saint-Pierre-et-Paul**, built in 1761, contains a fine old **organ**, which has been restored to its sixteenth-century glory.

STAZZONA, a kilometre east along the spur of the D506, was the centre of arms manufacture during the War of Independence – its name means "forge" in

Corsican. More recently it's made its money from the **Eaux d'Orezza** spring: as the faded old hotel signs indicate, people used to come up here for the curative waters, but nowadays the stuff is bottled and sold all over the island. To reach the spring just continue north for 500m and you'll see the gates on the left – you might also see a gang of local kids here, as mud-packs made with spring water are reputedly effective against adolescent acne. Whilst you're here you could pay a visit to the workshops of **Valle d'Orezza**, 2km to the southeast along the D46, where wonderful, traditional smoking pipes and boxes are carved from olive and chestnut wood.

Heading back through Piedicroce, take the D71 north for the **Couvent d'Orezza**, which stands in a green glade in a bewitchingly silent spot. Reduced to a craggy ruin by the Germans in World War II, the site has profound historic associations. In the eighteenth century the convent was a centre of resistance to the Genoese republic, and several *consulte* (rebel meetings) took place here – on April 20, 1731, twenty representatives of the clergy gathered here to discuss whether violent rebellion was against the fundamental principles of Christian morality, and it was here that Paoli was voted commander in chief of the Corsican National Guard. Napoléon and Paoli also met here in 1793 in an unsuccessful attempt at achieving a truce between their respective armies.

The summit of **Monte San Petrone** (1767m), one of the most thrilling viewpoints on the island, can be reached in about three hours from Campodonice, about 2km west of Couvent d'Orezza down a side road. A mule track from the centre of the hamlet clearly indicates the way.

Campana to the Col de Prato
Beyond Piedicroce the D71 continues to twist through the forests on the slopes of Monte San Petrone, past various abandoned hamlets. Just 2km from the Couvent d'Orezza the village of **CAMPANA** merits a stop for its Baroque **Église Sant'André**, which houses a fine *Adoration of the Shepherds* attributed to the Spanish seventeenth-century painter Zurbaran. After Campana head north for 2km, then veer right at the fork for the village of **CROCE**, which has a campsite and bungalows to rent – either phone the owner, M. Mattei (☎95 39 21 33), or ask at the *mairie* in the centre of the village.

One of the most distinctive villages of the Castagniccia is **LA PORTA**, about 6km from here; its multicoloured roofs make a pleasant change from the sombre grey stone of most Castagniccia hamlets. A **hotel** here, the *San Petrone* (☎95 39 20 19; ②), caters for hikers and visitors attracted by the famous **bell tower**, which at 45m high is visible above the greenery from quite a distance. Built in 1720, the ornamented tower adjoins the **Église Saint-Jean-Baptiste**, a definitively Baroque creation dating from 1648. If you want to sample the best of Castagniccia's cuisine, go to *Restaurant de l'Ampignani* in the village centre just south of the church; it's quite expensive but very good.

Taking the north road out of La Porta will bring you to the **Col de Prato** (985m), the highest point on the roads of Castagniccia. From the col, a walk to the ruined **San Petrucolo**, a church founded as far back as the sixth century, can be done in half an hour. Follow the narrow track south in the direction of Monte San Petrone, then after 100m take the track on the right into the maquis – follow this for a few steps then strike left, and you'll see the chapel straight in front of you.

Morosaglia and beyond

An approximately straight 2km west of the Col de Prato lies **MOROSAGLIA**, where Pascal Paoli's birthplace stands at the east end of the village in the hamlet of Stretta, signposted **Maison de Pascal Paoli**. Unfortunately the museum is usually closed, but you can try ringing the bell in the hope that someone might show you the small collection of letters, portraits and other memorabilia, including the very first Corsican newspaper, printed in 1794. Paoli's ashes, brought back from England in 1807, are entombed in a chapel on the ground floor.

Paoli was baptized in the Pisan-founded but extensively rebuilt church of **Santa Reparata**, situated up a track opposite the house. His brother Clement, described by Dorothy Carrington as "a matchless marksman who preyed for his enemies' souls as he shot them down", lived out his retirement here, in the large mansion that's now the village school.

A couple of fine Romanesque chapels are to be found beyond Morosaglia. The nearer, **Santa Maria di Valle-di-Rostino**, stands to the west of the D15, 5km along the road. Passing the village on your right, continue for 500m to reach the ruined chapel, accessible via a rough track. Dating from the tenth century, the apse displays some fine Pisan stonework created by narrow blocks interspersed with green and grey schist, adorned with slender columns and harmonious arcading. Amongst the primitive sculpture along the external roof band, Adam and Eve on either side of the Tree of Life feature most prominently. **San Tomaso di Pastoreccia**, 10km north of Morosaglia at the end of the zigzagging route through Pastoreccia, is a half-ruined building of grey schist, dating from the tenth century, its interior enlivened by a series of sixteenth-century **frescoes.** Some are in very bad condition, but you won't have any difficulty picking out most of the Apostles and saints (a young Saint John stands out in a gold surround), or deciphering the scenes from the Passion and the Last Judgement.

The Casinca

Bounded by the Golo and Fiumalto rivers, the **Casinca** covers the eastern slopes of Monte Sant'Angelo, an area swathed in olive and chestnut trees and embellished with stately villages. It's less popular with tourists than the Castagniccia, but is easier to get into if you haven't got your own transport, as there's a twice-daily bus from Bastia to **Vescovato**, many of whose inhabitants earn their living in the city. There's no accommodation on offer but it's a small area, easily coverable in half a day.

The Casinca villages

CASTELLARE-DI-CASINCA, just 1km up the D6 from the main coast road, about 15km north of Moriani-Plage, affords a wonderful view of the eastern plain and has a beautiful tenth-century church, **San Pancrazio**, notable for its triple apse. About a kilometre out of the village turn left for **PENTA-DI-CASINCA**, a place that ranks second in importance to the region. Its dark streets, crammed with lofty schist buildings dating principally from the fifteenth century, open out onto a large square which gives a fine view across the plain.

A kilometre east along the D206 you reach a junction where an abrupt left takes you onto the spectacular road flanking Monte Sant'Angelo. **LORETO-DI-CASINCA**, the next halt, perches on a spur overlooking all the villages of the

Casinca, its long main street affording a panorama right across to Bastia – the **bar** next to the church is an ideal place to make the most of it. A waymarked hike through the chestnut forest up **Monte Sant'Angelo** (1218m) starts 500m south of the village – it's about ninety minutes' fairly strenuous climbing to the summit.

Some 500m north of the village you can cut back east by taking a right turn and following the road across a ridge for 2km until you hit the D237 again. A right here will bring you to remote and lofty **VENZOLASCA**, whose slender, lancelike church spire is conspicuous from a long way off. Venzolasca is one of the few places in Corsica where you still see men dressed in traditional black corduroy, complete with silver studs and gun belt.

From here it's a short drive down to **VESCOVATO**, set amongst chestnut trees and olive groves. Capital of the Casinca, this was an important place in the thirteenth century when the bishopric of Mariana was transferred here in a move to escape the malaria-ridden plain ("vescovato" means bishopric in Corsican). The bishopric remained until 1570 when it was relocated to the more important town of Bastia. The village is livelier than most places hereabouts – its busy central square, shaded by lines of ancient plane trees, even has an outdoor café, a rare find in these parts.

On the south side of the square, a family coat of arms indicates the house of the historian Filippini, whose *Historia di Corsica* (1594) is a principal source of medieval Corsican history. A further wander through the village reveals various plaques commemorating eminent visitors such as Mirabeau, but Vescovato's main sight is the church of **San Martino**, reached by climbing a flight of steps north of the square. Enlarged by the bishops of Mariana in the fifteenth century, the church contains a fine marble tabernacle, carved by a Genoese sculptor in 1441 and portraying two Roman soldiers sleeping against the tomb.

travel details

Buses

Aléria to: Bastia (2 daily; 1hr 30min); Ghisonaccia (2 daily; 20min); Porto Vecchio (2 daily; 1hr 30min); Solenzara (2 daily; 40min).

Ghisonaccia to: Aléria (2 daily; 20min); Bastia (2 daily; 1hr 50min); Porto-Vecchio (2 daily; 1hr); Solenzara (2 daily; 20min).

Moriani Plage to: Bastia (3 daily; 1hr).

Solenzara to: Aléria (2 daily; 40min); Bastia (2 daily; 2hr); Ghisonaccia (2 daily; 20min); Porto-Vecchio (2 daily; 40min).

Vescovato to: Bastia (2 daily; 40min); Venzolasca (2 daily; 10min).

Venzolasca to: Bastia (2 daily; 50min); Vescovato (2 daily; 10min).

CHAPTER SIX

CENTRAL CORSICA

Central Corsica is a nonstop parade of stupendous scenery, and the best way to immerse yourself in it is to get onto the region's ever-expanding network of marked trails and forest roads. The ridge of granite mountains forming the spine of the island is closely followed by the epic **GR20**, a trail which can be picked up from various villages and is scattered with refuge huts, most of them offering no facilities except shelter. Whereas the summits of Monte Cinto, Monte Renoso and Monte d'Oro are only for experienced high-altitude walkers, you don't have to be an athlete to enjoy the peaks: Incudine and Rotondo pose fewer difficulties for the uninitiated, and the roads of this region, although in many places falling into disrepair, penetrate deep into the forests which carpet the mountain slopes, crossing various lofty passes that provide exceptional views across the island.

Corte, set in a dip at the centre of the island on the main road between Ajaccio and Bastia, provides the perfect place to begin exploring, as it's well placed to reach anywhere covered in this chapter and has the bulk of the region's accommodation – elsewhere it's rare to find more than one basic hotel per village. Capital of independent Corsica in the eighteenth century, Corte is a fortress village *par excellence*, with its walled citadel, set atop a twisted pinnacle of rock, piercing the landscape of overlapping mountains and forests. Though the second-ranking town of northern Corsica, it's a peaceful, slow-moving town where old traditions die hard, making it a fascinating introduction to the mentality of the island.

In the immediate environs of Corte the chief attractions are the **Vallée de la Restonica** and the parallel **Gorges du Tavignano**, but the most popular valley in central Corsica – on account of its comparative proximity to Bastia – is the **Vallée d'Asco**, which offers another superb gorge and rich wildlife. The Asco road culminates at Haut'Asco, a ski resort on **Monte Cinto**, Corsica's highest peak. Access to the upper reaches of Cinto is easier from the adjacent valley of the **Niolo**, a sheep-rearing region that was isolated for centuries until the construction of the road a hundred years ago. Like Corte, the Niolo is an essential visit for anyone eager to understand the soul of Corsica, so you might want to linger for a night or two in the main settlement of **Calacuccia**, a centre for walks and drives into the **Forêt de Valdo-Niello**, a dizzying forest of Laricio pines.

ACCOMMODATION PRICES

Throughout this guide, hotel accommodation is graded on a scale from ① to ⑥. These numbers show the cost per night of the **least expensive double room in high season**, and correspond to the following prices:

① under F200	③ F300–400	⑤ F500–600
② F200–300	④ F400–500	⑥ over 600F

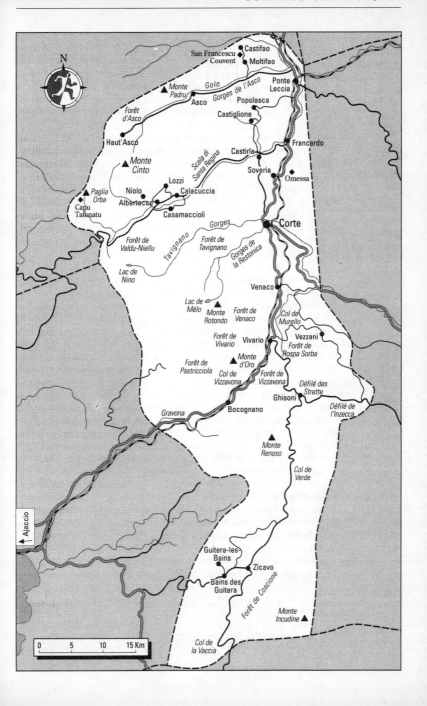

Such forests cover much of central Corsica, and one of the most superb drives on the island goes south of Corte from **Vivario** through the **Forêt de Rospa-Sorba**, the endless trees set against an omnipresent background of snowy peaks. The nearby village of **Ghisoni** is the place to make for if you want to tackle **Monte Renoso**, while **Vizzavona**, further south along the Bastia–Ajaccio route, is the springboard for Monte d'Oro, and offers countless walks into the luscious beech forest. Still further south, **Zicavo** is the base for **Monte Incudine**, the southern-most major peak.

Getting around central Corsica, you're limited to the *micheline* train, which crosses the mountains from Bastia to Ajaccio with a main connection at Ponte Leccia. Four daily trains stop at Ponte Leccia, Corte, Venaco, Vivario and Vizzavona, passing through a four-kilometre tunnel that is one of the major engineering triumphs of the mountain railway. The last stop before the descent to Ajaccio is Bocognano. No public transport serves the Niolo, but a twice-daily bus runs between Ponte Leccia and Haut'Asco.

The Vallée d'Asco

The **Vallée d'Asco** – the wettest part of Corsica – was once a region of intensive pastoral farming, but nowadays is a sparsely populated region making its way on the proceeds of small-scale cheese production and a regular influx of hikers. The River Asco starts life as the Stranciacone, which rises at an altitude of 2556m on the lower slopes of **Monte Cinto**, Corsica's highest mountain, then flows through the village of Asco and on through a fantastic **gorge** before flowing into the Golo close to Ponte Leccia. In the upper valley, beyond Asco, the scenery is most alpine – up here mouflon roam in carefully protected zones, and bearded vultures and royal eagles are sometimes to be spotted in the magnificent **Forêt de Carozzica**. The road comes to an end 15km west of Asco at the semi-operational ski station at **Haut'Asco**, from where trails lead into the forest and up the flank of Cinto – though the principal approach to the mountain is from the south (see p.187).

There is a bus service between Ponte Leccia and Haut'Asco, but you'll need a car to make a tour of the valley. Starting at Ponte Leccia, it's a good idea to detour up to the delightful villages of **Moltifao** and **Castifao**, before returning to the gorge and the road up to Haut'Asco.

Ponte Leccia, Moltifao and Castifao

PONTE LECCIA, lying 19km north of Corte at the junction of road and rail routes to Bastia, Corte and the Balagne, has nothing to recommend it except its service stations, where you might want to refuel before pressing on into the Vallée d'Asco. A couple of kilometres north, the D47 leaves the N197 to follow the River Asco, initially along a flatland scattered with eucalyptus trees. If you need a place to stay hereabouts, you're best advised to pass over the places in Ponte Leccia in favour of the *Cabanella* (☎95 47 80 29; ①), an *auberge* opposite the turning for Moltifao, 7km from the junction with N197 – it provides a decent bed and excellent home cooking for next to nothing.

A right along the D247 here takes you up the hillside to **MOLTIFAO**, an amphitheatre of ancient buildings set on a crest separating the valleys of Tartagine and Asco. Moltifao's church houses a beautiful sixteenth-century **triptych** and some sacristy furniture, including a wooden retable incorporating a fine primitive painting of the Virgin on a gold background. For a great view across to the Tartagine, carry on 3km north to **CASTIFAO**, a warm-toned settlement that once thrived on its copper mine and marble quarry.

The Gorges de l'Asco and Haut'Asco

Back down the main road, after a further 2km the road penetrates the **Gorges de l'Asco**, following every twitch of the river for 9km, between overhanging rock-faces of orange granite which soar to 900m. There isn't much to **ASCO** itself, an austere little place famed in the eighteenth century as home of the *paceri* (peace-makers), a tribunal of locally elected magistrates who mediated between families involved in vendettas. Its location, however, couldn't be better: built up the left bank of the river, the village lies at the base of a grandiose crest of mountains, with the crags of Monte Padro immediately to the northwest and the Monte Cinto massif and Capo Bianco to the southwest. A wonderful – if well-known – swim-ming spot can be found beyond the village, at the signposted **Genoese bridge**; the water is transparent green, fairly deep, but pretty cold even in midsummer.

Beyond Asco the D147 widens and hugs the **Forêt de Carozzica**, a magnifi-cent forest of maritime and Laricio pines, which extend up the valley walls up to the 2000m contour. Keeping close to the river, the road passes clearings and pools ideal for a picnic and a bathe. It then becomes increasingly difficult as you ascend to the few buildings that comprise **HAUT'ASCO** (or Asco La Neige), a ski station set amidst swathes of lush turf punctuated by stunted pines. A large impersonal hotel, *Le Chalet*, is open from June to September (☎95 47 81 08; ②) and rents out chalets during winter; the hotel restaurant is open only in the summer months. There are three slopes for skiing, each with its own lift, and for hikers the highest section of the GR20 passes close by. Five kilometres to the south lies the challenge of the Punta Minuta, part of the Monte Cinto massif, or you might attempt Monte Padro via the Vallée du Stranciacone.

The Niolo

The **Niolo** is the vast basin of the upper reaches of the **Golo**, a river that rises 2000m up in the mountains, is swelled by meltwater from the high peaks of Monte Cinto, Paglia Orba and Capo Tafonato, and expires to the south of Bastia, 80km from its source. The region's name – a corruption of the Corsican *niellu*, meaning "sombre" or "afflicted" – is now more appropriate than ever, for fire has destroyed much of the Niolo's forested land, leaving bleak landscapes of orange granite and shrivelled vegetation. Conifers and chestnut trees scatter the lower slopes of Monte Cinto, but of the great dark forest which once blanketed the whole basin all that remains is the **Forêt de Valdo-Niello**, a majestic swathe of Laricio pines in the southwest of the district.

The forest extends east of the frequently snowbound Col de Verghio, the high-est mountain pass in Corsica and one of two routes into the Niolo. The other one is the rocky corridor known as the **Scala di Santa Regina**, a vertiginous ravine some 21km long and 300m high, through which a road was built in the late nine-teenth century. Until then, people had used hazardous goat and mule tracks (the *scala*) to get into this region, whose isolation and consequent inbreeding perpetu-ated the singularly tall, blond and blue-eyed appearance of the Neolithic tribes known as the Corsi, from whom the Niolins claim direct descent.

The Niolins have always made their living from the breeding of goats. Shepherds formerly lived a solitary, harsh existence, trekking over the mountains with their herds to the milder coastal plains for winter – mainly to Galéria on the west coast but sometimes as far as Cap Corse – and returning to the high ground with their flocks in summertime. Some of the old, bare stone dwellings still pepper the slopes, but are mostly abandoned these days. In addition, Niolo's craft industry has all but disappeared – the main survival is the local gastronomic speciality, a sharp goats' cheese. On the other hand, ancient traditions have an extra vitality in the Niolo, and some of the finest *a paghjella* chanting can be heard here (see box below). Improvised singing competitions are still held at Casamaccioli during the three-day **Santa di u Niolu**, a country fair which takes place around September 8 and attracts crowds from all over Corsica, who come as much for the entertainment, drinking and gambling as for the livestock.

These days tourism is making itself felt at the far-flung capital of the Niolo, **Calacuccia**, an exposed little place offering basic accommodation as a base for exploration of the area. Apart from a trip to **Casamaccioli**, you could pay a visit to **Albertacce**, which boasts a small ethnographic museum, to **Corscia**, an impressive stack of hillside hamlets, or to the southeast face of **Monte Cinto**. Southwest of Calacuccia, the glistening **Lac de Nino** makes a rewarding hike from the **Forêt de Valdo-Niello**, a magnet for walkers and tourists in search of some shade.

Calacuccia and the Niolo villages

A clutch of grim grey buildings, **CALACUCCIA** benefits from its unusual location, set high on a wide plain at the heart of the Niolo, on the edge of the **Lac de Calacuccia** reservoir and in the shadow of the weird jagged ridge of the Cinque Frati mountains. The only historic sight here is the church of **Saint-Pierre**, built on an eminence at the western exit from the village and affording a fine view across the plateau; inside, a seventeenth-century wooden statue of Christ forms the principal attraction.

If you're after a **room**, head for *Hôtel des Touristes* at the centre of the village (☎95 48 00 04; ②); despite its austere facade it's a welcoming place, and has the best-value food. The *De la Scala* (☎95 48 02 76; ①), at the eastern edge of the village, is less expensive but a touch too functional. The poshest place is *L'Acquaviva* (☎95 48 06 90; ③), overlooking the lake as you leave the village on the road to Casamaccioli; its swimming pool is perhaps its most alluring point.

You get an exceptional view of Calacuccia's surroundings by taking an easy four-hour round-trip walk to the **Col de l'Arinella** (1592m). Directly south of the Lac de Calacuccia dam, follow the road leading to the left – after about 500m you'll notice a winding path leading up to the col from a sharp bend in the road. The col lies on the crest separating the Golo and Tavignano valleys, so you get a magnificent view of both, looking south towards Monte Rotondo and north towards Monte Cinto. You can either descend the same way or follow the rough track for 6km down to Casamaccioli, from where it's 5km back to Calacuccia.

Around Calacuccia

Occupying the greenest part of the Niolo, **CASAMACCIOLI** lies south of the lake in the middle of a chestnut forest. The small village square, edged by enormous chestnut trees, is the setting for the **Santa di u Niolu**, when the solitary café – empty for most of the year – almost comes apart at the seams. From the

CORSICAN FOLK SINGING

Singing has for many centuries provided a crucial mode of entertainment and expression for the shepherds of poor and remote areas such as the Niolo, and though it is dwindling in its purest form, Corsican song remains an integral part of the island's rich oral tradition.

As recently as the 1960s, remote village streets would still occasionally echo with the wild, searing incantation of the **voceru**, an improvised song by a woman in mourning for a loved one. In the more distant past, when the death of a son or husband often stemmed from a vendetta, the song would register not only the pain of bereavement but also urgency of revenge, aimed at spurring the surviving men to retribution. Today, though sometimes performed by folk groups, *voceri* are very seldom heard in their original form.

Death and separation have also provided inspiration for many shepherds' songs, often sung in the form of the three-part **a paghjella**, a form perhaps dating as far back as the megalithic age. It's performed by three male voices – the first (*a prima*) sets the pace for the chant, the second (*u boldu*) provides the base sound, while the third (*a terza*) sings the mesmerizing melody. Mass used to be sung this way in the more remote churches of the island; today you can hear *a paghjella* at its best at the Santa di u Niolu fair.

A third type of singing, known as **chiami e rispondi** (questions and answers), is also an important feature of the Santa di u Niolu. This takes the form of a competition in which two male contestants have to improvise a dialogue in strictly rhyming verse to a repetitive air. They may sing about anything, but it's popular to aim abuse at the assembled company or else proclaim about political issues. The one who first runs out of answers in this battle of wits is the loser.

Finally, the **nationalist movement** has not only revived interest in Corsica's vernacular heritage, but has also spawned an evocative and highly popular new hybrid of folk and rock styles – look out for hugely popular bands such as I Muvrini, A Filetta and Chiami Aghjelese at nationalist rallies and festivals.

church there's a splendid view of the amphitheatre of mountains to the northwest, while inside you can take a look at **La Santa**, a statue of the Virgin that is said to have transported itself here by a mule, following the destruction of its home convent in the seventeenth century.

Three kilometres west of Calacuccia, **ALBERTACCE**'s row of little cottages makes an interesting contrast with the fortress houses found throughout the rest of the island – people hereabouts thought the mountains were protection enough against uninvited guests. If you knock at the last house on the right coming from Calacuccia, you'll be let into a small folk **museum**, where the exhibits include shepherds' implements and clothes, with some evil-looking knives thrown in. Heading through the village, if you take a left up the D318 around the base of the Monte Cinto massif you'll come to **CALASIMA**, the highest inhabited village in the Niolo, giving a splendid view of the great valley from amid its goat enclosures.

A cluster of high-altitude hamlets 3km northeast of Calacuccia, **CORSCIA** warrants a visit for its phenomenally steep terraced houses and for the traditional Corsican dwellings – complete with high exterior staircases – in Costa, the uppermost hamlet, standing at 900m.

Monte Cinto

Monte Cinto (2706m), a line of broken crags marking the culminating point of the crest dividing the Niolo and Asco basins, is the loftiest if not the most handsome mountain in Corsica, and the ascent of its southeast face is the most popular climb on the island. Only experienced mountaineers should attempt this ascent, but most people can tackle the hike around the glacial basin on the lower slopes. However, route-finding can be difficult despite the paint flashes marking the way, and the terrain is loose, slippery, steep and rocky.

To drive as close to the mountain as possible, take the D218 north out of Calacuccia, then turn right along a rough track at the hairpin bend just before the hamlet of **Lozzi**, some 4km along. About 6km up this track you'll come to a place where you can park, just before the dry stone huts – formerly shepherds' refuges – known as the **Bergeries de Cesta**. From here a route traced in yellow paint leads off along a ridge, descending to the Erco River and then traversing an area of maquis before reaching the *Refuge de l'Erco*, about an hour's walk away. The unstaffed refuge is the starting point for those attempting the summit of Monte Cinto, roughly a three-hour climb. The waymarked path, a far gentler proposition, continues amidst enormous blocks of granite into the basin formed by Cinto and neighbouring Monte Falo, coming to an end at the waterfall at the foot of Monte Falo, 2km from the refuge.

The Forêt de Valdo-Niello and Lac de Nino

Southwest of Calacuccia the D84 follows the river into the **Forêt de Valdo-Niello**, where Laricio pines, some of them 500 years old, grow to a height of forty metres. From the **Maison Forestière de Popaja**, 10km from Calacuccia, trails branch off deep into the forest in all directions, with an easy 45-minute stroll marked to the **Bergeries de Colga**. More devoted hikers can pick up the GR20, which skirts the edge of the forest about 6km west of the *maison forestière* at a bend known as the Fer à Cheval (not signposted), in the approach to the Col de Verghio. Heading north, the GR20 plunges past pines and silver birch to a water-fall called the **Cascade de Radule**, a gentle walk of about ninety minutes there and back, passing close to the **Bergeries de Gradule**, a cluster of stone huts giving a stunning panorama of the massive hollow. Two hours beyond the water-fall, the **Ciottoli di i Mori** refuge is the starting point for ascents of Paglia Orba and Capo Tafonato.

To the south, the GR20 runs to **Lac de Nino**, source of the River Tavignano, but the lake can more easily be reached by taking the waymarked path from the *maison forestière*, a five-hour trek across relatively easy terrain. Marked with yellow paint, the path follows the Colga River past the **Bergeries de Colga**, a gathering of stone shacks at 1411m, then on – more steeply – up to the **Col de Stazzona** (1762m), between Monte Tozzo (2007m) and Punta Artica (2327m). At the top of the pass there's a weird scattering of black pointed rocks known as the devil's oxen – the story goes that the devil was challenged by Saint Martin to plough a straight line, and upon failing his oxen were turned to stone and he hurled his ploughshare in a rage through the mountain known as Capo Tafonato (the Pierced Mountain). It's only fifteen minutes farther to the lake, which from June to September is thronged with flocks of sheep and goats. The surrounding marshy turf declivities, known as *pozzi* (meaning "wells"), are the remnants of lakes gouged by glaciers which subsequently filled up with sediment. From here it's a tough eight-hour hike to Corte along the banks of the Tavignano (see p.195).

Corte and around

Situated amidst mountains and gorges at the core of the island, **CORTE** (Corti) has been the home of Corsican nationalism since the first National Constitution was drawn up here in 1731; it is also where **Pascal Paoli**, "U Babbu di u Patria" (father of the nation), formed the island's first democratic government later in the eighteenth century. Self-consciously insular and grimly proud, this is not the most welcoming spot, and the presence of a university doesn't noticeably improve the atmosphere, as the students tend to escape home at the weekends. For the outsider, Corte's charm is concentrated in the tranquil **ville haute**, where donkeys graze below the majestic **Citadelle**, amid deathly quiet cobbled streets.

A sprinkling of cafés and restaurants in the town provide a spark of life year-round, and the local **cinema** is also a popular meeting place, screening new films and boasting a hi-tech bar. The busiest time of year comes at the end of August, when Corte hosts the **Ghjurnate di U Populu Corsu**, a seven-day celebration of Corsican culture that has become a meeting place for separatists from all over Europe.

A brief history of Corte

Corte's reputation for belligerent independence was born in the ninth century when the occupiers of the strategic post allegedly saw off a group of Saracen raiders. Later on, the Genoese rulers were constantly harried by the local nobles, culminating in 1419 with the takeover by **Vincentello d'Istria**, the king of Aragon's viceroy. After Vincentello's execution in 1434, Genoa ruled relatively undisturbed until the French expedition of 1553, when Corte happily succumbed to Sampiero Corso, though within six years the Genoese were back in charge, and were to stay in control for a long time.

By the early eighteenth century, Corsican nationalism was on the rise in Corte, its success due in part to the town's isolation from the occupied coastal towns. Following a local insurrection in 1731, a National Constitution was drawn up here at the first National Assembly, and in 1752 Gaffori was elected head of state in Corte. After Gaffori's assassination in 1753, Pascal Paoli returned from exile and from 1755 to 1769 made Corte his centre of government. His revolutionary government set up the first Corsican printing press and the **Università di Corsica**, the first university to be established on the island.

However, in 1768, under the terms of the Treaty of Versailles, France bought Corsica from the Genoese, and after the battle of Ponte Nuovu in the following year the period of Corsican independence was at an end. Under the French the town became insignificant, and it's only recently that it has acquired a slightly more exalted status as *sous-préfecture* of Haute-Corse and as the seat of the revived university, whose aims are to re-establish the value of Corsican culture, partly through the compulsory teaching of the indigenous language.

Arrival, information and accommodation

Buses stop in the centre of town on cours Paoli, the main street, but the **train station** is at the foot of the hill near the university, from where it's a ten-minute uphill walk into town. If you're **driving** the best place to park is either at the top of avénue Jean Nicoli, the road which leads into town from Ajaccio, or in place

Paoli at the top of cours Paoli. Corte's **tourist office** (May–Oct daily 9am–noon & 2–6pm) is situated inside the citadel in the *ville haute*.

Finding a **place to stay** shouldn't be too difficult – there's not an abundance of hotels, but there are some inexpensive places in the centre of town, and they are rarely fully booked. You'll find the nearest **campsites** in the Vallée de la Restonica, about a kilometre out of town.

Hotels

Auberge de la Restonica, Vallée de la Restonica (☎95 46 20 13). Sumptuous comfort by the river, 1km southwest of town. It's best to book. ④.

Colonna, 1–3 avenue Xavier Luciani (☎95 46 01 09). Basic but comfortable rooms off cours Paoli. ①.

Ile de Beauté, route d'Aleria (☎95 46 09 26). Modern well-equipped hotel, close to station but in the least attractive part of town. ④.

Du Nord, 22 cours Paoli (☎95 46 00 68). Pleasant, clean place right in the centre. ②.

De la Paix, 1 av Général de Gaulle (☎95 46 06 72). Large, smart and central, set in an elegant part of town. Closed winter. ③.

Porette, 6 av du Neuf Septembre (☎95 61 01 21). Close to the station and university; unprepossessing but open all year round. ②.

De la Poste, 2 place Padoue (☎95 46 01 37). Huge old place, shabby but central with lots of character. ①.

Sampiero, 1 av Président Pierucci (☎95 46 09 76). Sixties-style modern block, with spectacular views from the balcony. Closed winter. ③.

Campsites

L'Alivetu, faubourg Saint-Antoine (☎95 46 11 09). Well-equipped but ugly, next to the university.

U Sognu, route de la Restonica (☎95 46 09 07). Closest to the main town, at the foot of the valley. Has a view of the citadel, and a recently opened restaurant.

U Tavignanu, chemin de Balini, Vallée du Tavignano (☎95 46 16 85). Basic camping in wild surroundings.

The Town

Corte is a very small town whose centre effectively consists of one street: **cours Paoli**, an often hostile street with almost all the town's banks, shops and cafés, and far too many cars. This thoroughfare runs alongside the **ville haute**, which is reached by climbing one of the cobbled ramps on the west side of the cours or by taking the steep rue Scoliscia from place Paoli.

At the north end of the *cours* lies **place du Duc de Padoue**, an elegant square of nineteenth-century buildings that's strangely out of place in this rough mountain town. Its statue, a grim bronze lump by Bartholdi, designer of the Statue of Liberty, is of Arrighi di Casanova, a general whose service under Napoléon earned him the title of Duke of Padua; his ancestral home can be seen in place Poilu in the *ville haute*. Apart from this square, there are only two spots in the lower town where you might want to hang around: the shady garden of the **Hôtel de Ville**, at the northern end of cours Paoli, which has a fountain made from an ancient Roman marble bath; and **place Paoli**, at the southern end, a more tourist-friendly zone packed with cafés, restaurants and market stalls, surrounding a cumbersome and self-satisfied statue of Paoli.

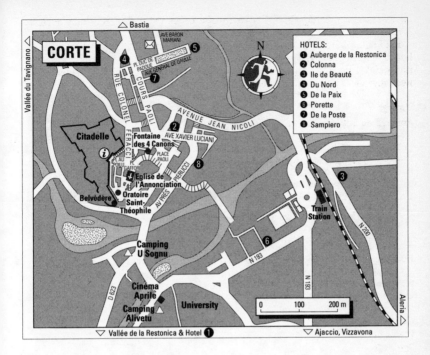

Ville Haute

Place Gaffori, the centre of the old *ville haute*, is dominated by a statue of General Gian' Pietru Gaffori pointing vigorously towards the church in the midst of the square's restaurant tables. On the base of the statue a bas-relief depicts the siege of the Gaffori house by the Genoese, who attacked in 1750 when Gaffori was out of town and his wife Faustina was left holding the fort. Faced with weakening colleagues, she is said to have brandished a burning torch over a barrel of gunpowder, threatening to blow herself and her soldiers to smithereens if they surrendered, a threat that toughened them up until Gaffori came along with reinforcements. The house stands right behind, and you can clearly make out the bullet-marks made by the besiegers.

Opposite the house, the **Église de L'Annonciation**, built in 1450 but restored in the seventeenth century, is where Joseph Bonaparte, Napoléon's brother and future King of Spain, was christened. Inside, there's a delicately carved **pulpit** and a hideous wax statue of Saint Theophilus, patron of the town, on his death bed. The saint's birthplace – behind the church in place Théophile – is marked by the **Oratoire Saint-Théophile**, a large arcaded building which commands a magnificent view across the gorges of Tavignano and Restonica. Born in 1676, Blaise de Signori took the name of Theophilus upon entering the Franciscan brotherhood, and went on to study in Rome and Naples, then to found numerous hermitages in Italy. In 1730 he returned to Corsica, where, after a few years' activity in the fight for independence, he died on May 9, 1740. He was canonized in

PASCAL PAOLI

"He smiled a good deal when I told him that I was much surprised to find him so amiable, accomplished and polite", wrote Boswell on first meeting **Pascal Paoli** in 1765. "For although I knew I was to see a great man I expected to find a rude character, an Attila king of the Goths, or a Luitprand king of the Lombards." By this time Paoli was forty years old and was famous throughout Europe, widely admired by the liberal intelligentsia of the time, among them Jean-Jacques Rousseau.

Paoli was **born in Morosaglia** with the cause of Corsican independence in his blood – his father Giacinto, a doctor, was a first-generation rebel, one of the three primates elected in 1731 by the independent assembly. At the age of fourteen Pascal accompanied his father into exile in Naples where the boy became a keen student of political enlightenment. At the time of Gaffori's assassination, Pascal was a 29-year-old sub-lieutenant in a Neapolitan regiment, but his brother Clemente was in the thick of the rebellion. Appointed one of four regents after Gaffori's death, Clemente invited his younger brother to take over the position of **General of the Nation**, a title he accepted in **1755** and was to hold for the next fourteen years.

Paoli's intention was to drive out the Genoese by force of arms, but despite his military background he wasn't an experienced soldier, and was anyway always short of the necessary supplies. However, he proved to be adept at the art of government, giving the island a **democratic constitution** which anticipated that of the United States of America, founding the university at Corte, building a small navy that was strong enough to break the Genoese blockade, and establishing a mint, a printing press and an arms factory. Furthermore, the system of justice instituted by Pascal Paoli was effective enough to bring about a decline in vendetta killings.

Then in **1768** everything collapsed. The French moved in once more, this time intending to stay after having bought out the Genoese under the terms of the Treaty of Versailles. Determined to crush the rebels for good, the French overwhelmed the Corsican troops at **Ponte Nuovo**, whereupon Paoli went into exile in London. However, his political life was not over.

In **1789**, at the start of the French Revolution, the people of Corsica were declared to be subject to the same laws as the revolutionary state, and it was in this changed political climate that Paoli returned triumphantly to the island in the following year. Initially he sympathized with the new republicanism, but the Corsican Jacobites – the Bonaparte family amongst them – owed too much to France to have much sympathy with separatist politics. Disagreements came to a head with Paoli's arraignment in June **1793**. His response was dramatic – setting up an independent government in Corte, he approached the British government for help. The British, driven out of Toulon by the French, were in search of a naval base in the area, and so there followed one of the more curious episodes of Corsican history.

The British sent **Sir Gilbert Elliot** to evaluate the situation, and agreement was quickly reached. English troops and naval forces moved in and after some fighting – during which the future Admiral Nelson lost the sight in one eye – the French moved out. A new constitution was drawn up that gave Corsica an attachment to the English crown, but with a large degree of autonomy. It's questionable whether Paoli was ever entirely happy with the course of events, but he was in a difficult situation, as the guillotine was waiting for him if France ever regained control. There seems no doubt that he expected to be appointed viceroy of the island, and when Elliot was given the job things began to turn sour. The parliament of 1795 elected Paoli as president, but Elliot objected; soon after, rioting was provoked by a rumour that Paoli's bust had been deliberately smashed at a ball given in the viceroy's honour. When the English began talking again to the republican French the game was over. In 1796 Paoli was persuaded to return to London, shortly before Elliot withdrew as Napoléon's army landed to secure the island for France.

Given a state pension, Paoli **died in London in 1807** at the age of 82, a revered figure. He was initially buried in his place of exile – there's a bust of him in Westminster Abbey – but his body now lies in his birthplace.

1930, the only Corsican to achieve sainthood, and on the anniversary of his death a commemorative Mass takes place in the oratory, followed by a procession from the Chapelle Sainte-Croix, carrying a huge figure of Christ.

For the best sight of the citadel, follow the signs uphill to the viewing platform, aptly named the **Belvédère**, which faces the medieval tower, suspended high above the town on its pinnacle of rock and dwarfed by the immense crags behind. The platform also gives a wonderful view of the converging rivers and encircling forest – a summer bar adds to the attraction.

In **place du Poilu**, the forecourt to the citadel, stands the house of the di Casanova family, where Napoléon's father – a friend of the Casanovas – lived in 1768 when he was Pascal Paoli's secretary. When the patriots were defeated by the French, Carlo and his wife Letizia were forced to flee, escaping across to the mountains to Ajaccio on muleback.

At the gates to the citadel stands the **Palais Nationale**, a great, solid block of a mansion that's the sole example of Genoese civic architecture in Corte. Having served as the seat of Paoli's government for a while, it became the **Università di Corsica** in 1765. Run by Franciscan monks, it offered free education to all (Napoléon's father studied here), and the enlightened monks taught the contemporary social thought of philosophers such as Rousseau and Montesquieu as well as traditional subjects such as theology, mathematics and law. The university closed in 1769 when the French took over the island after the Treaty of Versailles, not to be resurrected until 1981. Today several modern buildings have been added and it houses the Institut Universitaire d'Études Corses, dedicated to the study of Corsican history and culture.

Tickets for the **Citadelle** (April–Oct daily 9am–8pm; 10F) are sold at the **tourist office**, on the left of the entrance, where you can get a free map. The only such fortress in the interior of the island, it served as a base for the Foreign Legion from 1962 until 1984, but now houses the **Fonds Régionale d'Arts Corses**, which holds exhibitions of contemporary Corsican artists. Projects for the future include a Corsican historical museum, due to open in 1995.

The citadel is reached by a huge staircase of Restonica marble, which leads to the medieval tower known as the **Nid d'Aigle** (eagle's nest) situated at its highest point. The citadel, of which the tower is the only original part, was built by Vincentello d'Istria in 1420, and the barracks added during the reign of Louis Philippe. These were later converted into a prison, in use as recently as World War II, when the Italian occupiers incarcerated Corsican resistance fighters in the tiny cells. Adjacent to the cells is the **echauguette**, a former watchtower which at the time of Paoli's government was inhabited by the hangman. This was a job no Corsican would take – accustomed to killing with guns and knives, they found the practice of hanging someone to death too demeaning and dishonourable. A Sicilian duly volunteered, and in 1766 James Boswell visited the poor wretch: "a more dirty rueful spectacle I never beheld", he wrote of the despised man he found cowering in the turret with a "miserable bed and a little bit of fire" as his only comfort.

To complete a tour of the *ville haute*, take the steps to the left as you leave the citadel, crossing rue Colonel Feracci to arrive at the **Fontaine des Quatre Canons**, once the water supply for all the houses in the vicinity. From here you can either descend to the *cours* or carry on down rue Colonel Feracci for a look at the sixteenth-century **Chapelle Sainte-Croix**, notable for its lavish Baroque interior and its floor of Restonica marble.

Eating and drinking

Corte has a fair number of **restaurants** and more casual eating places, with the usual sprinkling of pizzerias and crêperies, nearly all of them on cours Paoli – place Gaffori is the only place in the *ville haute* with restaurants. Local specialities are **trout** and locally hunted **wild boar**, but if you just want a snack you could go to the pizza van parked opposite *Café de France* in place Padoue. The **bars** of cours Paoli are strictly for posing; place Paoli has three cafés – it is more touristy but at least you can sit and drink in comfort. Students favour the bar of the **cinema**, the white building on the road to Restonica just outside the centre of town.

Restaurants

Asia, 4 cours Paoli. Asian specialities; interesting menu if you fancy a change.

Le Bips, 27 cours Paoli. The most popular restaurant in town, beneath an intimidating bar known as the "rendezvous de chasseurs". Excellent Corsican food, fresh fish, pasta and pizzas. Inexpensive.

Le Gaffori, place Gaffori. The least expensive place in town, with 45F menus and loads of omelettes, salads and spaghetti. Local *charcuterie* especially good.

Le Passe Temps, 2 rampe Ste-Croix. Crêperie in a restored vaulted building; tasty variations on the normal fillings (eg wild boar); also serves soups and fish. Expensive.

Place a Piazetta, place Gaffori. Pleasant outdoor restaurant, presided over by grandmother of the premises. Lasagne with wild boar sauce recommended, as is the trout. Closed winter.

Cafés and bars

Café de France, junction of cours Paoli and place Padoue. Pleasant café with shady forecourt.

Le Pascal Paoli, place Paoli. Touristy, but does inexpensive steaks and snacks.

Rex, cours Paoli. Best of the posy bars along this street.

Listings

Banks All the main banks are on cours Paoli.

Bike rental *Corte location service*, 4 cours Paoli (☎95 46 07 13).

Bookshops *Librairie de la Presse*, 22 cours Paoli. Good selection of books about Corsica.

Bus information *Ollandini*, 2 av Xavier Luciani (☎95 46 02 12).

Car rental *Europcar*, 9 cours Paoli (☎95 46 02 79); *Hertz*, c/o *Cyrnea Tourisme*, 9 av Xavier Luciani (☎95 46 24 62).

Hospital Avenue du Neuf Septembre (☎95 46 05 36).

Pharmacies Several on cours Paoli.

Police 4 av Xavier Luciani (☎95 46 04 81).

Post office Av du Baron Mariani, off place Padoue.

Taxis *Taxis Corte* (☎95 46 07 90 or 95 61 01 41).

Train information At the station (☎95 46 00 97).

Travel agents *Corte Voyages* 14 cours Paoli (☎95 46 00 35), *Cyrnea Tourisme*, 9 av Xavier Luciani (☎95 46 24 62).

Around Corte

The **Gorges du Tavignano**, virtually on the town's doorstep, offers an exhilarating hike from Corte but is only accessible on foot. The less energetic can simply drive southwest to the **Vallée de la Restonica**. A torrent of jade-green water punctuated with enormous boulders, the Restonica is followed closely by the road out of Corte, which comes to a stop within striking distance of the stunning **Lac de Melo**, the **Lac de Capitello** and **Monte Rotondo** – a sprawling mountain that may not be much to look at from a distance but is a superb sight close up, with its ring of crags encircling a glacial lake.

Gorges du Tavignano

A deep cleft of ruddy granite 5km to the west of Corte, the **Gorges du Tavignano** offers one of central Corsica's great walks, marked in yellow paint flashes alongside the broad cascading River Tavignano. You can pick up the trail from opposite the Chapelle Sainte-Croix in Corte's *ville haute* and follow it as far as the Lac de Nino, some 30km west of the town, where it joins the GR20 (see p.86). There's a **refuge**, *A Sega*, situated 15km along the route, but check first at the tourist office to make sure it's open.

The first part of the walk crosses a small chestnut wood before hugging the left bank of the Tavignano. Massive rocks, fringed by dense vegetation, border the river. Some 5km into the walk the gorge begins, the scenery becoming wilder the further you advance, with bare rock faces surging up on each side and boulders cluttering the path. Some 10km from Corte the gorge comes to an end – from here you either go on to Nino or take the branch up to the Col de l'Arinella (1592m), a further 7km to the northwest. Forming the watershed between the valleys of the Golo and the Tavignano, the col affords fantastic vistas of the Niolo.

Gorges de la Restonica and Monte Rotondo

The glacier-moulded rocks and deep pools of the **Gorges de la Restonica** make this the busiest mountain road in Corsica – if you come in high summer, expect to see parked vehicles lining the road all the way up to the car park at the Bergeries de Grotelle, 15km from Corte at the base of Monte Rotondo, with hikers and cyclists filling in the background.

The gorges begin after 6km, just beyond where the route penetrates the **Forêt de la Restonica**, a glorious forest of chestnut, Laricio pine and the tough maritime pine endemic to Corte, recognizable by its conical shape. Not surprisingly, it's a popular place to walk, picnic and bathe in the many pools fed by the cascading torrent of the Restonica River, easily reached by scrambling down the rocky banks.

A HIKE UP MONTE ROTONDO

A relatively easy hike up Monte Rotondo begins 11km along the D623 from Corte, at the Pont de Tragone. Cross the bridge and take the first track to the left, following the wooden signs for the *Bergeries de Timozzo* refuge, which lies 1500m to the southwest. Beyond the *Bergeries* continue to climb close to the Timozzo torrent, crossing over from one bank to another according to the difficulty of the terrain for about 200m, after which the rest of the walk is marked by cairns. Veering away from the torrent for a short distance, you soon rejoin it at a point where it forms a waterfall. Another 250m on and the black crest of rocks of the summit are visible. Roughly the same distance again brings you to the Lac d'Oriente, then another 1km leads to the foot of the great walls of rock which form the base of the mountain. Here a gully to your right helps you attain the small col which gives easy access to the top. You can take the route down by the Pietra Piana refuge, 2km south beyond the huge glacial lake of Lavu Bellebone.

The classic ascent of **Monte Rotondo** (2322m) begins at the Tragone bridge, opposite the *maison forestière* about 11km along the D623, and takes about five hours there and back (see box below). For a less strenuous expedition, continue along the road to the ramshackle huts of the **Bergeries de Grotelle**, one of which has been converted into a café, providing welcome refreshments before or after a trek. From here it's an hour's clearly marked hike to **Lac de Melo** across a broad, sweeping, rocky slope scattered with dwarfed black pines. Enclosed by a moraine formed during the Ice Age, Lac de Melo is the lowest of the fifteen lakes of Monte Rotondo, and marks the point where the real mountains begin. It's a further thirty minutes to **Lac de Capitello**, which lies at a height of 1930m and is frozen over for eight months of the year; beyond here, the terrain is strictly for real climbers.

South of Corte

The main road south of Corte slices into the heart of the Corsican mountains, tracked by the railway through Venaco, Vivario, Vizzavona and Bocognano – a rattling ride that's worth taking even if you have your own vehicle. East from **Vivario** there's an incredible drive through the **Forêt de Rospa Sorba** to **Vezzani**, while to the southeast lies **Ghisoni**, a mountain base dominated by the peaks of Kyrie-Eleison and the craggy **Monte Renoso**. You have a choice of spectacular exits from Ghisoni: east through the **Defilé de l'Inzecca**, a thrilling shortcut down to the eastern plain; or south along the zigzagging route to **Col de Verde**, offering incredible views of the peaks. South of the col, **Zicavo** gives access to **Monte Incudine**, the southernmost high peak of the island.

Back on the N193 and the rail line, **Vizzavona** lies at the highest point of the road before its descent to Ajaccio. A beautiful forest lies on one side of this small mountain resort, and the great dome of **Monte d'Oro** looms to the west – but for the best view of this mountain you should head down to **Bocognano**, about 7km from the Col de Vizzavona.

Accommodation is very limited in these parts, with the odd hotel at Vezzani, Vivario and Vizzavona.

Corte to Vivario

Immediately south of Corte you ascend into a landscape of lush chestnut forests that lasts as far as the **Col de Bellagranjo** (723m), 9km along the route and just beyond **SANTO-PIETRO-DI-VENACO**. This appealing hamlet has a fine hotel called *Le Torrent* (☎95 47 00 18; ②), a stylishly old-fashioned place tucked beneath a tree-shaded terrace by the river.

South of here the road sweeps through **VENACO**, an elegant village of rusty buildings emerging from deep green verdure on the slopes of Monte Padro. You might want to halt here to admire the vistas – from the terrace of the Baroque church there's a spectacular view of the lower Vallée du Tavignano in the east.

About 5km from Venaco the road passes the **Pont de Vecchiu**, an arched stone bridge that flies over the River Vecchiu and under the iron bridge designed by Gustave Eiffel in 1888, putting the final touches to the Bastia–Ajaccio rail line. The river's gorge is dominated by **VIVARIO**, a large innocuous village located at the junction of the routes to the Forêt de Rospa Sorba and the Col de Verde, and thus a good base for walkers, who stay here at the basic *Macchie e Monti* (☎95 47 22 00; ①). Vivario's attraction lies in its forest setting, a savage environment that once supported its own wild man. In 1800 a ten-year-old boy went missing here after arguing with his parents and stayed missing for twenty years, until a group of hunters ensnared him by the Vecchiu. The unfortunate soul was carted off to be reunited with his parents but, unable to adapt to his new life, he perished after a few months. The only traversable spot across the Gorge du Vecchiu, a three-hour walk west of Vivario, is a three-metre jump still known as the *Saut du Sauvage*.

A shorter walk from Vivario takes you to the **Fort de Pasciolo**, an evocative ruin 1km south of the village beside the N193. Set in a wild site facing a great circle of peaks and overlooking the deep gorge of the Vecchiu, the fort was built around 1770 by the French, and was transformed into a prison to incarcerate the rebels of Fiumorbo (see p.170).

Vivario to Vezzani

East of Vivario, the D343 follows a tree-lined route around the side of Punta Muru mountain, passing through **MURACCIOLE**, where the view forms a pleasant prelude to the awe-inspiring panorama from the **Col de Morello** (824m), 2km north of the hamlet. From here, a rewarding half-hour walk goes to the **Occhio-Vario**, a rocky eminence providing an even more exceptional viewpoint – a narrow goat track leads north of the col to the point, which is marked by a white granite monument.

After the col the road penetrates the **Forêt de Rospa-Sorba**, a glorious forest of Laricio pines and chestnut trees. Distant snowy peaks most of the year feature all along the meandering road, which swoops in a semicircle towards **VEZZANI**. Fantastically located under the high ridge of Punta di a Ringhella, this mountain village has a couple of hotels, of which *U Sambuccu* (☎95 44 03 38; ②) is the better, as it has a good restaurant.

MONTE RENOSO

The easiest and most popular ascent of **Monte Renoso** (2352m) is up the north side, a relatively easy nine-hour circular walk from the Campannelle refuge. You get to the refuge by following the D69 south of Ghisoni for about 6km as far as the Pont de Casso, where you turn right onto an excessively windy road that traverses the **Forêt de Ghisoni**, a dense forest of pines, beech and alders. The refuge – once a shepherd's hut – lies 500m west of the spot where the road comes to an end, next to a makeshift ski station that rarely sees enough snow to function.

From here the track is marked with cairns, leading off to the southwest across the stream beneath the ski lift. Passing the idyllic Pizzolo springs, the track skirts the west shore of the Lac de Bastiani, a grey expanse of water framed intermittently by snowdrifts, before following the ridge to the **summit**. Here you'll be treated to one of Corsica's most amazing views – the panorama embraces the whole of the south of the island, taking in the Golfe d'Ajaccio and Golfe de Valinco on the west coast, and extending even as far as Sardinia. If you carry on south along the waymarked track, past the Punta Orlandino, you'll gain the **Col de Pruno** (2262m) in another thirty minutes or so. From here the path descends to the *Bergeries des Pozzi*, then strikes east to the Plateau de Gialgone, after which it joins the **GR20**, which shoulders Monte Renoso around the east side and brings you back to where you started.

Vivario to Monte Incudine

Just 1km south of Vivario the D69 cuts steeply east to the **Col de Sorba** (1311m), from where the panorama is stunning: in the foreground rise the needles of Kyrie Eleison, to the north the rail line can be made out, winding through the crags to Venaco, and to the south extend the forests of Pietro Verde and Marmano, with a towering backdrop formed by Monte d'Oro and Monte Renoso. Continuing south, the deteriorating and narrowing road descends through the forest to **GHISONI**, about 7km from the col. This large village, nestling in a vast hollow on a tributary of the River Fiumorbo, is dominated by Monte Renoso, and most of the people staying in the village's cheap and cheerful **hotel** – the *Kyrié* (☎95 57 60 33; ①) – are here to climb the mountain (see box below).

To Zicavo

South of Ghisoni, the narrow D69 wriggles up the slopes of the higher Fiumorbo valley, through the Forêt de Marmano, arriving after 12km at **Col de Verde** (1289m), where the Fiumorbo and Taravo valleys almost meet. An *auberge* at the top provides refreshments.

It's a very narrow and crumbling route down through the gorgeous Laricio pines of **Forêt de San-Pietro-di-Verde** and the adjoining **Forêt de Saint-Antoine** to **ZICAVO**, 20km from the col. Zicavo is the best base for excursions to Monte Incudine (see box below), with two **hotels**: the *Tourisme* (☎95 24 40 06; ①) is a simple and inexpensive place at the centre of the village, and does excellent food; the *Florida* (☎95 24 40 57; ②), north of the village overlooking the valley, offers glorious views.

MONTE INCUDINE

The massive four-kilometre-long hump of **Monte Incudine** (2136m) is crenellated by numerous peaks, the highest of which can be climbed in a generally easy-going ten-hour walk from and back to the San Petru **refuge**, to the southeast of Zicavo. You get to the refuge by turning onto the D428 from the D69 about 10km south of the village, then driving some 5km through the **Forêt du Coscione**, a beautiful expanse of beech trees carpeting the lower slopes of the Punta di Sistaja. From San Petru refuge, where you can leave your car, it's a straightforward climb, following the road south for 7km as far as the Col du Luana (1805m), where the route turns sharply south and you pick up the GR20 trail, waymarked in red and white paint. Three kilometres after the col the route becomes steep and crosses some difficult gullies choked with loose rock, but the view of the Bavella needles from the summit's cross makes the exertion worthwhile. Walkers following the GR20 on to the Col de Bavella might want to make use of the Asinao **refuge**, a short way down the south face of Incudine, above the Asinao stream; after that, the next resting point is the *auberge* at the col itself (see p.146).

Vizzavona and around

Monte d'Oro dominates the route south of Vivario to **VIZZAVONA**, about 10km away. Shielded by trees, the village is invisible from the main road, so keep your eyes peeled for a couple of tracks on the right, one of them signposted for the train **station** – the place where the bandit Bellacoscia surrendered to the police at the age of 75 (see p.200). With its handful of *auberges* and restaurants,

Vizzavona is an ideal place to spend a few days walking in the forest, and for this very reason it does sometimes get crowded in summer, but there's usually a **bed** to be found at the *Monte d'Oro* (☎95 47 21 06; ③), a huge place in the hamlet of **LA FOCE**, deep in the forest 3km south along the main road. With its magnificent terrace looking out onto the mountain, this is the first-choice hotel, but the alternatives are perfectly acceptable: the *Moderne* (☎95 47 21 12; ②) opposite the station, or the even less expensive *Beauséjour* (☎95 47 21 13; ①), a tiny place attached to the station, serving authentic Corsican cuisine.

Forêt de Vizzavona

A glorious forest of beech and Laricio pine, the **Forêt de Vizzavona** is the most popular walking area in Corsica, thanks to the easy access by main road or train. A lot of people come here to tackle the ascent of Monte d'Oro (see box below), but there are many less demanding trails to follow, one of the most frequented of these being the walk to the **Cascade des Anglais**, which is connected to Vizzavona by a marked trail but is more commonly approached from La Foce, 3km south of the village. Some 200m down the hill from the hamlet, you turn left onto a forest road which plunges towards the river, where the waymarked GR20 leads to the waterfall where the River Agnone crashes into emerald green pools, providing excellent bathing spots.

Less than a kilometre west of La Foce lies the highest pass on the Ajaccio–Bastia road, the **Col de Vizzavona** (1163m), which is usually jammed with picnickers, most of whom take a postprandial stroll along one of the various short walks laid out from here. Fifteen minutes south of the col along the forest trail you come to a magnificent **viewpoint** over the forested peaks, with the ruins of the Genoese **Fort de Vizzavona** prominent on a rise in the valley below. You can reach the fort itself in just fifteen minutes along a wide path north of the picnic tables. A walk to **La Madonuccia** – a mound of scrambled rocks that's supposed to look like the Virgin – takes about thirty minutes from the col, following the trail signposted "Bergeries des Pozzi", which branches off southeast. Another marked path from the col takes you to the **Fontaine de Vitulo**, the source of the Foce stream, which joins the River Gravona further down the mountain.

To get the best out of the forest, though, you should walk to **Col de Palmente** (1460m), a relatively strenuous four-hour there-and-back hike along the GR20 from the *maison forestière* just south of Vizzavona on the main road. The path

---

MONTE D'ORO

The fifth highest peak on Corsica, **Monte d'Oro** (2389m) offers one of the most rewarding hikes on the island, the view from its summit taking in all the island's principal peaks – Cinto, Rotondo, Renoso and Incudine – as well as Ajaccio to the west and the Tuscan islands beyond the east coast. However, it's a difficult ascent which should on no account be attempted by the inexperienced, and is best tackled during the summer, although you're still likely to encounter snow on the highest slopes.

There are two ways of getting to the summit from Vizzavona. The easier takes about three hours from the Cascade des Anglais, following the GR20 along the River Agnone past the Bergeries de Portetto **refuge**, then veering off up a steep rocky gradient to the Col du Porc (2159m), about 1km west of the main peak. The alternative route, marked with yellow paint flashes, takes four hours from Vizzavona, traversing the ravine of the Ghilareto and the Speloncello valley before wheeling round up the north face. A narrow corridor known as the *scala* presents a hazardous final approach to the summit.

winds through magnificent woodland before rising to the col, which affords fantastic views of Monte Renoso and the Forêt de Vizzavona.

Bocognano

From the Col de Vizzavona, the route winds southwards for 6km before reaching the appealing ochre cottages of **BOCOGNANO**. Set on a plateau amidst a chestnut forest, the village gives a perfect panorama of Monte d'Oro's pale grey domes, and is well placed for walks to the **Cascade du Voile de la Mariée**, where the River Gravona crashes from a height of 150m in a series of cascades. The best approach to the falls is a thirty-minute walk south from the main road 3km south of Bocognano, just before the Pont de Vitiluccia.

Bocognano is indissolubly associated with Antoine and Jacques **Bellacoscia**, born here in 1817 and 1832, fathered by a man who earned the family surname – meaning "beautiful thigh" – by also fathering eighteen daughters by three sisters with whom he lived simultaneously. Antoine, the elder son, took to the maquis in 1848, having killed the mayor of the village after an argument over some land. With his brother he went on to commit several more murders in full view of the hapless *gendarmes*, yet remained at liberty thanks to the support of the local population. In 1871 Jacques and Antoine managed to gain a safe pass into Ajaccio to organize an expedition to fight for the French in the war with Prussia. They returned from the war with their reputations restored, and took up residence in the family home, from where they continued to flaunt the law. In 1888 the police finally succeeded in ousting them from their house, which was converted into a prison. Antoine eventually surrendered at Vizzavona station on June 25, 1892, whereupon he was acquitted and exiled to Marseille in true Corsican tradition. The fate of Jacques is unknown.

travel details

Trains

All train services run four times daily.

Bocognano to: Ajaccio (45min); Bastia (3hr 15min); Corte (1hr); Ponte Leccia (1hr 30min); Vivario (30min); Venaco (55min); Vizzavona (15min).

Corte to: Ajaccio (2hr); Bastia (2hr); Bocognano (3hr 30min); Ponte Leccia (15min); Venaco (15min); Vivario (30min); Vizzavona (1hr).

Ponte Leccia to: Ajaccio (2hr 15min); Bastia (1hr); Bocognano (1hr 30min); Corte (30min); Venaco (45min); Vivario (1hr); and Vizzavona (1hr 15min).

Venaco to: Ajaccio (1hr 30min); Bastia (1hr 40min); Bocognano (40min); Corte (15min); Ponte Leccia (45min); Vivario (15min); Vizzavona (25min).

Vivario to: Ajaccio (1hr 15min); Bastia (2hr); Bocognano (30min); Corte (30min); Ponte Leccia (1hr); Venaco (15min); Vizzavona (15min).

Vizzavona to: Ajaccio (1hr); Bastia (2hr 20min); Bocognano (10min); Corte (1hr 15min); Ponte Leccia (1hr 15min); Venaco (30min); Vivario (15min).

Buses

Corte to: Ajaccio (2 daily; 2hr); Bastia (2 daily; 2hr).

Ponte Leccia to: Haut'Asco (2 daily; 1hr).

PART THREE

THE

CONTEXTS

THE
HISTORICAL
FRAMEWORK

Invasion and resistance are recurring themes throughout Corsica's history. This has always been an island of particular strategic and commercial appeal, with its sheltered harbours and protective mountains, set on the western Mediterranean trade routes within easy reach of several colonizing powers. Greeks, Carthaginians and Romans came in successive waves, landing on the eastern coast, driving native Corsicans into the high interior and battling against new predators in their turn. The Romans were ousted by Vandals, and for the following thirteen centuries the island was attacked, abandoned, settled and sold as nation states and empires squabbled over Europe's territories, and generations of islanders fought against foreign rule and against each other. In the light of this turbulent past, it seems inevitable that Corsica's early history, unexplored until this century, should have its own pattern of invasion and occupation.

BEGINNINGS

For thousands of years the relics of Corsica's **Stone Age** were simply accepted as an inexplicable aspect of the island's landscape. In 1840 Prosper Mérimée, then Inspector of Historic Monuments, described the simple **menhirs** (from the Celtic *maen hir* – "long stone") of the southwest and tabulated various primitive stone monuments elsewhere in Corsica, but the

origins and functions of these stone slabs and figures remained unknown until 1954, when French archeologist Roger Grosjean set about excavating and recording the megalithic sites. Only when his excavations started in earnest did a picture emerge of a complex prehistoric society that developed its religious and cultural framework over several millennia.

THE FIRST SETTLERS

It's now believed that Corsica's **original inhabitants** arrived from northern Italy in the **seventh millennium BC**, long before the monument-building era; making their shelters in caves and under cliffs, they survived by hunting, gathering and fishing. A thousand years later came new settlers with new skills, building villages, planting crops and herding cattle. The practice of **transhumance** – driving sheep to graze on the uplands in summer then down to coastal pastures in the winter – may have been started in this era, and was followed by Corsican shepherds almost to the present. In the **fourth millennium**, the creators of the island's **megalithic** buildings migrated into the Mediterranean area from Asia Minor and the Aegean. There are numerous interpretations of the stone monuments and tombs that were erected during the next 2000 years, but the most widely held opinion is that they were connected with the veneration of ancestors and the spirits of the dead, and perhaps centred on an Earth Deity or Mother.

At first the dead were buried in underground tombs or **cists**, and were represented, commemorated or maybe guarded by single menhirs placed nearby. Clusters of these tombs and menhirs have been found in the southwestern Sartenais region and near Porto-Vecchio. Cist burial later gave way to the custom of setting stone sarcophagi or **dolmens** ("table stones") above ground and covering them with earth; about a hundred of these, measuring about six feet by eight, have been discovered (now exposed after the erosion of the soil), one of the best examples being at **Fontenaccia**. At a later stage the menhirs acquired human forms and features: some were given swords or daggers, some were carved with rudimentary shoulder blades or ribs, and no two statues were the same. The function of these eerie warrior figures, most of which were found at **Filitosa**, can only be imagined. Suggestions range from representations of dead spirits to trophies of war, each one marking a defeated invader.

THE TORRÉENS

The culture embodied by these carved menhirs reached its peak towards 1500 BC, when new aggressors – portrayed, perhaps, by the stone warriors – landed in the south and made their first base near Porto-Vecchio. Naming this civilization the **Torréens**, after the dry-wall **torri** (towers) they raised in various parts of the island, Roger Grosjean posited that they were the same people as the sea-going Shardana who are known to have attacked Egypt in the late second millennium BC, and that the bronze weapons with which they subdued the islanders were the weapons depicted on the sword-bearing menhirs of Filitosa.

Their towers, each one built around a central cavity with smaller chambers to the sides, were found to contain remnants of fires, and may have been used to cremate the dead or even sacrifice the living. Fragments of the earlier, Neolithic structures, perhaps destroyed as the Torréens advanced along the island, were incorporated in their walls. Grosjean has traced the invaders' progression to the west, as they drove the megalithic natives further into the interior and finally to the north, where the natives were left to pursue their own beliefs and practices in peace. Stone menhirs were still being created in northern Corsica as the Iron Age got underway, centuries after the Torréen invasion, while in the south of the island – according to Grosjean – rivalry between Torréen settlements precipitated another migration, this time south to the island of Sardinia.

GREEKS, ROMANS AND SARACENS

In 565 BC Corsica's first major colony was founded at Alalia (Aléria) by Greek refugees from **Phocaea**. For a few decades these settlers made a successful living, planting vines and olive trees and enjoying a brisk trade in metals and cereals, but within thirty years they were fighting off an invading fleet of **Carthaginians** and **Etruscans**. By 535 BC, devastated by their losses in battle, the Greeks had abandoned Alalia to the Etruscans, who in turn were briefly succeeded by Carthaginian settlers in the third century BC.

By now Corsica had attracted the attention of the **Romans**, who sent in troops under the command of Lucius Cornelius Scipio in 259 BC. The indigenous islanders, enslaved or driven into the mountains by each successive invading power, joined forces with the Carthaginians and their leader Hanno to resist Roman occupation. Although the east coast was soon conquered and settled, it took another forty years before Corsica (together with Sardinia) could be brought within Roman administration, and another century of rebellion passed before the island's interior was overpowered.

For over 500 years Corsica remained a province of the Roman Empire. A string of ports was established along the south coast – subsequently flattened by invasion and malaria – and a settlement built at **Mariana**, to the south of present-day Bastia, though Aléria remained the largest settlement. From the third century AD onwards, **Christianity** was introduced to the island and bishoprics were established at Mariana, Aléria, Nebbio, Sagone and Ajaccio.

This comparatively stable period in Corsican history came to an end as the Roman Empire disintegrated and the **Vandals** started to harass the coast. By 460 the Vandals were established on the island, only to be defeated by Belisarius and his Byzantine forces in 534, but absorption into the Byzantine empire did little to protect Corsica from the Ostrogoths and later from the **Lombards**, who managed to annexe Corsica in 725 – by which time the coastal settlements were suffering frequent raids by the Saracens (or Moors). In 754 Pépin the Short, King of the Franks, agreed to hand Corsica over to the **papacy** once it was free of the Lombards; when the Lombards were driven out twenty years later, Pépin's son, Charlemagne, honoured the promise.

Within thirty years of its transfer to papal sovereignty, parts of Corsica were being overrun by the **Saracens**. These invaders retained their grip for another two centuries, despite the brief triumph of **Ugo della Colonna**, reputedly a Roman aristocrat sent to "liberate" the island by Pope Stephen IV, but more likely a semi-legendary figure based on Count Boniface of Lucca, who gained a foothold on the island in 825, building the fortress of Bonifacio on its southern tip.

Whatever the facts may be, Ugo della Colonna became a useful point of reference for the local Corsican families, who began to assert their authority as the Moors retreated under pressure from an allied force of Pisans and Genoese at the start of the eleventh century. During the Saracens' rule the native islanders had been confined to the interior, where they had developed a system of administration based on mountain communities, with elected leaders who took every opportunity to make their status hereditary. This period saw the rise of such mighty clans as the **della Rocca** and **Istria** families, the dominant dynasties among the feudal lords known as the **Cinarchesi**, most of whom claimed descent from Ugo della Colonna. As their feuds and rivalries intensified, some swore allegiance to the pope, who in 1077 placed Corsica under Pisan protection; others turned for support to the Genoese, who claimed their own right to the island.

THE PISAN PERIOD

In 1133 Pope Innocent II split Corsica's bishoprics between Pisa and Genoa, an action that did nothing to stem the enmity of the two republics. For two centuries, while Corsica remained **officially governed by Pisa**, the Genoese stayed on the offensive, capturing Bonifacio in 1187 and Calvi in 1268. Nevertheless, the Pisans were able to impose a framework of government built around the local parish or **pieve**. A massive programme of church-building got underway, each church providing the focus for its *pieve*, which in turn linked several village communities.

In the meantime, the Corsican nobles continued to flex their muscles. **Sinucello della Rocca**, a vassal of Pisa who held lands in the southwest, took advantage of the running dispute with Genoa and made his own bid for power, taking arms against other Corsican nobles and switching his loyalties between Pisa and Genoa as necessary. He eventually gained control of almost the whole island, drawing up a constitution and earning the name **Giudice** (Judge) for his sense of justice, but his success had made him few friends, and the rival *signori* soon turned against him. When Genoa defeated the Pisan fleet at **Meloria in 1284** and finally took control of the island, della Rocca retreated to his original base in the southwest and was eventually betrayed by his own illegitimate son. Captured by the Genoese, he died in prison in 1306.

THE GENOESE PERIOD

Despite **Genoa**'s decisive victory at Meloria, the republic's struggle to control Corsica was by no means over. In 1297 the island, along with Sardinia, was handed by Pope Boniface VIII to the **Kingdom of Aragon**, setting off yet another territorial war – one which was to rumble on for two hundred years more. While Genoa held fast against Aragonese attempts to realize their claim to Corsica, the *signori* continued to fight it out among themselves. A people's revolt led by **Sambocuccio d'Alando** drove out the battling nobles of the northeast, and led to a political split between two areas of the island. In the northeast, the area known as *Diqua dai Monti* ("This side of the mountains"), the ancestral lands were taken over by village communities to form the **terra di commune**, officially protected by the Genoese, who founded and fortified Bastia in 1380. The southwest – *Dila dai Monti* – remained the **terra dei signori**, ruled in effect by the Cinarchesi, who looked to the more distant power of Aragon for support.

Generations of *signori* kept up a relentless effort to bring the whole island under their rule. Backed by Aragon, **Arrigo della Rocca** gained considerable successes against the Genoese in 1376, and then his nephew, **Vincentello d'Istria**, gained control of most of the island as viceroy of the King of Aragon from 1420 until 1434, when he was captured by Genoese forces and publicly beheaded. In 1453, in a bid to overcome such ambitious nobility, Genoa put Corsica into the hands of the **Bank of Saint George**, a powerful financial corporation with its own army. For ten years the Bank imposed a tough military government, building a series of coastal watchtowers, restoring battered fortifications and containing the fractious warlords.

SAMPIERO CORSO

Events in Europe brought this era to an end: **Henry II of France**, at war with Charles V, struck a blow against the Habsburg emperor's Genoese allies by sending a fleet to capture Corsica. Leading the invasion was mercenary **Sampiero Corso**, who took possession of the entire island except Calvi and Bastia. French rule lasted all of two years, before Corsica was passed back to Genoa under the Treaty of Cateau Cambrésis in 1559. Corso, however, was rather less inclined to relinquish his supremacy, and led a successful uprising against the Genoese in 1564, again securing control of most of the island. He was finally defeated by a vicious Corsican custom – the **vendetta** – according to which any act of violence or dishonour had to be avenged by the victim's relations. Corso was murdered in 1567 by the brothers of his wife Vannina d'Orso, whom he had strangled in the belief that she had betrayed him to his Genoese enemies. His killers were heftily rewarded by the Genoese.

GENOESE CONSOLIDATION

In the late **sixteenth century** the Corsican population was reeling from years of war, pirate attacks, famine and malaria. The Genoese republic, now governing the island directly, was finally able to impose an administration of sorts. A governor was installed in Bastia to oversee the network of provinces and parishes, leaving local government to the Corsican communities and their assemblies (*consulta*). Attempts were even made to clamp down on the vendetta, but with no success – hundreds of murders were committed each year in the name of honour.

Nevertheless, in comparison with the previous pattern of civil war and invasion, the 170 years of direct Genoese rule were relatively peaceful. Corsicans enjoyed a certain degree of freedom to run their own affairs, and the rural economy developed and prospered – factors that were eventually to undermine the Genoese supremacy. Influential families, beneficiaries of the boom in agricultural trade, formed an articulate and ambitious new class. Excluded from the top ranks of government and resentful of Genoa's trade monopolies and high taxes, they provided the leadership for a Corsican society growing in political maturity and aspirations. Circumstances came to a head in the early eighteenth century, when discontent exploded into armed rebellion.

THE WARS OF INDEPENDENCE

The hated Genoese taxes were the trigger for **revolt in 1729** when, having suffered a series of failed harvests, one village near Corte refused to pay. Its defiance developed into a full-scale uprising and the reinforcements sent in to suppress it were soon overpowered. Rebellion spread quickly across the island and was formalized in **1731**, when a popular assembly declared **national independence**, adopting a constitution and forming a parliament with a representative from each village. The Genoese, beseiged in their coastal fortresses, turned for help to Emperor Charles VI, who responded with six battalions which helped recapture Saint-Florent and Algajola from the insurgents. Under pressure from the emperor's troops, the Corsicans agreed to a settlement in 1732, winning several concessions from the Genoese, including access to public office.

The fighting resumed as soon as the emperor's soldiers had withdrawn but the rebels made little progress, being short of resources and blockaded by a Genoese fleet. Salvation arrived in 1736 in the bizarre form of **Theodor von Neuhof**, a Westphalian adventurer brought up in the French royal court, who had spotted in Corsica's chaos an opportunity for glory. Having persuaded Tunisian financiers to back his venture, von Neuhof sailed into Aléria with ample supplies of money, arms and ammunition. The rebels had little choice but to accept his offer of support and they crowned him **King of Corsica**, though his authority was severely restricted by a new constitution, an executive council and an elected legislature. King Theodor's reign lasted eight months, by which time a lack of military success and depleted funds had provoked the hostility of many Corsicans; in November 1736 their monarch left the island, promising to find new allies.

Still the Corsicans and Genoese were in stalemate, each side unable to raise enough funds or forces to influence events decisively – until, in 1738, Genoa appealed to Louis XV of France and received several regiments commanded by the Comte de Boisseux. The following year, after the deployment of a further detachment of French troops, a thousand Corsicans were forced to flee the island. Among the refugees was **Giacinto Paoli**, one of the first leaders of the revolt, who went into exile in Naples with his teenage son Pascal.

The French pulled out of Corsica in 1741 but before long the major European powers were fighting over the island again, hoping for a strategic advantage in the War of the Austrian

Succession. A British fleet carrying Austrian and Sardinian troops joined forces with the Corsican patriots, who elected **Gian' Pietru Gaffori** their commander. The 1748 Treaty of Aix-la-Chappelle marked an end to British involvement in the struggle, but the Corsicans continued their campaign, drawing up a new constitution in 1752. Gaffori led a determined drive against the Genoese, eventually capturing their stronghold at Corte, despite the fact that his son had been abducted and held hostage within the city walls. His heroic reputation among the Corsicans was matched by that of his wife, who prevented her household from surrendering to enemy troops by threatening to light a barrel-load of gunpowder and blow them and herself to smithereens.

PAOLI'S INDEPENDENT CORSICA

The rebels lost their dynamic commander in 1753, when Gaffori was assassinated, and in 1754 **Pascal Paoli**, son of the exiled Corsican leader, was called back to Corsica to take over leadership of the rebellion.

Paoli returned with a keen sense of constitutional theory and a thorough political education. Having been elected leader of the nation in 1755, he introduced a constitution according to which every man over 25 had a vote and every parish could send representatives to the public assembly, which in turn elected an executive council of state. Paoli himself was in charge of military and foreign matters, but all other policies required the assembly's agreement. Rapid steps were taken to boost the islanders' flagging morale and pitiful resources. Schools were built and a university was founded in Corte; a mint and a printing press were established; mines and an arms factory were put into production. The death penalty was rigorously enforced for vendetta killings, which finally began to decline. Under Paoli's command the Corsican patriots and their enlightened system of government found admirers among the liberals and radicals of Europe. Jean-Jacques Rousseau toyed with the idea of moving to the island and writing its history; James Boswell came to meet Paoli and sang his praises in his journal of the visit, published in 1768.

In the meantime, events were overtaking the Corsicans. French forces occupied five coastal towns in 1764 and in **1768** the

Genoese ceded their rights to the island, selling their claim to France under the Treaty of Versailles. An invading force landed within a month of the treaty's being signed, taking possession of Cap Corse. Paoli's men – and women – kept up the pressure, hiding out in the maquis and launching guerrilla attacks on the French, but when a new detachment of troops was sent in there was little hope for the Corsicans, who suffered a terrible defeat at the battle of **Ponte-Nuovo** in May 1769. Pascal Paoli was obliged to flee to England.

FRENCH RULE TO THE TWENTIETH CENTURY

Though sporadic resistance continued even after Paoli's departure, Corsica was brought fairly painlessly within the monarchy as a *Pay d'Etat*, with its own biennial gathering of churchmen, nobles and commoners. As part of its programme of assimilation, the French offered Corsica's noble families scholarships to its prestigious military schools. Among the successful applicants was the son of Paoli's ex-secretary – **Napoléon Bonaparte**.

During the twenty years of rule by the French monarchy, the drive for independence gradually subsided, and when the revolutionaries ousted Louis XVI in 1789, Corsica urged the Assembly to make the island a fully integrated part of the French state. The royal ban imposed on political exiles was lifted, and Paoli returned to be elected President of the Corsican Conseil-Général. His authority was at first accepted by the Paris Convention, but soon Paoli fell out of favour after a Paris-instigated campaign to conquer Sardinia ended in failure. When it became known that Paoli was to be arrested, the Corsican Assembly came to his defence, naming him **Father of the Nation**. Paoli's supporters turned on the French and pro-French on the island; the Bonaparte family, who had long since transferred their loyalty to France, left their Ajaccio home to the looters and were hastened to Toulon by Napoléon, by then serving in the French army.

THE ANGLO-CORSICAN INTERLUDE

Aware of the superior strength of French forces, Paoli called on his old English allies for help, and in 1794 **Sir Gilbert Elliot** arrived with reinforcements who quickly captured

Saint-Florent, Bastia and Calvi (where Nelson lost an eye). In return for this intervention, Britain demanded a stake in the island's government, and in June **1794** an **Anglo-Corsican kingdom** was proclaimed.

To the bitter disappointment of Paoli and his supporters, Sir Gilbert was made viceroy of the new kingdom, with the power to dissolve parliament, nominate councillors and appoint the highest officers of state. When the Corsican members of parliament responded by electing Paoli their president, Sir Gilbert threatened to pull out his troops, and they were forced to back down. A series of riots followed, and a nervous Sir Gilbert persuaded the king to exile Paoli once again – this time for good. But the damage was already done: Paoli loyalists joined the French in their attacks on British soldiers and in September 1796 Sir Gilbert and his troops sailed away, leaving the island to be retaken by France.

THE NAPOLEONIC ERA AND ITS AFTERMATH

Apart from a brief stay in Ajaccio in 1799, **Napoléon** paid scant attention to his homeland during his period of power. A number of uprisings on the island during the 1790s were put down with brutal force, and opposition to Napoleonic rule led to widespread revolt by an alliance of Royalists, Paolists and British supporters in 1799. This, too, was stamped out and its leaders executed. In 1801 the constitution was suspended and Général Morand arrived to administer a harsh military rule. His reign of terror lasted until 1811, when the almost equally unpopular Général César Berthier took his place. In the same year the island was made a single *département* of France (it had been divided into two in 1796), with its capital in Ajaccio. Resistance to the French continued, and in 1814 the citizens of Bastia appealed to Britain to intervene on their behalf. A detachment of British troops was sent, but in April of that year Napoléon abdicated and the soldiers were recalled.

After 1815 and the **restoration of the French monarchy**, the governing state made some attempts to develop the island's economy, opening mines and foundries, setting up a railway, introducing an education act and building roads and schools. But most of their

schemes had little success, and Corsica remained a marginal and largely neglected part of the French economy. For Corsicans, the real opportunities lay in France, and young islanders began to turn away from the old villages, seeking their careers and education on the mainland. The romance and drama that visitors such as Edward Lear and Prosper Mérimée discovered in mid-nineteenth-century Corsica veiled a grim picture of poverty, malaria and violence – the vendetta, though on the decline, was still claiming up to 160 victims a year. In the last half of the century **emigration** surged so dramatically that within sixty years the population had been halved.

THE TWENTIETH CENTURY

In 1909, as a result of a commission set up by Georges Clemenceau, French Minister of the Interior, the French government promised more investment and development for Corsica. This plan was set aside with the outbreak of **World War I**, which itself reduced Corsica's population still further, taking over twenty thousand lives.

During the 1920s and 1930s Mussolini set his sights on Corsica, and World War II brought occupation by eighty thousand Italians and eight thousand German troops – almost half the number of the island's inhabitants. Once more, Corsican rebels took to the maquis, earning worldwide fame for their relentless guerrilla activity against the Axis powers, and lending the name **Maquis** to other resistance movements. In 1943 the Italians surrendered, and in the following year Corsica was the first French *département* to be liberated by the Allied forces. American soldiers moved in and began the process of real change in Corsica's economy, chiefly by using DDT to clear the east coast of malarial mosquitoes.

In the postwar years, Corsica was earmarked by the French government as a target for development, and in 1957 two state-sponsored organizations were set up to exploit its potential: **SOMIVAC** – the *Société pour la mise en valeur agricole de la Corse* – introduced modern agricultural techniques; **SETCO** – the *Société pour l'équipement touristique de la Corse* – provided funds to build a tourist industry. Both organizations met with considerable distrust, seen as threats to an ancient way of life that had evolved and survived during centuries of hostile occupation. Nevertheless, the development gathered pace, and after 1962, when Algeria gained its independence, the situation was complicated by a massive influx of refugees from the ex-French colony. Over 20,000 settlers poured into Corsica during the next twenty years, many of them buying up the newly developed land and hotels, adding to Corsican fears of losing control of their resources. Summer **tourists** began to arrive in steadily rising numbers, topping the half-million mark in the early 1970s (and now heading for 1.5 million).

CALLS FOR AUTONOMY

It was against this background of change and insecurity that demands for greater administrative power were increasingly voiced from the 1960s. A party of nationalist students started the call for decentralized government, for restrictions on the east-coast tourist developments, for a Corsican university (Paoli's had been closed by the French), and for compulsory schooling in Corsican language and history. A number of **autonomist movements**, varying in tactics and demands, entered the political scene, and from the mid-1970s the more moderate factions won substantial support for their manifesto of a national assembly, investment in controlled development and protection of the land. Meanwhile, a group of activists operating as the **FLNC** (*Front de Libération Nationale de la Corse*) embarked on a programme of bombing campaigns, targetting the tourist villages and foreign-owned properties that they believed to be destroying Corsica's land and culture.

In the early 1980s the autonomists profited from a change of policy in France favouring increased decentralization. A Corsican university was re-established in 1981, providing a channel for the ambitions and political ideas of the younger generation. In the following year, Corsica was the first of the French regions to be granted a national assembly, with limited powers over policy, administration and finance. Nonetheless, dozens of explosions heralded the election of 1984, as allegations of fraud and corruption were levelled against the politicians.

In 1987 another spate of bombings led to the banning of the separatist party **MCA** (*Mouvement Corse pour l'Autodétermination*), and attacks on holiday homes and official buildings have continued into the 1990s. But the past twenty years have seen a slow progression towards a re-evaluation of Corsican culture and the island's attainment of increasing control over its own affairs. A statute passed in 1990 gave a great degree of autonomy to Corsica, and in 1992 the nationalists won 13 of the 61 seats in the regional assembly. Though many young Corsicans still seek jobs and education on the mainland, those who stay can now study the language and customs that had seemed to be dying out, and enjoy a standard of living that has risen markedly since the 1950s, largely as a result of the tourist boom. Parts of the island might seem in danger of becoming bland, international-style holiday resorts, and the abandonment and spoliation of large tracts of agricultural land presents a real problem, but the revival of a strong Corsican identity has led to a reassessment of the island's future – which is guaranteed to be as controversial and unyielding as its past.

Nia Williams

CORSICAN WILDLIFE

The **Parc Naturel Regional de la Corse**, established in 1972, now embraces about a third of Corsica, largely down the mountain spine but reaching the sea in the northwest. Managing important sites such as Scandola, the Restonica valley, the Finocchiarola isles in the north and the Lavezzi isles in the south, the park authorities ensure the survival of the mouflon and other endangered species, and increase the accessibility of the wildlife of Corsica, through the publication of excellent books and booklets and through the maintenance of footpaths. The ruggedness of Corsica's heartland naturally restricts intensive exploitation, but even in areas where human intervention has occurred, the island's terrain is extraordinarily rich. The lush chestnut woodland of the Castagniccia, for example, is the result of plantation, and the tangled, headily scented maquis which clothes more than half of Corsica might seem a natural cover, but is in fact what comes in after fire or on abandoned grazing land.

THE HABITAT ZONES

Corsica's landscape has three well-defined habitat zones, the lowest of which is the Mediterranean zone, which runs from the sea to an altitude of 1000m. Corsica is noted for its clean seas and varied marine life. At places along the coast you'll find pristine sand dunes, lagoons and estuaries, all three of which are now hard to find elsewhere in the Mediterranean. Trees sometimes grow right at the edge of the beach: the highly resinous **Aleppo pine** prefers rocky ground at this level,

while the **stone pine** (or umbrella pine) is often seen growing singly but sometimes in groves – some of the best specimens are at Palombaggia beach near Porto-Vecchio. Stands of tall Australian **eucalyptus** can also be found in many places, planted late last century judging by the size of the trees.

However, the typical indicator of the Mediterranean climate is the **olive tree**. Solitary olive trees can be found everywhere in Corsica's Mediterranean zone (the oldest giant is near the deserted convent below Oletta at the foot of Cap Corse), while the largest groves are in the Balagne and near Propriano. At these lower altitudes erect "funeral" cypresses are often planted alongside family tombs, and three species of oak also identify this zone – the **cork oak** (its trunk dusky red when newly stripped), the evergreen **holm oak** (which has spiny leaves on sucker shoots and is found in both shrub and tree forms) and the **kermes oak** (rarely tree sized, and with holly-like leaves).

Introduced shrubs and trees which thrive in this Mediterranean climate include **orange** and **lemon** in groves and gardens, red or purple **bougainvillea** in gardens, **palms** in town squares, pink and white **oleanders** and the gigantic cactus-like **Mexican agave** on roadsides.

It's in the Mediterranean zone that the **maquis** comes in after fire or when fields or open grazings are abandoned. Its most easily recognized plants are the shrubs of the **cistus** family, carrying pink or white flowers with crumpled petals which are shed at the end of each day. Some cistus have highly scented gummy stems and leaves – the Montpellier cistus, which likes acid granite soils and has masses of small white flowers, is perhaps the smelliest of all.

Cistus bushes often indicate open, newish maquis, which in time will grow into an all-but-impenetrable scrub, with yellow-flowered **brooms** (some of which are wickedly thorny), the taller **strawberry tree** (the red strawberry-like fruits are edible but pappy), the pungent **mastic** and **myrtle**, **rosemary** and white-flowered **tree heather**, which grows two metres tall or more. In the "tall" maquis, cork, holm oaks and other trees come in, and as their crowns broaden they begin to shade out the shrubs below them, until eventually woodland or forest results.

Towards the top of the Mediterranean zone these trees might be joined by **maritime pine**, which unusually keeps large cones of different ages on its branches, and it keeps those branches even when they are starkly dead – the Restonica valley has many examples. **Sweet chestnut** also makes an appearance (it is most widespread between 500m and 800m), as does bracken. Groves of ancient chestnuts can be found near most of the hill villages, where the production of chestnut flour used to play an important part in the economy. Nowadays the chestnuts are given over to pigs, and many of the trees display dead antler-like branches as a result of attacks of mildew and parasites.

At around 1000m the **mountain zone** succeeds, as oaks and chestnuts give way to forests of the native, tall-trunked **Laricio** (or Corsican) **pine**, maybe mixed with **beeches** and **firs**. The Aitone, Valdo-Niello, Bonifato and Tartagine are among the most magnificent of these forests, featuring centuries-old Laricio pines that are the tallest conifers in Europe, reaching up to 40 metres.

Above 2000m stretches the **alpine zone** – open and largely rocky, perhaps with scatters of ground-hugging bushy alders, and often with a wonderful variety of flowers.

WILD FLOWERS

Many Corsican plants are distinctive of the island – of the 2000 species of wild flowers found here, eight percent are native to Corsica or shared only by Corsica and Sardinia. Which species you'll see will depend on the soil, the bedrock, the altitude and of course the time of year. Spring is glorious, with wild flowers everywhere, and many species celebrate a "second spring" after the summer drought: **cyclamens** and **autumn crocus** appear with the autumn rains, for example, and the handsome **bush spurges** of Cap Corse are in vivid green leaf in winter and spring, but reduced to bare twigs in summer.

FLOWERS OF THE MEDITERRANEAN ZONE

On the seashore in summer, the dramatic **yellow-horned poppy** is worth looking for, with its very long curved seed pods. Colourful **sea stocks** and **sea lavender** grow on shingle and on rocks, where carpets of **stonecrop**

– with fleshy red leaves and heads of small blue flowers – also make a handsome showing. The **sea holly**, one of the most beautiful of all wild plants with its grey-green spiny leaves and blue flower heads, sometimes forms low mats a couple of metres across – you'll see it on the open sands at Cargèse, for example. Here and at the back of other sandy beaches you can also find the white **sea daffodil** flowering in August, and almost anywhere you might come across carpets of **hottentot fig** with its brilliant lilac or yellow-orange flowers.

In spring various wild flowers brighten the clearings among the colourful **maquis** shrubs. If the maquis is invading old grazing land, or if the open patch is overgrazed and impoverished, there will probably be **asphodel** growing; its delicate white flowers are withered husks by summer, although the tall spikes remain. Many of Corsica's fifty or so species of **wild orchid** flower in the maquis; one of the most handsome is the pink **butterfly orchid**, and there are always a good number of the unmistakeable hooded **serapias** group, which are purple or dark red. French **lavender** is common, its small almost black flowers carried below striking purple sails, and in some areas wild **gladiolus** can be seen along the roads or even as a weed in the ploughed fields – it has smaller flowers than the garden hybrids but is easily recognizable.

The verges and rocky cuttings of roads and lanes through the maquis and between the fields are home to **wild pinks** (some of the mountain pinks are endemic to the island), **ferns**, **honeysuckle** and **eglantine** (a wild white rose looking rather like cistus). Wild **asparagus** is often found growing around the olive groves, while in spring **tassel hyacinths** and white **Florentine iris**, the original fleur-de-lis, flower on open soil (the iris is also popular in gardens).

FLOWERS OF THE MOUNTAIN AND ALPINE ZONES

In the chestnut woods and amongst the pines of the mountain zone grow the handsome green tufts of the **Corsican hellebore**, a poisonous species endemic to Corsica and Sardinia. **Foxgloves** may be found here, and in spring scatters of **cyclamen** mix with **violets** along the streamsides, together with hosts of delicate white or lilac **anemones** in some areas. **Autumn crocus** and **squill** also flower here and elsewhere towards the end of the year. Wherever you find beech trees at this height you might look for wild red **peony**.

Although the mountain zone is harsh, there can be a surprising variety of flowers when the snow melts, many of them endemic – indeed, half of those you see might grow only in Corsica and Sardinia, such as a Corsican alpine groundwort and a blue mountain columbine. And many common enough in the Alps are not found here, suggesting that these two islands separated from mainland Europe at a far distant time in the past.

BIRDS

As a result of the closed breeding of its island populations, Corsica's birds often display certain differences from those of mainland Europe. Songbirds such as the blackbird have a song that's distinct from that of related European species, and the birds' normal habitats are in many instances extended in some way. In Corsica the blackbird ranges from coastal maquis to the high mountains, while the explosive "chetti" call of the small brown **Cetti's warbler** is heard not only in the reed beds around the coastal lagoons but also in the maquis up to 500m. The most renowned Corsican example is the elusive **Corsican nuthatch** of the Aitone and other high pine forests. The **treecreeper** is another, while there are also forms of **great spotted woodpecker** and **wren** shared with Sardinia. Corsica is the place to add the **Dartford warbler** to your list – it is a localized and rare resident in the south of Britain; here it is common in the coastal maquis but as a darker, smaller sub-species.

Because of its position, Corsica is probably visited by the majority of trans-Mediterranean **migrants**, many of which make landfalls on the headlands or lagoons. The **spring and autumn** list includes common and curlew sandpiper (the latter the commonest migrant wader here), reed bunting, marsh and Montague's harriers, pied flycatcher, grey heron, black kite and tree pipit. Of the birds that come to **winter** on the island, the sparrow-like dunnock is one of the commonest in the maquis, and amongst the other regulars are snipe, cormorant, common starling, gannet, pochard, tufted duck, teal, black-necked grebe, redwing and song thrush. Others such as the wood pigeon are resident, but numbers swell in winter when incomers fly in to gorge on the plentiful crops of acorns.

SEABIRDS AND WETLAND SPECIES

In general most **coastal birdlife** is centred on remote headlands and islands. Scandola, for example, has osprey, peregrine, rock dove and blue rock thrush (which also nest on bare slopes inland to 1800m). Shearwaters nest in some places, but you'll see fewer **gulls** than you might expect. Herring gulls nest at Scandola and Capo Rosso and other remote sites, and you may spot the Mediterranean gull (black-headed in summer) and the slim-winged Audouin's gull, which nests on several offshore islands. Shags too nest on rocky shores and are often seen flying low over the sea.

Despite widespread drainage for vineyards, fruit and other crops, the string of lagoons of the east coast remain as one of the most extensive wetland units of the whole Mediterranean, attracting great crested and little **grebes**, pochard and mallard, and the water rail with its incredible pig-like cry. Reed, moustached, Cetti's and other **warblers** call from the reed beds while marsh harrier and hobby hunt across them. In winter, Biguglia and the other lagoons are an important station for ducks, grey heron, wintering kingfisher and others.

MAQUIS SPECIES

The maquis in its various forms offers ideal nesting for **warblers** and birds such as red-backed shrike, pipits, buntings and even the highly colourful bee-eater. The **linnet** picks out more open areas, as does the **stonechat** and the red-legged **partridge** (the grey has been introduced for shooting in some places). These birds all follow the maquis as it spreads up the valleys and slopes inland, but where it grows tall and is invaded by holm oak and other trees (as seen in the Fango valley, for example) the scrub warblers such as Dartford and Sardinian warblers leave while the blackcap and subalpine warbler remain. Being evergreen, the maquis maintains its insect larder in winter, when many of its resident birds are joined by migrant cousins.

Kestrel and buzzards (widespread but nowhere very common) patrol above the maquis, as does red kite, which prefers the lower scrubby maquis to the taller growth. At night the clear bell-like notes of the **Scops owl** and the call of the nightjar echo across the maquis, mingling with the constant croaking of frogs.

The chestnut groves are comparatively empty of birdlife, but look for the endemic **tree-creeper** here, and also the **mistle thrush** and the **wryneck**, the last now rare almost everywhere.

MOUNTAIN SPECIES

In the mountain and alpine levels grey wagtail and dipper forage in the spray of the torrents, where the crag martin is often seen as well. The pine forests have **goldcrest**, **coal tit** and the endemic **nuthatch** – this last, found from the Tartagine in the north to Ospedale in the south, is smaller than its mainland cousins and is more often heard than seen. Sparrowhawk and goshawk have a presence in these pine woods, as does the crossbill.

A feature of some parts of the **high mountains** are *pozzines* – small tablelands of peaty turf cut by meandering streams. Here **lark** and **wheatear** are often seen, with even blackbird and chaffinch if there are scrubby alders for cover. The blue rock thrush, though nesting on the coast at Scandola and elsewhere, can be met as high as 1500m. The central mountains are the domain of the yellow-beaked **alpine chough** and the rare **lammergeier** and **golden eagle**. Bonelli's eagle is reported from the Asco valley, but it is not known if it nests.

GARDEN SPECIES

Gardens attract many birds, such as blackbird, warblers, hooded crow and turtle dove – these last are widely shot when they fly in in spring, but there are always some to be heard in summer. (The collared dove is a recent colonist and still uncommon.) Gardens also attract the spotted flycatcher – the Corsican form scarcely lives up to its name, with few if any speckles, but it is quickly recognized by its lively flycatching sorties, usually returning to the same post. In the Nebbio and a few other spots the **hoopoe** with its dramatic crest is also seen in gardens at dawn. The towns attract **house martin** and **swifts** – both the familiar Eurasian swift and the similar pallid swift.

MAMMALS

Woodmouse, shrew, rabbit, brown hare, weasel and hedgehog are as familiar in Corsica as elsewhere in Europe, but there are no squirrels. Squirrel-like nests in shrubs or low trees may be those of the black rat, while a sighting of a small brownish animal with squirrel-like bushy tail would be the **fat dormouse**, though it is shy and nocturnal. The slimmer garden or **oak dormouse**, with white underside to body and tail, is also resident. Both these animals may search houses for a hibernation den in autumn, and you often hear them scratching around in the attic. Bats are common everywhere: in the gorge of the Bonifato forest behind Calvi, for example, they swarm out at sunset.

The fox is seen, and there are reports of a wild cat in remote parts of the island such as the Aitone forest – it may turn out to be a tribe of striped feral cat, domestic stock now living wild. There are similar indecisive reports of pine marten in these forested areas.

Around 500 **mouflon** – a wild sheep, the males sporting massive curved horns – are found in two main areas, at Asco and at Bavella. They might be the relic of an original wild population which began to be domesticated in Neolithic times, or they may be the descendants of escapees from those first domestic flocks.

The **wild boar** (*sanglier* in French) is found throughout the maquis and in the lower mountains, and has something of a cult status in Corsica. Many villages organize weekly hunts over the winter, culling an estimated 10,000 each year from an average population of 30,000. Even though the males are smaller than their continental cousins (a common island trait this), the Corsican boar can still reach 80kg, and is a formidable animal, being armed with tusks for rooting and grubbing – you'll come across the disturbed ground during walks in the maquis. It is a Corsican habit to let the domestic **pigs** roam free in the chestnut and beech woods on the mountain flanks, so there is certainly interbreeding between boar and pig, yet about 40 percent of the wild boar stock remains untainted.

The native **red deer** – the smallest of all red deer – became extinct only a few decades ago, but some Sardinian stock can be seen in a paddock near Quenza in the south.

Offshore, the common and striped **dolphins** and the common **porpoise** patrol, if no longer as regularly or in the numbers that were once seen, and the endangered monk seal of the Mediterranean was last seen in Corsican waters in 1982. The fin whale, however, is often seen with young off Cap Corse in spring.

REPTILES AND INSECTS

Corsica's hot rocky landscape suits reptiles, and **lizards** are always seen scuttling across walls and rocks. The **Tyrrhenian wall lizard** is a sometimes abundant species found only in Corsica and Sardinia, and the mountain lizard is also endemic, but their variable colouring makes identification of lizard species difficult. Their cousins, the plump but flattened **geckos**, are most often noticed high on room walls and ceilings, which they patrol after sunset, dealing with mosquitoes and other irritations.

There are no poisonous snakes on the island. The **grass snake** is seen in damp places, while the **whip snake** – a slender snake often with a barred pattern – is found on sunny hillsides and other dry habitats. It will attempt to bite if annoyed – its French name is *colereuse*, "quick-tempered one".

Hermann's tortoise is a fairly common sight in some areas, and a centre for tortoise breeding and release has recently been created near Moltifao in the Asco valley. The European pond **terrapin** might be seen in secluded pools and other still waters that have overgrown banks.

Endemic to the island is · the **brook salamander**, olive grey and brown and with a clear yellow stripe down its spine, found near running water up to 2000 metres. The rather larger **fire salamander**, with dramatic black and yellow skin, might also be seen.

A CHECKLIST OF WILDLIFE SITES

FORESTS

Aitone – magnificent specimens of Laricio pine; in the remoter reaches (towards Monte Cinto), wild boar, eagle and mouflon. See p.187.

Bavella – impressive though fire-damaged hunting reserve; chance of sightings of mouflon and eagle. See p.144.

Bonifato – classic "chaos" of rocks and forest, pines and maquis. See p.92.

Castagniccia – chestnut woods. See p.175.

Ospedale – pines and other trees. See p.166.

Tartagine – bat caves and magnificent pines. See p.91.

Valdo-Niello – the largest of the island's forests, with fine examples of Laricio pine. See p.188.

Vizzavona – some of the finest pines and beech. See p.198.

OTHER WILDLIFE ZONES

Asco valley – possible sightings of mouflon, eagle, lammergeier; Laricio and maritime pines. See p.184.

Biguglia and the east coast lagoons – birdlife. See p.47.

Bonifacio – limestone cliffs with rare flowers. See p.153.

Les Calanche – flowers and coastal birds. See p.99.

Cap Corse – remote maquis, good for birds (maybe eagles attracted by remoteness); nature reserve on Finocchiarola isles. See p.56.

Désert des Agriates – a largish area of thin maquis growing on rocky, impoverished terrain; good for flowers and nesting birds. See p.67.

Fango valley – good walking through mix of maquis and forest habitats. See p.93.

Iles Sanguinaires – distinctive island vegetation. See p.120.

Lavezzi isles – nature reserve off Bonifacio. See p.161.

Niolo – alpine choughs and other mountain birds. See p.185.

Restonica – Corsican and maritime pine. See p.195.

Scandola – supreme nature reserve of international importance; classic lava column geology; osprey and other birds; marine life. See p.94.

Most piercingly vocal are the **edible frog** and the **common tree frog**, which has enormous vocal sacs for its small size. The **green toad**, with spotted green and white skin and shrill warbling call, is also reasonably common.

The frog chorus takes over from the summer daytime chorus of the **cicadas**, especially loud in the vicinity of their favourite umbrella pines. The cicadas are just one of a host of grasshoppers, bushcrickets, beetles, bees and butterflies which make Corsica – and other Mediterranean lands – so fascinating for anyone with any interest in natural history. Some butterflies will be familiar from northern Europe, such as the migrant painted lady and the red admiral; of the Mediterranean species, one of the most handsome is the large, strongly flying **two-tailed pasha**, which feeds on the strawberry tree of the maquis. **Hummingbird hawk moths** of various kinds are commonly seen in gardens, hovering in front of the flowers.

Damselflies and mayflies are a common sight dancing over the streams, and the dramatic and fierce **hawker dragonflies** – a birdwatcher's insect if ever there were one – may spend the day hunting across the maquis, far from water.

Geoffrey Young

BOOKS

Very few books about Corsica have been written in English, and the great majority of them are currently out of print, so you'll have to resort to second-hand book shops or libraries if you want to get stuck into the titles listed below. Out-of-print titles are marked o/p in the listings below. For those few that are in print, the UK publisher is given first in each listing, followed by the publisher in the US, unless the title is available in one country only, in which case we have specified the country concerned. If the same publisher produces the book in the UK and US, the publisher is simply named once.

TRAVEL BOOKS AND JOURNALS

James Boswell, *An Account of Corsica, The Journal of a Tour to that Island and Memoirs of Pascal Paoli* (o/p). Typically robust and witty account of encounters with the Corsican people, including absorbing insights into the psychology of local hero Pascal Paoli. Excerpts published in *Journals of James Boswell* (Mandarin in UK).

Thomasina Campbell, *Southward Ho!* (o/p). Jolly account of the island as seen through the eyes of a Victorian walker, with plentiful descriptions of wild flowers and scenery – but little on the inhabitants.

Dorothy Carrington, *Granite Island* (Penguin). A fascinating and immensely comprehensive book, combining the writer's personal experiences with an evocative portrayal of historical figures and events. By far the best study of Corsica ever written in English.

A. Dugmore-Hardie, *Corsica the Beautiful* (o/p). Gushing eulogy of Corsica's landscapes, flora and fauna.

Emma Eleanor Elliot, *The Life and Letters of Sir Gilbert Elliot* (o/p). Observations on Corsica from the British viceroy's office (1794–96), compiled by his granddaughter.

Edward Lear, *Journal of a Landscape Painter* (o/p). Account of a Corsican visit in the 1860s, augmented by beautifully atmospheric engravings.

John Lowe, *Corsica: a Traveller's Guide* (o/p). Rather trite commentary on the Corsican people and their ways, but one of the few English-language books to tackle the present-day island.

Alan Ross, *Time Was Away – A Journey Through Corsica* (o/p). Gloomy impressionistic account of a visit to postwar Corsica, with drawings by John Minton. Recently in print from Collins Harvill, so there may still be the odd copy lying around.

Geoffrey Wagner, *Elegy for Corsica* (o/p). Amusing impressions of life in Corsica from an ex-pat's point of view.

ARCHEOLOGY

Roger Grosjean, *La Corse avant L'Histoire* (o/p). The most influential discussion of the island's prehistoric sites, from the man who excavated most of them. The explanations are clear and precise, and aided by photographs.

Jean Jehasse, *Aléria Greque et Romaine* (o/p). Heavy-going in-depth study of the Roman site of Aléria.

Genevieve Moracchini-Mazel, *Les Monuments Préchrétiens de la Corse* (o/p). An important work on Bronze Age Corsica, including an interpretation of the statue-menhirs of Filitosa.

Genevieve Moracchini-Mazel, *La Corse Romane* (o/p). The island's Pisan Romanesque architecture discussed with drawings and descriptions of building techniques.

Xavier Poli, *La Corse dans l'Antiquité* (o/p). Rather stuffy but authoritative study of prehistoric Corsica.

HISTORY

Dorothy Carrington, *Napoleon and his Parents on the Threshold of History* (o/p). Lucid study of Napoléon's early years in his native country.

Corelli Barnett, *Bonaparte* (o/p). An anti-Napoléon biography with vivid insights into his life in Corsica – good pictures too.

Vincent Cronin, *Napoleon* (o/p). Enthusiastic and accessible biography; you might still find copies of the recently deleted Penguin edition on the shelves.

Peter Geyl, *Napoleon – For and Against* (Penguin). A compendium of various French scholars' views on Napoléon.

M. Maclaren, *Corsican Boswell* (o/p). Places Boswell's reactions to Corsica within their historical context; an amusing read but difficult to find.

Valerie Pirie, *His Majesty of Corsica* (o/p). An illuminating biography of Corsica's ephemeral king, Theodor von Neuhof.

Peter Adam Thrasler, *Pasquale Paoli – an Enlightened Hero* (o/p). A rather laboured biography, but does include some interesting facts about Corsica in the eighteenth century.

LITERATURE

Alphonse Daudet, *Letters from my Windmill* (Oxford University Press). Tale of a lonely Corsican lighthouse keeper, with colourful description of the Îles Sanguinaires, near Ajaccio.

Alexandre Dumas, *The Corsican Brothers* (o/p). Far-fetched tale of two outlaw brothers in nineteenth-century Corsica. The original text – *Le Freres Corses* – is available from Flammarion.

Gustave Flaubert, *Memoires d'Un Fou* (o/p). Flaubert romanticizes the bandits, the maquis, the mountains and the sea in letters to his sister.

Prosper Mérimée, *Colomba* (Oxford University Press). Short novel based on a real-life blood feud which divided the village of Fozzano in the 1830s. A son returns to Corsica and is expected to avenge the death of his father.

WALKING AND CLIMBING

Robin G. Collomb, *Corsica Mountains* (West Col). Covers all the principal mountain peaks, with information on different approaches and ascents, backed up with diagrams.

Noel Rochford, *Landscapes of Corsica* (Sunflower in UK). Car tour routes, suggestions for picnic spots and specific walking routes. Good for ideas for gentle walks, but its directions are sometimes confusing.

Walks in Corsica (in the Robertson McCarta *Footpaths of Europe* series in UK). The long-distance *GR20* and *Tra Mare e Monti* hiking trails described in detail, with colour 1:50,000 maps printed alongside. Essential for serious hikers.

LANGUAGE

Since 1974 it has been compulsory for school-children to learn Corsican up to the level of the *baccalauréat*, and at Corte University all students are obliged to study the language. Corsican nationalists use the language for their campaign literature, folk singers always sing in Corsican, and there's a newscast in Corsican on television every evening. Yet the language is struggling to survive in competition with French, a more international language and the official language of the island. French is spoken and understood everywhere in Corsica, where few speak English, even in the tourist offices – so you'd do well to familiarize yourself with the information given below before you leave.

FRENCH PRONUNCIATION

One easy rule to remember is that **consonants** at the ends of words are usually silent. *Pas plus tard* (not later) is thus pronounced pa-plu-tarr. But when the following word begins with a vowel, you run the two together: *pas après* (not after) becomes pazapre. **Vowels** are the hardest sounds to get right. Roughly:

a	as in h**a**t	*eu*	like the **u** in h**u**rt	*ou*	as in f**oo**d
e	as in g**e**t	*i*	as in mach**i**ne	*u*	as in a pursed-lip
é	between g**e**t and g**a**te	*o*	as in h**o**t		version of **u**se
è	between g**e**t and g**u**t	*o, au*	as in **o**ver		

More awkward are the **combinations** in/im, en/em, an/am, on/om, un/um at the ends of words, or followed by consonants other than n or m. Again, roughly:

in/im	like the **an** in **an**xious	*on/om*	like the d**on** in D**on**caster said by
an/am, en/em	like the d**on** in D**on**caster when		someone with a heavy cold
	said with a nasal accent	*un/um*	like the **u** in **u**nderstand

Consonants are much as in English, except that: ch is always sh, c is s, h is silent, th is the same as t, ll is like the y in yes, w is v, and r is growled (or rolled).

A BRIEF GUIDE TO SPEAKING FRENCH

BASIC WORDS AND PHRASES

All nouns are divided into masculine and feminine. This causes difficulties with adjectives, whose endings have to change to suit the gender of the nouns they qualify. If you know some grammar, you will know what to do. If not, stick to the masculine form, which is the simplest – it's what we have done in this glossary.

today	*aujourd'hui*	man	*un homme*	less	*moins*
yesterday	*hier*	woman	*une femme*	a little	*un peu*
tomorrow	*demain*	here	*ici*	a lot	*beaucoup*
in the morning	*le matin*	there	*là*	cheap	*bon marché*
in the afternoon	*l'après-midi*	this one	*ceci*	expensive	*cher*
in the evening	*le soir*	that one	*cela*	good	*bon*
now	*maintenant*	open	*ouvert*	bad	*mauvais*
later	*plus tard*	closed	*fermé*	hot	*chaud*
at one o'clock	*à une heure*	big	*grand*	cold	*froid*
at three o'clock	*à trois heures*	small	*petit*	with	*avec*
at ten-thirty	*à dix heures et demie*	more	*plus*	without	*sans*
at midday	*à midi*				

NUMBERS

1	*un*	11	*onze*	21	*vingt-et-un*	95	*quatre-vingt-quinze*
2	*deux*	12	*douze*	22	*vingt-deux*	100	*cent*
3	*trois*	13	*treize*	30	*trente*	101	*cent-et-un*
4	*quatre*	14	*quatorze*	40	*quarante*	200	*deux cents*
5	*cinq*	15	*quinze*	50	*cinquante*	300	*trois cents*
6	*six*	16	*seize*	60	*soixante*	500	*cinq cents*
7	*sept*	17	*dix-sept*	70	*soixante-dix*	1000	*mille*
8	*huit*	18	*dix-huit*	75	*soixante-quinze*	2000	*deux milles*
9	*neuf*	19	*dix-neuf*	80	*quatre-vingts*	5000	*cinq milles*
10	*dix*	20	*vingt*	90	*quatre-vingt-dix*	1,000,000	*un million*

DAYS AND DATES

January	*janvier*	November	*novembre*	August 1	*le premier août*
February	*février*	December	*décembre*	March 2	*le deux mars*
March	*mars*			July 14	*le quatorze juillet*
April	*avril*	Sunday	*dimanche*	November 23	*le vingt-trois*
May	*mai*	Monday	*lundi*		*novembre*
June	*juin*	Tuesday	*mardi*		
July	*juillet*	Wednesday	*mercredi*	1993	*dix-neuf-cent-quatre-*
August	*août*	Thursday	*jeudi*		*vingt-treize*
September	*septembre*	Friday	*vendredi*	1994	*dix-neuf-cent-quatre-*
October	*octobre*	Saturday	*samedi*		*vingt-quatorze*

TALKING TO PEOPLE

When addressing people you should always use *Monsieur* for a man, *Madame* for a woman, *Mademoiselle* for a girl. Plain *bonjour* by itself is not enough. This isn't as formal as it seems, and it has its uses when you've forgotten someone's name or want to attract someone's attention.

Excuse me	*Pardon*	please	*s'il vous plaît*
Do you speak English?	*Vous parlez anglais?*	thank you	*merci*
		hello	*bonjour*
How do you say it in French?	*Comment ça se dit en Français?*	goodbye	*au revoir*
What's your name?	*Comment vous appelez-vous?*	good morning/ afternoon	*bonjour*
		good evening	*bonsoir*
My name is . . .	*Je m'appelle . . .*	good night	*bonne nuit*
I'm English/ Irish/Scottish Welsh/American/ Australian/ Canadian/ a New Zealander	*Je suis anglais[e]/ irlandais[e]/écossais[e]/ gallois[e]/américain[e]/ australien[ne]/ canadien[ne]/ néo-zélandais[e]*	How are you?	*Comment allez-vous? / Ça va?*
		Fine, thanks	*Très bien, merci*
		I don't know	*Je ne sais pas*
		Let's go	*Allons-y*
yes	*oui*	See you tomorrow	*A demain*
no	*non*	See you soon	*A bientôt*
I understand	*Je comprends*	Sorry	*Pardon, Madame/je m'excuse*
I don't understand	*Je ne comprends pas*		
Can you speak slower?	*S'il vous plaît, parlez moins vite?*	Leave me alone (aggressive)	*Fichez-moi la paix!*
OK/agreed	*d'accord*	Please help me	*Aidez-moi, s'il vous plaît*

FINDING THE WAY

bus	autobus, bus, car	hitchhiking	autostop
bus station	gare routière	on foot	à pied
bus stop	arrêt	Where are you going?	Vous allez où ?
car	voiture	I'm going to . . .	Je vais à . . .
train/taxi/ferry	train/taxi/ferry	I want to get off	Je voudrais descendre
boat	bâteau	at . . .	à . . .
plane	avion	the road to . . .	la route pour . . .
railway station	gare	near	près/pas loin
platform	quai	far	loin
What time does it leave?	Il part à quelle heure ?	left	à gauche
		right	à droite
What time does it arrive?	Il arrive à quelle heure ?	straight on	tout droit
		on the other side of	l'autre côté de
a ticket to . . .	un billet pour . . .	on the corner of	à l'angle de
single ticket	aller simple	next to	à côté de
return ticket	aller retour	behind	derrière
validate your ticket	compostez votre billet	in front of	devant
		before	avant
valid for	valable pour	after	après
ticket office	vente de billets	under	sous
how many kilometres ?	combien de kilomètres ?	to cross	traverser
		bridge	pont
how many hours ?	combien d'heures ?		

ACCOMMODATION

a room for one/two people	une chambre pour une/ deux personnes	sheets	draps
		blankets	couvertures
a double bed	un lit double	quiet	calme
a room with a shower	une chambre avec douche	noisy	bruyant
		hot water	eau chaude
a room with a bath	une chambre avec salle de bain	cold water	eau froide
		Is breakfast included?	Est-ce que le petit déjeuner est compris?
For one/two/three nights	Pour une/deux/trois nuits	I would like breakfast	Je voudrais prendre le petit déjeuner
Can I see it?	Je peux la voir?		
a room on the courtyard	une chambre sur la cour	I don't want breakfast	Je ne veux pas de petit déjeuner
a room over the street	une chambre sur la rue	Can we camp here?	On peut camper ici ?
first floor	premier étage	campsite	un camping/terrain de camping
second floor	deuxième étage		
with a view	avec vue	tent	une tente
key	clef	tent space	un emplacement
to iron	repasser	youth hostel	auberge de jeunesse
do laundry	faire la lessive		

HEALTH MATTERS

doctor	médecin	stomach ache	mal à l'estomac
I don't feel well	Je ne me sens pas bien	period	règles
medicines	médicaments	pain	douleur
prescription	ordonnance	it hurts	ça fait mal
I feel sick	Je suis malade	chemist	pharmacie
I have a headache	J'ai mal à la tête	hospital	hôpital

QUESTIONS AND REQUESTS

The simplest way of asking a question is to start with *s'il vous plaît* (please), then name the thing you want in an interrogative tone of voice. For example:

Where is there a bakery?	*S'il vous plaît, la boulangerie?*
Which way is it to the Eiffel Tower?	*S'il vous plaît, la route pour la tour Eiffel?*

Similarly with requests:

We'd like a room for two	*S'il vous plaît, une chambre pour deux*
Can I have a kilo of oranges	*S'il vous plaît, un kilo d'oranges?*

Question words

where?	*où?*	when?	*quand?*
how?	*comment?*	why?	*pourquoi?*
how many/	*combien?*	at what time?	*à quelle heure?*
how much?		what is/which is?	*quel est?*

CARS

garage	*garage*	put air in the tyres	*gonfler les pneus*
service	*service*	battery	*batterie*
to park the car	*garer la voiture*	the battery is dead	*la batterie est morte*
car park	*un parking*	plugs	*bougies*
no parking	*défense de stationner/ stationnement interdit*	to break down	*tomber en panne*
		petrol can	*bidon*
petrol station	*poste d'essence*	insurance	*assurance*
petrol	*essence*	green card	*carte verte*
fill it up	*faire le plein*	traffic lights	*feux*
oil	*huile*	red light	*feu rouge*
air line	*ligne à air*	green light	*feu vert*

GENERAL NEEDS

bakery	*boulangerie*	bank	*banque*
food shop	*alimentation*	money	*argent*
supermarket	*supermarché*	toilets	*toilettes*
to eat	*manger*	police	*police*
to drink	*boire*	telephone	*téléphone*
camping gas	*camping gaz*	cinema	*cinéma*
tobacconist	*tabac*	theatre	*théâtre*
stamps	*timbres*	to reserve/book	*réserver*

THE CORSICAN LANGUAGE

Corsican, originally a Latin-based language with resemblances to Romanian, developed an Italianate vocabulary and syntax during Pisan and Genoese occupation. Arabic and French influences have added to the complexity of Corsican, which for centuries was predominantly an oral tongue until around two hundred years ago –hence the confusing variety of spellings for place names, despite attempts at standardization. The commonest variants come about through the transposition of ll and dd – as in "casteddu" and "castellu". Buildings and monuments are often labelled in different languages (San Pietro/San Pietru), and on maps you'll find mountain passes, rivers and regions marked in a mixture of Italian, French and Corsican – the "u" ending (pronounced as in English "zoo") is a frequent indicator of Corsican usage. Deep in the country, many old people are still easier with Corsican than French, so a few phrases will be met with surprise and pleasure. Pronunciation is generally as for Italian, but look out for two tricky clusters of consonants – chj/chi and ghj/chi pronounced ty or dy.

CORSICAN WORDS AND PHRASES

BASICS

yes, no, OK	*iè, nò, và bé*	day	*ghjurnu*
please, thank you	*fate u piacè, a' ringraziavvi*	week	*simana*
where, when	*induve, quandu*	month	*meze*
what, how much	*chi, quantu*	yesterday	*ieri*
here, there	*custi, custà*	day before yesterday	*avant'ieri*
this, that	*quellu/quella,*	next week	*simana'dopu*
	quessu/quessa	next month	*meze'dopu*
now, later	*ora, dopu*	nothing	*nulla/nunda/nudda*
open, closed	*apertu, chiusu*	morning	*a mane*
with, without	*cù, senza*	evening	*a sera*
good, bad	*bonu, male*	night	*a notte*
big, small	*grande/maio, piccola/chjucu*	car	*a vittura*
cheap, expensive	*bonu mercatu, cara*	girl/boy	*zitella/zitellu*
hot, cold	*caldu, fredda*	it's good	*he bonu*
more, less	*piu, menu*	something	*qualcosa*
today, tomorrow	*oghje, dumane*	I want	*vogliu*

GREETINGS AND RESPONSES

hello, goodbye	*bonghjornu, a'vedeci*	I (don't) understand	*(nò) capiscu*
good evening	*bona sera*	Do you speak English?	*Parla inglese?*
goodnight	*bona notte*	My name is . . .	*Me chjamanu. . .*
sorry	*me dispiace*	What's your name?	*Cumu a chjamanu*
excuse me	*scusame*	I am English	*Sò Inglese*
How are you?	*Comu si?*	Let's go	*Andemu*

QUESTIONS AND REQUESTS

Do you have?	*Avetene?*	. . .with two beds/double	*cù duie letti*
Give me (one like that)	*Datemi*	. . .with shower/bath	*cùlla duscia/bagnarola*
That's enough	*Basta*	It's for one person	*Ci ne vole una/*
What would you like to drink?	*Chi vulete beie?*	(two people)	*duie una persona*
I'd like a lemonade/coffee	*A me una lim nata/caffè*	How long are you staying?	*quantu ci avete da stà?*
How much?	*Quantu costanu?*	. . . for one night (one week)	*. . .pé una notte*
Is there?	*C'he?*	It's fine – how much is it?	*Và bé quantu costanu?*
. . .a room	*. . .una camera*	It's too expensive	*He troppu caru*

DIRECTIONS

Where is..?	*Induv'é?*	How long will it take	*Quantu ci vole à*
It's near	*He vicinu*	to get to Ponte Leccia?	*ghjunghje*
It's far	*He lontana*		*à u Ponte à a Leccia ?*
left, right, straight on	*sinistra, dritta, sempre drittu*	What's the time ?	*Chi ora he ?*
		It's three o'clock	*Sò trè ore*

MONTHS AND SEASONS

January	*Ghjennaghju*	July	*Ghjugliu*	winter	*imbernu/Ingnernu*
February	*Febbraghju*	August	*Aostu*	spring	*veranu*
March	*Marzu*	September	*Sittembre*	summer	*estate*
April	*Aprile*	October	*Ottobre*	autumn	*auturnu*
May	*Maghjiu*	November	*Novembre*		
June	*Ghjiugnu*	December	*Dicembre*		

NUMBERS AND DAYS

1	unu (una)	15	quindeci	90	novanta
2	dui (duie)	16	sedeci	100	centu
3	trè	17	dicessette	101	cent'e unu
4	quattru	18	diciottu	102	cent'e dui
5	cinque	19	dicennove	Monday	luni
6	sei	20	vinti	Tuesday	marti
7	sette	21	vintunu	Wednesday	mercuri
8	ottu	22	vintidui	Thursday	ghjovi
9	nove	30	trenta	Friday	venneri
10	dece	40	quaranta	Saturday	sabatu
11	ondeci	50	cinquanta	Sunday	dumenica
12	dodeci	60	sessanta		
13	tredeci	70	settanta		
14	quattordeci	80	ottanta		

WORDS OF THE COUNTRYSIDE

Bird	acellu	Plateau	pianu
Mountain	montane	Cliff	scuglialu
Mountain pass	bocca, foce	Bridge	ponte
Mountain peak, summit	capu, cima, monte, punta	River	fiume
		Tree	arburu
Forest, wood	furesta, valdu	Beach	a marina
Lake	lavu	Village	u paese

INDEX

HELP US UPDATE

We've gone to a lot of effort to ensure that this edition of *The Rough Guide to Corsica* is accurate and up-to-date. However, things do change — places get "discovered," opening hours are notoriously fickle, restaurants and rooms raise prices or lower standards. If you feel we've got it wrong or left something out, we'd like to know, and if you can remember the address, the price, the time, the phone number, so much the better.

We'll credit all contributions, and send a copy of the next edition (or any other Rough Guide if you prefer) for the best letters. Please mark all letters "Rough Guide Corsica Update" and send to:

Rough Guides, 1 Mercer Street, London WC2H 9QJ
or, Rough Guides, 375 Hudson Street, 4th Floor, New York NY10014

DIRECT ORDERS IN THE UK

Title	ISBN	Price	Title	ISBN	Price
Amsterdam	1858280869	£7.99	Mediterranean Wildlife	0747100993	£7.95
Australia	1858280354	£12.99	Morocco	1858280400	£9.99
Barcelona & Catalunya	1858280486	£7.99	Nepal	185828046X	£8.99
Berlin	1858280338	£8.99	New York	1858280583	£8.99
Brazil	0747101272	£7.95	Nothing Ventured	0747102082	£7.99
Brittany & Normandy	1858280192	£7.99	Paris	1858280389	£7.99
Bulgaria	1858280478	£8.99	Peru	0747102546	£7.95
California	1858280907	£9.99	Poland	1858280346	£9.99
Canada	185828001X	£10.99	Portugal	1858280842	£9.99
Corsica	1858280893	£8.99	Prague	185828015X	£7.99
Crete	1858280494	£6.99	Provence & the	1858280230	£8.99
Cyprus	185828032X	£8.99	Côte d'Azur		
Czech & Slovak	185828029X	£8.99	Pyrenees	1858280524	£7.99
Republics			St Petersburg	1858280303	£8.99
Egypt	1858280753	£10.99	San Francisco	1858280826	£8.99
England	1858280788	£9.99	Scandinavia	1858280397	£10.99
Europe	185828077X	£14.99	Scotland	1858280834	£8.99
Florida	1858280109	£8.99	Sicily	1858280370	£8.99
France	1858280508	£9.99	Spain	1858280818	£9.99
Germany	1858280257	£11.99	Thailand	1858280168	£8.99
Greece	1858280206	£9.99	Tunisia	1858280656	£8.99
Guatemala & Belize	1858280451	£9.99	Turkey	1858280885	£9.99
Holland, Belgium	1858280877	£9.99	Tuscany & Umbria	1858280915	£8.99
& Luxembourg			USA	185828080X	£12.99
Hong Kong & Macau	1858280664	£8.99	Venice	1858280362	£8.99
Hungary	1858280214	£7.99	West Africa	1858280141	£12.99
Ireland	1858280958	£9.99	Women Travel	1858280710	£7.99
Italy	1858280311	£12.99	Zimbabwe & Botswana	1858280419	£10.99
Kenya	1858280435	£9.99			

ough Guides are available from all good bookstores, but can be obtained
irectly in the UK* from Penguin by contacting:

enguin Direct, Penguin Books Ltd, Bath Road, Harmondsworth, West
rayton, Middlesex UB7 0DA; or telephone our credit line on 081-899 4036
)am–5pm) and ask for Penguin Direct. Visa, Access and Amex accepted.
elivery will normally be within 14 working days. Penguin Direct ordering
cilities are only available in the UK.

he availability and published prices quoted are correct at the time
f going to press but are subject to alteration without prior notice.

For USA and international orders, see separate price list

DIRECT ORDERS IN THE USA

Title	ISBN	Price
Able to Travel	1858281105	$19.95
Amsterdam	1858280869	$13.95
Australia	1858280354	$18.95
Berlin	1858280338	$13.99
Brittany & Normandy	1858280192	$14.95
Bulgaria	1858280478	$14.99
California	1858280907	$14.95
Canada	185828001X	$14.95
Corsica	1858280893	$14.95
Crete	1858280494	$14.95
Cyprus	185828032X	$13.99
Czech & Slovak Republics	185828029X	$14.95
Egypt	1858280753	$17.95
England	1858280788	$16.95
Europe	185828077X	$18.95
Florida	1858280109	$14.95
France	1858280508	$16.95
Germany	1858280257	$17.95
Greece	1858280206	$16.95
Guatemala & Belize	1858280451	$14.95
Holland, Belgium & Luxembourg	1858280877	$15.95
Hong Kong & Macau	1858280664	$13.95
Hungary	1858280214	$13.95
Ireland	1858280958	$16.95
Italy	1858280311	$17.95
Kenya	1858280435	$15.95
Mediterranean Wildlife	1858280699	$15.95
Morocco	1858280400	$16.95
Nepal	185828046X	$13.95
New York	1858280583	$13.95
Paris	1858280389	$13.95
Poland	1858280346	$16.95
Portugal	1858280842	$15.95
Prague	185828015X	$14.95
Provence & the Côte d'Azur	1858280230	$14.95
St Petersburg	1858280303	$14.95
San Francisco	1858280826	$13.95
Scandinavia	1858280397	$16.99
Scotland	1858280834	$14.95
Sicily	1858280370	$14.99
Spain	1858280818	$16.95
Thailand	1858280168	$15.95
Tunisia	1858280656	$15.95
Turkey	1858280885	$16.95
Tuscany & Umbria	1858280915	$15.95
USA	185828080X	$18.95
Venice	1858280362	$13.99
Women Travel	1858280710	$12.95
Zimbabwe & Botswana	1858280419	$16.95

Rough Guides are available from all good bookstores, but can be obtained directly in th
USA and Worldwide (except the UK*) from Penguin:

Charge your order by Master Card or Visa (US$15.00 minimum order): call
1-800-255-6476; or send orders, with complete name, address and zip code, and list
price, plus $2.00 shipping and handling per order to:
Consumer Sales, Penguin USA, PO Box 999 – Dept #17109, Bergenfield, NJ 07621.
No COD. Prepay foreign orders by international money order, a cheque drawn on a US
bank, or US currency. No postage stamps are accepted. All orders are subject to stock
availability at the time they are processed. Refunds will be made for books not
available at that time. Please allow a minimum of four weeks for delivery.

The availability and published prices quoted are correct at the time
of going to press but are subject to alteration without prior notice.
Titles currently not available outside the UK will be available
by January 1995. Call to check.

* For UK orders, see separate price list

SLEEP EASY
BOOK AHEAD

You **are**
A STUDENT

You **travel**
THE WORLD

You **want**
TO SAVE MONEY

Here's
how

The International
Student Identity Card

International Student Identity Card
Internationaler Studentenausweis/Carte internationale d'étudiant

ISIC

1
9
3
S 2185082

Family name/Nom de famille
Sian
First Name/Vorname/Prénom
Sharoush
Born/Geburtsdatum/Né le
20/8/1973
Nationality/Nationalité/Nationalité
French
Studert a/Hochschule, Schule/Etabli d'enseignement
University of Paris

STUDENT

Available at Student Travel Offices Worldwide.

Entitles you to discounts and special services worldwide.